# Pentecostal Newspapers

Messengers of an Outpouring

Volume One

Michael D. Fortner

Trumpet Press, Lawton, OK

Copyright 2022 by Michael D. Fortner
All rights reserved.
Version 1.1

Special Thanks to:

Flower Pentecostal Heritage Center
https://archives.ifphc.org/index.cfm

And

Consortium of Pentecostal Archives:
https://pentecostalarchives.org/

for making Pentecostal resources available online.

The following images are courtesy of the Flower Pentecostal Heritage Center; used by permission:

* Birdsall and Boswell in Dallas.
* Maria Woodworth-Etter poster


1. Pentecostal History. 2. Christian History. 3. Revival History. 4. Signs and Wonders.
Fortner, Michael D., author.

ISBN: 978-1-7343990-8-0


Due to having several pages of Table of Contents, several small notices and reports had to be left out of the listing or it would have been much longer.

Trumpet Press is a member of the Christian Indie Publisher's Association (CIPA).

www.michaelfortner.com

# Table of Contents

Introduction ............................................................................................. 7
Chapter 1: Pentecostal History Part 1
    The History of the Apostolic or Pentecostal Movement ....................... 11
    Tongues in History ................................................................................ 12
    The Work of the Spirit in Rhode Island ............................................... 16
    First Pentecostal Convention ................................................................ 17
    Forty Years Ago in the Cumberland Mountains .................................. 19
    Incidents of the Spirit's Work from 1890 to 1900 ............................... 21
    Incidents of the Spirit's Work from 1901 to 1904 ............................... 23
    Houston, Texas and W. J. Seymour ..................................................... 26
    Reminiscences of an Eyewitness .......................................................... 29
    The Pentecostal or "Latter Rain" Outpouring in Los Angeles ............ 34
    My First Visit to the Azusa Street Pentecostal Mission ...................... 39
Chapter 2: Pentecostal History Part 2
    The Work Spreads to India .................................................................. 44
    How Pentecost Came to Calcutta ......................................................... 49
    Christians in India Are Given "Gift of Tongues" ................................ 52
    When Pentecost Came to India ............................................................ 57
    Additional from Los Angeles Concerning the Early Pentecostal Work ........... 62
    The Tongues of Pentecost Duplicated ................................................. 64
Chapter 3: Pentecostal History Part 3
    Pastor Barrett and the Work in Europe ............................................... 66
    Pentecost in Sunderland: (excerpt) ....................................................... 70
    The Pentecostal Movement Invades Ohio ........................................... 72
    The Experience of W. Jethro Walthall ................................................. 75
    How and When Pentecost Came to Cleveland .................................... 78
    Details From Various Sources .............................................................. 81
    The Pentecostal Work in Fort Worth, Texas ....................................... 83
    Further Incidents From the Early Days in Azusa Mission .................. 86
    My Convictions .................................................................................... 88
    The Great Revival at Azusa Street Mission: How it Began
        and How it Ended ........................................................................... 90
    Pentecost in Persia ................................................................................ 94
    Pentecost in Russia ............................................................................. 109
    How the Outpouring Came to Chili, S. America ............................... 110
    Apostolic Power Brings Apostolic Persecution ................................. 115
Chapter 4: Pentecostal Newspapers 1906-1909 ................................... 121
    Evangelist T. W. McConnell's Testimony ......................................... 122
    Pentecostal Faith Line: ....................................................................... 123
1907 ..................................................................................................... 124
    A Wonderful Baptism in England: ..................................................... 125
    Success at Laurens: ............................................................................ 126
    Pentecostal Work in Florida: (excerpt) .............................................. 126
    Susie Bain's Testimony: ..................................................................... 128

## 1908 ........................................................................................................... 128
- A Rescue Mission Worker's Recent Experience: ........................... 128
- Report from the Channel Islands: ................................................. 129
- Hong Kong China: ......................................................................... 130
- Testimony of Smith Wigglesworth ................................................ 131
- Testimony from Bournemouth: (A Visit to Sunderland) ................ 132
- From Brother Smith Wigglesworth ............................................... 133
- The Lame Walk: ............................................................................. 134
- Miracles of Salvation, Healing, Provision and Protection ............. 136
- What God is Doing in South Africa: by John G. Lake .................. 141
- A Helpful Vision, In a Sculptor's Studio: [Main part] ................... 143
- Jesus the Way, the Truth and the Life: (excerpt) ........................... 146
- Confirming the Word by Signs Following ..................................... 147
- An Inspiring Night's Service: (excerpt) ......................................... 149
- A Remarkable Dream: (Mrs. Eugene Nix) ..................................... 150

## 1909 ........................................................................................................... 152
- The First One to Speak in Tongues: [as it was then believed in 1909] ............ 152
- Atrophied Optic Nerve, Spinal Trouble, and Gastritis Healed ....... 155
- The Lord's Healing ........................................................................ 157
- A Gospel Worker's Dream ............................................................. 164
- They Were All With One Accord in One Place ............................. 165
- Rejected for Speaking on Tongues ................................................ 168
- Telling the Lord's Secrets .............................................................. 169
- Healed of Arsenic Poisoning: ........................................................ 176
- The Lord Reigneth! ........................................................................ 177

## Chapter 5: 1910
- A Potato Miracle ............................................................................ 180
- Raised from the Dead .................................................................... 181
- Australia, A Young Man's Baptism ............................................... 183
- Spoke the Zulu Language ............................................................... 184
- Echoes From the Jungles of India .................................................. 184
- Warning: ......................................................................................... 186
- A Prophetic Message ..................................................................... 187
- Pentecost in Holland: ..................................................................... 188
- My God Shall Supply All Your Needs: ......................................... 190
- A Remarkable Case of Healing (At Glad Tidings Mission) .......... 194
- Jottings From the Mountains of Tennessee: (A Vision of the Blood) .............. 194
- The Power of Pentecost in Indianapolis: ....................................... 196
- The Homestead Pa. Campmeeting: (excerpt) ................................ 197
- Testimony of a Baptist Minister: (Alvin L. Branch, Colon, Mich.) ............... 198
- Looking Up to Jesus ....................................................................... 199
- The Stone Church: (That produced The Latter Rain Evangel.) .... 201

## Chapter 6: 1911
- A Testimony by Mrs. Marie Burgess Brown: ................................ 202
- A Message in the Spirit .................................................................. 205
- A Remarkable Dream: (Mrs. L. E. Eames, Oneieda, New York) .. 205
- How God Led Me to Pentecost: (Sarah E. Keatley) ...................... 208
- That Big Black Bear: ..................................................................... 212

Reminiscences of a Faith Life #1: (Miss Elizabeth Sisson) ............................ 214
Reminiscences of a Faith Life #2: (Miss E. Sisson) ..................................... 217

## Chapter 7: 1912
The Outpouring of The Spirit in Los Angeles: ............................................. 219
Conversion of A Chinese Woman: ................................................................ 220
Reminiscences of a Faith Life #3: (Miss E. Sisson) ..................................... 221
Reminiscences of a Faith Life #4: (Miss Elizabeth Sisson) ........................... 222
Witnessing for Jesus in the Southland: (Feb. 27, 1912) ................................ 224
Pulling Up the Tares: ................................................................................... 227
Snares in the Path of the Christian Worker; God's Leading
  and the Result: (excerpt) ........................................................................... 228
I Will Guide Thee With Mine Eye (Heeding the Voice of God): ................... 233
Pentecostal Outpouring in Dallas, Texas: ..................................................... 234
In the Hands of the Potter ........................................................................... 235
The Finnish Gold Story: .............................................................................. 241
GLORY AND UNITY at the EUREKA SPRINGS CAMP! ......................... 244
Trip to the Southwest: ................................................................................. 245
The Good of Speaking With Tongues: ......................................................... 246
Revival Fires From Heaven Still Burning .................................................... 248
GOD'S MIGHTY POWER, Dallas, Texas .................................................... 250
Notice About Parham: .................................................................................. 252
North Missouri and Iowa Camps Victorious ................................................ 252
God Visiting Kansas: [and other places] ...................................................... 253
Missionary Reports ...................................................................................... 254

## Chapter 8: 1913
Miraculous Interpretation of English ........................................................... 257
Providential Protection from Storms ............................................................ 257
Los Angeles Campmeeting ........................................................................... 260
A Blessed Revival in Chicago ...................................................................... 261
Wonderful Miracles Worked in Jesus' Name ............................................... 262
Diversities of Operations but the Same Spirit ............................................. 264
The Day of Chicago's Visitation .................................................................. 265
Neglect Not the Gift that is in Thee ............................................................. 277
Additional Notes of July Meetings ............................................................... 283
A Blessed Revival in Chicago ...................................................................... 285

# Pentecostal Newspapers

# Introduction

This two-volume series is 95% direct quotes found in Pentecostal newspapers of the early 20th century outpouring. It contains a history of the outpouring that was written by those who participated in it, or were eyewitnesses. A normal history book is only a survey of events that happened way back when, but the articles in this book, taken from several different Pentecostal newspapers.

While reading these stories of healing, miracle provision, and divine intervention, you will laugh, cry, shout, and be amazed. God truly worked signs and wonders among Pentecostal people and ministers all over the world, not just a few big named ministers. These articles show that divine healing and even unknown tongues existed long before the outpouring "officially" began in 1906.

When a backwoods preacher prayed for a smashed elbow, those present could hear the bones snapping into place. On the day the Holy Spirit fell on the West Coast, a Pentecostal convention was being held on the East Coast of the US, and it was not the first. (These people spoke unknown tongues. There was another group that called themselves Pentecostal in the late 1800s because they believed they had the Holy Ghost, but they did not speak in tongues.)

The above is just part of the real history of the outpouring that is revealed in the Pentecostal newspapers. The articles also show how it spread into different cities and nations all over the world. The Weekly Evangel was the paper of the Assembly of God (then became The Pentecostal Evangel); the editor collected a history of the movement which it published in a series of articles in 1916. They asked people to write what they knew, and many sent in their stories.

The editor used some of the articles in his book, Apostolic Faith Restored, (1916). But the paper continued to publish more such articles, and I found similar articles in other papers that provide even more history.

After the history, I give many articles with testimonies of healings, baptisms in the Holy Spirit, revivals that took place, including a few inspiring stories of hero missionaries. You will read firsthand accounts of how God answered prayer in miraculous ways, over and over again. These stories will inspire you and build your faith.

Individuals give their testimonies of how they hungered for more of God, and sought Him until they finally received the baptism in the Holy Spirit. Some of these people got their Pentecost in a campmeeting or a revival meeting, but some received at home alone with God. This is yet another point that proves false, the claim that Charles Parham started the movement, and that everyone that spoke in tongues in those years got it from him or someone he laid hands on. Once people heard it was available, many people sought and received it direct from God.

These historically significant stories give many more details than you will learn from reading the usual summary-type history of the movement. However, because it is only the words of the articles found in the newspapers, it is not and cannot be a comprehensive history. I am sure many details will be left out since I only use papers from 1906 through 1923.

Occasionally I will give some clarifying details to help the reader have a more complete picture of the movement, or sometimes just to clarify the specific information given. Many of the articles were written by people who were not trained writers, so sometimes I include a word or sentence of my own in square brackets [***] giving more detail or explanation, or even a whole paragraph after the notice: Book Editor. However, if it just says "Editor," it is the editor of a paper.

However, these brackets ( ) inside a paragraph are original to the text. When the word "wrought" appeared I substituted the correct modern word, which is usually "worked." There are also many paragraphs that were as long as the page, so I simply found good places to create a paragraph without making any actual changes in the text.

Many early 20th century Pentecostal missionaries went to China, India, Africa, and South America, all without knowing they would receive any financial support. They were called Faith Missionaries, yet, many were successful. One lady and her husband went three years without so much as a letter or a dollar from home; when the husband died she made a trip from the heart of Africa to Chicago with virtually no money; God provided for her every step of the way.

You will read about other great heroes of faith who are unknown today, such as the preacher who took his family by train to another city without a cent in his pocket, even for train fare; God provided everything as he went. He then began a revival and was able to build a new church that was paid for in one year. These heroes did not just take great risks on blind faith, they were following God's specific instructions.

You will read many visions and dreams, which were common in this outpouring. You will read of Americans speaking in tongues and speaking perfect Chinese or Greek, and of Christians in China or India who were speaking in tongues and speaking perfect English.

You will not only read about the victories, but also the troubles and the struggles. Some ministers were beaten, arrested and put on trial; dynamite was put under one church in an attempt to explode it. One fellow claimed to have been born blind and then claimed a great creative miracle of new eyeballs and received much attention for his claim, but it was later shown that he lied, which brought charges of fraud to the work of divine healing.

There are many heresy-hunters today that will point to every move of the Spirit and say it is not of God, but they have never been in a genuine move of the

Spirit, so they have no practical basis upon which to judge. If you want to know what a genuine move of God looks like, then you will find it in the pages of the Pentecostal newspapers.

These papers existed long before there were any Pentecostal denominations. Each paper contains many reports of revival meetings all across the nation, but I include only a few as representative examples. You would need to take the reports of revivals and campmeetings and multiple them by 10 or 100 to get the true number, as they did not publish a notice about every single revival.

Several times you will read about a "heavenly choir," which does NOT refer to a wonderful-sounding normal choir, but one of the manifestations of the Holy Spirit in that age. The Holy Spirit would move upon many people at the same time to sing in unknown tongues; they would, of course, sing the same original Holy Ghost written tune. And the majority of the people singing could not in their real human ability even sing well, but this heavenly choir was truly angelic. The manifestation continued at least into the 1940s, because I heard Oral Roberts tell of sitting with his wife in a tent meeting and they both became part of such a choir. Sadly, this manifestation no longer is present in any Pentecostal or Charismatic church today; see if you can figure out why, while reading this book.

As the chapters go along, you should begin to notice that the Pentecostals of that period were different from the Pentecostals and Charismatics of today. So keep aware and try to see if you can understand how they were different.

This book only contains a few articles related to doctrine, and only one or two specific Bible teaching articles, as good as many of them are; this book mainly contains what can be classified as eyewitness reports and personal testimonies of what God was doing among the Pentecostal people during the years covered.

Even though the articles are not focused on doctrine, a lot of their beliefs are revealed in the testimonies, both the Holiness and Pentecostal beliefs. Reading this book is like taking a crash course in old-time Pentecostalism! Healing, speaking in tongues, financial miracles, unusual manifestations-- it is all here.

Some readers may suspect that I have intentionally picked out all the articles that have visions or dreams in them, but there were so many, I did not include even 50% of those I found. I only included the most interesting and useful ones, as well as a few simply as examples of what was common.

A few dreams and visions contain information that are actually important for us today, such as the one titled, *The Last Great Spiritual Conflict*, that predicts great deception coming into the Pentecostal movement-- from the inside. This was seen over 110 years ago, therefore, we are living in part of it; and I provide a detailed explanation in a separate book titled, *The Last Great Spiritual Conflict: A Vision and Prophecies* (coming in 2023). But you can read the vision by itself, with no interpretation, in Volume Two; since it was published in 1916. The only chapter I have written is the final one called Final Observations of Volume Two.

A few really long articles were edited for length because the writer would drift into preaching, or was just not a good writer and used too many words. So, in the interest of including as much of the best stuff as possible, and retaining the interest of the reader, some articles have a few sentences or paragraphs removed, indicated when three dots . . . appear. A few times I include only a paragraph or two from an article because I found the information interesting or useful.

Volume One goes about halfway into 1913, and Volume Two then begins in 1913 and goes through 1923.

# Chapter 1

# Pentecostal History: Part 1

### The History of the Apostolic or Pentecostal Movement
#### By B. F. Lawrence

*Book Editor*: I left out the first two parts of this multi-part history because they only deal with a basic teaching on tongues and how it came on the Day of Pentecost; which is already well-known.

This history, as collected here, I consider to be especially noteworthy because the writers had access to information which would be impossible to acquire today. The following notice was published in more than one issue of the paper:

In our effort to produce a real and comprehensive account of the great Pentecostal Movement, we need, and need badly, the help of every one of the Lord's people who are in possession of any information which ought to appear in these columns.

We therefore make the following appeal to the various agencies which can be of help to us. We are bold in making these requests because we feel that the general Pentecostal Body will be the real beneficiaries in the publication of this work.

First, we wish every Pentecostal exchange would publish this notice. That they would themselves take time to write a brief record of their history and present scope, and that they would send us the names of those who would be able to give us specially valuable information.

Second, we wish every pastor would send us an account of the origin, location, former pastors, founders, and approximate membership of his work. This is meant for every assembly of like precious faith with us whether you recognize the General Council of the Assemblies of God or not. We will carefully give your affiliation or make it plain that you are an independent body, if you will send in your report. If there is no pastor at your place, fellow members of the body, write the report yourself.

Third, we wish every missionary to do what we requested the pastors to do, adding the dates of their going to their works, and the times of their absences therefrom.

Fourth, where there are field directors, superintendents, overseers, chairmen of conferences, and State Councils, we wish you would take time to report the history, scope, and approximate membership of your charge.

We address this general call for information in the hope that it will be considered by each one of you as a personal invitation. We have had the privilege of being connected with the work from the time of its advent in Indianapolis, Ind. in the latter part of 1906 and are acquainted with many of the Lord's ministers, but there are many more of whom we have no knowledge. It is plain therefore that we cannot make the request by letter to each of those from whom we desire a response.

Let us make this plain, this is no effort to procure a census of the Pentecostal Movement, nor is it an effort to build up the General Council of the Assemblies of God at the expense of others. This is a bonafide effort to produce a real history of the whole movement.

Of course, if any one thinks it wrong to write such a history, let him appear before the judgment bar of Christ and assail Matthew, Mark, and John for their histories of the life of Jesus; and Luke for his gospel and for his history of the Pentecostal Movement in the first thirty years of its existence. Send your reports and articles direct to the editor of this department, B. F. Lawrence . . .

*Book Editor*: B. F. Lawrence published his history as, *Apostolic Faith Restored: A History of the Present Latter Rain Outpouring of the Holy Spirit known as the Apostolic or Pentecostal Movement.* Then about ten years later another book was published by Stanley Frodsham called *With Signs Following*, which is more complete, and was updated to the third edition in 1946.

## Tongues in History

### B. F. Lawrence

Pursuant to our plan to trace a few details of the work of God from the days of Pentecost to the present outpouring of the Spirit, we present the following:

It is obvious that the preparation of a detailed chronological record covering 1500 years would involve a [great] deal of time, labor, and research; and the publication of such a record would require as much space as we are prepared to give to this whole history. The space for publication and the facilities for research we do not possess; moreover, as we declared in our first installment, it is the Scriptural rather than the historical aspect that interest us.

Before we take up the details which we have allowed ourselves, we desire to call your attention to the following facts.

First: The primitive Christians were persecuted by Rome, in the persons of her emperors, governors, magistrates, and citizens, largely because of the circulation of false reports concerning them. They were said to be atheists; to offer infants in sacrifice, and then to eat their flesh; to be guilty of gross immorality, even to incest; to be enemies of the State; and to be responsible for fires, earthquakes, flood, and pestilences.

Second: The greater amount of our information regarding the "heretics" who took their stand against the established (and generally corrupt) order of things in the middle ages, is derived from their enemies. And it must be remembered that these informants were often as destitute of righteousness, sound judgment, and love of the truth as were those who circulated such false reports about Paul and his brethren.

Third: The Protestant scholars who have investigated these records have, in the majority of cases, been as prejudiced against the phenomena [speaking in tongues] in which we believe as were the ones who wrote the derogatory accounts of the revivals. Understand, in many cases, these investigators believed in the doctrines of the "heretics" while condemning the "excitement" under which they labored.

This disposition to slight and undervalue glossolalia, (speaking on tongues) is apparent, not only in their manner of handling the reports of its appearance in history but in their criticism of the New Testament manifestations as well. (See Encyclopedia Britannica and Catholic Encyclopedia, article Gifts of Tongues.) This fact robs their condemnation of medieval and modern tongues of much of its weight with those who believe that God, "divided to every man severally as He willed" and that tongues were included in the giving.

Fourth: The stories now disseminated in many places regarding the present work of God are of the same family and bear the same general characteristics of those told against the primitive and medieval Christians. We are all hated by the world, and for the same reasons.

**Encyclopedia Britannica**

Vol. 27 Pages 9 to 10, 11th edition says that glossolalia, (tongues) "recurs in Christian revivals of every age, e.g., among the mendicant friars of the thirteenth century; among the Jansenists and early Quakers, the converts of Wesley and Whitefield, the persecuted Protestants of the Cevennes and the Irvingites. Along with this phenomena came reports of healing, miracles, and prophecy.

**St. Francis Xavier**

The Catholic Encyclopedia says that St. Francis Xavier, who was born April 7, 1506 in Navarre and died Dec. 2, 1552 on the island of Sancien just off the Chinese coast preached in tongues unknown to him. The sphere of this man's labors embraced Spain, Portugal, Japan, India, Ceylon. He is accounted one of their greatest and most successful missionaries of all time, and, of course, this manifestation of tongues is received by Catholics as a genuine work of the Spirit.

**Southern France**

With its mountains and valleys was a famous breeding ground for so-called "heretics" from the twelfth century on down. Indeed, some of those old congregations are still in organic existence. In this territory the Waldenses and Albigenses were nearly coexistent in point of time, beginning about 1170 and continuing until the 15th century. The Camosards appeared at a somewhat later date and held on until 1705 or later. Each of these sects had those among them who spoke in tongues.

## The Jansenists

Just prior to the disappearance of the Camosards, a man by the name of Cornelius Jansen, a French Catholic, began to set forth his ideas. It was not his intention to separate himself from the Roman Church, but he did insist on personal knowledge of God and communion with Him. This contention provoked a storm among the sacramental religionists of Rome, and the Jansenist doctrines were condemned by the Pope. Those who held to the proscribed doctrines were at last unable to refute the charge of heresy and many fled to Holland. The persecution waxed fiercer, the power of God fell, and many spoke in tongues and prophesied. This occurred in 1702-1705.

## The Quakers

Over in England the fire was burning at the same time. George Fox, the first Quaker, had begun his ministry in 1647. He insisted on personal salvation, communion with God and the leading of the Holy Spirit. He also, in opposition to the Puritans, Baptists and other nonconformists of the day, believed in present, complete deliverance from sin. He was opposed to war for any cause, would not take oath, and the people whom God raised up under his ministry were the only ones for a long time who refused to meet secretly in times of persecution. This persistence in public worship brought much suffering to them, but was one of the great factors in bringing about religious liberty in England.

For a long time the Quakers had no regular organized existence; and it was easy for any one to obtain a reputation of being a Quaker by simply attending their meetings. Many men of no principle did so attend and were the source of great reproach to the true children of God. This condition is also true of the Pentecostal Movement.

Later, when an attempt was made to correct this to provide an orderly worship and government, there was strong opposition on the part of some very good men who seemed to be afraid of the same things some of the Pentecostal people are afraid of today.

The Quakers further refused to set out a written creed and did not attempt to bind the consciences of their people in minor matters.

In their worship, they permitted women to preach and pray on equal terms with the men, and sometimes had great manifestations of the power of God. So great was that power at times that both saint and sinner would fall prostrate, and frequently those falling would shake, or "quake" as they called it then. Speaking in tongues was frequent among them, not only in England but in this country.

From 1647 to 1662, a period of fifteen years, four hundred of these godly persons were known to have died in prison, while another hundred died as the result of the violence of mobs. During this time a total of 4500 were imprisoned, and in 1685 when a petition was addressed to the king praying for relief and protection, there were 1460 in confinement.

This brief account shows that these people were, in many respects, our true fathers in the faith; the burden of their preaching and practice was identical with our own. This exception should be noted, however; they neither baptized nor took the Lord's Supper. Truth requires that we add that this lack was less from objection to the sacraments than to the place assigned to them by other religious bodies of their time.

**Wesley and Whitefield**

During the 18th century both Wesley and Whitefield accomplished great works for the Lord. Whitefield was one of the most eloquent, powerful, successful preachers the church has known. His converts were numbered by the thousands, and some of them received the baptism in the Spirit and spake in other tongues.

Both the Encyclopedia Britannica and the Life and Epistles of St. Paul admit the presence of glossolalia among the early Methodists. The latter work in the People's Edition, pp. 451-452 has the following in the footnote: "If, however, the inarticulate utterances of ecstatic joy are followed (as they were in some of Wesley's converts) by a life of devoted holiness, we should hesitate to say that they might not bear some analogy to those of the Corinthian Christians."

It might be noted here that speaking in tongues was not always followed by a "life of devoted holiness" on the part of some in the Corinthian Church. See 1 Cor. 3rd to 6th chapters. Both from the Scriptural record and modern observation we know that tongues are not the evidence of a mature Christian character. If, as we believe, they are an evidence of the baptism in the Holy Spirit, then they often came at an early age of the development of that character. See Acts 8, 10, 19. Those who contend otherwise injure the truth and create an improper impression in the minds of those who are or will be in contact with the phenomena of tongues.

**Edward Irving**

Sometime after the revivals of Wesley and Whitefield the work broke out in Scotland. Edward Irving became acquainted with it from that source in 1830. He was a divine of the Established Scottish Church, but for some time had been dissatisfied with the condition of things in his heart and church. When he heard and saw the wonderful works of God he fell in line with them, though at a considerable sacrifice. His church excommunicated him in 1832 on the charge of heresy and he was chosen pastor of the Congregation in Newton Street, London, in the following year. The name chosen by the movement at that time was, "Catholic Apostolic Church." Irving was an eloquent, forceful speaker, a man of great natural ability, the friend of such men as Carlyle, Henry Drummond, and Coleridge. Carlyle said of him that, "His was the bravest, freest, brotherliest human soul mine ever found in this world, or hopes to find."

About this time the great Charles G. Finney, Presbyterian, was engaged in a revival campaign which resulted in the salvation of five hundred thousand souls. He says of himself that he "literally bellowed out the unutterable gushings of his heart." Inasmuch as he taught that the baptism in the Spirit was an experience subsequent to regeneration, it is evident that he spoke in tongues.

Though arising at different times, under different circumstances, rebuking different abuses, holding different doctrines along some lines, these all, to a greater or less extent, enjoyed the presence and power of God, and suffered for it. We follow in the steps of a goodly company.

Some have wondered at the diverse doctrines held in these days by people who all agree on the speaking in tongues. Here in history we have our counterparts in this respect. I think that some of our hairsplitting is amusing to the great God who has seen so much of it in the long centuries which have elapsed since Pentecost, and that He, seeing our hearts, blesses us in spite of these things, just as He blessed these men of old. (*The Weekly Evangel*, Jan. 15, 1916)

## The Work of the Spirit in Rhode Island
### B. F. Lawrence

In this chapter we will satisfy ourselves with presenting an account of the work of God beginning in 1874. It is written for us by a present minister of the movement, R. B. Swan, Pastor of the Assembly meeting at 7 Winter St., Providence, R.I.

My own heart was made to burn within me as I read the following. It is so very like the present work of God. I want you to notice especially the dates. There is a mistaken impression that this Movement is a mushroom growth, originating in California in 1906. This is not the case. God, who in sundry places, at diverse times, poured out His Spirit with the sign of tongues, sent the outpouring at Los Angeles after He had prepared for it by smaller, but by no means less genuine, works in other places.

The letter from Brother Swan follows:

"I was converted and joined the Stewart Street Baptist Church in Providence, R.I. in 1864, and remained a member for several years; after which I left them under the following circumstances-- I providentially came in contact with a small company of believers who were looking for the soon coming of Jesus, and who were teaching the receiving of the Holy Spirit and the gifts as taught in 1 Cor. 12th chapter. This appealed to myself and wife, and we, with them, became earnest seekers for the baptism of the Spirit.

"In the year 1875 our Lord began to pour upon us His Spirit; and wife and I, with a few others, began to utter a few words in the "unknown tongue." I recall one incident at that time, in connection with this gift, of a sister (who at present is a member of my assembly) who was worked upon by the Spirit to speak. She did not want this gift and refused to do so. One evening at a gathering held at my home, she was again worked upon, but she kept her lips closed. We labored with her to yield to the Spirit, and when she did, she broke forth in a volume of words in the unknown tongues which continued for quite a time. Her name is Amanda Doughty. Her husband is an elder in my assembly. They live at 1104, S. Broadway, East Providence, R.I.

"In the year 1874-5 while we were seeking the baptism, there came among us several who had received the baptism and the gift of tongues a number of years before this and were very helpful to us. They are now sleeping in Jesus, but at your request for names I will append them as follows: William B. Doughty of

Maine, father-in-law of Amanda Doughty above noted; Zina Ford of Concord, N.H.; William Hawkes of East Boston, Mass.; Eliza Libby of Lawrence, Mass.; Rose Jenkins of Vermont; Rosa Childs of Hartford, Conn. (By the locations here given, it is evident that there was considerable territory reached with this light at that early day. Editor's Note.)

**First Pentecostal Convention**

"In the summer of 1875, I with some others, felt then the time was due for calling the "Gift People" (as they were then called) together. How was it to be accomplished? Only a few of us, and no money in sight; certainly we must do it by faith, for did not the Lord [know] so? In taking account of stock, I had eight dollars and Brother Dinsmore had six. I bought 50 postal cards and had the campmeeting call printed on them which said, "Come for all things are free, and without money and without price." They were sent into all of the states where we knew of any who were in sympathy with the Spirit's work and manifestations.

"We hired Adelaide Grove in the suburb of Providence, lumber was hired to seat it and to make frame for tents, a long frame was made for the eating tent, and with my eight dollars and the brother's six, we bought cotton cloth enough to cover it. A big tent was hired and we were ready for the King's business. On came the saints until the camp was full. The meeting was extended to two weeks. All were fed free, with lodging, and at the close we were six hundred dollars in debt and no money in sight, as we had taken no collections.

"On the last Sunday a call was made to meet in the big tent. The bills were presented; the six hundred dollars was raised in a short time and we left the grounds free from debt.

"The point I wish to make is this, during these two weeks [of] meetings, many thousands came from the city and outlying districts and saw the marvelous works of the Holy Spirit; many messages were given in the unknown tongues; some were slain and baptized in the Holy Spirit -- it was Pentecost indeed.

"In addition, some years before the outpouring in Los Angeles, Bro. T. F. Plummer, who is now connected with the Pentecostal Assembly at the Franklin Union Building, Boston, Mass. was given the gift, and so continues. Also Sister Mattie Osgood of Millbrook, Maine received before 1906."

The following account is given by the same brother, published by *Word and Work* [another Pentecostal newspaper]:

"In the year 1882 a great burden came upon me, and for three days I was bowed under the Holy Spirit's power. I was led to go to a chapel in West Duxbury, Mass. hamlet called Ashdod), which has since been described by reporters as "being five miles from everywhere." This chapel had been closed for some years, and sin was reigning; a revival followed, the house was filled, and some conversions followed.

"In this same year above mentioned, Bro. J. Osgood and wife moved there from New Hampshire. W. Marsh and wife were already there, and a small company who united with us, and the work began. [...] the vessels were gotten together for the work that was to follow as the years went on, preparatory for the 'latter rain' that was to fall upon His people.

"The writer became pastor and leader of this work and the others rallied around him; efforts were made to keep in touch with those who in those days were called 'gift people' who believed in all of the gifts of the Holy Spirit and God's mighty power which would follow a baptism and filling. We knew of many who were scattered abroad in many States; how could we bring them together and have days of Pentecost?

"We had a chapel and a few homes where we could lodge them, and not much money; but we had not forgotten God's message to Zerubbabel when he was bidden to 'finish this house . . . for who hath despised the day of small things?' This work of bringing the people together must be accomplished by conventions; we began this work in 1886, we sent out notices to the saints to meet in a three days assembly. Only a few came to this first gathering, for we were out in the wilderness, 'five miles from everywhere' (five miles from four depots) at different points of the compass. The few that came we entertained without money and price. All was free, and that method has continued up to the present time, but on the last day of the conventions a free-will offering is taken and in every case all bills have been met.

"As the years pass, on they come, all were hungry for the 'bread from heaven' and the 'living water.' We must enlarge our borders; an old house near the chapel was empty, the sisters cleaned it, beds were brought from our homes. What the house could not hold were taken to our homes in teams, food was cooked by the few families of our assembly. But our barns were not large enough to hold the wheat, and the work of setting up and taking down was taxing. Heroic measures must be taken to meet the oncoming saints who were jumping fences of the old pastures which were eaten to the roots, and were now coming into the wilderness to get some clover that was springing up. [*Book Editor*: He is speaking of spiritual things.]

"Temporary measures were at an end, for a house and about two acres of land were bought near the chapel, and the work began. Donations were asked for, a prompt response came from those who appreciated the situation and under the direction of Bro. C. C. Foster, who is a master builder and who had been with us from the beginning, we took our saws and hammers and erected a large building containing a large dining room capable of seating nearly ninety persons at one sitting; a nice kitchen, pantry, and sitting room below, and room above to lodge sixty. This surely will do now, and the first convention [in this new facility] was April, 1897. It was soon filled to its capacity, and a second lodging house was built, and in a year later a third house was built, all having nice beds that will accommodate over two hundred people.

"Saints from many states and a few from abroad have met with us, and if the Lord tarries and the 'Later Rain' continues to fall, other precious gatherings will be held. A large number have received their baptism and fillings, and on April 9, 1906, when the Holy Spirit fell at Los Angeles, we were holding a convention on

## Forty Years Ago in the Cumberland Mountains
### Sarah Haggard Payne

The first that I remember of public work for God was when I was about ten years old. My father was an ordained Baptist minister and preached at McMinnville, Tenn., for years, but did a larger work as an evangelist in the mountains of Tennessee, and I went with him to sing many times. I have seen people crowd into his meetings because of "strange doings," they called it. My father, a great powerful man physically, would preach the pure Gospel, reading and quoting often from the Word, and then he would call on me to sing. Then he would fall on his knees and pray, and it seemed he grew taller and taller, and his voice louder and louder, and heaven opened and the power began to fall like rain.

If any of the converts spoke in tongues, I never knew it, but father and mother often did. I have heard my father speak in tongues in the pulpit and interpret it, and have heard my mother sing in tongues, but we never mentioned the thing to anyone as tongues, but as the effects of the power of God, the work of the Spirit. And we children thought our father was talking in Greek or Hebrew, but he told me (I was his chum selected from the children) that God was talking through him; and we thought mother was a little off. Mother told me one day when I came up behind her and heard her singing in an unknown language, that God was singing in her heart, and now I understand since I have received the baptism.

My father traveled all over the mountains in all kinds of vehicles, sometimes walking, leading me by the hand and carrying me over the rough rocks, and he scattered Bibles and literature, some of it being his own writing, on healing and temperance, in all the places he went into. Often, he would preach in the homes of the poor mountaineers and sometimes in the woods, many times never even announcing his name; and if I was with him I would sing, for even then I loved to sing of Jesus, although not born of the Spirit. I wandered in sin's paths until 1904, when I was "born again." "Ye must be born again," Jesus said, no matter how godly your training may have been.

All his meetings were conducted as mentioned above; signs and wonders followed his preaching. He was strong on divine healing. One man was healed of hydrophobia [fear of water] instantly; drunken men cursing and raving would be stricken with the jerking and fall as though dead, and rise sober and saved, shouting and singing praises until the lonely mountain woods would be alive with songs to God for His wondrous works to the children of men. He was a real Paul-like man. He preached powerful temperance sermons all over those mountains, and also in the town in which I was raised, and by doing so, created bitter enemies.

At one time a saloon keeper told him he would beat him to death if he preached another temperance sermon in that town, but father was led by the Holy Ghost and soon felt led to preach on a temperance subject, and did, giving many instances of awful suffering of wives and children in the town where this same saloon keeper sold intoxicants to the husbands of these wives. And he gave names, for father never minced words, but spoke with no uncertain sound. The next afternoon this saloon keeper met him on the street and slapped him, and father turned the other cheek, but for a wonder the man refused to strike him again.

His life in the mountains was always in jeopardy, and my presence-- a little innocent girl who never dreamed of danger, and loved every one, and sang all the time on the road, my voice ringing out through the woods joining the birds, God's "fowls of the air," and at their homes, at churches, and everywhere-- saved him from harm. I heard this on my trip in the year of 1912, when I visited my twin sister who lives on the side of the Cumberland mountains. [It appears, that bad men would have attacked him, if he had been alone.]

On this visit, I was remembered as the little singer who went with Pastor J. R. Haggard on his trips, and I sang for them again over the telephone, the office turning over number after number of the party phones for as long as one hour at a time, and I sang, "I fell in love with the Nazarene." "Nowhere to lay my head," and others. [Back then, you could have a private line or a "party" line, which was cheaper and allowed many phones to be connected by the operator. It appears she sang to many people at the same time over their party lines.]

God got glory and proved His words from the rainbow of fire He showed me in 1904, when He promised He would scatter the songs to the uttermost parts of the earth. Night after night the songs rang out to them. Then they sent for me to come, and I rode in all kinds of vehicles over the roughest roads I ever saw and had meetings in homes, school houses, churches, and out in the woods, and the little birds joined me again in my praises as they did when I sang for my sainted father forty years ago. God never forgets; if not the fowls of the air surely not His little ones.

I found an old lady, nearly a hundred years old, who was brought into [one of] my meetings to hear the music. She could not see, [but] she remembered my father and me, and said when she learned I was that child, that my voice sounded the same as then, only as if I had been to heaven and saw the glory there and had come back to tell it in song. I sang over the line from Sparta, Tenn., where my husband and I had taught in Dibbell Normal College twenty-five years before, to McMinnville, Tenn., the town in which I was raised, to a lady who said the voice sounded like a voice from the heavenly world, and more voices than one. God's ways are not our ways.

I credit my turning to God, my singing-evangelist leanings, my spiritual bent and visionary inclinations to the prayers of my father. When he was not preaching, visiting the poor and sick, he was on his knees. My mother often asked us children, and if the others knew not, I did, where father was, and invariably one or the other would say, "Oh, he is praying somewhere!" If we hunted him we would find him praying in the old barn, down on his knees in the sweet new hay, his face upturned and tears streaming down his face; and through all my worldly life in after years, I simply could not drown my dear old father's prayers. I could not get away from them. He prayed, "Oh, God, the Father and Creator of all things, answer my prayer by the power of the Holy Ghost, for the sake of thine only begotten Son, save my children and their children, and their children's children." So they will all be saved, and mother will do as she used to tell us she would do, introduce us to Jesus.

Requests came from all over the mountains to me on this visit in 1912 to sing, and I sang the songs given me by inspiration only, to people three to four hundred miles apart from each other and from me, and as I sang, shouts of joy would come ringing over the line to me as a friend held the receiver to my ear. I played on an auto harp and the people said it sounded like a great, grand orchestra of a thousand strings and the voice sounded as though coming from heaven, and truly it did, because I had the fire of the Holy Ghost in my baptized soul. Hallelujah!

God plans our lives long before we are conceived and if we are barricaded by the earnest prayers of Godly parents, Satan cannot thwart God's plans for us. Hallelujah! Mothers, fathers, look to your colors! Keep true! Be sure you are worthy to be parents! Father and mother were true from beginning to end, and have gone home to God and their reward. May God bless this testimony to His glory.
-- S. H. P. Ocean Park, Cal. (*TWE*, Feb. 17, 1917)

## Incidents of the Spirit's Work from 1890 to 1900
### Daniel Awrey, Ohio and Tennessee

In 1889 our Brother Daniel Awrey, of blessed memory, was converted and began a life for God which has been singularly blessed and owned of his Lord. He has preached the gospel around the world and has suffered persecutions for the gospel's sake in many localities, and at many times. He left this life to be with his Lord, December 4, 1913 in Liberia, West Africa.

About nine months after his conversion, or on the last night of the year 1889, he was reading a religious book which brought his mind into a mood proper for communion with the Lord. As the bells were ringing the old year out and the new year in, the Spirit spoke to his heart, assuring him that God had for him a new and better experience. He raised his hand and said, "Then, by the grace of God I am going to have it." The next day his testimony was that he felt so clean all day. As he expressed it, he seemed to able to look through and through himself.

That night (Jan. 1, 1890) he attended a prayer meeting where volunteer prayers were called for. He, among others, responded and as he began to pray, his faith rose, claiming an immediate fulfillment of the promise given the night before. Suddenly, the Spirit of God fell upon him and he began to pray in an unknown tongue. The Spirit, which had been working in Providence, R. I., and Duxbury, Mass., had now, in Delaware, Ohio, found another tabernacle and was furthering His effort to bring in the gracious revival which we are now enjoying. So far as we can trace, there was no human connection between this work of the Lord and that in Providence and Duxbury, though both were simultaneous.

Ten years later, Mrs. Awrey received the Spirit and spake in another tongue. In 1899 the Awreys were living at Benah, Tennessee. About a dozen received the

Spirit there with the accompaniment of other tongues. It should be stated, however, that Brother Awrey did not teach at that time that tongues were the evidence of the baptism, though he did teach (either then or shortly afterward) that the baptism was subsequent to what he knew as Sanctification. The manifestations of tongues here recorded appeared to be a sovereign operation of the Spirit.

Brother Awrey, when he came in contact with the present outpouring, fell in line with the people of God and was able to give them a vast amount of very beneficial counsel drawn form his sixteen years walk in the Spirit prior to 1906.

### Sister Sarah A. Smith, N. Carolina and Tennessee

In the neighborhood of 1900 there was another outbreak of the Spirit's work in tongues. Mrs. Sarah A. Smith, a returned missionary from Egypt, writes to the following effect. A little prior to the above date she was a member of an organization called "The Fire Baptized Association." At the time when the Spirit fell, the Association had been disbanded.

Over in North Carolina there was a body of people who had withdrawn from the Baptist Church on account of their faith in the doctrine of the second work of grace. Former members of the Association frequently went over from Tennessee (where they lived) to hold meetings for them.

At the time we speak of, two brethren were holding a meeting there. Their names were Joe Tipton and W. B. Martin. One night, while the meetings were in progress, a woman began to pray, and presently broke out speaking in another tongue. Those present believed at the time that it was a revival of the original Pentecostal blessing and Brother Tipton and others soon received the experience.

They returned to Tennessee to the place Sister Smith was staying at the time, and there she, with a number of others (perhaps 40 or 50), were baptized in the Spirit. This was about six years before the work came to Indianapolis, Indiana in December, 1906.

We insert here a few words from her own testimony:

"I remember hearing them say that nearly everyone fell under the power (that is, over in North Carolina), and the thought came to me that I had been unwilling to fall, for the Lord had been trying me by putting His power on me in a peculiar way, so that I would spin around like a top; two or three times He had done it, and every time I would back up to the wall to keep from falling. But when I heard their testimony, I told the Lord I would fall or do anything, but I wanted what He had for me.

"Of course, He tried me again, and of course, I yielded and fell and spoke at once. In a few days, the power for interpretation came upon me and I interpreted everything I spoke. It was such a wonderful thing to me that I seemed to be in a new world. The coming of Jesus seemed so near, and God revealed many things to me that have since come to pass. One of them was that I and many others would cross the ocean and tell these wonderful things in other countries." [No reference given.]

She further says that to the best of her remembrance, Brother Tomlinson and Lemons were baptized in the Spirit at that time.

## South Dakota

Between 1900 and 1903, the Spirit fell in South Dakota upon a band of people, who afterward went to Africa. I have not been able to get in touch with the man who could give me full information concerning this work, but I think that these people were Norwegians. I know that the man who accompanied them to Chicago was, and that he afterward preached in La Grange, Illinois. He name was Bakke. These people, at least Mr. Bakke, did not believe that tongues were the evidence of the baptism, but regarded them as gifts given in the sovereignty of God.

## Numerous Other Incidents

There have been numerous reports from many places regarding individuals who spoke in tongues. For instance, a woman in Nebraska, a member of the Baptist Church, was attending a Methodist protracted meeting when, during the preaching, she began to shout, and wound up by speaking in other tongues. Again, one of my friends tells me that her mother heard many of the Quakers in Canada speak in tongues sixty years or more ago.

While it is true that most of those who received the baptism prior to 1900 did not regard tongues as the invariable accompaniment of the baptism in the Spirit. Those who received in South Carolina and Tennessee did so regard them, at least to the extent that when they first heard one speak in another tongue, they did what Peter did at Cesarea, viz. Believed that the Gift of the Holy Spirit had been given to them as to the disciples at the beginning. (*TWE*, Jan. 29 and Feb. 5, 1916)

# Incidents of the Spirit's Work from 1901 to 1904
### B. F. Lawrence

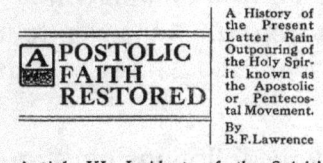

## A Wonderful Healing Among The Gift People

We have seen that in divers places and at diverse times, God had poured out His Spirit in the time between 1875 and 1900. Indeed, we have had fragments indicating that the speaking of tongues was known prior to 1875 in a quite wide degree.

The gift people, of whom Brother Swan wrote in his account of the work in Rhode Island and Massachusetts, were a well known body before his time, as he admits. In the state of New York live a woman who told the following story regarding her association with them; the story is vouched for by good authority.

She said that, in her youth, a body of them worshiped in her neighborhood and were despised and hated by the professors about them [other Christians near them]. It was regarded as a disgrace to attend their meetings, and the better class of persons generally refused to do so.

Her sister was at that time a confirmed invalid -- a hunchback. Hearing of the healings reported to be performed by the Gift People, she desired her father to take her to one of their meetings in the hope that she might find help. This he refused to do. The woman who told the story was then a wild, high-spirited girl, on the lookout for a chance to have a lark. When her father refused to take her sister to the meeting, she promised her that she would herself take her at the first opportunity.

One Sunday morning, therefore, when the old folks went to their regular place of worship, she went out and got a rig ready [a horse and buggy], carried her sister out to it and drove her to the Gift meeting. When they arrived, they saw a man who had his limb broken who was carried into the meeting. The people went to prayer, and presently one from among them arose, went to the man with the broken limb, laid hands on him, and in the name of Jesus bade him arise and walk. He did so, much to the astonishment of the visitors. (I, myself, have seen such things done in the last four years. Editor.)

Then, turning to the invalid sister, he laid hands upon her, bidding her to be straight in the name of Jesus. She was instantly healed. This brought such conviction upon the heart of the girl who had brought her there that she fell prostrate under the convicting hand of God, and when she arose she had yielded her heart to God. It was the custom of these people to pray over the new converts, and after prayer, to decide which gift they should receive. They did so with her and decided that she should have the gift of tongues. They laid hands on her according to the scripture and she spoke in tongues. This account was given to a minister in New York State by the woman herself a few years ago, and is doubtless true.

**Topeka and Galena, Kansas**

In the close of the nineteenth century the following question was propounded to the students of the Bible School in Topeka, Kansas. "What is the Bible evidence of the baptism in the Holy Spirit?" That question was at the time agitating the minds of many, and in its answer the threads we have traced through various states were tied together.

My understanding of the happenings of the occasion is as follows. The students had finished their regular studies and had some little time left before the holidays. This important question was given them to study over in these remaining days. On the first of January, 1901, Miss Agnes N. Ozman, now Mrs. La Burg of Texas, felt that she must receive the gift of the Spirit and called for some present to lay hands upon her according to Acts 19. They did so, and she was filled with the Spirit and spoke with other tongues. On the third of the month, thirteen others received a like experience, among them Mrs. Fannie Dobson of Joplin, Mo., who is at present in Crane, Mo. helping Brother Banta.

As a result of their study and experience, they declared that the speaking in tongues was a part of the baptism in the Spirit in the sense that it invariably accompanied it. This was a bold stand for a little, unknown company of people to take, and it resulted in much persecution. However, many thousands now agree with them.

This experience naturally created considerable excitement in Topeka when it became known, and the meetings were crowded. Government linguists were brought in who testified that the people were speaking in real intelligent languages. The Kansas City papers published this report and interest increased. Every prospect pointed to a great revival, but unwise counsels prevailed and the work was for a time hindered. However, there is now a strong assembly at Topeka.

Unsuccessful meetings were held in Kansas City, Mo. Excelsior Springs, Mo., and Nevada, Mo. under the leadership of Charles F. Parham, who was at the head of the Bible School in Topeka where the work broke out.

In the fall of 1903 Mr. and Mrs. Arthur of Galena, Kansas, opened their home and a meeting began. A tent was procured and erected about October 20, 1903 at the corner of Galena Ave. and Third St. Here the meeting continued until Thanksgiving, when the weather forced them indoors.

The Grand Leader building on Main St. was rented and the meeting continued. This place never accommodated the crowds, though it was 50 x 110 [feet] in size and the doors were never closed while services were going on.

The meeting ran about three months and in the neighborhood of one hundred received the baptism in the Spirit, many being saved and healed. From this meeting the news went to many other localities, and the success of the new movement seemed assured.

The work at Galena continues under the care of the same Mrs. Arthur who first opened her house to it. They are now worshiping in the Pearl Theater building on Main St. Our beloved Brother H. A. Goss, now of Hot Springs, Ark., was converted in the meeting held here in 1903.

From Galena the work spread to Joplin, Mo., where in 1904, a successful meeting was held. Both these works have gone through bitter testings; some who promised well have fallen away when persecution threatened; ministers have come and gone; doctrines and issues have left their mark upon them; but they still stand, lights in dark places, enjoying the presence of God.

Next week we will give an account of the moving of the work to Texas and the outspreading to Los Angeles. (*The Weekly Evangel*, Feb. 12, 1916)

\*\*\*

Fifteen years ago, the spiritual people of the world realized the need of a world-wide revival. Prayer bands were formed in many cities which continually presented that need before God, making strong intercession that God would pour out His Spirit upon all flesh. In response to that heart cry, the heavens were opened and the Holy Spirit was poured out, the grace of God was revealed in the salvation, healing, and anointing of the Holy Ghost of countless numbers of souls in all countries of the earth. And we are witnesses to these things. (*TPE*, Feb. 17, 1917, page 1)

## Houston, Texas and W. J. Seymour

### B. F. Lawrence

From 1901 to the spring of 1905 with struggles, persecutions, failures, [the] few successes, seemed a long time to the toiling, faithful few who carried the spark of the holy fire. It seemed that the sodden world would not ignite, that revival fires would never catch; that labor and prayer bore small fruitage in return for the time and strength expended. But, from small beginnings God has frequently brought great endings. Sometimes, we are compelled to plant and plant until we are in despair; but "God giveth the increase."

The spring of 1905 marked the beginning of an important spiritual era for Texas. A handful of workers, carrying the blessed tidings of Pentecostal experience restored, came to Orchard and there held the first meeting of the Movement in the State.

Galena, Kansas, and Joplin, Mo., had combined forces to send them forth. Bedding, eatables, money, were gathered together, and the trip to Orchard was somewhat in the nature of a pilgrimage or an invasion. Some success attended this effort and the invaders, with renewed courage, advanced upon Houston.

**Houston, Texas**

Here they found a body of Holiness people who had open ears and hearts. Brother Carothers says of this Assembly that, "Being already thoroughly established in the grace of God, this congregation afforded a basis for a lasting work in the new Movement, something which it had not found up to this time."

Perhaps three hundred souls received the precious baptism in the Holy Spirit in the city of Houston alone before the work began in Los Angeles. Our Bro. W. F. Carothers, who has served as field director for Texas, and as a member of the Presbytery of the General Council, was pastor of the Holiness Assembly mentioned above, and came into the light in the first meeting. Also Bro. D. C. O. Opperman entered the Movement a few months later.

The Movement was now truly a movement. Order and harmony prevailed. Field Directors and State Encampments helped to preserve the integrity of the movement and to repress lawlessness. Systematic attempts to evangelize were made, for the most part with success. For instance, from the Kansas State Encampment, workers were sent to Zion City, Ill. A gracious revival resulted and some of the fruits of that revival have since served God in the "ends of the earth."

It is a significant fact that all the great impulses toward Bible order and unity have emanated from the territory covered by this old "Apostolic Faith Movement," or from men trained directly or indirectly under its influence.

**William J. Seymour**

Bro. Seymour, an African preacher of Houston, became interested in the new Movement and its doctrines, and allied himself with it. Bro. W. F. Carothers and

C. H. Parham instructed him in the doctrines held by the Movement at that time. (They are substantially the same today.) Preparations were under way to send him to those of his own color in Texas, when circumstances arose which changed the whole history of the movement.

Parties in Los Angeles, having heard of the work of God, sent money to Bro. Seymour so that he could come west with the glad tidings he had learned in Houston. They were under the impression that he had, while in Houston, received the baptism of the Spirit. Such, however, was not the case. He did not receive, in fact, until some time after the Spirit fell in Los Angeles.

Bro. Seymour was rejected by all the Holiness bodies of Los Angeles for preaching that tongues invariably accompanied the baptism in the Spirit. Thereupon he began a series of prayer meetings in Bonnie Bray Street, and it was here that the Spirit first fell in Los Angeles, on the evening of April 9th 1906. Afterward, because of the need for more room, they moved to the famous Azusa Street Mission at 312 Azusa St. Detailed accounts of the Los Angeles revival will appear in forth coming issues of the paper.

Many have made the claim that this blessed revival originated among the colored associates of Bro. Seymour. These reports, as we have seen, are unfounded in fact. The name of the movement and its doctrines were communicated to Bro. Seymour by the brethren in Houston, Texas. One of the Houston saints, Mrs. Lucy Farrow, followed Bro. Seymour to Los Angeles and became one of the most helpful of the workers there.

We might add that Sister Jennie Moore, now Mrs. Seymour, was the first one in Los Angeles to receive the Baptism in the Spirit.

Following we append a selection from an article by W. F. Carothers published in *Apostolic Faith*, Vol. 2, No. 2, Oct. 1908 issued in Houston, Texas.

**To Zion City**

"From the state encampment held in Baxter, Kansas, in the early autumn, 1906, precious workers carried the news of Pentecost, and the blessed experience with them to Zion City. They found those people in the midst of discouragements and confusions, brought by the common enemy of us all, and the new message came as an unspeakable blessing to them. With almost universal consent the Zion people here and elsewhere have accepted the experience, and no more blessed work has been nor is being done than is going on in their midst and through their instrumentality in many parts of the globe.

"Later in the winter of 1906, or after nine months of unity with the original movement the work in Los Angeles separated from us, under circumstances which the present writer believes justified them, but about which it would be painful to write.

"They first called themselves the 'Pacific Coast Apostolic Faith Movement' and had evangelistic and pastoral directors just as the original Movement had.

"God continued to bless them and visions of greater service for God came before them and they changed their title to 'The Divine Apostolic Faith Movement,' but in a short while they dropped all this and with it practically all resemblance of an orderly and united Movement.

"While we believe that in the end good will come from the division, yet temporarily it brought great damage in many ways:

"1. It was an entering wedge which well nigh disrupted Christian disciple and Bible order in the whole Movement. At once certain freelancers, who had before been held in check, leaped to the front and introduced great confusion and disorder. God has singularly overruled this feature, however, and has continued to bless the precious saints who have gone out from Los Angeles to the uttermost parts of the earth.

"From Zion City and the other Movement on the one hand and from Azusa Street, Los Angeles, on the other, by the word of mouth, and by letter, by the Spirit and by the Word, over all lands and across the seas, the tidings have been carried until they have circled the globe.

"It must be remembered that this is only a brief outline of the progress of events. Space forbids us going into the blessed details and telling of the sacrifices, the persecutions, the victories and blessings, the failures and successes that have marked the progress of the Movement. We do not deem it wise, nor have we the disposition to give the names of the actors for the simple reason that all the glory belongs to God -- and all the evil that has been palmed off simultaneously belongs to the devil, whence it will ultimately return. Suffice it to say that heroes have been made [of] both men and women, boys and girls, whose deeds are recorded in the Lamb's book of life, and many more are rising up to carry the fully restored Gospel of our blessed Lord to the uttermost bounds of the earth -- after which we look for Him to return.

"We believe that the foregoing account of the origin and spread of the present-day Pentecostal experience, although necessarily very brief, will throw a great deal of light upon the subject to thousands of interested people over the world. At the same time we trust that it will put us of the older part of the Movement in the right light before our brethren who are not acquainted with us.

"While it is true that God has carried the message and experience clear out beyond the confines of the original Movement, and poured out of His Spirit upon thousands who have never heard of the origin of the present Movement, yet we have not been led to disband our forces and cease our labors -- as some have advised us to do. There is much ground to be occupied all around us, young workers called into the vineyard need training and guidance, young congregations need building up and new territory in our very midst needs evangelizing while our united resources should be behind the missionaries who have trusted God and gone to foreign lands.

"But though we maintain our original name and united Movement, it does not mean any lack of appreciation for all of the blessed work being done by others in different branches of the great vineyard. We love them all who are in divine order and are pressing the battle on lines that honor God and earnestly covet the love and prayers of every branch of the work.

"While we preach unity and believe in it, yet we have no desire to see it come at the expense of elevating any man or combination of men above their fellows, and this is the real obstacle to unity. We believe there is a practical spirit of unity among all the various forces in the experience and perhaps that is sufficient for present purposes.

"It may be that we of the older part of the Movement place a little more emphasis upon Bible order and thoroughness in the work, and stand more for Christian discipline that will weed out the goats, than do some of the newer works, but this is only natural. Please be sure that we are as firm as ever against 'organization' as it has been practiced in the modern church movements and which saps spirituality." -- W. F. Carothers. (*TWE*, Feb. 19, 1916)

## Reminiscences of an Eyewitness

### B. F. Lawrence

We are indebted to Brother H. A. Goss of Hot Springs, Arkansas for the following lines:

In the fall of 1903, Charles F. Parham came to Galena, Kansas and opened a tent meeting. I was an infidel and had no concern about religious work; but this meeting was something unusual, so I went once in awhile just for curiosity, and later, when the meeting was moved to a large double storeroom on Main St., I went oftener with some of my fellow High School students to see the "show" as it was called.

The Galena Revival was a wonderful meeting; hundreds were saved and baptized in the Spirit, also there were many cases of healing.

The speaking in tongues was a marvel to me, as I did not believe in supernatural power. However, these things soon convinced me that there was an Almighty, so tongues proved a sign to me. 1 Cor. 14:22.

I remember watching a big Peoria Indian preacher receive the baptism of the Holy Spirit and begin to talk in other languages and shake as if some great machine had hold of him. His whole frame shook for more than two hours, his hands all this time being held above his head. These wonders, put me on my face seeking God, and after more than a week, God saved me. I had much unbelief to fight through, but, thank God, He brought me out victorious. At once I began to seek my baptism in the Holy Spirit and to read my Bible.

On New Year's Eve there was a watch meeting held which included foot washing and the ordination of twelve people to the ministry. Among the twelve were John James and E. Pierson, a former Quaker minister. These men are in the Pentecostal ministry today. That was a wonderful night; at six in the morning there were about four hundred people present.

Wonderful altar services were held. I have seen as many as a hundred line up before the platform at a time, waiting their turn to be prayed for, for healing. And hundreds found their desire.

After the great revival, the work spread to the surrounding country and to Joplin, Mo. where a great meeting was held. There are Assemblies in these places to this day.

In the spring of 1905 Mr. Parham went to Orchard, Texas to visit some friends, and while there held some meetings. Later, he returned to Galena and held a kind of campmeeting in July. Many people from nearby towns came to this camp, at the close of which Mr. Parham selected about fifteen preachers and workers to take back to Texas with him. They stopped at Orchard again and held another meeting; then with additional help moved on to Houston to open a work there.

Bryan Hall was rented at a cost of $50 per week, and in a short time the city was stirred and much people were added to the Lord, healed and filled with the Spirit.

Among the most noteworthy cases of healing was that of a Mrs. Delaney, a woman well known in the city. About two years previous to her healing she had been injured in a street car wreck and had sued the Street Car Co. for damages.

Sometime before the meetings opened, she had a vision, in which she saw Mr. Parham, and the Lord showed her that this man would pray for her and that she would be healed.

As she was being wheeled down the street one day (paralysis and a wheel chair were the results of her accident), she came to a street meeting and saw the man that the Lord had showed to her in her vision. She stopped and listened to the preaching, inquired where the meetings were being held, and after a few days was brought to the hall. A few of the brethren carried her, chair and all, up the stairs. She was prayed for and was instantly healed, and has been walking ever since. This caused a still greater stir among the people.

As the work spread over the city, W. F. Carothers, who was pastor of a Holiness church in Brunner, a suburb of Houston, invited some of the worker out to his place. Great blessings were upon the work in those days.

After the revival, Mr. Parham left the work in charge of some of the helpers, and with some of the young Texas converts, came back to Kansas and held a great Camp meeting in Columbus, Kansas, and this city also was mightily stirred.

At this time I had yet cut loose for the Lord's work, but I knew that God had called me, and others, who felt the same way about it, came to me and asked me to consider getting free to go to Texas, as there was another company arranging to go. I decided to do so, and on October 15, 1905, a company of twenty-two of us left Columbus on the Frisco 'Meteor' for Texas. I felt that I was really forsaking all to go and do His bidding. I had a great deal of opposition in getting out into the work, my friends telling me that I was making a great mistake in my determination; but I knew that God had called me, and I felt so good to get away from discouragements and obey the Lord.

We stopped at Orchard for a few days and had a blessed time. One of the preachers of our company received the baptism in the Spirit on the train after leaving Orchard. We had to change trains at Alvin, and while waiting for our train we held a street meeting. Many of the citizens were interested and desired us to return and hold a revival.

At Houston the brethren received us joyfully, and we had a few days conference at the Brunner Tabernacle. At the close of the conference several bands of workers were formed to go to nearby towns and hold revival services; about six being in each company.

Oscar Jones and myself, with a few others, went back to Alvin; rented the opera house and opened fire on the enemy. Soon there was a great revival on; the power of God was falling, people were getting saved, filled with the Holy Spirit and speaking in other tongues; the sick were being healed and the town was in a stir. About two hundred were saved and one hundred and thirty-four received the baptism in the Spirit. Some very precious workers came out of this meeting, among them W. B. Jessup, Standley Bennett, Miss Milicent McClendon who became a powerful preacher, Hugh Cadwalder, later a missionary to Africa, and my wife, about a year later. Many others were launched out as [a] result of the meeting.

We had some mighty and wonderful manifestations of the power of God in the Alvin revival and a great work was established.

From Alvin we went to Galveston where, later, we had some trouble with fanaticism, but Mr. Parham acted with great wisdom and corrected it as soon as he found it out. He was very careful to keep the work clean and free from extremes. All through the work at this time we had manifestations of the gifts of the Spirit as recorded in 1 Cor. 12. (TWE, Feb. 26, 1916)

(This article continues in the next issue (below) of March 4, 1916.)

## The Houston Bible School and W. J. Seymour

The Bible School at Houston was a great blessing to all of us, as Mr. Parham was a very interesting teacher. Also a revival was carried on in the city in connection with the school and a great work was done on the streets. Many more were saved and filled with the Spirit and spake in tongues. Mr. Parham taught that all would speak in tongues when filled with the Spirit.

This school is the place where Mr. Seymour, later of Azusa St., Los Angeles, received the light about the baptism in the Spirit. I remember very clearly his coming to the classes at 9 A. M. and he and Mr. Parham preached to the colored people of the city, and some of them received the light. Mr. Seymour was already a minister, but was seeking the baptism.

He soon wanted to go to Los Angeles, but was urged not to do so until he received the Baptism. However, he did go before receiving, and later opened the Azusa St. work. Later, Mrs. Lucy Farrow, a colored baptized saint that had cooked for the company of workers while holding meetings at Bryan Hall in Houston, and who had been in Mr. Parham's family for several months, went to Los Angeles to assist Seymour in his work there. This was about Feb., 1, 1906.

February 15, 1906 a company of us went to Wallis to open a work. I stayed there two weeks and then came back to Houston to the school. Soon the school closed and all the workers were sent out to various towns around about.

Another young man and myself went to Angleton, a new field, to open up a work. Here after several weeks of bitter opposition, the power began to fall and God gave a great revival.

At the close of the Houston School there were about fifty preachers and workers in the field, and as the companies were in new fields they were having great revivals

## He Receives the Baptism on a Train

A convention was announced to be held in Orchard, Texas, April 13-15. Many of the preachers and workers came together, and we had a great time. I sought my baptism almost all night and day, as it seemed I could not go back to Angleton without the experience. On Monday, while we were all at the depot waiting for the train (which was late), Mr. Parham started services which continued until the belated train arrived. After we were on the train, the power began to fall and some were singing, while others were praying and still others were seeking for the baptism in the Spirit. God answered and the Spirit was poured out and some of the seekers received the baptism and began to speak in other tongues. I saw that the power of God was mightily in the car.

Brother Caywood, of Houston, came to me and told me to praise the Lord. I did not feel like doing so, but he urged me, and so I began and soon the power was coming on me stronger and stronger. Directly, my strength was about gone and I could not speak another word. Another was of glory struck me and I relaxed every muscle, fell back in the chair and said, "Lord, have Thy way." Directly [there was] another wave of the power of God which took hold of my tongue. The glory filled my soul, so that it cannot be described, while the fire of God seemed to be burning me up. Presently, my tongue was loosed and I began to speak in languages I had never heard before. O, the joy of that experience is more than I can tell.

In about an hour, twelve more on this train received the baptism. Among them, P. M. Stokely and Joe Rosselli. Both are now in our ministry.

We soon had to change cars and others with me from Angleton got off. I could not speak English at all, and could only tell them what to do by motioning with my hands. On the train we now took, more of our company received the baptism.

We shortly after this heard of the power falling at Los Angeles and our hearts were made to rejoice in the blessing of God on the work.

At this time (the beginning of the Outpouring in Los Angeles) there were 60 preachers and workers in Texas, and I think I am safe in saying that there were more than a thousand who had received the baptism in the Spirit and had spoken in other tongues.

## The First State Encampment

The first State Encampment was announced for Brunner (Houston) in July 1906. We all gathered there again and the power fell mightily. Here Mrs. Farrow came and gave us a detailed account of what was happening in Los Angeles. She was endued with an unusual power to lay hands on people for the reception of the Holy Spirit. At one time I saw a row of about twenty-five lined up before her, she laid hands upon them and many began to speak in tongues at once.

Hundreds and thousands of Houston people came to hear the Gospel. From the campmeeting the preachers scattered again with this great message, some of them going to other states.

Mr. W. F. Carothers was appointed General Field Director, and I was made field Director for Texas and Kansas. This was the first step toward church government for the general work. Heretofore, Mr. Parham has been the only general leader, and he, with the advice of others, selected us.

The work now spread to Zion City and Chicago. Mrs. Mabel Smith Hall, a woman used of God in a marvelous way in Texas in speaking in tongues, interpretation and preaching, went to Zion City with others, and later to Chicago, and was first to bring the message to that City.

**The Work Greatly Hindered**

When we learn of Mr. Parham's failure, our hearts were almost broken, and we could hardly believe it; and then the trials began. Some took sides with Mr. Parham and some believed the charges. Mr. Carothers was some what in the lead, and tried to bring peace again, but the matter grew worse, and Mr. Carothers and myself, in an endeavor to hold the work together, announced a Bible School at Waco, Texas.

> *Book Editor*: Mr. Parham was accused of sexual immorality. It is true that some ministers have fallen into sexual temptation, but it is also true that some have been falsely accused, as Mr. Parham claimed.

The school was a blessed one, but we had another fight along another line, viz. speaking in tongues as the evidence of the Baptism in the Spirit. Some contended that all did not speak in tongues, while we held that all should. Thank God, it came out victorious that tongues were the evidence of the baptism in the Spirit, though not the only one.

Brother D. C. O. Opperman assisted us in the school, as he was at this time seeking his baptism. Later, he, in company with A. G. Canada and workers, went to San Antonio to open a work. L. C. Hall, a Zion Elder, came to this place and received the baptism in the Spirit.

After the school, the work in Texas was somewhat torn up over Parham's failure, and many of the preachers and workers were discouraged. I wrote a circular to the workers to go on and to stay in the field until Mr. Carothers and Mr. Parham got the trouble settled. At this, I was accused of desiring leadership at the expense of others. This hurt me, so after a few weeks I resigned. The work went to pieces as far as order was concerned. Most all of the workers left the field, with the exception of my own company, and we had many discouragements, but kept in the fight for the Lord.

Soon we had a meeting and disfellowshipped Mr. Parham, but this did not help matters as far as the general work was concerned. But at the campmeeting in July, Brother A. G. Canada, who had been free from all this trouble in Texas (having gone back to North Carolina after the San Antonio meeting), was elected

Director of the Texas work, and the brethren that stood with us lined up for the battle again, and our God led us our to victory.

In 1908 Brother Opperman announced a Bible School at Houston and another step of progress was made in the power of God, as some of the gifts of the Spirit were given and proved a great blessing to the work.

And thus, the full Gospel continued to spread around the earth. -- H. A. Goss

## The Pentecostal or "Latter Rain" Outpouring in Los Angeles

*Brother Frank Bartleman of Los Angeles, Cal., has kindly supplied us with the following valuable information about the beginning of the work in that city:–*

I have been requested to write briefly what I know about the present Pentecostal outpouring of the Spirit that has swept around the globe in the last nine years. In doing so, I shall write from a personal knowledge only. I reached California in the spring of 1903, with my little family. We located in Sacramento. Shortly before Christmas, 1904, we came to Los Angeles. Just after the first of the new year our oldest daughter died. It was a terrible blow, but it drove me to God. I had been preaching the gospel since 1895. Had been converted in Philadelphia..

In my sorrow at the loss of our oldest child, I threw myself on God and consecrated myself to His service anew. Beside the coffin of my dear one God definitely entered into a new contract with me. He began to reveal to me a deeper, wider service than I had ever known before. The burden of "soul travail" came upon me. I felt I could only live by being used of Him for lost souls, and He showed me that He would grant my desire. He promised that it should not seem long to me until my work was over and I should meet my darling child again.

Then He began to open up to me a wonderful "forward" vision in faith and prayer. He showed me it was in His purpose again, as of old, to pour out His Spirit among us mightily. We had gotten quite pessimistic before this. Few people seemed to be expecting anything better for the last days.

The spirit of prophecy came upon me. I began to prophesy of mighty things from the hand of God. I seemed to receive a "gift of faith." And the travail of soul was wonderful. It consumed me. This began in January, 1905. I began meetings in a little Mission in Pasadena, Cal., at once, after the funeral of our little child. I felt I must be at work for God.

### The Travail of Soul

The Lord wonderfully poured out His Spirit. A number of workers were dug [sic] out in those meetings that later received the Pentecostal baptism and are Pentecostal preachers in the field today. They caught the vision and the faith also. We began to cry, "Pasadena for God!" Meetings were started in a Methodist Church of which these workers were members. They got under the burden. About two hundred souls knelt at the altar in two weeks' time. The Lord began to stir up His people in different churches in the city. The results were directly traced to the prayers of these young men. They were on fire. Our cry was for a "Pentecost." The Lord was clearly directing.

About April, I first heard of the wonderful revival in Wales. It stirred my soul to its very depths. I laid my life in God's hands and asked Him to use me if he could to help further the same wonderful Spirit in America. A few weeks later, while reading S. B. Shaw's book on the "Great Revival in Wales," God spoke to me and asked me to contract definitely with Him that I would never go back to the plow again, but that I would spend all my remaining years in His service only. I have never turned back since that time. I dare not. We have been tempted, but God has proven faithful.

**Inspiration From the Welsh Revival**

In June, 1905, Pastor Smale, of the First Baptist Church in Los Angeles, returned from England, where he had been attending the revival in Wales. He started prayer meetings in his church to wait on God for an outpouring of the Spirit similar to that they were having in Wales. God wonderfully anointed him to exhort the people. He was full of faith for mighty things. I immediately began to attend his services and found them exactly in line with my own vision and aspirations for God.

These prayer meetings ran for a number of weeks, and there was much spontaneous worship, also some very wonderful healings. But the burden that gathered volume daily, and the cry, was for a "Pentecost" for Los Angeles, and for the world. "Pentecost" is the very word we all had on our lips, given by the Holy Ghost. Spiritual workers began to gather to this little company from all over the city. They came from many different denominations and missions. It was a gathering together of those to whom the Lord had spoken. Faith increased rapidly for extraordinary things. God made Pastor Smale a regular Moses to lead us toward the "promised land."

But soon the church dignitaries could tolerate the new, spontaneous order no longer. They ordered it to cease, or the Pastor to resign. The consequence was the Pastor wisely resigned to go on with God, and the Lord and the people went with him. The "cloud" moved. A "New Testament Church" was formed. Here God wonderfully led and blessed, up to the Spring of 1906.

All this year the travail of soul was heavily upon me. In fact, for at least fifteen months, day and night, almost without intermission, the hand of the Lord was upon me to "bring forth." I had no rest day or night from these "groanings that could not be uttered." My precious wife believed that I would die. Days and nights I rolled on my bed in an agony of prayer for the lost world. I seemed as separate from my family almost as though I had been in a distant country for a year. But God spared my life to "eat of the fruit" of my groans and tears. I wrote many tracts during this time, and a number of articles for the papers. God shut me off from preaching much. I could only prophesy of the "things to come." I was tired of my own preaching and that of others. We needed a reviving. We needed the "anointing."

**Encouragements to Faith**

I had a number of most wonderful visions during this year also. Mostly while in travail of soul. One night, after a specially heavy burden in prayer that seemed to almost take my life, the Lord Jesus Himself appeared to me and strengthened me. I lost all sense of time and space. When I came to I had to pinch myself to see if I was flesh and blood. For days I walked with an invisible presence at my side. Human voices sounded harsh and grating. Human contact pained me. I had been with the Lord.

Gradually the stream was rising, ready to overflow all banks as He promised. The clouds of blessing were gathering overhead, accumulated by the prayers of many. There was great expectation. But still the situation seemed to wait for something. It would be a great mistake to attempt to attribute the Pentecostal beginning to Los Angeles to any one man, either in prayer or in preaching. Personally, for months the matter seemed to be accumulating within me. The tide of the Spirit was rising, but it could not yet burst forth. I was not abandoned for it. None of us understood fully what we were seeking or just what to expect. We wanted God to come forth; but just in what way we did not know. We never do. He could not come the same as in Wales, for conditions were very different in Los Angeles.

They did not break through at Pastor Smale's Assembly. There was too much reserve there. God had taken them as far as he could. We had marvelous meetings both there and in private prayer meetings, however, all through the year. More than once we saw and felt God's glory. At times the "cloud" was visible to the naked eye. "Pentecost" did not drop down suddenly out of heaven. God was with us in large measure for a long time before the final outpouring. It was not a mushroom of a night by any means.

Much that would be of interest in this connection must be omitted for lack of space. Finally in February, 1906, seven of us met after prayer service at the New Testament Assembly, and, joining hands, agreed that God should be petitioned to pour out His Spirit speedily "with signs following." I don't think we, any of us, knew what we meant by that. But we felt something out of the ordinary was needed to awaken the people. God gave us that prayer.

**Help Came From Texas**

Somewhere about this time, perhaps a little earlier, Bro. Seymour came to Los Angeles from Texas. He was a quiet colored man, very unassuming. He had been invited by some saints in Los Angeles, who supposed he had already received his Pentecost in Texas. They began to hold quiet meetings in cottages, waiting on God for the outpouring with signs following. Bro. Seymour felt the Lord had sent him to Los Angeles for a special purpose at that time. He was in the closet sympathy with the burden that was on all of our hearts.

He himself had never spoken in "tongues", but he believed in it and had met he Apostolic Faith saints in Houston, Texas, who were already so speaking and had the teaching from them. He believed that "tongues" should accompany a real Pentecostal baptism, according to Acts 2:4. This he asserted not at all in a dogmatic way. He himself did not speak in "tongues" until weeks after others had begun to in our midst.

Finally he began to meet with a little company of white and colored people in an humble cottage in Bonnie Brae St. They decided to wait on God for ten-

days' special petitioning of God and in yielding themselves to Him. The time had come. God had found the right company at last. The most spiritual of the saints were among this company. Suddenly, one night in these meetings, the Spirit of God was poured out and some began to "speak with other tongues, as the Spirit gave them utterance." The news spread like fire naturally. The expectant saints began to gather. They opened public meetings in old Azusa St., in an old Methodist Church that had been for a long time in disuse, except as a receptacle for old lumber, plaster, etc. It was very dirty. A space was cleared large enough to seat a score or two of persons. We sat on planks resting on old nail kegs, if I remember correctly. But God was there. The work began in earnest.

**The San Francisco Earthquake**

It was on the 9th of April, 1906, that the Spirit was first poured out in Bonnie Brae. On April 18th we had the terrible San Francisco earthquake. It had a very close connection with the Pentecostal outpouring. God covered the fire at old "Azusa Mission" and protected it during the first few days of its existence until there was no danger of its being stamped out by the enemy. Then He let loose His judgments in California. This shook the whole state, as well as the nation. Men began to fear God. California was very wicked. Their consciences needed to be knocked at. This paved the way for the revival. Otherwise they would have mocked us. There was "no fear of God before them."

Workers began to gather from all parts of the city, from throughout the state, and in fact from all over the nation, to "Azusa Mission." Bro. Cashwell came from North Caroline, got his "baptism," and carried the fire back and spread it all over the Southland, especially the South Atlantic States. Sister Ivy Campbell went back to her home in Ohio and spread the flame throughout that whole eastern country. Others came in from different sections and carried the news and the blessing everywhere. Missionaries returned from many parts of the heathen world, sent directly and impressively by God, to tarry for their "baptism." It was a time of wonderful gathering. God alone had ordered it. "Gather My saints together unto Me." Ps. 50:5. Thousands were saved and baptized with the Spirit, all speaking in other tongues.

**Azusa Became the Center**

God suddenly shut up many little Holiness Missions, Tent meetings, etc., that had been striving with one another a long time for the preeminence. It would not work any more. They had to come together. God only could tame them. There was little going on anywhere else, but at Azusa St. All the people were coming. Even Pastor Smale finally came to "Azusa Mission" to hunt his people up. Then he invited them back to let God have His way. The fire broke out at his own Assembly also. When God dries a place up it is dry. This [is what] many churches who opposed the Azusa work soon found out to their sorrow. And many are yet sorrowing over it. They would not take God's way. They were "also among the prophets," but when the Lord came He did not come through them. This killed them. They would not go to "Azusa," nor let "Azusa" come to them. "Azusa" was despised in their eyes.

But "Joseph" has got the corn. The "seven years of plenty" have not swept around the world. Missionaries returned, [they came] by faith for bread, and for the healing of their bodies in sickness, [then went] to all parts of the world. They carried the Pentecostal message and power with them. Almost every country on the globe has been visited by them. The work is almost stronger in some other countries than it is even in America. It has been my personal privilege to "see the mighty works of God" in Pentecostal power in England, Scotland, Wales, France, Holland, Switzerland, Germany, Norway, Sweden, Finland, Russia, Egypt, Palestine, Ceylon, India, China, and in the Islands of the Sea, outside of the United States and Canada.

The Pentecostal power burst forth in the Christian and Missionary Alliance in New York state. Bro. Barratt came from far off Norway and received the "baptism" there. He carried it back and spread the fire in the whole of Scandinavia, and even into Russia. Vicar A. A. Boddy, of Sunderland, England, went to Norway and caught the inspiration. Returning home the fire fell all over the British Isles from his testimony. Even in wicked Paris the "Promise of the Father" has been freely given. In fact, in every part of the world, from the frozen north to the torrid south the good news and the Pentecostal missionaries have gone.

In every one of the five Continents the Pentecostal message has become familiar. There is possibly not one of the Seven Seas but what has been voyaged by these missionaries. Some have circled the globe many times in the last few brief years "since the fire fell." The writer himself has been privileged to circle it once with the Pentecostal message. It is simply wonderful how the truth has spread. And who could have done it but God?

Every part of the Continent of "dark Africa" has its Pentecostal witness. South America is also represented. Central America is not left out in the message. Alaska, Persia, Siberia, Japan, all have been visited graciously. China has been honeycombed with 150 Pentecostal missionaries. Tibet has not been forgotten. Even old Jerusalem has heard again the sound of "speaking in other tongues as the Spirit gives utterance." Many have already laid down their lives in these foreign countries for the Pentecostal gospel. Among them Bro. Brelsford in Egypt, the land of the ancient Pharaohs and the birth place of Moses. Oh, hallelujah!

The "seven years of famine" seem to have already set in. "Wars, and rumors of wars." The "last days" are upon us. Soon the opportunity will be gone. I am so glad I got the "Pentecostal baptism" nine years ago in the first outpouring of the Spirit in Los Angeles. It set me going for God in the "Last Call," the last great battle. "Get oil within your vessels. 'Tis the Midnight Cry!" -- Frank Bartleman, L.A. (March 11, 1916)

## My First Visit to the Azusa Street Pentecostal Mission

*We are indebted to Bro. A. W. Orwig for the following account*:

It was in September, 1906. I had heard of the meetings during the early part of the same year, when there was "no small stir" concerning them. The daily papers of the city had characterized them as scenes of wild fanaticism, enacted by ignorant and crazy people. Especially was the reputed speaking in unknown tongues bitterly denounced as a fraud, and was sacrilegiously caricatured. Besides this, many church-members spoke disdainfully of the meetings, some declaring them to be of devil. This naturally influenced others to condemn them; some, however, suspended judgment, wholly or in part, for the time being; I was among the latter.

During the month and year above mentioned, a large, four-page paper was issued by the mission, a copy of which accidentally or providentially fell into my hands on a Friday afternoon. At once I began to read it with considerable interest, and in a very short time was convinced that God was in the work. I continued to read nearly all Saturday until my heart burned within me, and I said to my wife, "I am going to Azusa Street Mission on Sunday and see and hear for myself."

I arrived at ten o'clock, and at that early hour found the house practically full, with many more coming later, some glad to secure standing room. I remained until one o'clock, returned at two and stayed until five, thus spending six solid hours on that one day. And I was more than ever persuaded that the movement was of God.

I will not now attempt to describe sermons, testimonies, prayers, and songs, only to say that they were usually attended with divine unction to such a degree as to move and melt hearts in every direction. The altar of prayer was generally crowded and other space designated for seekers, both saint and sinner. Many of both classes who came out of curiosity, and some possibly to ridicule, were smitten to the floor by the power of God, and often wrestled in agony and prayer until they found that for which they sought, -- some for pardon and others for deeper experience in God, by whatever name the latter might be called.

Often it was termed sanctification, holiness, or the baptism of the Holy Ghost. Quite prominent was the teaching that the baptism in the Spirit was upon the sanctified life, and evidenced by the speaking in another tongue, however brief, as on the day of Pentecost. Not all, however, who gladly attended the meetings and derived profit thereby, fully or at all accepted this teaching. Nor did they specially identify themselves with the movement, although often endorsing it in general terms.

The subject, or doctrine, of divine healing received special attention and many cases of deliverance from various diseases and infirmities were more or less continually reported. Likewise was the doctrine of the pre-millennial coming of Christ ardently promulgated.

One thing that somewhat surprised me at that first meeting I attended, and also subsequently, was the presence of so many persons from the different churches, not a few of them educated and refined. Some were pastors, evangelists, foreign missionaries, and others of high position in various circles, looking on with seeming amazement and evident interest and profit. And they took part in the services in one way or another. Persons of many nationalities were also present, of which Los Angeles seems to be filled, representing all manner of religious beliefs. Sometimes these, many of them unsaved, would be seized with deep conviction for sin under the burning testimony of one of their own nationality, and at once heartily turn to the Lord.

Occasionally some foreigner, although [only] somewhat understanding English, would hear a testimony or earnest exhortation in his native tongue from a person not at all acquainted with that language; thereby be pungently convicted that it was a call from God to repent of sin; often such repentance followed just as on the day of Pentecost. I could give interesting details of such instances if space permitted, and may possibly do so at some other time. (We have received another article from Bro. Orwig which appears below.)

Of course some persons attending the meetings in those early days of the revival, mocked and [made trifling objections], also as on the day Pentecost, and are doing so at the present. But this is true of every mighty work of the Holy Spirit. It would be unlike Satan not to stir up derision and opposition. By this I am not saying that there have been no indiscretions and positively no counterfeiting of the Holy Spirit's work; the devil is an expert in imitating that work. And undiscerning persons have not known the difference between the true and the false. The genuine is therefore, sometimes doubted even by some Christians; and what is true as to unfortunate things connected with the so-called Pentecostal Movement, is just as true of some things occurring in the various Christian denominations.

**Further From Los Angeles About the Pentecostal Work**

In the above I spoke of my first visit to Azusa Street Pentecostal Mission in the year 1906, and the very favorable impressions made upon me. My heart is often stirred with praise and gratitude as I think of their beneficial effect upon me at the time. Especially did the enchanting strains of the so-called "Heavenly

Choir," or hymns sung under the evident direction of the Holy Spirit both as to words and tune, thrill my whole being. It was not a something that could be repeated at will, but supernaturally given for each special occasion and was one of the most indisputable evidences of the presence of the power of God. Perhaps nothing so greatly impressed people as this singing; at once inspiring a holy awe, or a feeling of indescribable wonder, especially if the hearers were in devout attitude.

Most vividly are other scenes recalled of the mighty power of God upon the minds and hearts of both sinner and saint. Often the hardness of heart, the levity, of the former were completely overcome by the burning truth of God, and men and women were gloriously swept into the kingdom of grace with whirlwind power. Not that the preaching was great, humanly speaking, but because mighty prayer, faith, singleness of eye and truly anointed speech were used of God for the salvation of souls, the edification of believers, and the receiving of the Holy Spirit with various manifestations. Not a few of the so-called "Holiness People," who perhaps thought they had about all there was to be obtained, found the meetings a great blessing to them. Others of this class stood aloof for different reasons; some because of not understanding the movement; some from more or less prejudice; others because the occasional speaking with other tongues proved a stumbling block to them.

**Incidents, With Remarks**

1. *"It will soon blow over."* -- Either in 1906 or 1907, a beloved brother preacher said to me, "The Lord has shown me that this movement will soon blow over." Of course he erred in two things, namely, his claim as to what the Lord had shown him, as also what he thought would happen to the movement in a year or two. But the brother was simply a representative of many others. Of course I need not specially refer to the fact that "this movement" soon spread to many parts of the country and to other lands. It is admitted that some defects were connected with it, as is natural with any enterprise or work in which fallible humanity has a part. The same is true of the various Christian churches. But the imperfections of the "Apostolic Pentecostal Movement," or even some of its seemingly strange features, is no evidence whatsoever that God was not and is not with it. But how many foolish and even pernicious things are found in some churches! And in not a few cases no effort seems to be made to eliminate them.

2. *The Invitation of a D.D.* -- I now recall what I heard a prominent Baptist preacher say at one of the Sunday afternoon meetings in the Azusa Street Mission in 1906. Standing in the back part of the church, perhaps for lack of room elsewhere, and while listening to the very glowing testimonies, he called out, substantially, "I wish some of you persons on that rostrum would come over to my church this evening and speak to the people who gather outside for a meeting before the services begin inside." And, he continued, "No one will lay his hand on your shoulder and say, 'Be brief, brother,' for you may continue to speak as long as you please, even though there is no service inside." That was indeed a significant endorsement of what was occurring at the Mission. He was magnani-

mous enough to go and see and hear for himself, instead of persistently remaining away and condemning without personal and unprejudiced investigation. I mention this as being in happy contrast with the unfair, stolid condemnation and even uncharitable and sinful derision of some professor of religion. Oh, the loss and injury often sustained by some persons because of the malignant demon of [racial] prejudice possessing them!

3. *A Prominent Methodist's Declaration.* -- He was a high official in the principal church of the city, and at one of he meetings at old Azusa's humble, almost barn-like place of worship, he declared that he thoroughly believed the work was of God, and wished the same holy fire and marvelous work of grace would break out in his church and other churches. He seemed to be greatly captivated, although a man not given to excitement, but a prudent, influential business man. Occasionally the "holy fire," of which he spoke, did seize some persons of social, religious and intellectual standing, besides those among the more "common people." Many, of course, did not identify themselves with the movement, as such, though frequently attending the services, but remained in their own churches as better "lights" and more efficacious "salt" than they had hitherto been. Not infrequently, however, some left their church and attended the meetings regularly, and became one with the "Pentecostal" people, or, as some persons would say, with "the tongues people," sometimes with no unfriendly feeling. No ecclesiastical organization, strictly speaking, was "joined," for here was none to join, and is none to this day, although a brotherly union of spirit is usually maintained.

4. *A Daily Paper's Reporter Captured.* -- It was during the early days of the meetings at Azusa Street Assembly. He had been assigned to "write up" an account of the meetings held by those supposed ignorant, fanatical, demented people. But it was to be from the standpoint of the comic or ridiculous, -- the more highly sensational the better. It was doubtless supposed that this would the more freely meet the tastes of the readers of the paper. And the reporter went to the meeting with feelings in harmony with those of his employers. He was going to a "circus," as he and others would say, so far as genuine worldly amusement is concerned. But, fortunately for himself, he witnessed some very touching and solemn scenes, and heard the Gospel truth so powerfully presented in the Holy Ghost by different persons, that his frivolous feelings gave way to devout ones.

After a little while a Spirit-filled woman gave such a mighty exhortation and appeal to the sinner to turn to God that the reporter was still more greatly impressed. Suddenly she broke out, not voluntarily, but truly as the "Spirit gave utterance" (Acts 2:4), in a different language, one with which she was utterly unfamiliar. But it was in the native tongue of the foreign-born reporter, who was also proficient in the English language. Directing her earnest gaze upon him, she poured forth such a holy torrent of truth, by way of exposing his former sinful, licentious life, that he was perfectly dumbfounded, no one seemingly understanding the language but himself.

When the services were over, he at once forced his way to the woman, asking her if she knew what she had said concerning him while speaking in that particular foreign language. "Not a word," was her prompt reply. At first he could not believe her, but her evident sincerity and perfectly grammatical and fluent speech thoroughly convinced him that she absolutely knew nothing of the language. Then he told her that she had given an entirely correct statement of his wicked life, and that he now fully believed her utterances were exclusively from God in order to lead him to true repentance and the accepting of Jesus Christ as his Savior. And he at once faithfully promised such a course. Going from the meeting he informed his employers that he could not give them such a report as they expected him to present. He added, however, that if they wanted a true and impartial account of the meeting he would gladly give it. But they did not want that, and also plainly told him that they did not need his services thereafter.

**Closing Words: What a Bishop Said**

I had intended to give a few more instances in which the speaking in another or unknown tongue, as supernaturally effected, and resulting in salvation to the sinner, as also in being a help to some Christians, among other things removing prejudice and even active hostility with both classes of persons, but lack of space forbids. The Lord willing, and having an invitation from the "Evangel" representatives to furnish material, I expect to resume the subject of the Pentecostal work under various aspects. More interesting incidents will follow. The "tongues" question will receive further attention by way of correcting wrong notions concerning it, pro and con.

By way of closing let me say that I was informed, several years ago, that one of the bishops of a certain denomination had advised people not to condemn the movement, but to let it alone, lest they misjudge and hinder a work that may be of God. -- A. W. Orwig,. . . Los Angeles, Calif. (*TWE*, March 18, 1916)

# Chapter 2

# Pentecostal History Part 2

**The Work Spreads to India**

*Bro. and Sister Garr were the first Pentecostal missionaries to carry the news of the Pentecostal outpouring to India and China. We are indebted to them for the following remarkable account:–*

> "Forasmuch as many have taken in hand to set forth in order a declaration of those things which are most surely believed among us, even as they delivered them unto us, which from the beginning were eyewitnesses and ministers of the Word. It seemed good to us also to write of those things which our eyes have seen and our hands have handled of the Word of God." Luke 1:1-2.

We were permitted to be among the first to witness God's mighty power as poured out at Azusa Street, Los Angeles, and also were chosen of Him to be the first Pentecostal missionaries to cross the seas to tell to missionaries and natives of India and China that God had visited the earth and given the "Latter Rain."

For years, in the Holiness Movement, our hearts had hungered to be filled with all the fullness of God, and though told by leaders that the experience of sanctification was the same as the great infilling received by the disciples on the day of Pentecost, the blessed Spirit of God was true to our hearts and God's precious Word revealed to us that there was an experience beyond what we possessed, which would bring with its reception a power hitherto unknown.

After much prayer and fasting and very definite seeking of God's face, we were led to come to Los Angeles and take charge of the Metropolitan Holiness Church, several months before the outpouring at Azusa.

These months were very special seasons of prayer for a revival on our souls and the work in our charge, and although we could not state very definitely what our own hearts needed, still we followed our convictions like the Psalmist, who said, "When Thou sayest, Seek ye my face; my heart said unto Thee, Thy face, Lord will I seek." Psa. 27:8.

He "whose eyes run to and fro throughout the whole earth to show Himself strong in behalf of those whose hearts are perfect toward Him," found us in this waiting, hungry attitude and led us with the then small company at Azusa to enter into an experience with Himself which was more than we could have asked or thought.

## Messengers of An Outpouring

These were wonderful days in the Spirit -- the new worship through the manifestation of tongues and the Heavenly song, was marvelous to us, but there had been in our seeking that longing for power to win lost souls.

It was for this we tarried. It was with this prayer on our lips one night -- "Oh! God, Thou has called us to preach Thy Gospel, souls are going down, but we cannot go without the power from on high" -- that the Spirit descended upon us and we felt and knew that the promise of our Father was fulfilled. He had come and, with Him, the power for service.

After a few days of this joy and fellowship, the blessed Spirit began to give such travail for souls and such reaching out for the nations of the earth as we had never known, though God had given much soul agony in the Holiness movement. The Spirit made us to know we were to be witnesses unto the uttermost parts of the earth.

It was not long before we were on the seas, our hearts burning with longing to carry this glorious Gospel to India and China. We had, as it were, suffered the loss of all -- all our old Holiness friends rejected us, the old doors were closed, but God was setting before us an open door which no man could shut.

It was like beginning life over, a new ministry in the power of God's Spirit, not limited to a small fraction of the Holiness people, nor to one country as before, but the "World our parish" and a message of God's outpouring for all nations. Blessed be our God, who prepared Cornelius in a vision for Peter's message, so also, He went before us into India to get ready the soil in hearts for the seed of this blessed Pentecostal Truth.

On reaching India, we found it was the Viceroy's season in Calcutta, when the missionaries had come in from all parts of India to make a special effort for souls. This was so truly the hand of our God.

They were much in prayer for a revival so that it could have been said of us, "I sent you to reap that whereon ye bestowed no labor; other men labored, and ye are entered into their labors."

God moved in a mysterious way before He brought us into contact with those to whom we were sent.

With no funds with which to open up in India, we were kept in much prayer for God's opening. One day we were directed to a prayer meeting where we found quite a body of missionaries whose testimonies revealed not only their own deep hunger for souls, but a longing for a revival in Calcutta, and there was real faith that God was going to give them their heart's desire. We were strangers among them and therefore said nothing, but our hearts kept telling us that this was our company and God had given us a message for these hungry ones.

The next morning we went to another mission home and the way opened for us to tell of God's visitation in America. With the exception of one or two, we found the whole company very receptive, and when the Spirit spoke through us in other tongues, the reverence and deep hunger with which it was received proved to us that we had found the people to whom God had sent us.

At the night service an opportunity was given to tell of the outpouring of the Spirit at Azusa St., and at the close an elderly gentleman, Bro. Hook, the Pastor of Lal Bazaar Baptist Church, Calcutta, came forward and offered his church to us for the preaching of this blessed "Truth." We had believed for a tent or a store building to open, but this fine Baptist church to which we were taken on the following Sunday morning, and such a saintly old Pastor, this was beyond our fondest dreams; but oh, so like our God who always does more than we can ask or think.

There was nothing said in our hearing of the closing of the other meeting, of which Pastor Stockmeyer of Germany and Mr. Ward of Coonoor were the leaders, but on entering Lal Bazaar Baptist Church for our first service, we found the same body of noble missionaries, who like the Bereans, "received the Word with all readiness of mind, and searched the Scriptures daily whether those things were so."

Many of them were very ripe in experience, having received very rich anointings from the Lord, but the Gift of the Holy Ghost, with the accompanying sign of speaking with other tongues, had not been received. Lal Bazaar Church proved to be an ideal place for tarrying before God.

Hours were spent in prayer each day. They were wonderful seasons! Sometimes silence would reign for a long time, but there were the deepest heart searchings after God, which He abundantly rewarded.

We had quite a cosmopolitan audience, composed of missionaries from all denominations, officers and soldiers of the English army, Englishmen and Americans in business in Calcutta, Eutrasians and East Indians, but God was coming in answer to prayer to "pour out His Spirit upon all flesh."

Before any one received the Baptism in the Spirit, there was much confession and restitution and a very wonderful revival. Many were saved. The church floor looked like a battle field. "The slain of the Lord were many."

Among them were quite a number of very fine young men from the army, some of whom are today Pentecostal missionaries in India, having bought their discharge. The first man to receive the baptism in India was a captain in the English army.

The night he was slain under the mighty power of God was one to be remembered. It was the first witness, and there was much fear in the hearts of his loved ones when this fine soldier fell to the floor, slain by God's power. As one brother bent over him and asked, "Is it all right, Captain?" back came the answer, filled with God's anointing, "All is well."

His dear wife and daughter soon entered into the same experience. God granted to the wife some very marvelous visions during those days.

We could not work at the altar; in fact there seemed no need. The deep repentance, the strong cryings of those seeking salvation, the many slain on the floor, showed us the work was being carried on by the Spirit and we needed only to stand by and worship our God that we were permitted to live and see His workings.

One very marked case of restitution is worthy of mention. An Englishman who was attending the meeting had deserted from the English army many years before, marrying his wife under an assumed name, and had also taken supplies from the railroad company that employed him, to the amount of 1,000 Rupees (over $300).

During the preaching of a sermon on "Hell," he was seen to fall forward on the seat in front of him and cry out bitterly. At the close of the service, he asked if he had to confess his life, and on being told that "he that covereth his sins shall not prosper, but whosoever confesseth and forsaketh shall find mercy," he went home to confess to his wife and son. It was a great sorrow to the wife who felt she could not forgive, but God dealt with her and the father, mother and son fell at the altar, and the glory of God filled them, and a happier family could not have been found.

The thousand rupees was restored and we went with the brother several hundred miles to "Wellington," the headquarters of the English army, where he delivered himself up to the commission officer.

Though our brother was a man weighing over two hundred pounds, and in charge of three hundred natives, still the officer, after hearing the testimony of our brother, pronounced him unfit for service, and in answer to the prayers of God's people he was released. (*TWE*, March 25, 1916) [Continued in the next issue:]

## Brother Max Wood Moorhead

Bro. Max Wood Moorhead, afterward editor of the *Pentecostal Witness* of India, the first issue of which was published during the revival at Calcutta, received his baptism very early in the meetings, and from that day until now has been used through his testimony, and pen, for the spread of this blessed "Truth."

God used Bro. Moorhead to open a large house in Calcutta, when persecutions became so fierce that it seemed impossible to go on in the church, although the Pastor stood by us nobly.

God rewarded him by giving him the blessed Spirit, and since then Lal Bazaar Baptist Church has been an open door for Pentecostal Truth. Most of the conventions since held in India have been within her sacred walls.

Bro. Moorhead threw open this home for hungry ones and they came from all parts of India, received their baptism, and went back to their stations in the power of the Spirit to tell their co-workers of God's marvelous workings at Calcutta. Hunger was created in the hearts by these living witnesses, and they too would come and receive.

Our services were held in the large drawing room of this "Home." Wonderful results followed the baptisms of these missionaries. Frequently the power of God would be poured out on their whole school in a short time after they received.

In the case of Miss Easton, head of the American Mission Board in Calcutta, who had charge of a large girl's school, we think there were forty of her girls entered into the baptism in a few days from the time Miss Easton received.

Miss Costello, who had charge of the Orphanage of the same missionary board, found the same power attended her ministry.

The dear Indians under her care were filled with God's power. Miss Salatti, at the head of the Salvation Army Rescue Work, experienced the same among the

Rescue Women, some lay for hours under God's power, worshiping the Lord in new tongues. These are a few out of the many that proved indeed that power does come with this mighty baptism.

One missionary, after receiving her baptism, returned to her station and took her regular morning service with the school. She said nothing to the girls of what God had done for her soul, but just praised the Lord.

There was a new unction, and a new power in their missionary that took hold on the hearts of those Indian girls, and that night lights were seen in the dormitory at a late hour. This was against the rule, and the missionary went to investigate. She found the girls pouring out their hearts in prayer. Confession and restitution followed and God poured out His Spirit on that whole school.

During the Calcutta revival Pandita Ramabai, so well known to Pentecostal readers for the wonderful outpouring at Mukti (her school), wrote us, inviting us to come and preach to her school. None of her missionaries nor the dear Indian Christians had received the Spirit with the sign of tongues.

We were in the midst of a mighty revival and felt we could not go, but God stirred the hearts of quite a number at Mukti to pray for a revival. Each day these praying ones were joined by more of the girls, and God poured forth upon them such a revival as is seldom seen, scores were baptized into the Spirit, though they had never heard it preached nor seen a witness.

When God later on permitted us to go there and preach, the power of God on the work was wonderful.

It was no uncommon sight to see hundreds in prayer at once, many of them in other tongues and mightily under the control of God's Spirit. Cases in which ignorant Indian girls prayed or praised in pure English were among them.

Seventeen miles from Ramabai's, a the boys' school of Bro. Albert Norton, sixty of the boys were baptized in the Spirit in a short time. Confessions and restitution and a very great spirit of prayer, in fact the supernatural spirit of prayer, was beyond anything seen in America; were always followed by a mighty visitation of God's power. Results followed the outpouring of the Spirit, for which the missionaries had spent years of labor, but the Spirit accomplished it in these dear Indians in a short time.

One of the marked characteristics of the baptism, both among missionaries and native Christians, was the great burden of souls. This was most convincing to other missionaries. One missionary wrote us after returning to her work, that she knew more love and travail for souls in the few short weeks since her baptism than in all her previous years of ministry to India's needy souls. When she came to our meeting she saw some seekers under the power of God and she made this remark, "What could I do with that in my work?" (referring to the manifestation).

That night she retired to her room to pray, and the Spirit gave her a vision of a "Christless" grave, with India's millions pouring into it. The Spirit led her out in prayer for these until at two o'clock the next morning, she received the baptism in the Spirit, and came from her room -- a transformed woman -- a new power, and floods of God's love in her being.

And what shall we more say? For the time would fail us to tell of the mighty works done by the Spirit at Allehabad, when days and nights the school at dear Miss Chuckerbutty's were in a mighty supernatural spirit of prayer; when cries of penitent ones were mingled with shouts of victory, victory for Jesus Messiah (in their own native tongues).

We scarcely knew when we would get a meal or rest. As we look back over the scenes there and remember how God answered by fire, baptized many with His Spirit, we thank God we were privileged to be with these dear ones.

Then of Coonoor, in the hills, where the missionaries gather for a rest. It was here that battles were fought on our knees, and victories won. Missionaries fought thru great opposition to come to our meetings; were even met at stations along the railway and warned; -- all manner of evil was said against us, but our answer was a mighty Spirit of prayer for these dear ones. God told us we were not to be "weary in well doing, for in due season we would reap if we faint not."

He came and poured waters on thirsty souls and floods upon the dry ground, making their hearts to blossom and bloom like a rose.

The missionaries became witnesses with the power to the death and resurrection of Jesus. Witness after witness arose in India, who had a mouth and wisdom which all their adversaries could not gainsay nor resist. More and more they multiplied until some of India's strongest missionaries are today baptized in the blessed Spirit, with the sign of speaking in other tongues.

We could not close this article without mentioning the faithful company who stood by us in those pioneer days of Pentecost and who went with us through India and the Island of Ceylon with the flame of God's love burning in their hearts and who suffered much. It makes us to realize afresh that mighty things can yet be accomplished on our knees, through faith in Jesus' name. The husbandman waits for the precious fruit of the earth until he receive the early and latter rain.

May we carry this glorious Pentecostal Gospel to hungry hearts. In every nation, in every church and mission there are hungry ones as we were.

The King is a the door, may we give Him no rest day nor night until all are brought in, made ready for His blessed coming.

Pray for us! Yours in His glad service, Mr. and Mrs. A. G. Garr, 126 N. Flower St., Los Angeles, Cal. (*TWE*, April 1, 1916)

## How Pentecost Came to Calcutta
### Max Wood Moorhead

While the Spirit was being poured out in Latter Rain with the sign of tongues upon a company of lowly people in Los Angeles, California, I was crossing the ocean from New York to England on a trans-Atlantic liner. This was in April 1906. I did not hear of the outpouring until several months later. Shortly after my arrival in London I was awakened to an intense hunger for more of the Spirit of Jesus and was convicted of unlikeness to Him. I remember that I wrote a letter to the most spiritually-minded man in London that I knew, entreating him to pray for me.

It has occurred to me since then, that with this marvelous outpouring of the Holy Ghost as on the Day of Pentecost, the members of the Body of Christ scattered throughout the entire world must have felt a thrill of life.

The following August, when in Colombo, Ceylon, a missionary told me that someone in California had spoken in tongues and I said, "If this is true, the gift of tongues will become the heritage of the Church just as in the latter part of the Nineteenth Century divine healing became the heritage of the Church." At that time it had not occurred to me that there is a Scriptural connection between the Pentecostal baptism of the Holy Ghost and the sign of tongues.

During the Christmas holidays in 1906 a company of missionaries and Christian workers assembled in Calcutta from North and West and South and a few came who were resident in Ceylon. The object of this gathering was to wait on the Lord for more spiritual power for service. Pastor Otto Stockmayer was our leader and he expounded the Bible daily to a company of hungry waiting people, whose hunger was not satisfied at the close of those waiting days early in January. And yet it had been profitable to wait in the Spirit of prayer day after day.

At this juncture Mr. and Mrs. Garr appeared in Calcutta, having come direct from Los Angeles, sent, they said by the Spirit of God. With joy and boldness they witnessed to Pentecost, connected with the heaven-born, Spirit-inspired utterance in tongues. The members of the group who had been waiting on God daily, received the witness which these friends brought, except the leader, who rejected it.

A resident of Calcutta said to me, "Mr. and Mrs. Garr are earnest people but they are a little off the lines; you take your Bible and go and put them straight." So I called on them, but when Brother Garr and I got down to pray the Spirit gave him utterance in tongues which was accompanied with such a manifestation of the glorious presence of our Omnipotent God that one felt like Jacob at Bethel when he exclaimed, "This is the Gate of Heaven." I came away feeling I had made a mistake and that I was the one who needed to get on New Testament lines!

Among the number of seekers was Pastor Hook of the Carey Baptist Chapel in Bow Bazaar. William Carey had preached in this chapel one hundred years ago, and Mr. and Mrs. Garr were invited to hold meetings in this historic building, which was situated in a beautiful grove; immediately in the rear of the chapel was the parsonage.

I had never up to this time witnessed such manifestations of God's presence and power as were given in this series of meetings. In one of the earlier ones of the series, after a quiet Bible talk given by Brother Garr, a spirit of intense conviction seized some who were present. A young British soldier was suddenly made conscious of a dishonorable transaction many years before, and after confessing a wrong he had done and promising the Lord to make restitution, he dropped suddenly on the floor as if he had been shot.

A lady missionary was seen to grow pale as she made a humiliating confession. A young man, an Indian, confessed as if his heart had been wrung, to a sin revolting as well as shocking in its wickedness. Confession of sin was a marked feature of these early meetings. A middle-aged man confessed that he had deserted from the British Army as a lad; his conscience gave him no rest until he had confessed to Government Headquarters and had offered to make restitution.

On one occasion the Spirit was felt in the Carey Chapel like a rushing, mighty wind; and night after night scenes were witnessed which reminded one of what one had read of the ministry of the Wesleys and Whitefield and Jonathan Edwards during the eighteenth century. People screamed and groaned under the preaching they heard, and some acted as if they thought the judgment day had actually come and was though they saw flames bursting forth from the bottomless pit. At other times sobs and groans, wailing and weeping, were mingled with triumphant shouts and sounds of hallelujahs, and these sounds blending simultaneously made the din terrific.

Hymns of praise were mainly sung and hymns which exalted the Person of Jesus rather than hymns of experience to which most of us had been habituated. Many confessed to having found peace through believing, and there were some marked supernatural manifestations. I remember to have seen a sister in the meeting enveloped in a rose colored light while she sang a hymn whose melody was so unearthly in its sweetness that it seemed to come from heaven. Dreams were related of a prophetic character and visions of Jesus were granted to a favored few.

The band of seekers waited on from day to day expecting the "promise of the Father" and they were not disappointed. Crowds of people visited the Carey Chapel, many of whom came to scoff and to criticize. The persecution which attended this work of grace was severe and unrelenting; and alas! Opposition and persecution proceeded from individuals who bore the name of Christian. Under the operation of the blessed Holy Spirit seekers would be prostrated and others would lie in a trance, while the preaching continued at intervals.

I have seen visitors walk around the room and stare at seekers, acting like people in a theater who hold their lorgnettes to their eyes as they view the shifting scenes of comedy. On one occasion the criticism was audible, when a Church of England clergyman in the midst of a meeting suddenly announced, "This thing is unscriptural and must stop!"

But the meetings did not stop; on the contrary God's people went from strength to strength and from victory to victory. However, so persistent were the attempts to frustrate the plans of God that it was considered wise to change to a place of meeting where things could be kept more completely under control. Accordingly, in February a commodious house in Creek row was hired and though enemies followed us even to this private house, several of the seekers came through into Pentecost with the sign of tongues; the spirit of prayer and praise increased and the Gospel message continued to be rung out.

Early in March 1907 most of the seekers outside of Calcutta returned to their respective stations, and gradually the fire spread to nearly all the provinces of the Empire. There have been witnesses to Pentecost among those resident in Bengal, Bombay Presidency, Madras Presidency, Central Provinces, United Provinces, Orissa and the North-West Frontier Province. About ten times as many Indians as Anglo-Saxons have received the baptism. Among Indians who have received are those belonging to various countries whose vernaculars are: Bengali, Oriyan, Tamil, Telegu, Badaga, Bhil Malayalam, Kanarese, Marathi, Gujerathi, Hindi, and Hindustani. (*TLRE*, Dec., 1913)

## Christians in India Are Given "Gift of Tongues"
### William T. Ellis

(Special to *The Times*, Joseph B. Bowles)
WONDERFUL PSYCHIC AND RELIGIOUS PHENOMENA AMONG THE ORPHANS AND GIRL-WIDOWS OF PANDITA RAMABI'S ASYLUM, AS DESCRIBED BY AN EYEWITNESS-- IGNORANT NATIVE PEASANTS SPEAK ENGLISH, GREEK, HEBREW and SANSKRIT -- STORIES THAT PARALLEL PENTECOST -- AN EXTRAORDINARY "REVIVAL" OVER WIDE EXTENT OF TERRITORY

The above heading appeared over a very remarkable article which was published in June 1907, in the *Erie Daily Times* (Pa). This article has never been published in any Pentecostal paper before; but, by special permission of the author, we are enabled to secure it for the benefit of the *Evangel* Family. The fact that Mr. Ellis is not a Pentecostal man, gives greater weight to the article, as he was not prejudiced in favor of the work. Mr. Ellis says,

> "I control the copyright of the article on religious revival in Pandita Ramabai's work in India, which was one of a series of travel articles that I wrote for a series of daily newspapers. I haven't read the article for years, and, as you will observe, it is merely a record of what I saw and heard, without committing myself to any of the positions involved.
>
> "I have no objections to your reprinting the article in the 'Weekly Evangel,' with adequate credit and with the copyright line and 'Used by permission!'" -- Kedgaon, India, June 15, 1907.

I have stumbled upon an extraordinary religious manifestation, as remarkable as anything in connection with the great revival in Wales. So startling and wonderful it is that I feel quite unwilling to pass an opinion upon it, so I shall simply narrate, soberly and consecutively, what I have seen and heard concerning this "baptism with fire," and pouring out of "the gifts of tongues," whereby ignorant Hindu girls speak in Sanskrit, Hebrew, Greek, English, and other languages as yet unidentified.

The name of Pandita Ramabai, "the Hindu widow's friend," is known among educated people all over the world. She is the most famous of all Hindu women. There is an International "Pandita Ramabai Association," which cooperates with her in her work of rescuing, training, and caring for high caste widows. She, more than any other woman, has made known to the world the horrors of the child widow's lot in India. Herself a high caste widow, of rare gifts and education, her appeal has been made to people of culture; nor was her work regarded as strictly religious or missionary, not being associated with any religious body.

# Messengers of An Outpouring

## A World-Famous Work

Ten years ago, at the time of the great famine, Ramabai took hundreds of famine orphans, and ever since she has had about 1,400 widows and orphans and deserted girls under her care, as well as 100 famine boys. All caste lines are now down, and the whole immense work is known as the Mukti mission, although in certain respects the original enterprise for widows maintains its separate identity.

Because of the fame of Pandita Ramabai, and because of the greatness of her work, I conceived it to be my duty to take the hot journey out to Kedgaon. Were it not for the more important incidents which follow, I should tell at some length the story of this great settlement, with its wide acres of farm land, its many modest buildings, and its varied forms of industry. Study and work are the rule for every girl; clothes for that multitude must all be woven on the spot, and the industrial plant is large. An uncommunicative English woman guided me faithfully to every spot of the settlement that she thought of interest, from the cornerstone to the steam engine and the dyeing vats. But not a word did she say that would lead me into a knowledge of what is by all means the most noteworthy fact concerning this great institution.

## Stumbling Onto A Revival

Of course, I was aware of the unusual religious experiences reported from many Christian communities in India; but I had never associated this sort of thing with Pandita Ramabai's work; probably because some of her foremost supporters in America are identified with the "new theology" which has scant room for the campmeeting type of "old-time religion." My first clue was a pamphlet which I chanced to pick up, relating strange spiritual experiences on the part of some of Ramabai's girls. I began to ask questions, which were answered, I thought, with seeming reluctance and discovered that this revival was still under way.

For half an hour I had been hearing strange sounds, now of one person shouting in a high voice, now of the mingled utterance of a crowd, and now of song. At last it settled down into a steady roar. "What is that I hear?" I asked. "It is the girls' prayer meeting," was the answer. "Could I visit it?" I pointedly asked my guide, after hints had proved unavailing. "Why -- I -- suppose -- so. I'll see." In a few minutes I found myself witnessing a scene utterly without parallel in my experience of religious gatherings.

In a large, bare room, with cement floor, were gathered between thirty and forty girls, ranging in age from twelve to twenty. By a table sat a sweet-faced, refined, native young woman, watching soberly and without disapproval the scene before her. After a few minutes she also knelt on the floor in silent prayer.

The other occupants of the room were all praying aloud. Some were crying at the top of their lungs. The tumult was so great that it was with difficulty that any one voice could be distinguished. Some of the girls were bent over with heads touching the floor. Some were sitting on their feet, with shoulders and bodies twitching and jerking in regular convulsions. Some were swaying to and fro, from side to side or frontwards and backwards. Two or three were kneeling upright, with arms and bodies that must have been the most exhausting physical exercise. She, like others, also swung her arms violently, often the gestures of the praying figures were with one or both hands outstretched, in dramatic supplication.

Not infrequently, several girls would clap their hands at the same time, though each seemed heedless of the others. At times the contortions of the faces were painfully agonized and perspiration streamed over them. One girl fell over, asleep or fainting, from sheer exhaustion [that was his assumption].

All had their eyes tightly closed, oblivious to surroundings. Such intense and engrossing devotion I had never witnessed before. It was full 15 minutes before one of the girls, who had quieted down somewhat, espied me. Thereafter she sat silent, praying or reading her Bible. The discovery of the visitor had this same effect upon half a dozen other girls during the next quarter of an hour. At my request the guide, after a time, asked the leader if I might talk with her, and while a dozen of the girls were still left, praying aloud and unaware of the departure of the others, the leader withdrew.

**A Strange Story**

My first interest was to know whether the girls had been "speaking in tongues" that day, for I had thought that I detected one girl using English. Yes, several of the girls had been praying in unknown tongues, this young woman quietly informed me. Then, in response to my questionings, she proceeded to tell me that these meetings are held twice daily by girls who have been "baptized with the Holy Spirit and fire;" it is common for them to speak in tongues which they do not understand, and also to be smitten dumb, so that they cannot speak at all, even in their own language.

During the early part of the meeting at which I was present, one of the girls had been obliged to write her message, because her tongue was holden. Sometimes the girls will go about their tasks for days, unable to utter a word, although they understand perfectly everything that is said to them, and are able to pray in other tongues, and when they especially pray for the power to do so, they are able to speak in religious meetings. The girls show no effect whatever of the terrible strain they undergo during these prayer meetings, and they all do their regular daily work. The burden of their prayers is intercession, that all the mission, and all India, may be converted and experience a great revival and receive the Pentecostal baptism. So much I learned from this young woman.

**Apparitions of Fire**

Before relating my interview with Pandita Ramabai herself, let me quote from a narrative of this spiritual experience, which has been written by one of the teachers and printed at the Mukti Mission press.

"Many are being anointed with the spirit of intercessory prayer, spending hours, lost to time and surroundings, pleading for the unsaved. Young men and young women are receiving the gift of the Spirit, speaking with tongues, interpreting tongues previously unknown to them; the sick are being healed, and unclean spirits cast out in answer to prayer.

"In January, 1905, Pandita Ramabai spoke to the girls of Mukti concerning the need of revival, and called for volunteers to meet with her daily to pray for it. Seventy volunteered, and from time to time others joined, until at the beginning of the revival there were 550 meeting twice daily. In June Ramabai asked for volunteers from the Bible school to give up their secular studies and go out into the villages about us to preach the Gospel. Thirty young women volunteered, and we were meeting daily to pray for the 'enduement of power,' when the revival came.

"On the 29th of June, at 3:30 am., the Holy Spirit was poured out upon --- ---, one of these volunteers. The young woman sleeping next to her awoke when this occurred, and seeing the fire enveloping her, ran across the dormitory, brought a pail of water, and was about to dash it upon her, when she discovered that --- --- was not on fire. In less than an hour nearly all the young women in the compound gathered around, weeping, praying, and confessing their sins to God. The newly Spirit-baptized girl sat in the midst of them, telling what God had done for her, and exhorting them to repentance. The next evening, while Ramabai was expounding John 8, in her usual quiet way, the Holy Spirit descended and the girls all began to pray aloud so that she had to cease talking. All in the room were weeping and praying, some kneeling, some sitting, some standing, many with hands outstretched to God. Promises and word of help were of no avail."

## The Most Famous Indian Woman

Ramabai herself is a quiet, strong personality. She dresses after the Hindu fashion, but in white, and her hair is short, for she is a widow. She elects to sit on a low stool at the feet of the person with whom she converses, for the sake of better hearing. While we were talking, her grown daughter, Manoramabai, her first assistant in the work, sat on the floor with her arms about her mother, and occasionally interjected a pertinent word.

Ramabai (the suffix "bai," means "Mrs." or "Miss") speaks simply, naturally and directly. So she told me of the growth of Shadai Sadan, the work for widows, and of the Mukti mission, the whole supported by faith. Then, passing on to visit to Keswich, England, two years ago, she related how she had united with a band of spiritually minded persons who were praying for a world revival. In 1905 she began to pray especially for an outpouring of the Holy Spirit upon Mukti, six months later the answer came as indicated above. Now, praying bands of Mukti girls, accompanied by teachers, go to villages as distant as fifty or 100 miles, conducting revival services.

"We do not make a special point of the gift of tongues; our emphasis is always put upon love and life. And undoubtedly the lives of the girls have been changed. About 700 of them have come into this blessing. We do not exhibit the girls that have been gifted with other tongues, nor do we in any wise call special attention to them. We try to weed out the false from the true, for there are other spirits than the Holy Spirit, and when a girl begins to try to speak in another tongue, apparently imitating the other girls, without mentioning the name or blood of Jesus, I go to her and speak to her, or touch her on the shoulder, and she stops at once;

whereas, if a girl is praying in the Spirit I cannot stop her, no matter how sharply I speak to her or shake her."

*Book Editor*: It appears that P. Ramabai did not have a deep knowledge of the tongues. Sometimes the Holy Spirit gives the unction and you must speak in tongues, but you can pray in tongues whenever you want. It also appears that the Holy Spirit with fire was poured out in India before Azusa Street.

## The Wonderful Gifts of Tongues

"My hearing is peculiar," continued Ramabai, "in that I can understand most clearly when there is a loud noise (a well-known characteristic of the partially deaf) and I move among the girls, listening to them. I have heard girls who know no English make beautiful prayers in English. I have heard others pray in Greek and Hebrew and Sanskrit, and others in languages that none of us understands. One of the girls was praying in this very room (the room of one of the English staff) a few nights ago, and although in her studies she has not gone beyond the second book, she prayed so freely and clearly and beautifully in English that the other teachers, hearing wondered who could be praying, since they did not distinguish the voice." [They did not recognize who was speaking.] "Yes," spoke up the occupant of the room, "and she prayed by name for a cousin of mine whom I had forgotten, and of whom I had never once thought since coming to India."

When I asked why, in Ramabai's opinion, tongues that served no useful purpose being incomprehensible to everybody should be given, whereas the gift of tongues on the day of Pentecost was so that every person in that polyglot multitude should hear the story in his own speech, she replied, "I, too, wondered about that. But it has been shown to me that it is to rebuke unbelief in the gift of tongues," she herself has been given the gift.

## Many Parts of India Afire

All these wonders I have set down impartially, as phenomena of great interest to all who give thought to religious or psychic themes. Neither Ramabai, nor the native teacher who led the meeting which I described, is an emotionalist, so far as I could perceive. Both, in fact, are persons of more than ordinary reserve, culture, and discernment, nor can I explain the relation between what is happening at Mukti and the revivals that are being reported from various parts of India, most of them characterized by astonishing confessions of sin, on the part of Christians and by prolonged and even agonized prayer, with pronounced physical emotion.

Let me summarize the phenomena of this Indian "revival," as I have learned them from various missionaries, and in particular from Bishop Warne, of the Methodist Episcopal church, who is issuing, in America, a booklet upon the subject. Most notable is the fact that the breaking out of the revival in many widely separated communities, occasionally in the absence of the missionaries, has been preceded by praying, rather than preaching. Most religious "awakenings" are associated with some one personality; the Welsh revival had its Evan Roberts; but there is no corresponding figure in India. One 13-year-old girl, Sansuki, of Khassia Hills, is reported to have been the means of 900 conversions. The prominent place which young girls in praying bands -- timid, untutored, Indian girls, reared to believe in the complete subjection of women -- have had in this revival, is noteworthy. Instance after instance could be given of the girls' continuing whole nights in prayer; of their having seen visions, and particularly of their having been invested with a strange, beautiful and supernatural fire, are reported from various directions.

**Making Presbyterians Dance**

There has been a pronounced physical side to the demonstrations, as I found at Kedgaon. Entire audiences have shaken as if smitten with palsy, strong men have fallen headlong to the ground. Even lepers have been made to dance. Leaping, shouting, rolling on the floor, beating the air and dancing have been common. Concerning dancing, Bishop Warne said, "Personally, I have not seen much of the dancing; that is reported as mostly having taken place in Presbyterian churches!" It is a fact that the dignified Presbyterians, even the Scotch church missions, have been foremost in these revival experiences.

The revival has continued in various parts of the empire for more than a year; I have reports from Lucknow, Allahabad, Adansol, Moradabad, Bareilly, Khassia Hills, and Kedgaon. The Methodists baptized 1,900 new converts during the year, besides the notable result of having secured more than 300 new candidates for the ministry.

Dramatic in the extreme have been the confessions of sin, and reconciliations between enemies.

Everywhere there is agreement that the lives of the people have been markedly altered for the better. "The revival," says one, "has given India a new sense of sin." The spontaneous composition of hymns has been a curious feature of some meetings; Bishop Warne thinks that "there will be a new hymnology in the vernacular as an outcome of this revival." (*TWE*, June 24, 1916)

## When Pentecost Came to India

Miss Sara Coxe, in the Missionary Conference, May 17, 1918

It was the year before Pentecost fell in our Missionary Training Institute at Nayack on the Hudson, when the young men and women who were gathered there were down before Lord, seeking and searching, and yearning for something more, new power or new light. Those days of great heart-searching, days of great cleansing, days when God poured out in a real way of His Spirit upon the Institute, and the next year came the great Pentecostal revival when the Lord met so many of our pastors and missionaries and students who were called to the regions beyond. And that was the year we went to India.

So when we got into Bombay, after having seen just a little bit of God's work in the homeland, the missionaries said, "Do you know anything about Pentecost; about the latter rain, and what God is doing at home? We are having sprinklings all over India." I said, "Yes, we have seen just a little bit in America," and they were all looking for something from God.

One little missionary who had been in India for eighteen years, who had charge of one of our large schools, and was about the best woman missionary we had, said, "Lord, I am dry. Will You not please do something for me?" God came down upon that woman and anointed her, and do you know she was absolutely transformed. She wasn't dry any longer. You could feel in the compound and in every corner of our work that God had anointed her and baptized her with the power of the Holy Ghost.

About forty-eight of our missionaries said to me, "Sara, what would we do if we hadn't received the Holy Ghost when Pentecost fell?" [He refers to 1906.] We had a flood, we became submerged and came up with new life. When we were dry we thought we were no good at all, and of course we were not. It is just as He says, "Not by might nor by power, but by My Spirit," and friends, in this great audience, if all the people will bend and go down before the Lord they will find that He will pour out His Spirit again; He will do a mighty new thing, and it will reach even unto the ends of the earth. . . .

When Pentecost came it fell like a flood on our whole compound, and we had a great many revivals. I was like an oasis in an awfully dry desert. Our girls had been taught to pray, and every year God sent us some kind of revival; in all there were about eight or nine. One year we had a big revival of prayer. The girls prayed until God came down and hearts were broken, and many were brought to the Lord Jesus. Then we had a revival of faith, where the faith of the missionaries was stirred and strengthened.

Then we had a revival of repentance. I called it the old junk revival. Indian girls are just like girls in this country, sometimes they quarrel. We used to have balls of soap, and some of the girls would take each other's soap, and in this revival they brought the soap they had stolen, and would say, "I took somebody's soap, I want to get right with God." There was one little girl who had taken a slate pencil, and others had taken needles and pins.

In India the Hindu women wear jewelry of all kinds; their ears are laden with rings until sometimes the lobe of the ear reaches down to their shoulders; they wear rings around their ankles and on their wrists; this is a custom, and sometimes the Christian girls like to wear bracelets. They would say, "May we have them; they cost only a couple of pice?" [coin no longer used, 1/64$^{th}$ of a rupee] We would say, "Settle it with God," but as soon as the revival came, off came those bracelets. They did not want them any more. They called it the revival of restitution and repentance, but I called it the old junk revival.

Ofttimes it is only a piece of junk that will keep us from God's best, some little, trifling thing will keep even the Pentecostal people from going all the way with God. When we got down to pray one little girl said, "I told a lie," and another little girl said, "I never do anything right, I am always disobeying my mother."

After a while we had a revival not only in church but the Spirit of God came down everywhere. Under one tree you would see a group of girls praying, in our school, in our go-down, in the kitchen and in the bungalow, all on their faces before God, pleading that He would work. When they had straightened everything up they said, "Now we are all cleaned up, let us have new revival," and then the fire of God came down and deluged our compound.

One day one of our best evangelists, his face all aglow looked to the north and south and east and west of our compound and said, "The Lord Jesus is going to work in this place." Just then it seemed the light of God settled upon us and it wasn't very long until seventy-five girls were baptized in the Holy Ghost, and every missionary in the bungalow as well. The news went out and the heathen came and inquired what this was. We told them it was the power of God.

I was the last one to receive, but I didn't worry. I knew He was coming to me. I wasn't troubled, but my little class of fifteen girls were sitting cross-legged on the cement floor of our sitting-room one day, and they said, "What is the matter with her that she has never yet received the baptism in the Holy Ghost?" And one little girl said, "There is nothing the matter at all, all she has to do is get into the boat with the Lord Jesus and go sailing down the stream." Whenever they spoke of anyone being baptized they always called it getting into the boat. So they said, "Let's all drop our work and pray for her." They asked me to sit down and they all gathered round me and began to pray for me, and soon I was lost in the presence of God. Those girls prayed and prayed, "Lord, won't you baptize her now?" Finally the Lord met me and I got into the boat.

We had one missionary on the field six years, and she was so tired and worn. She said, "If it were only next year I'd go home." One night God came down on her and it seemed as if every bit of her would be shaken to pieces, first gently, then more vigorously, and finally she was absolutely submerged by the power of God, and she got up with a glow on her face I had never seen before. She had walked with God all her life, but said, "I never have received anything like this. I never knew it could be so wonderful." We were rooming together and the next morning she said to me, "I don't feel tired, and I have many letters to write, but I'd much rather preach the Gospel. I feel the power of God resting on me." I told her to go and preach and I would write the letters, and she went out to preach.

As she went, she met an old sweeper woman who had heard the Gospel. I wish you could have seen that woman -- dirty, unkempt, repulsive in the natural. This missionary, who is now Mrs. Schoonmaker, said to her, "Do you know Jesus Christ loves you? He is coming back very soon, won't you give your heart to Him?" That woman began to tremble and shake, and she dropped her broom and said, "Where is this Jesus that I might find Him?" And then and there she sought the Lord Jesus Christ. Then Mrs. Schoonmaker went out and met a small caravan journeying along. As they stopped by the river she told them about Jesus. The power of God was on her life in mighty way, and they said "We never in our lives heard anything as wonderful as that. Won't you please tell us again," and she did, and when she came home she said, "I never knew God could be so great and that He could do such wonderful things."

This missionary and I roomed together, and I was often very ill, and many times when I could not stand for myself she stood in God for me. Before that revival came, in time of sickness we had such battles for healing. God did answer prayer, but many times we had to fight through a long severe illness; but after

Pentecost fell the power of God was so mighty upon us that our girls got healed at once. It seemed the power of God was upon our lives all the time.

There was one girl who was stung by a scorpion. The pain from a scorpion's sting is very intense and it generally lasts for many hours, and she cried as though her heart would break, "The scorpion bit me. What shall I do?" We put our hands on her head and the pain left her. And so it was all through the compound. The Spirit of God rolled in power over the native people; over the girls and over the boys.

There were several hundred boys in our Boys' School, and one afternoon when the missionaries were at prayer in the bungalow, it seemed as though the heavens opened and a mighty, rushing wind filled the room. Mr. Turnbull said the wind came from the north, and they looked toward the church and there the boys were praying and that rushing wind came over their heads and tongues of fire were seen, and many of them with Mr. Schoonmaker were baptized with the power of the Holy Ghost. Do you wonder when I say we were drowned in India? Ah! we knew we had a fountain that was unsealed right within us that would never, never dry up! Have you that fountain within you? If you haven't, seek his face. Say, "Lord, what wilt Thou have me do?" I am sure He wants to do a new thing for you.

We had in our compound a young man, a great, big, tall fellow; he belonged to a caste who were very proud; he had never been under the hand of God, although he had been in the mission for years. He came to us when he was a tiny, famine boy, hadn't strength enough to reach out his hand. He had named the name of Jesus, was baptized in water, but he had a yellow streak in him which often caused him to do wrong. It was after the senior missionaries had left the field, and every night he used to put his cow in the wheat fields that were connected with the mission, but I never could catch him at it. I never could put my hand on the thing and say, "You did it." I felt he was a hypocrite and in the natural I wanted to shake him, but I didn't. Some one said, "Why don't you speak to him?" But I didn't seem free to do it. You know there is only one thing to do for a man like that, and that is to pray. So we began to pray, "Lord, deal with that man." The native girls heard about it, and they began to pray, "Lord, deal with that man." Every morning, as he came to take his orders from me, he would *salam* me very politely, and his hypocrisy deeply stirred me, but there was nothing to do but pray.

One day the missionaries said, "Miss Coxe, we are going to have a conference and we will build huts for you. Bring your best girls and come up." So we told the native Christians, that they might go and we went up. We had a man out from America, a Quaker evangelist, and he preached about walking with God, and the message struck home to every heart.

It was a big conference of native Christians, boys and girls from the mission, with about ten missionaries and when we got down before God the native church was in the center, and this young man was there. The Spirit of God took hold of him at the back of the neck and shook that boy until I thought his life would be shaken out of him, and he confessed everything he ever did that was wrong. He got down and confessed one thing and then tried to get up, but the Spirit would thrust him back and he confessed something else, and the last thing he confessed was, "I did, I did, I did put my cow in Miss Coxe's wheat field." Then the Spirit of God came upon him and he wasn't only cleaned up, but he received the baptism in the Holy Ghost. About six months ago I received a letter from a missionary, "Miss Coxe, do you remember So-and-so?" Could I ever forget him. "He is going on with God. The other day he left his wife and children in our care and has gone out to preach the Gospel to his own people." Didn't it pay for us to hold on in prayer? . . .

I remember a Conference we had just two years before I left the field. We were having a large Bible school and at the close of the school we had our Conference, and we had everything planned for it. One of the missionaries was to preach three sermons about the coming of the Lord ; another, three sermons on consecration; and another, three sermons on Divine Healing; and a fourth was to speak on the line of Salvation. We had a native evangelist who was filled with the power of God, and he wrote a month ahead, "I am praying for the Conference. Won't you pray?" Of course we would. He wrote again, "I am praying night and day. Won't you pray?" When we came up to that Conference we knew that that evangelist had prevailed with God for those meetings. You could feel God's power on the place as soon as you put your foot there, and not one of those missionaries gave the messages they had planned.

But there was a missionary there who never expected to preach, felt she didn't know the language well enough, but God poured His Spirit through her. She would open up her Bible and talk for a half hour just the message He wanted. Oh it was wonderful!

There was a native woman in this Conference who had come for miles in the interior, terribly possessed with demons. I wish you could have seen that woman, bound hand and foot, spiritually bound, and we felt her influence was going out over that meeting. She was so against the things of God. Every time this missionary who was anointed mentioned the blood of Jesus, that woman hissed, and one day one of the men said, "We will pray this through." The evangelist and the missionaries got down before God, and one afternoon the woman sat near the front, during a blessed message. Again, as anything was said about Jesus or His blood, this woman would hiss as only a native can.

The message was over and all prostrated themselves in prayer, and from the back of the room the Lord picked up an evangelist and led him right in front of the woman; another came also and the Lord brought Mrs. Schoonmaker, who had gone out, back into the meeting, right in front of the woman. I was sitting over in the corner with my eyes tightly shut. One of our native evangelists talked to that woman in Hindustani, and in a little while God came down in that place and the enemy was cast out of her life; she was absolutely delivered.

She stood up and asked for a drink of water, and then asked us to pray for her. Mrs. Schoonmaker said, "Isn't it strange he should have talked to her in Hindustani and not Gujarati," but the woman said, "No, it is not strange. We have priests and they do wonderful things, and about three years ago I said in Hindustani, 'If

I could only do what those priests do,' and I invited the enemy to come into my life and take control." So when he rebuked the enemy of course he did it in Hindustani. The instrument the Lord used wasn't a Hindustani boy, but he spoke perfect Hindustani that afternoon.

We had one boy about twenty-one who was in the back of the church and away from God, and he simply leaped up to the front and there was a mighty break. All we could do was to get low before God. That is the way he turned our Conference upside down.... (*TLRE*, June, 1918)

## Additional from Los Angeles Concerning the Early Pentecostal Work
### A. W. Orwig

For a third time I write about the work in question, even though not formally identified with any of the assemblies here or elsewhere. My knowledge of the work in this city is chiefly derived from occasional attendance at some of the various meetings and from the literature that is sometimes published. From the beginning, however I have read different Pentecostal papers published both in this country and a few in other countries. And while I have received considerable benefit from the meetings and the periodicals, I have not always been able fully to coincide with all the doctrines taught. But it is well known that these dear people do not themselves agree in all phases of doctrine. Nor is this always essential. Love and unity of spirit are more important.

1. *Not Knowing French, Yet Speaking French.* -- It was during the very early Pentecostal movement in Los Angeles that a woman, who knew only the English language, actually addressed a man in the French language. He was her grocer, a Frenchman, but understood English well. While both of them were crossing the street, in opposite directions, she suddenly spoke to him in his native tongue. But it was in the form of a Gospel message, with a view to his salvation. Utterly surprised, he asked, "Since when have you been able to speak French?" To this she replied, "I do not know that I spoke French, for I don't understand a word of that language." To this the man answered, "You certainly spoke in very excellent French, warning me to repent of my sins and to give my heart and life to God." Verily "tongues are a sign" to the unbeliever.

2. *"Would Not Tolerate Speaking in Tongues."* -- Years ago a brother preacher, whom I very highly esteem, came to Los Angeles from another state, and who had never been to a meeting held by the people under consideration. Discussing with him the subject of speaking in a new or unknown tongue at meetings, he said, "I would not tolerate such gibberish in any of my meetings." Knowing that he was not familiar with certain conditions, and had not specially studied the subject from a Scriptural standpoint, I told him that he would doubtless assume a grave responsibility in attempting to interfere with what might be a demonstration of the Holy Spirit. He then admitted that his language was very likely too strong. But other persons have said practically the same thing who have never been to one of those meetings; but some, on going several times, have completely

changed their opinions. And sometimes some of the most hostile ones have been so mightily [worked] upon by the Holy Spirit, even to their physical being, [causing them] to speak in an unknown tongue very freely, and became the most ardent defenders of this divine manifestation.

That there may occasionally be counterfeit or Satanic manifestations is admitted, but this is no proof whatever that there is not an actual utterance given by the Holy Spirit through certain persons in another language. Only a genuine thing can be counterfeited.

3. *Not Opposed by Rev. Dr. George D. Watson.* -- On someone telling me, a number of years ago, that Dr. Watson did not allow the speaking in other tongues in his meetings, I assured the person that he was in error, for I had heard some thus speak without the slightest protest. Some of the "Pentecostal" people sometimes attend Brother Watson's expositions [he gives] on the deepest and most blessed themes of the Sacred Oracles, frequently on prophetical subjects.

4. *A Preacher Rebuked by an Interpreter.* -- During the campmeeting, in the outskirts of Los Angeles in 1907, the Lord gave a certain brother the interpretation of a number of testimonies spoken in language unknown to the speakers. It was a great surprise to very many persons thus to witness this wonderful manifestation of the Divine Presence. A holy awe rested upon the audience. A brother who expected to preach on the occasion made some seemingly unnecessary apologies as to not being fully prepared, etc. Instantly, someone arose and spoke in a strange tongue, directing his gaze at the man standing behind the pulpit who expected to preach. Then followed the interpretation which was to the effect that no apologies should be made by anyone who was conscious that God wanted him to preach; also that if the preacher had truly met God in prayer and meditation, He would use him to the Divine glory. The preacher was evidently moved by the solemn interpretation and acknowledged the fault mentioned. The incident may be of value to other preachers.

## "Tongues" The Great Stumbling Block

The "tongues" feature of the Pentecostal movement has been, and still is, the great stumbling-block to many persons. But they forget, or have never known, that it has a real Scriptural side to it, both pro and con. Certainly, there is Scripture for the speaking in an entirely unfamiliar language, under certain circumstances, and often not understood by anyone present. But the fact or importance of such speaking should not be unduly magnified, nor may it be entirely ignored. We should abide by the Word of God, whether we understand the subject or not. Generally, the leaders in the movement disapprove and deplore all excesses in the matter, including all unseemly bodily demonstrations.

5. *"Don't Talk About Tongues."* -- In the first year of the work in Los Angeles, I heard W. J. Seymour, an acknowledged leader, say, "*Now, don't go from this meeting and talk about tongues, but try to get people saved.*" Again I heard him counsel against all unbecoming or fleshly demonstrations, and everything not truly of the Holy Spirit. Wise words, indeed. There had been some extremes, and still are in other places, but these things no more represent the real Pentecostal work than do the

follies in various churches represent genuine Christianity.

Bro. Seymour constantly exalted the atoning work of Christ and the Word of God, and very earnestly insisted on thorough conversion, holiness of heart and life, and the fullness of the Holy Spirit. And yet, some uninformed persons uncharitably declare that the chief or whole thing consists in talking in tongues and is of the devil.

6. *Favorable Editorial Comment.* -- Three cases, among papers outside of the movement in question, allow me briefly to quote. An editor of a holiness paper in the East wrote thus: "If you fail to take up with the 'tongues' feature, stand with Gamaliel and wait. We know of no reason why the Lord should not send to the faithful today what He once sent to Jerusalem and Corinth."

The well-known Rev. Dr. A. B. Simpson, of New York City, declared in his paper thus: "There is no reason to believe that these special gifts were ever intended to be discontinued. Many of the most remarkable, as miracles and even the gifts of tongues, have occasionally re-appeared in modern times."

The Rev. Dr. A. S. Worrell (now deceased), whom I saw at several meetings at Azusa Mission, wrote to his paper that he firmly believed the movement was of God. He further stated: "There are real gifts of tongues here in Los Angeles and other gifts of the Holy Spirit."

And thus, I might continue to present testimony from persons of deep piety and learning as to their belief (and some from actual experience) that the speaking in unfamiliar tongues is still one of the manifestations of the Holy Spirit. But I must forbear for the present. -- 1220 W. 37th Drive, Los Angeles, Calif. (*TWE*, April 8, 1916)

## The Tongues of Pentecost Duplicated

The following remarkable narrative was sent to me by R. W. Nichols of the Galena, Kansas, Assembly of God. I, myself, have met Bro. Nichols; heard him pray and seen his face shine. Also, the narrative bears the endorsement of Mrs. Mary Arthur, for many years the leader of the work in Galena.

She says, "I commend to you Bro. Nichol's testimony as being worthy and true; he is a most earnest and humble Christian; one whom God can use to His glory."

Sister Arthur needs no commendation to those among us who know her; to those who have not that privilege, we say that she is a wise, level-headed, godly, Spirit-filled woman. So this story may be accepted as true.

*The narrative follows:*–

"I thought it would glorify God to write of an experience I had shortly after receiving the Baptism in the Spirit. I was filled with the Spirit about Oct. 31, 1914.

"In the beginning of November, I met a Syrian woman at my home when I returned to dinner. She had taken sick and had stopped in to wait for a friend. Finding that she was sick, I started to ask her if she knew Jesus could heal her. Part of the question I asked in English and then the Spirit led me off into her own native language.

"The Spirit thereupon told her of Jesus and His power to save and heal and warned her of his soon coming. Presently her friend came in and heard a large measure of the warning.

"When work time came at one o'clock, I sent [my] brother-in-law in my place and continued talking and praying with the two for sometime. Part of the prayers I offered were in the Syriac [language].

"A week later, lacking one day, I met two other Syrians. My mother was acquainted with one of them and she stayed patiently while the Spirit again warned them of Jesus. She said that she had met the first two and they had told her how frightened they were when the Spirit had told of the soon coming of Jesus.

"I was ignorant of their way of worship, but while talking to the second couple the Spirit led me through many manifestations, such as counting beads, crossing myself, etc. I told them that they were deluded and that the priest was taking them to hell. They were so bound and set in their way of worship, that the message had little effect upon them at the time.

"Months afterward, I met a young Syrian man who spoke pretty good English. He told me that the person for whose healing I prayed in the first instance immediately recovered."

Here is a well authenticated case of glossolalia identical with the manifestation upon the day of Pentecost. The young man was, and is, ignorant of the Syriac; he spoke -- as the Spirit gave utterance -- of Jesus and the wonderful things of God. The fact that the message did not result in the immediate salvation of all the hearers does not take it out of the Pentecostal class; some on that day "mocked." Further, the woman for whom prayer was offered, recovered.

In spite of the learning of the wise, I believe that God is the "same yesterday, today, and forever." (*TWE*, April 8, 1916)

# Chapter 3

# Pentecostal History Part 3

### Pastor Barrett and the Work in Europe

We have the privilege here of presenting something of the personal testimony of Pastor Barrett and a letter from him dealing with the work in Europe. Also, a letter from Miss Yunna G. Malick, now in the country, but who was born, saved, and baptized in the Spirit in Palestine.

Bro. Barrett was born in Albaston, Cornwall, England, on the 22$^{nd}$ of July, 1862. His parents were both English and belonged to the Wesleyan Methodist Church. When he was five years old, his parents removed to Norway; he has made his home there ever since.

He was converted when twelve years old, and was, in his sixteenth year, stirred to a deeper consecration and a larger life for God. He soon entered the ministry and presently had great success in winning souls for his Master.

In 1905 he visited America to raise funds for the erection of a large hall in Christiania, intended for the center of a great mission work in that city. He was at this time a member of the Wesleyan Methodist Church.

His mission here, though supported by appeals from several bishops and other leading men, was not successful. This grieved his heart and really began a work in his heart which made room for the blessed light and truth of "Pentecost."

We here append an account of his experience in his own words. This extract is taken from "When the Fire Fell," a pamphlet containing a detailed narrative of the Lord's dealings with him.

### Pastor Barrett's Own Testimony

All this time I remained underneath the cleansing and protecting Blood of the Atonement, knowing that Christ alone could impart the blessing I sought. Acts 2:33; John 7:37-39.

I had not mentioned to anybody, except by correspondence, that I was seeking the full Pentecost. But at last I felt I must. A sudden tremor passed through my body when I did it. Oh, how precious those days are to me still!

Taking a nap in the afternoon, I awoke, feeling my jaws working on their own account. The physical sign of the coming blessing had therefore commenced, before anybody had prayed with me or laid their hands on my head. Calling on Mrs.

L\_\_\_\_\_, the wife of a physician, who had received her Pentecost, I conversed with her about the subject and requested her prayers. The devil taunted me by saying: "The idea of a minister going to ask a woman to pray for him!" I bade him begone. She prayed with me and sent me to a meeting conducted by a friend of hers. But it was at the meeting the next evening I first felt at liberty to tell those present what I was seeking. This was on the 15th of Nov., 1906. About fifteen persons were present. Some seeking sanctification, other the baptism of fire.

We could not close the meeting and I determined, God helping me, to stay till the victory was won.

I requested the leader, a little before 12 o'clock, to pray for me with laying on of hands. After that, I had no more strength in me, I lay on the floor by the platform in a reclining position. At about half-past twelve I asked a Norwegian brother there and Mrs. L. to lay hands on my head and pray for me once more.

My jaws and tongue began to work, but there was no voice. The brother said, "Try to speak!" But I would not force matters myself. There was to be no humbug in this. The Holy Spirit was to do the speaking Himself, or rather, make me speak.

## The Holy Spirit Comes

Just then both of them saw a supernatural light over my head, and in this, Mrs. L. says, she saw a crown of fire, and a cloven tongue the length of her hand.

Immediately I was filled with light and power and began to speak clearly and distinctly with a great volume of voice, in a foreign tongue. The power came so suddenly and powerfully that I lay on the floor speaking in tongues incessantly for some time. In fact, I kept on, mostly speaking in tongues, singing, and praying, with very little intermission, until 4 o'clock in the morning. Nine persons remained until three o'clock, and are witnesses of the whole scene. I must have spoken about eight different language during that time. Some present believed the number was greater. All were spoken with great distinctness.

It seemed as if an iron band lay over my jaws. Both jaws and tongue were worked by this unseen power. I could very easily detect the various sounds and forms of speech, and the different position of the tongue, and at times also the vocal chords. One of the languages had a deep gutteral sound, and came slowly, in one the nasal sound predominated, another rushed forth like a [torrent], others came more regularly and smoothly. Once the twisting of the organs of speech, in order to produce the sounds, made the muscles of the throat ache. They were of course not used to it.

I knelt, stood, or sat in a chair while this was going on. I stood erect sometimes, speaking so forcibly that several thousand person could easily have heard all I said. I felt such strength throughout my body that I now understand, by personal experience, where David and Samson obtained their strength.

But the most wonderful moment, the most rapturous of all, was when I suddenly commenced to sing a beautiful baritone solo, using one of the most pure and delightful languages I have ever heard. The tune and words were entirely new to me, and the rhythm and cadence of the verses and chorus seemed to be perfect.

I was perfectly conscious of all that was going on, but was led by the Spirit of God, filling my whole being with His presence. I felt at times as if on fire inside, but there was no pain. It was a mighty sense of the holy purity and gracious love of God within.

Now and then I had seasons of prayer. But it was the Holy Spirit praying within me. I received an illustration of Romans 8:26-27. I don't remember having prayed in that way before. New York and the United States, Norway and all Scandinavia and Europe, my loved ones and friends, lay like an intense burden on my soul. What power was given in prayer! That night will never be forgotten by anyone present.

God's presence overwhelmed me completely. I then threw myself on the floor with the cry, "At last! At last!" It seemed as if the heavens would open above us and the glory of God appear before us.

## Letter From Pastor Barratt

*In answer to a letter asking him about the rise and progress of the work in Europe, he sent us the following*:

After receiving the baptisms of fire in New York, I returned back to Norway and commenced meetings in Christiania; immediately the fire fell there and the revival commenced. From this center it spread all over Europe. Brother Johnson commenced shortly afterward in Schofde, Sweden, while numbers carried the fire from Christiania to other parts of Norway.

About three months after the outbreak of the revival in Christiania, I commenced to travel. [I] visited Stockholm and other towns in Sweden. I then went to Copenhagen and the revival began there. From there I went to Sunderland, England, and the revival commenced there.

Two sisters, Miss Thille and Miss Dagmar Gregerson, (both are now married and are missionaries in India) took the fire to Germany and Switzerland. I did not have time to go there then, nor had I time to visit Holland. But later on I visited India (by invitation), and the Holy Land and stopped some time in Switzerland, making the work more secure there. I also visited Germany and some years after, Holland.

The revival spread from Sunderland, England, to Holland. That is, Brother Pollman received his baptism in Sunderland and the revival, which had entered Holland from Switzerland, was brought into a purer line of influence.

In Germany, God raised up great workers; among the foremost might be mentioned Pastor Paul.

Later on, I visited Finland and Russia. A great revival broke out in Finland, especially after Pastor Smidt's work there. I have visited Finland several times since and crowds have attended and remarkable revival scenes have taken place.

But in no country have I seen a deeper work than in Norway. The revival has spread all over the country, more or less, and God is constantly glorifying his holy name in our midst.

How much of the labor, groaning prayers, mighty preaching, fastings, trials, victories [cannot be fully] covered by this brief letter, only the day will declare. We hope in time, to present fuller details of the work abroad. This, however, will take time, and we can only do the best we can.

(That much of interest may be developed is evident from the following letter from Miss Malick. Bro. Barrett covers the time spent in the Holy Land with a half dozen words; I wish that we had side lights on all his trips as we have this little one upon this visit to Palestine.)

## Miss Malick's Letter

A friend placed in my hand a copy of the Weekly Evangel of Jan. 22, 1916, in which I read of your desire to acquire as much information as possible about this Pentecostal Movement. So I thought to send you a brief account of my experience along this line, hoping that it will add a little to the interest in the subject, and bring honor and glory to God for His wonderful works among the children of men.

Away in the Holy Land, in the lower slopes of Mt. Lebanon, there is a small town, Shwifat by name, about six or seven miles from the Mediterranean coast. In this town I was born, brought up, and there I taught school for several years.

I was saved as a child and my heart's desire was and always has been to reach every creature with the Gospel news. I tried to do so, as much as I had a chance. At one time I worked in Hebron, South of Jerusalem, for six years among the Mohammedans. I was there with Mrs. Murry, a blind lady, who died a few years ago in India. All this time there was in my heart a craving for more of the Holy Spirit and power in service.

In the year 1909 this desire became more intense. I was at home then in Shwifat. Talking to a friend about it one day, she said, 'Let us pray definitely about it.' This suggestion settled deep in my heart and I started to wait on God for an outpouring of His Holy Spirit. I made this a regular thing at an appointed time in my room. This went on for several weeks. One day I received a Latter Rain paper from across the ocean, [I] do not know who sent it to me. It was the first of the kind I had ever seen, and [it] contained the first news which I had received of the outpouring of the Holy Spirit as on the day of Pentecost. I cried unto the Lord, saying, 'If this thing is going on in the world, I must have it too, for thou art no respecter of persons; it is the thing I have been praying for all this time.'

A week after this, Pastor Barrett of Norway, on his way home, stopped in our town to spend a few days with some friends. He had been in the United States and while there had received the baptism in the Holy Spirit and spake in other tongues.

We arranged to have prayer meetings for a week. What was supposed to be the last day of the meeting came, and no one had received their baptism as yet. That morning my younger sister and I were the only ones in the upper chamber besides the pastor and the household members. The rest of the seekers had perhaps given up, and perhaps some were busy. But, praise the Lord, he never gives up, not even the ones and the twos, for as soon as we knelt down to pray the power of God fell on my sister and she began to speak in tongues. In a few minutes, I too, lost control of my tongue and the Spirit was interceding through me with utterances unknown to me.

When this was known outside, the afternoon and evening meetings were crowded with people. Some came out of curiosity, others were in earnest. The meetings were extended another week; a few received the baptism. You may be sure the devil caused no small stir over it, but the Lord held steady the faithful ones, those who were willing to suffer loss for His name's sake.

(Five years later Miss Malick came to this country and spent some time in the Rochester Bible Training School. She expects ultimately, to return to Palestine.) (*TWE*, April 15, 1916)

## Pentecost in Sunderland (excerpt)
### A. A. Boddy, Vicar of All Saints

In 1906 the Lord laid it upon the hearts of some of our beloved Christian Brothers to meet together for prayer. When I could. I often joined them, but their steadfastness was God-given. They met in All Saints' Vestry, *and for months and months they held on to God, often with little to encourage*. How they clung to the promises, and so did I and my dear wife also. Isaiah 62:6, 7. was exemplified. "I have set my watchmen upon thy walls, O Jerusalem, which will never hold their peace day or night. Ye that make mention of the Lord keep not silence, and give Him no rest till He establish and till He make Jerusalem a praise on the earth." I thank God for these fellow watchmen.

We were tarrying until we should be endued with power from on high. We were praying for a revival, and we did not know how God was going to answer our prayer, but we were *sure He would answer and the answer has come. And the answer is from Him*.

How well I remember taking into their little gathering one of the first papers telling of what seemed to be an apostolic outpouring of the Holy Spirit in the West. We praised God for this answer to prayer for revival and took courage.

At last the Lord led me into touch with this work of God which now had traveled over the Atlantic to Norway. I prayed Him to lead me to Christiania, and that if this was His work it might soon spread to our land. In a most remarkable way He arranged for the journey, and undertook during my absence.

Thomas Ball Barratt, born in Cornwall, but now a Mission preacher in Norway, was the instrument God was mightily using. Under the good hand of God I took the long journey overland in wintry weather and received His own great blessing in these Spirit-filled meetings. It was a mission room in an upper chamber. Perhaps about 120 were present. I had given out the teaching about the healing of the sick, and had spoken in the power of the Holy Ghost, and then we went to prayer. I asked those who had received the Holy Spirit with the sign of the Tongues to lay hands on me for a Baptism of the Holy Ghost. The Blessed Holy Spirit came upon me just then, filling me with love, joy and peace.

This inflow of the blessed Holy Spirit occurred March 5, 1907, but not until Dec. 2d, nine months later, did the Lord give me the sign of the tongues.

# Messengers of An Outpouring

Back in England in the months that followed, our prayer meetings were filled with power. I was mightily anointed several times. On one occasion I received a special witness from the Lord of my sanctification. *It was when we were adoring the Lamb that the power of God overwhelmed me, and caused me to sink helpless on the floor.* It was thus that God specially met me, filling me more and more until the sign came, and the full vessel at last overflowed.

One Sunday four of us were led together to pray at 9:30 P. M, in the Vicarage and we continued until nearly one in the morning. We had had a blessed day of worship and witness. The window blinds were not drawn down. I was opposite the window and so looked out at the church. A wonderful light suddenly filled the room and lingered over the church roof.

One brother fell to the floor very suddenly, crying with tremendous vehemence, "It is the Lord, there is no deception, brothers, it is the Lord Himself." This continued on and on, the light lingering over the roof of the church, an emblem it seemed of blessing that was to be connected with this place. Only one saw the Lord, we three saw the light only. Then a brother kneeling at my right hand fell to the floor suddenly also and cried in wonderful tones of awe, "It's the *blood*. Oh, it's the *blood*."

Being guided, I believe by the Lord, I asked Pastor Barratt from Norway to come over and help us. He came to a very hungry and prepared people, and he was graciously used at once as a channel of God's blessing, to be a pioneer of work which has continued ever since. He was with us just seven weeks and many received the Holy Ghost with signs following. On Sept. 11, 1907, my dear wife was thus blessed and had a wonderful revelation as to the blood.

On the 13th of September, in one of our large meetings in the Parish Hall in the presence of my people, I offered myself definitely to the Lord, as the Spirit came to me causing deep breathings and laying hold of me more and more. I prayed there for those who were opposing the work of God, I asked for more love, the love of Christ to be mine. I was led to make a full surrender of everything to the Lord. I quite hoped to receive the sign of the tongues, but was not given that night. I must confess that I was disappointed. It seemed hard to be taking so prominent a part in this work of God and yet not to have the sign which the Lord gave to many others before He gave it to me.

September 21st came around again and I hoped that the Lord who had powerfully anointed me now four times would speak through me. It was the anniversary of my baptism in 1892. That evening my two dear daughters both received the Holy Ghost with the signs in a small gathering in the Vicarage. A more touching scene was witnessed by a thankful father and mother. Very remarkably He gave me that day one strange word as I woke from a dream in which I was overwhelmed by the glory of the Lord, and I cried out almost in fear because of the nearness of God. I believe I was beginning to say "Maranatha," the Lord is at hand.

This was the beginning of the fullness of the blessing. I realized that I had indeed received the blessed Holy Ghost and I soon found that as I whole-heartedly recognized Him it was true; but He kept me waiting for a fuller sign of the gift of tongues. Forty-nine were graciously dealt with by our God before He took my tongue and spoke a strange language with it.

I hope that the precious memory of the glorious Spirit-filled meeting in All Saints' Vicarage, Dec. 2, 1907, will never fade away. I lay before the Lord feeling that I could not get low enough. I had special reason to believe that at last He was going to give me the sign. So on that Monday night He took my tongue as I yielded and obeyed. First speaking quickly but quietly and then more powerfully. The whole meeting at this point was adoring and praising God with great joy. The Lord was raising His hands in blessing above the meeting as we were conscious of His presence. My voice in tongues rose with theirs as a torrent of words poured out. So far it had been between me and the Lord, and I was indeed grateful that after nine months the sign I had hoped for had come at last. Hallelujah to the Lamb!

During the past twelve months the atoning work of God's Incarnate Son has, in a new way, been ever our theme. The precious blood of the Lord Jesus has been our constant and only plea, and we have as never before adored the "Lamb that was slain." (*TLRE*, Feb, 1909)

## The Pentecostal Movement Invades Ohio

In this week's issue of the Evangel, we greet you with an account of the incoming of the work of God in Ohio. We are fortunate in obtaining so much along this line. Sister Ivey Campbell was the God-chosen pioneer of the new light; and it was Brother McKinney's people who first, as a body, accepted the message. We have letters from both of them; Sister Campbell's follows immediately:–

In the years 1904 or 1905, the echo from the Wales revival caused a deep hunger to settle upon the children of God, resulting in a prayer for a world wide revival. The prayer was, "Lord, send a revival, and let it begin in me." God heard that prayer and began to pour out His Spirit upon all flesh.

On April 9th, 1906, God poured out His Spirit in a new way on a little tarrying company in Bonnie Bray St., Los Angeles, Cal. As the news spread, we heard of it in June and we cautiously found our way to 312 Azusa St. God was indeed manifesting Himself to His sanctified ones in a way much spoken against.

As we went, the hunger increased and we searched God's Word, finding it even as they had told us. It was on the 26th of July 1906, that God poured out His Holy Spirit upon me and possessed my whole being. (He is seeking a people for His own possession.)

I had been called to work for Him when I was sanctified some years before. I was at the time of receiving the baptism, in the work at the Soldiers' Home at Sawtell, Cal. I now felt the call to go to Ohio, my native state, and witness to them of the outpouring of the Holy Spirit. Many there were waiting on God to send someone to them with the experience.

I first witnessed in my home town, East Liverpool, Ohio. Two received the baptism in the Spirit there; others were hungry and the altars were full of hungry seeking, but they shut the doors upon us. Rev. C. A. McKinney, a returned missionary to Africa, came to the mission in East Liverpool, found the doors shut and asked me to go to Akron and witness to his people in the first week in December, 1906. He left me my fare, and I went to his place.

A meeting was in progress with Evangelist Ed Ferguson in charge. I could not get in line with him, but gave my testimony and the hunger among the people increased. In three days, two [people] received the baptism; God took charge of them and they spoke in other tongues. One language spoken was Hawaiian; there were some men there from the Islands who confirmed it. Many were healed, and the Lord took charge after the evangelist left on Sabbath evening and a new order of worship was in progress. We just stood still and saw the salvation of the Lord. The altars were crowded in every service, which in a few days lasted from 9:30 A. M. until mid-night, sometimes indeed, until morning.

Salvation flowed like a river; sins were confessed; people were reclaimed, sanctified, baptized, and healed in almost every service. God worked with us, confirming His word with signs following. The tide kept rising, crowds increased and often as many were turned away from the church as could get in. Delegates came from neighboring cities and villages to see if these things were true.

Pastor C. A. Cramer, pastor of the Christian and Missionary Alliance at Cleveland, O., and some from the Friends Church in Cleveland came, workers were sent to them and the fire began to fall there. Also, visitors came from the Missionary Home at Alliance, Ohio. Finding that it was the Word of God which was being preached, and that the promise was for them today, they went home and began tarrying-meetings. In February a convention was held there.

A paper called *Pentecostal Wonders* was published by Brother McKinney and Rev. Kilborn in Akron. This soon consolidated with the New Acts, published in Alliance, Ohio, and Alliance and the Missionary Home there were made headquarters.

In the winter we held conventions, and in the summer, campmeetings, which were largely attended. It was said that there were over ten thousand on the ground the first Sunday. Five hundred were encamped. We had all things common and the table was provided for, while large sums of money were put into the mission field, a debt was lifted from the Home, and still there was money left in the treasury.

Other place were opened in other states; Indiana, Pennsylvania, New York and many other places in Ohio. God graciously worked, getting to Himself a name, and a people ready for the coming of the Lord.

The Lord has since suffered the work to be tried, but we can rejoice that it is His and not of human origin; He went to the Father and sent the promise of the Father down from Heaven. We are witnesses of these things, and so also is the Holy Spirit. And now we commend all to Acts 20:32.

(*The following account by Brother McKinney supplements the one just given by Sister Campbell*:)

In the fall of 1906 I was the pastor of the Gospel Church of South Street, Akron, Ohio. My people were spiritual and were, in holiness and righteousness, walking in all the light they had. In this condition, a deep spiritual hunger seized myself and my people. Oh, that God would reveal himself in power to us in the coming days of our revival meetings.

So great was the hunger for God that we set apart whole nights for prayer, and to my surprise, a number of people attended. God wonderfully met us and had we known the Spirit's workings, we might have received the baptism in those nights of tarrying before God.

In the providence of God, I received the first issue of the paper published by the Azusa Street Mission in Los Angeles. It was sent to me by a dear friend, Brother Morris, of Montana, the one who had led me out into the experience of holiness. While reading the paper I felt the witness of the Spirit to my soul that it was the truth; the same witness came to my wife. I took the paper over to the church and read it to my people; they greatly rejoiced, and felt that it was the revelation of God to their hearts.

I said to my wife, "If I had the money, I would like to go to Los Angeles and attend these meetings and see for myself." But my wife said, "Oh, husband, if this is God we are just as near to heaven in Akron as we would be in Los Angeles. Let us wait and pray, God will meet us."

Well, hallelujah, He did meet us. His providence was so precious. A young man who was preparing to go to Africa wanted me to help him secure the money for his outfit and transportation, and accordingly we were visiting several missions and laying the need of the African field before them.

We were to speak at the Liverpool Mission on Saturday evening and Sunday. On getting off the train at Liverpool, we were surprised to find many there to meet us. They were much excited, and we wondered what was the matter. Upon inquiry, we were informed that one of their best mission workers had returned from Los Angeles with other friends, and that they were filled with this new doctrine of the baptism of the Holy Spirit and speaking in other tongues.

The dear brethren were wondering if it was expedient to open the mission for services, lest this strange doctrine get into it. When they told me that they had been trying to get me over the phone to tell me not to come, I could see the providence of God in letting my phone get out-of-order and my heart leaped for joy. I told them that they need not fear, God would take care of His own work, and they seemed to be willing to leave the meeting in my hands.

It was on Sunday morning when God began to bless us that I knew that this little band of Pentecostal people were there, for one sister broke out praising God in other tongues and another burst forth with a song in the Spirit. It fell upon my ears like music from another world, rapturous and heavenly. It went thru me like mighty thrills.

I finally located them in the congregation and the people were expecting me to say something to them. However, I waited till the meeting was over and then went to Sister Ivy Campbell and asked her for her address. She gave it to me, but the enemy made her think that I was going to call on her and reprove her for interrupting the meeting.

We were being entertained in one of the best homes in the city, but after dinner, I excused myself and went to hunt that address. Sister Campbell was on her knees praying that the Lord would give her grace to meet the preacher when he came. Great was her surprise when she opened the door to hear me say, "Praise the Lord, I am so glad that the Lord has sent you here." She was so delighted that she burst forth in other tongues, praising God. When we were seated, I opened my heart and told her how the Lord had spoken to us through the little paper from Los Angeles, and that my people were waiting on the Lord and praying for someone to tell them about this outpouring of the Spirit.

I told her that I felt that God had truly sent her to Ohio, but that the Liverpool people did not understand her and were afraid to receive her. Also, that my people were ready to receive her, and invited her to Akron. We were about to start special revival services with Evangelist Ed Ferguson as our evangelist, and I promised her that if she would come, she should have the afternoon services.

Sister Campbell came to Akron, and it was wonderful to see the power of God manifested in the services. The people crowded the altars and the first row of chairs. It was a sight to me to see my best people receiving their baptism and speaking in tongues. I could not but realize that it was God. I had always taught my people that they received the baptism in the Holy Spirit when they were sanctified, but now I began to see that I had never believed that it was to be received with Bible evidence. Who was I to withstand God?

Brother Ferguson, the evangelist, and I lay on our faces, but it was so hard for us to make any progress, we had so much theology in our heads which hindered us.

I witnessed my mother as the Spirit fell upon her and she began to speak in other tongues. There were in the church that afternoon, two young men from the Hawaiian Islands, and as my mother began to speak, they were greatly delighted and seemed to understand what she was saying, "You speak Hawaiian," and began to speak to her in their native tongue. But the power of the Spirit had lifted, and my mother could not understand them. They told her that she had spoken in their tongue, and had told them that Jesus was coming and for them to get ready to meet him. Other things also, she said to them about their sins. They at last fell under conviction at the altar, gave their hearts to God and were beautifully converted.

Brother Ferguson had to leave us for Cincinnati and Sister Campbell continued the meetings for two months. There were hundreds at the altar night and day and it was impossible for us to tell how many were saved or received the baptism. The crowds were so large that the police had to stand at the door taking care of those who could not get into the church.

People from surrounding states received the baptism and took the news home with them. From Akron it spread to Cleveland, Alliance, and Findlay and thence, to the uttermost parts of the earth through the missionaries who went out form those places. (*TWE*, April 29, 1916)

## The Experience of W. Jethro Walthall

*In response to my request for information regarding the work of God in Pentecost measure throughout the earth, I received the following from W. Jethro Walthall, a Holiness Baptist preacher:–*

I was filled with the Holy Spirit in the year 1879. I sought the Pentecostal type of experience, not by any name, nor according to any theory, but I received the fullness of experience and power. I always felt that I had the experience and power. I always felt that I had the experience corresponding with the records given in the Acts of the Apostles. The realization of Christ's presence was continuous and I would often fall under the mighty power when the Spirit came upon me.

At the time I was filled with the Spirit I could not say what I did [have?], for I was carried away out of myself for the time being, but once since, under great spiritual agitation, I spoke in tongues; it did not seem to bring any deeper experience. Speaking in tongues has not been general among us, though many have spoken and we have had some interpretations and many visions, with manifestations of other kinds.

The ordinary Methodist and Baptist teaching was all that I knew, and, of course, that served to diminish my experience and to paralyze my faith rather than build me up.

In the meantime I began preaching, a work to which I was called when the blessed Spirit filled me. I always felt that there was a lost chord in the Gospel ministry. My own ministry never measured up to my ideal, nor did the teaching of my church (Baptist) measure up to my experience.

Finally, the Holiness revival came my way. It approximated my ideal more nearly than anything else, but I could never accept its theory of sanctification; nor could I accept its abridgment of the supernatural. So we were necessarily called Holiness Baptists, in contradistinction to other Holiness people. I never appreciated the name, although it still lingers with us.

The light of the full Gospel ministry began at this time to drawn upon me, and I had the courage to preach it. This caused me to be ostracized from the Baptist ministry. This was in the year 1895. All who acquiesced in my teaching were also disfellowshipped, and one whole church was dropped from association connection. The revival spirit was so great, and fellowship was so free in this church, that others of the kind began to spring up here and there, and soon an annual convocation was inaugurated.

We continued to press our way into full Gospel ministry, looking for the restoration of the supernatural in the same, when the Spirit's downpour came in 1906. It was the expected with us; our ideal was, for the first time, realized. We did not, however, accept the second cleansing theory that so many associated with it. When the finished work agitation began, while many enthusiasts pressed it beyond true measure, it met our ideal of theology.

Almost simultaneously with the great spiritual downpour, speaking in tongues began among us. With it came wonderful healings, among them two advanced cases of cancer, consumption, paralysis, etc.

A careful study of the Pentecostal Movement in general, and a special inquiry into the objects of the General Council, impresses me with the idea that we are, in reality, one people, with one or two discrepancies, as follows: While you maintain that speaking in other tongues is the Bible sign of the baptism in the Holy Spirit, and that physical healing is in the atonement, we have always regarded the supernatural, tongues and healing included, to be confirmatory signs of the preached Word, in its fullness, as in Mark 16:15-20; but we have no special contention with you on that point. We feel that the one thing needful for the saints is the real baptism into the Spirit, and whatever is the will of the Spirit to follow, will be the inevitable. We feel also that technicalities should not be a bar to the unity of the faith in the body of Christ. Amen. -- Yours in the blessed hope of His coming. W. Jethro Walthall.

Brother Walthall sent me a copy of the minutes of the Annual Convocation he mentioned in his letter, and on page 4 I read this: "All the preaching services were interesting and highly spiritual, but Sunday noon and night were attended with special supernatural manifestations, such as speaking in tongues, singing in the spirit, and falling in trances."

On page four, also, "A very interesting healing service was held, in which quite a number were anointed, with prayer offered for healing, with some very blessed and immediate results."

On page 5: "We also believe in striving to establish and maintain the spirit of unity among full Gospel people everywhere. Therefore, we recommend that this body appoint one or more men to open personal or written correspondence with the General Council of the Assemblies of God, known as the Pentecostal Movement, to ascertain the advisability of forming fraternal relations with that body." Brother Walthall was appointed as correspondent. We are publishing this account of God's dealings with them in the hopes that we can find ground for co-operative fellowship.

## Holiness Baptists in The Carolinas

In subsequent letters, Brother Walthall told me that there was a body of Holiness Baptists in Georgia which had [actually] come into existence before the one to which he belonged. Also, of another body of like faith in the Carolinas. Both of these bodies had manifestations of the Spirit's presence, including the speaking in tongues. His letter relative to the Carolina work follows: *

A great holiness revival was on in and around Greenville, S.C., in 1894 and 1895. A Baptist minister, Robert R. Singleton, was the prominent leader. He was excommunicated from his church, and there became such a following that Parish Mountain Holiness Baptist Church was formed, three miles from Greenville. In 1905 there was such a spiritual upheaval in that church that a number spoke in tongues. The pastor told me that one young man, who could neither read nor write, was [worked] upon by the Holy Spirit, and so filled with the Spirit of interpretation, that as the pastor would call the names of the letters in the English alphabet, the young man would give their Hebrew equivalents. It was marvelous to hear Brother Singleton tell of the manifestations in that revival. (This was before the outpouring in Azusa Street.)

The revival subsided somewhat in a year or so, and finally, just after restoration of tongues in 1906, an extremist, who had been vacillating, came to the church and began to preach tongues as a sign of the baptism in the Holy Spirit. He rigidly enforced the idea, and denounced all others as false. [This is actually the doctrine of the Assembly of God and other modern Pentecostals.] If his contention was true, it was not the thing to do there, on account of their past teaching, coupled with the fact that they had tongues already, without seeking for them in that way. The pastor opposed the teaching, and so he had the church retrograded somewhat, until in 1911 they called me there for a campmeeting. I began to preach the full Gospel, free from extremes on both sides. During the progress of this great revival the spiritual tide returned in full force with divers tongues, many visions and other manifestations of the Spirit.

This church grew into a movement of several churches, but from what I can learn, the revival tide has, comparatively speaking, passed over and the work lags somewhat.

There is also a large movement of Holiness Baptist churches in Southern Georgia, in which speaking in tongues and other great spiritual manifestations have played an important part in the progress of their work. Tongues were introduced there, however, after the Los Angeles downpour.

These three movements of Holiness Baptist churches sprang up almost simultaneously, without any knowledge of each other until some years after their inception. (*TPE*, May 6, 1916)

\*\*\*

I truly appreciate Brother Walthall's kindness in supplying us with this information, and it strengthens my faith in the wonderful present works of God. Here were three movements, unknown to each other, and yet each were, led by God, walking in the same light, enjoying the same measure of the Lord's Spirit. All through the course of my researches into the origin of this great movement, I have been struck with this thing. Hebrews 1:1 is in my mind as I think about it. "God, who at sundry times and divers manners spake in time past unto the fathers by the prophets, hath in these last days spoken unto us by His Son;" -- God who in time past spoke in divers places, in scattered groups of Christians struggling towards the light, has in these last days, spoken a great and united movement into existence, in which these scattered bands of saints can find fellowship, edification, counsel, upbuilding. The brooks of many years are now flowing together into a stream to which the attention of thirsty thousands is being drawn. Here is water at last, and in abundance. See to it, each of you in your place, that this stream, produced so evidently under the direction of God, does not go dry and those thirsty ones be turned empty away. (Ibid)

## How and When Pentecost Came to Cleveland
### James Leonard

Prior to the pouring out of the Holy Spirit after the fashion of Acts 2:4, "And they were all filled with the Holy Spirit and began to speak in other tongues as the Holy Spirit gave utterance," in 1906 many who are now members of the "Pentecostal Church" of Cleveland, Ohio, were members of the denominational churches, and yet were associated together as a branch of the Christian and Missionary Alliance.

## Messengers of An Outpouring

We believed in the so-called fourfold Gospel -- Jesus as Savior, Santifier, Healer, and coming King. Many of our company rejoiced in a firm conviction that Acts 1:5 had been made real in their lives and [their] experiences. We so testified and exhorted others to receive the Holy Spirit. Nevertheless, in the fall of 1900, we (both pastor and people) became conscious of the fact that we were impotent, powerless, and in a large measure were in our own souls dried up spiritually.

W. H. Cramer, our pastor, felt this so keenly that he appointed every night meetings for the purpose of waiting on the Lord for an outpouring of the Spirit. Through the months of November and December a little handful of earnest, hungry souls came together night after night, to wait at the feet of Jesus for power for some outpouring from Him that would satisfy our hearts and make us more nearly the witnesses that we felt we ought to be.

Just how God was going to answer this heart cry, none of us had the least conception (for we had not yet heard of Pentecost). The most any of us looked for was, perhaps a reviving such as we had been accustomed to receive in the past. While we were holding these nightly meetings, Pentecost fell in Akron, Ohio. Miss Ivey Campbell, who had received the baptism in Los Angeles, came to Akron and began witnessing to the saints, and the fire fell. We heard about it, and, like the people in Jerusalem, began to say, "What meaneth this?"

Brother Cramer went to Akron to investigate, and being convinced that this was of God, and was the real baptism in the Holy Spirit, reported so to us, assuring us this was what we needed, and this experience would be the answer to the cry of our hearts. Some of us, seeing that the accounts in the Acts of the Apostles were really our examples, were quickly convinced; while we did not repudiate anything that God had accomplished in us, we were able to see that we had not gone further in experience than had the disciples when Jesus said to them, "But tarry ye in the city of Jerusalem until ye be endued with power from on high."

Those of us who were thus convinced at once began to seek for the baptism. Others, however, hesitated and, because of cautions from those in whom they had confidence, and because of the strange manifestations, were filled with fear, and, I am sorry to say, have never received the baptism.

About the middle of December, 1906, Brothers McKinney and Sawders of Akron began a series of meetings in the Friend's Church, Cedar Ave. At these meetings some of the students and others received the baptism, but the church authorities repudiated the work, declaring it not of God. In the meantime our meetings at the mission were continued. Brother Cramer was the first of our number to receive the baptism.

Miss Cooper (now Mrs. Emery) of Akron came to us in January, 1907, and Miss Ivey Campbell in February, as helpers for Brother Cramer. On Sunday afternoon, January 13, 1907, the fire first fell upon us as a company, three of our number being prostrated by the mighty power of God. However, none of these came through at this time. That night the fire fell again, and Brother L. C. Grant, now of Pittsburg, Penn., about midnight received his baptism, speaking in other tongues. By the end of January several more among us had gotten through. After this it became almost a nightly occurrence for one or more to receive the baptism, all speaking in tongues and magnifying God. Many also had wonderful visions of Jesus. Some notable healings were also witnessed.

It was a wonderful experience, for us who had never seen God work after this fashion before, to see the prostrated bodies, so many at times that it was impossible to avoid stepping over them. The strange manifestations, the speaking and singing in other tongues, accompanied with shouts of praise, altogether made a deep and lasting impression upon our hearts; particularly the invariable testimony, of all who came through to the baptism at that time, to the *imminent coming of Jesus*, with exhortations from old and young to speedily prepare for this great event.

This, of course, was soon noised abroad and we were written up in the papers without regard for truth. The prostrations, the manifestations, and everything pertaining to the conduct of the worshipers was distorted and exaggerated and made as sensational as the minds of the reporters could conceive. All this, of course, drew the excitement-loving and curious to our meetings. We were looked upon, and talked about, as fanatical, crazy, etc. As we passed the "sons of Belial" on the streets we were hooted at, and sometimes they would mimic the speaking in tongues, but hallelujah, God poured out His Spirit all the more.

Many members of the churches out of curiosity came to see, most of them went away without having met God, but praise God some of them stayed or came back, got right with God and received their baptism. The room was filled with sinners every night and what they saw and heard caused many of them to repent and seek the Lord. Some of these were baptized, as they were at the home of Cornelius.

The first series of meetings continued about three months. Scores of God's children from far and near came, waited, and went away filled with the Spirit, speaking in tongues and magnifying God; so the light and testimony was carried to many other souls. Bless God!

How many there were who received the blessed Spirit in those days we never knew, as we did not keep a count.

Brother Cramer remained with us until God called him to other work. He was succeeded in the pastorate by Brother D. W. Kerr, Oct. 1, 1911. After Brother Kerr came to us we organized into an independent church and incorporated under the name of "The Alliance Tabernacle Church," since changing the name to "The Pentecostal Church." We believe that the baptism in the Holy Spirit according to the fashion of Acts 2:4 is for every child of God who will pay the price. *(TWE,* May 13, 1916)

\*\*\*

Cleveland is today one of our strongest assemblies. It is in hearty sympathy with the work of the General Council [of the AOG], and the pastor, Brother Kerr is an honored member of our Presbytery. We thank God for His loving kindness as manifested in His works in Cleveland. (Ibid)

> *Book Editor*: The above account very much reminds me of the Revival that took place at the Brownsville Assembly in Pensacola in the 1990s.

# Messengers of An Outpouring

## Details From Various Sources
[How Pentecost Came to Different People]

There is one thing which impresses every student of this mighty movement, and that is the sovereignty of God. Even in the Acts of the Apostle the story of the primitive church is largely a history of Peter and Paul. The history of the Reformation centers around a few illustrious names. The same thing is true regarding the great revivals under Wesley, Whitfield, Edwards, Finney. However, in this outpouring of the Holy Spirit the reverse is true. Very few great names stand out in this story, and those only for a little while. It is pre-eminently a work of God. Men may come and men may go, but the work of God goes forward any way.

This is made plain in the sketches we present to you this week. From widely separated geographical locations, ignorant of the work of God in each other, led by the Spirit alone, these people have met at last, as the three wise men met, at the feet of Jesus.

### A. P. Dennis, of Scottsburg, Ind., writes as follows:

Attending a meeting conducted by the evangelist, M. B. Woodworth (now Woodworth-Etter) in the fall of 1886, I received a wonderful anointing and enduement of power. I had been saved nine months previous to this experience. From this time on, I labored for Jesus, and He honored us with many souls. Sometimes I have seen a roomful slain like men in battle under the mighty power of God.

One night in October, 1888, while many were slain [likely also in an Etter meeting?], I became as a drunken man. I began to stutter, so stammer, and then suddenly began speaking in other tongues. Always after this, there seemed to be a greater anointing upon me, but I concluded that it was only a strange operation of the Spirit. In 1912 I attended a campmeeting conducted by Brother Haywood in Indianapolis, Ind., on purpose to receive the baptism in the Holy Spirit. I received Him in great glory and spake in tongues. Then I knew that it was the same that I had received in 1888.

Since then my wife has gone home, [before she died] an angel, or white form [was] standing at the foot of the bed, saying, "I am sent for thy wife." Before leaving, she asked many questions about the "bright ones" about her.

I now see many lonely days, but Jesus seems more precious than ever before. I had thought she would remain with me till Jesus came, "but the dead in Christ shall rise first, then we who are alive and remain shall be caught up together with them in the clouds to meet the Lord in the air; and so shall we ever be with the Lord."

> *Book Editor*: Notice that he had the power of God on him and spoke in tongues in 1888, but did not understand that he had actually been baptized in the Holy Spirit with the tongues as evidence, so he failed to continue to speak in tongues all during those years. It appears that God could have sent the outpouring through Sister Etter, but she did not teach on the subject, so people did not know that it was available then. Once it became an "official" outpouring, she

did teach on it and prayed for people to receive and many were baptized in her meetings.

## An Azusa Witness:

*This letter from Mrs. C. J. Hagg, of Los Angeles, throws an interesting side light on the work of the Lord in old Azusa Street Mission:*

"I received the baptism in the Holy Spirit on the first day of May, 1906. I was in the first meeting held in Azusa Street Mission, and was convinced that night that the work was of God. That very first time, the shower fell on me, and I fell under the power.

"I tarried ten days at Bonnie Brae Street, on the tenth day, I fell under the power again. A few days after that, at home, I spoke and sang in tongues. Then God made me a piece of clay. It was all so wonderful.

"I was the fourth white woman to receive the baptism. I have had the privilege of being in these meetings from the first.

"In August, 1906, I went to Fort Worth, Texas, my home town. Praise God, He poured out His Spirit, and through much persecution and travail of soul, He brought forth.

"While there, on two occasions, a woman from the Indian nation heard me speaking in her language. She testified that I spoke the same thing afterward in English, thus confirming the message. God has seen fit to speak and sing many tongues through me, which have been understood. At one time God took all my English away for a period of three days, so that I could only speak in tongues, and had to write to my family and friends. This was a sign to unbelievers and a message of warning.

"Two and one-half years ago God called me to the Russians, Armenians, and Jews. I have a mission at 132 Glen Street, Los Angeles. God is working, and some are being saved, while others have received the baptism."

## A Vision of Jesus:

Mrs. Hoy is a member of the Assembly of God in Springfield, Mo., and is a precious woman of God. The following are her words:–

I have seen many visions while in prayer with my eyes closed, but this time my eyes were open.

I received my baptism at the home of my sister, Mrs. Susie Wells, one and one-half miles south of Mammoth Springs, Ark., on the night of July 30, 1913, at about eleven o'clock.

The next day was bright, not a cloud in the sky. About 10:30 or 11 in the morning, sister and I were in the front room talking about our wonderful God and His unspeakable gift. Presently, our conversation languished and sister [went] into the other room. Just at that moment, without thinking what I was going to say, I called out, "Jesus is coming soon." Sister answered in tongues, coming back into the front room. As I spoke, I stepped to the front door, which was in the east wall of the room, pushed open the screen, and looking up, with these natural eyes open, saw Jesus in the air, robed in white, and appearing as though He was about to descend to the earth.

I do not think that my sister saw Him, but to me He was as plain as any living person on the earth. All glory to our blessed Christ. (*TWE*, May 20, 1916)

## The Pentecostal Work in Fort Worth, Texas

We have this week a letter from Brother A. P. Collins, and a report from Burt McCaffery, both dealing with the work in Fort Worth, Texas. The Lord has been very gracious to that place, and we are glad to spread the news of His doings.

*Brother Collins Writes*:

The Pentecostal truth was first brought to Ft. Worth by Mrs. Hagg of California, in the fall of 1906. Some two or three accepted the truth and were baptized in the Holy Spirit. They are still faithful. Through one of these baptized saints, Sister Roll, my attention was called to what God was doing in Chicago and Los Angeles.

About this time, Brother E. N. Bell had gone to Chicago to seek the baptism. In April, 1908, Doctor A. S. Worrell, a distinguished Baptist preacher and scholar, came to our home and prayed for my wife. She was immediately healed of appendicitis, after two leading physicians had said that she could not get well without an operation. During this visit I inquired particularly of Dr. Worrell concerning the reported outpouring of the Holy Spirit in Chicago and Los Angeles, from which places he was returning after a tour of investigation. He said, "Beyond all doubt, God was pouring out the Spirit, and people were speaking in tongues, as in the days of the apostles." This intensified my hunger for the deeper things of God.

For some years there had been, in Christendom, a concert of prayer for a world-wide revival. My heart was yearning for the same. Eagerly I scanned the papers to see signs of the revival. Two leading Baptist papers, the Argus of the South, and the Watchman, of the North, were the first to publish to the Baptist world the wonderful things God was doing in heathen lands -- baptizing in the Holy Spirit.

I called the attention of the church to what God was doing, and frankly told them that I was a candidate for all the Lord had for me. [I was] A Baptist preacher for twenty years -- pastor of the church at Hardly at the time -- a new brick church house just completed, the body well organized for work, salary arranged for, a nice home of my own, a little reputation, three daughters married, a wife and six other children at home; this announcement blighted all my prospects, worldly and denominational. Reputation went, friends deserted me, but I had a fresh glimpse of my Lord; I must go on, could not turn back.

I now went out on a trip of inspection and visited the Topeka camp where, day and night, I waited on the Lord for a period of ten days. Blessed days they were to me, "days of heaven upon earth." After this I returned home, resigned my pastorate, took my hammer and saw and went to work, still seeking God. Wife turned in with me and received the baptism before I did. This greatly encouraged me and she was so much help to me. My eldest daughter, living nearby, also received the Holy Spirit. My heart leaped for joy to see my precious family going down after God; and how God did bless them.

On March 13, 1909, at Houston, Texas, after about eleven months of preparation, the Lord heard my cry and filled me with His Holy Spirit. Then I sold my home, moved into Ft. Worth, and, in the month of July, the Holy Spirit set me over the little flock there. Many hundreds have been saved, healed, and baptized in the Holy Spirit in this Assembly and many have gone out from it to preach the full Gospel. -- Arch P. Collins.

**Brother McCafferty's Report**

The first Pentecostal meeting that was brought to my notice was held in that part of the city known as Glenwood, somewhere about the year 1908 or 1909. This meeting was held on the corner of Vickery Boulevard and Belzise Terrace. I know nothing of the success of this meeting from my own observation, so I quote from Brother Harvey Shearer, who was, as I afterward learned, in change of the meeting. He says:–

"My wife and I were called to Ft. Worth, Texas to hold a meeting. We pitched our tent in a part of the city known as Glenwood. We had been there but a few days when the power of God fell . . . and stirred up that part of the city wonderfully.

"A Baptist church was on the corner and only one had received the baptism in the Holy Spirit. We were somewhat discouraged, but I told them that God would take care of a patient and praying band of workers. They prayed much during this meeting, and a few weeks after that, a mighty revival broke out in the city, scores found the Lord and the fire has never ceased to burn."

Among those who were baptized in the early part of the outpouring of the Spirit in Ft. Worth were Brother W. R. Potter, pastor of a little Holiness mission in the downtown district (this place was afterward used as an assembly hall for the saints), W. L. Woods, Edwin Hardesty, Kit Hardesty, Brother Robertson (whose daughter, Henrietta, afterwards went as a missionary to Egypt), Will Watson, and many others who are now in the Lord's work.

The Interstate Campmeeting in Fort Worth was the next meeting that came to my notice. One day I chanced to find a small handbill blowing about; on reading it I found it to be an announcement that the sixth annual encampment of the Apostolic Faith would be held in Ft. Worth, at the old Tyler Park, services to be held in the old dance pavilion. This was to be in the month of July, 1910.

I at first paid little attention to the announcement, but as my mother began to attend, she would tell me of the way in which the services were conducted, saying that the people would gather at the altar bench and all pray at the same time. (See Acts 1:14; 4:24.) She also said that she had heard a young boy preach with great power, and that it was equal to, if not better than, the old and experienced preachers.

These sayings aroused my curiosity, and I determined to investigate. I attended that night; from the time I first set foot on the camp grounds the Spirit began to deal with me. The very air seemed to be filled with the presence of God; it seemed to me as though I was walking on holy ground. The singing, praying and burning testimonies, with the glory of God shining in each face, presented each an awe-inspiring scene that it seemed to me that Jesus was surely coming soon. As the preacher expounded the truth under the great unction of the Spirit, I could see that this was what my heart had been crying for for so long. This was indeed "Books of prophecy fulfilled at last."

In this meeting many were saved and baptized in the Holy Spirit and lay for hours under the power of God, [until finally] coming through speaking in other tongues as the Spirit gave utterance. It was during this meeting that God saved me, breaking the chains of habits and delivered me from sin, baptizing me in the Holy Spirit a few nights after. At the same time he healed me of several diseases. Several of my kindred were also saved and baptized.

**The Work Begins to Spread**

From this camp the work began to spread. Workers were sent to Smithfield, Keller, Birdwell, points in Kansas, and other northern points. L. C. Hall, F. F. Bosworth, Charles A. Smith, E. G. Birdsall remained in Ft. Worth. Brother Hall pitched his tent on Dagget and S. Main Streets, here God saved and baptized many.

L. C. Hall, Charles A. Smith and Floyd Baker presently left for South Texas, so we obtained another tent and pitched it in the same place. God continued to meet with us and many more were saved and filled with the Spirit. I am told that as many as thirty were baptized in the Spirit in one week. Many manifestations of the Spirit were in evidence, the long altar was filled night after night, large crowds attending. The revival began after the camp meeting in July and continued until cold weather.

By that time it was decided that an assembly hall should be built, so a lot on Bryan Avenue and Elizabeth was leased and a building erected. About two years prior to this, A. P. Collins had been called by the church to serve as their pastor. He now, with W. R. Potter as assistant, took charge in the new quarters. Elders and deacons were set apart to the work of the Lord and the church was truly set in order.

From this assembly the word of God has sounded out to the regions beyond and the work in the city has, from the time of the first outpouring, gone on in power and sweet unity. Error and false teachers have tried to get in, but through prayers and faithful watchings of Pastor Collins and the support of the elders, these things have been kept out and the assembly still stands for the truths of the old book.

Brother Collins has acted as pastor from the first establishment of the work until the present time, except for a short stay in Malvern, Ark. God has blessed him in his efforts and, assisted by the saints, has fought many successful battles against sin in the city and the country round about -- eternity will reveal the results.

The assembly is now located at 915 S. Main St., and souls are still being saved and baptized in the Spirit as in the days of the apostles. -- B. L. McCafferty.

We might add that representatives from this assembly have gone out into sixteen different states and to two foreign countries. (*TWE*, May, 27, 1916)

## Further Incidents From the Early Days in Azusa Mission

We are indebted to Mrs. C. J. Hagg, the sister who took the light of this truth to Fort Worth, Texas, for the following report of the Lord's work in old Azusa. While we have seen that this Pentecostal revival did not originate in Los Angeles, there is in our hearts a very tender spot for the Azusa work, and the greatness of God there revealed stirs our hearts to joy and gladness.–

One morning, while services were being held in the "Upper Room" at Azusa Street, a stranger came in and apparently engaged in taking notes of the meeting. A young girl, probably ten or twelve years of age, was praying for her father to receive the baptism in the Spirit. She arose, went to this stranger and spoke to him in his own tongue. Addressing him by his first name, she told him that he should preach the Gospel. After this, I heard him testify that no one in Los Angeles knew his first name and that his wife even, never used it. I waited at the door to ask him if I had understood him rightly regarding the language, and he told me that I had.

On another occasion, I heard a young man speak a wonderful message in another tongue. No one gave the interpretation, but, at the close, a Jewish woman said that he spoke to her a wonderful message about the Messiah. Later, this incident was published in the Apostolic Faith paper and a Jew in Chicago wrote to the Jewess asking if the report was true, saying that if it was, he would come and seek this also. I heard this letter read, and saw the Jewess who brought it to Azusa.

I assisted in answering the Azusa mail for awhile. This mail came from all over the world, from people in every walk of life. One letter, I remember, came from a woman in England with a handkerchief enclosed. Another sister and myself prayed over this and sent it back to her. In due time we received a letter from her son in Whittier, Cal., and later one from the woman herself. Both said that she was healed.

Another time we received a letter from a man in Boston, Mass. His wife's mind was afflicted and she was in the hospital in Boston. He was in bad condition, his money was gone, he had been compelled to give up his practice (he was a doctor), and it seemed that his life was wrecked. They had turned to Christian Science (falsely so-called) for help, but had received none. When we answered his pitiful letter we laid hands on it and prayed that the Holy Ghost would accompany it. When the man received it he was led to lay it upon the wife's body. The answer soon came from him that his wife was able to leave the hospital. About six weeks later they came to Azusa, within three weeks he was saved and received the baptism in the Spirit, while God dealt with her. I have had the pleasure of having them in my home and have heard their testimony.

I answered another letter from Providence, R.I.; the letter and a paper resulted in an outpouring of the Spirit there. Also at Newport News, Va., the Holy Ghost fell on them as on us at the beginning, through a letter and a paper.

Many came, through the course of the meetings, to investigate and to write and speak against these things that to them seemed to be impossible. At one time a priest came to see what he could see. The Spirit used a young girl to speak to his heart and life. The Spirit spoke to him in another tongue and narrated to him his life story, telling him among other things, that he was a murderer. The language she used was an unwritten one, he had learned it on some island among barbarous people.

He went out, but came back and asked the girl if she had ever been there. She told him that she had not, but that God was speaking to him. He thereupon confessed that what she said was true. Immediately, another person spoke to him in another language which he understood and told him that if he did not repent he would lose his soul and go to hell. He was saved and baptized in the Spirit and spoke in several languages as the Spirit gave utterance. (And the movement which has such works of God in it as this is criticized by cold hearted professors who have not seen a genuine conversion in ten years. -- Editor.)

A professor of Greek attended some of the services; he came to prove that it was impossible for this to be true and to speak against this way. I got up to testify and immediately the Spirit came upon me and I began to speak in tongues. The professor afterward told the preacher with whom I was acquainted that I spoke the most perfect Greek; he had come in an unbeliever, but went out believing. It is written, *"tongues are for a sign, not to them that believe, but to them that believe not."*

Lastly, I want to mention two visions which I had after I was baptized in the Spirit. The first Sunday after I received the baptism, I was sitting in the meeting with my eyes closed. I saw Jesus with a halo of light which was as the sun that shineth in his strength. His eyes were so full of compassion that I could not describe it. He met me on the cross, we were one and seemed to be hanging there together. I felt my head fall over and we went into the grave and arose, He saying, "I have burst the bonds of death."

At this time there was a sister sitting behind me who, outward appearance, seemed to be dying. The Spirit told me to turn and look; I did so and was told to kneel and put my hands on her head. I did so and immediately she opened her eyes and said, "I am dead." [She had also seen the vision.]

(Such a vision as this was bound to edify the seer. It brought to her heart more forcibly than any thought or teaching, her unity with the Lord in His death and burial and resurrection. We all need to have this consciousness, whether it come by vision or not, as a condition for baptism in water. Editor.)

The other vision I saw while at home, sitting in front of the stove. I saw a crown of the color of blood, it changed to purple, then to a dark grey shade. I opened my eyes and saw the crown fade from one color to another till it disappeared. Then these words were spoken, "The crown that fadeth not away," with many others that space is lacking to speak of.

I was an eyewitness to most of these things here written. All things are possible to God and to them that believe God. This is joy unspeakable and full of glory. He is my portion. -- Mrs. C. J. Hagg. (*TWE*, July 1, 1916)

## My Convictions
### George B. Studd

My friends have asked me to put into print my convictions (and how I came by them) as to The Pentecostal Movement, which is causing such a stir in the religious world today, especially in that section of it which is, or aims to be, truly spiritual, such as the Holiness churches and missions, etc. And I feel now that God would have me do so.

In July, 1906, before leaving England to return to California, I was informed by letter of a mission in Los Angeles, where people were claiming to speak with "Tongues," and that it was a sensational thing which was doing much harm to the work of God here. I remember that My first impression about the matter was this: Well, we are nearing the end of this dispensation, and I expect the Holy Spirit to be mightily poured out and the church to be restored to its apostolic glory and spiritual power, with all the gifts of the Spirit, before the Lord's return.

When I reached Los Angeles a few weeks later I was told [that] much in this movement was detrimental and dangerous, tending to wild confusion, and savoring of spiritualism, hypnotism, and the like. When I suggested that notwithstanding, "speaking in tongues" was surely a Scriptural experience, I was told that this was all spurious. As I thought it over, I said that if there was the spurious, there must be also the genuine; for Satan is the wisest of counterfeiters and he would certainly never trouble to imitate something which either did not exist at all, or had no real value.

### Five Good Points

I went to some of these meetings in the old Azusa Street Mission (which now has almost a world-wide reputation), at first going with great caution and some fear. But when I came to review what I had seen and heard there, I noticed the following good points which characterized their meetings and their literature:

1. They always honored the Blood of Christ.
2. They honored the Holy Ghost, giving Him room to work, and expecting Him to work.
3. They were certainly a missionary people, with a burning desire to spread the Gospel far and near.
4. They were earnestly looking for the coming of the Lord, and continually witnessing thereto. It seemed a watchword with them, especially when God blessed any one they would so often say, "Oh, Jesus is coming so soon."
5. As to money, they took no collections; neither did they ask for money, not even hint for it. [Yet all their bills were paid and they published a paper.] Truly, they were trusting God alone for supplies; and they all seemed poor in this world's goods.

As I looked at these five points, I could not help saying, "That does not look like the devil's work; I only wish that every church and every mission had the same solid foundation stones."

## Transformed Lives

Then I began to meet one and another of the saints who had received this Pentecostal baptism with the speaking in "tongues." I saw at once in some whom I had known well as consecrated Christians, how wonderfully their lives had been transformed and beautified by the Holy Spirit.

To one whom I had known as a sanctified woman, and on whom I now saw a new joy and liberty, I said after a few minutes' conversation, "Sister, you have something which you never had before," to which she replied, "Yes, indeed I have; I have been baptized with the Holy Ghost and fire, and it is wonderful; He is within and is so real to me, and Mr. Studd, he came to me with the manifestation of tongues." And so soon as she witnessed to the Spirit's speaking in tongues, I saw that He blessed her and her face was suffused with holy joy.

So I had to acknowledge that this Pentecostal movement with its strange manifestations (of physical shaking and speaking in tongues) was not all spurious. For now I was often meeting brothers and sisters in Christ, whose testimony I had no reason to doubt, and whom I saw that God had certainly blessed greatly, and they made my heart hungry for Christ.

The outward manifestations did not attract me, nay, in my ignorance I disliked them; and the first time I ever asked prayer for the baptism I said, "So far am I from seeking the gift of tongues, while I covet the blessing which I see that God has given to you, I would prefer (and I say it reverently) that He would give it to me without the tongues." Of course, I would not say such a thing now, for I see the blessing that comes with the speaking in tongues, and I know that I must not in any way limit the Holy Ghost. And whether I understand them or not, the Lord's manifestations are always for some good purpose. . . .

I saw too, that they had a wonderful spirit of prayer upon them; I never have seen such people to pray. Such liberty and unction in prayer, and such continuance in prayer . . . And of their spirit of praise, worship and adoration I will only say that though I have lived and labored with spiritual workers and very prayerful people in many places for twenty years, I have never seen such praise and such worship as among these Pentecostal people -- never. . . .

Thus, the more I saw of the, and attended their meetings, the more hungry I became for the baptism myself, and the more settled in my convictions that the work was of God. And so it was that later in the summer of 1907 when I found that my dear friends and fellow-laborers in the mission work of which I had been a part for many years, were decided to stand definitely and openly opposed to this work, I had with pain to separate from them. . . .

But, is not the devil also manifest in this movement? Yes, indeed, he fights it from without and from within (whenever he can get in) more bitterly than he is fighting any of God's work in the world today. . . . He is the same old devil, who is ever working with all his might to oppose and to hinder God's work, by open opposition and ridicule, and by the more subtle method of counterfeiting what God is doing. But if we keep fully surrendered to God's will with a faith that claims and trusts the shelter of the precious blood, we shall be kept from all his wiles and his hatred. I know that God has given me this comfortable assurance for myself.

Is there no danger then? Why, yes, can you be in an real battle without danger? And this is a tremendous battle with a tremendous array against us, nothing less than the principalities and powers of darkness. . . .

Those who are not conversant with this Pentecostal movement may think that it's just a small affair in a corner and among a few ignorant and emotional people; many Christians in Los Angeles ignore it as beneath their notice. To such I would say that God is working mightily in Los Angeles and in many places all over the world with the same manifestations, baptizing with the Holy Ghost (with the Pentecostal sign of speaking with other tongues) those of His children who will abandon themselves unreservedly to Him and seek their Pentecost. . . .

His Pentecostal outpouring at the close of the dispensation to prepare His chosen ones for the spiritual conflicts of the last days, which will usher in the coming of our Heavenly Bridegroom, and prepare the way for His kingdom on earth. . . . (This article was taken from the April 9th, 1906 issue of *"Jesus is Coming."* (*TWE*, July 15, 1916)

## The Great Revival at Azusa Street Mission: How it Began and How it Ended

*Book Editor*: This article needs some introduction; William H. Durham, of Chicago, received the baptism at Azusa, then returned to Chicago and had a great revival there. Later he moved to Los Angeles, and while William Seymour was traveling on a speaking tour, Durham was in charge, and it seemed a fresh outpouring had begun that was stronger than the original:

(*Pentecostal Testimony*, Vol. 1, No.8, 1911. Edited and published by William H. Durham, Los Angeles.) \*

On February 14th, [1911] we began meetings in Azusa Mission. From the first day the power of God rested upon the meetings in a wonderful way. The altar was crowded every service, and after the first few meetings, it was necessary to provide extra altar space, and soon we moved the seekers' meetings to the second floor, where there is a large room fitted up for that purpose. The work in Los Angeles was in a sad condition. Those who had been the leaders, in most cases, had proven so incompetent that the saints had lost all confidence in them, and this had resulted in a state of confusion that was sad indeed to see. Scores were really in a backslidden state, and yet in their hearts they longed to follow Jesus. Scores of others were, and for months had been, crying to God to send some one who would preach the truth and lead His people on. The suffering of the many had been great indeed.

As the message began to go forth, the saints came from all directions, and inside of a few days the place was crowded to the doors, and many turned away. Sometimes there would be more than a hundred at the altar at a single service. One after another would stand up in the meetings and confess that they had gotten their eyes off Jesus, and go to the altar, and in almost every case the anointing of the blessed Spirit would be renewed, till soon the very air was filled with notes of praise and shouts of victory.

From the very first, sinners were saved, and an average of at least ten a week were baptized in the Holy Spirit and spoke in tongues, as He gave them utterance. Week after week went by, and still the interest did not wane, but on the contrary the power increased, till the glory of God literally filled the place. At times the Spirit would move upon the saints, and they would sing in the Spirit, and praise the Lord in the most wonderful way I ever heard. At times there could be no regular order of service; no one could preach or even testify. All we could do was to sit with our souls bathed in a sea of heavenly glory, and praise the Lord with all our hearts.

As stated above, the sufferings of many of the saints had been great. Their joy now knew no bounds. They saw in these wonderful meetings the direct answer to the earnest prayers they had sent up to God for months, and now they knew their labor had not been in vain, and the light of Heaven began to shine from their faces in a way most marvelous to behold. God had told some of them He was going to do a work in Azusa St. Mission, and they now rejoiced in the fulfillment of His promise. Some saw visions of the cloud of glory hanging over the place, and had revelations of what God was going to do, every one of which came true. Time and space forbid our giving anything like a detailed account of the meetings. As many as twenty-two were baptized in the Holy Spirit in one week. Some of the hardest sinners were saved. I believe that literally hundreds who had more or less backslidden were restored, and many real cases of healing were witnessed.

When we arrived in this city, we tried hard to be in fellowship with the Upper Room Mission, of which Mr. Fisher was then pastor, but we were denied the privilege of speaking there, and refused fellowship, on the grounds that we were crooked in doctrine, in that we did not believe that sanctification was a definite, second work of grace. So when the meetings began Mr. Fisher, with many others who believe the second work of grace theory, seemed to feel it their duty to do all in their power against us. As a result, we were condemned and denounced in the most bitter terms. The people were warned against us, and told that those who were getting the baptism under our ministry were getting false baptisms. This was not confined to Los Angeles, but all up and down this coast, my teaching has been denounced as from the pit, and all sorts of charges have been made against me. In a word, the most bitter persecution and opposition has raged against me from the day God began to work so marvelously in Azusa St.

Some one will ask, what doctrine I preach that has brought all this upon me. In answer I will say that I preach the finished work of Calvary, that we come into Christ and are fully saved in conversion, and that the next step is to be baptized in water, and then in the Holy Spirit; that we do not, according to the Scriptures, have to seek for any intermediate experience. We exhort, to stand on the Word of God rather than to something He has given us, to abide in Him, and not in some experience. We believe that in conversion we come into Christ, and are saved and sanctified, and that we are to reckon ourselves dead, and in living faith abide in Christ, and live and walk in the Spirit.

This doctrine commended itself to the saints. The power of God fell, as it was preached. In one case after another God demonstrated His truth by saving and filling people with the Spirit in the same meeting; thus proving His power to work today, as He did in the days of the Apostles, as recorded all through the book of Acts.

Soon the people from the Upper Room Mission began to attend the services, and almost everyone who did so was at once convinced that the mighty power of God was there. Brother George B. Studd, who was associated with Mr. Fisher in the work, came, and was convinced that God was working. He had long been a seeker and had suffered much for the sake of the truth. God showed me that He wanted me to be in fellowship with Brother Studd and that He wanted to baptize him in the Holy Spirit in our meetings, and later that He wanted to separate from the Upper Room and from Mr. Fisher. True to what He showed me, God baptized him in our meeting, and a little later separated him from Mr. Fisher, and he has been with us ever since, rejoicing and praising God.

Meantime, Sister Fisher came to our meetings and was baptized in the Holy Spirit, and wonderfully blessed of God. Then came the janitor, the usher, and some of the elders and preachers from the Upper Room, and received their baptism. Mr. Fisher came up to the light, and at one time acknowledged it, then turned away, and hardened his heart and opposed the work more bitterly than ever, and today, if I am rightly informed, he is out of the ministry altogether. It is an awful thing to resist the power of God. Those who do so, do it at their own peril. Will the readers of this article please pray for this dear man, that the Lord will restore him?

As the meetings went on, the people on all sides began to ask what Brother Seymour would probably do, when he returned from the East. He had begun to write and wire for money to come home on. Some said he would oppose the work, others said he would accept it. The Spirit put a great burden upon my soul, and showed me clearly that he was trying to get home to get possession of the work, and that if he could not do so, he would do all in his power to stop it. I told this to several people before he arrived, and after he arrived, before he had taken his stand.

Meantime Brother Seymour came, and instead of making the honest confession he owed the people, for the way he had compromised and denied the truth, and then taking a humble place, till such time as he had regained the confidence of the people, he attempted to push himself on the people, and preach to them against their will, and a little later, notified me that this was his work, and that he wanted his place. I tried to reason with him, telling him that it would ruin the work to place him in charge at that time, but he showed a very bitter spirit and condemned and judged the people, saying that if the people did not want to hear him they could leave. When he said this I knew that it was useless to try to reason with him further. I saw plainly that God had shown me the truth concerning him. He does not care in the least for the work of the Lord, but wants a place in it. If he cannot have the place, he will not hesitate to tear down the work.

The next day I asked for an expression from the congregation, as to whether they wanted him to take charge of the work, or me to continue. With the exception of ten, the congregation, consisting of several hundred people, voted that the meetings should continue, as they were. The glory and power of God continued to rest mightily upon the meetings, and that day several were baptized in the Holy Spirit. This was Sunday.

When we came to the Mission Tuesday we found that Seymour had influenced a few of the officers of the Mission, men of his own color, to stand with him, and they had locked and bolted the door. It developed that for days, while we were preaching, praying, and seeking God in the Mission, Seymour had been scheming and planning as to how he could get possession of the building, if he could not get the work. This last move was necessary to let all men see what manner of man he has come to be. Many of us who knew him when the power and glory of God was so mightily upon him years ago, could never have turned away and left him with God, if he had not done something that would convince us beyond a doubt that he had gotten into such a condition that the power of God had entirely left him, and that he was no longer worthy of the confidence and respect of the saints. I have been the last of all the brethren, that I know of, to give him up, and have always found an excuse for his failures and blunders; but now I am compelled to acknowledge that the brethren have been right, and that, though once a mighty man, he is such no longer. Sadly do I pen these lines, and I hope every reader will pray that the Lord will restore him.

We all saw in this move a tremendous effort on the part of Satan to force us into a compromise. Failing in this, he succeeded in having us turned out of the place that was paid for with consecrated money for a place of worship. Thus we were turned into the street in the very midst of one of the greatest revivals we ever saw. It took us some little time to see that this was really God's way of separating us from an element who were not loyal to Him, and into a larger and better place as well. For a day or two there was a little confusion, as many could not understand what had happened. Then God led us to a large, airy hall at the corner of Seventh and Los Angeles streets which we could lease for a year, and we did so. By the help of the Lord we had it ready for the Sunday services, and from the first meeting the power and glory of God has been mightily upon us. In another article I will give an account of the present condition of the work in Los Angeles, as space forbids in this article.

With joy I have told of the beginning of the great revival at dear old Azusa St. Mission, and with real grief I have told of how it ended, and why. Let none of the saints condemn me, or think I have desired to condemn Mr. Seymour or Mr. Fisher or anyone else. The circumstances have forced this most unpleasant duty upon me. The news of the outpouring at Azusa brought rejoicing wherever it went; and so many letters of inquiry have reached me, that I feel it my duty to tell the saints everywhere just what happened, and who is responsible for it.

*Book Editor*: According to *The Revival Library* (www.revival-library.org), the reason Seymour locked out Durham was because Seymour had been preaching the Holiness doctrine of sanctification after salvation, but Durham had been preaching that there is no other works of grace: there is only the cross, water baptism, and Spirit baptism; this is called the "finished work" and it spread and is the main view in Pentecostalism today. After Durham moved to another location, the crowds and the anointing followed, and Azusa Street dwindled to nothing, and Seymour died in 1922.

Pastor Durham traveled back to Chicago for a two-weeks revival in June of 1912, and it was called "the greatest revival of modern times." He was greatly overworked and got pneumonia; he was able to deliver a final message and said he believed God was going to take him home. He only wanted to live long enough to say goodbye to his people in Los Angeles; he returned on July 5th and died on July 7th, but the work continued.

So the question is, was he wrong to takeover the work Seymour started? And did God take him because he took over the work, or some other reason?

## Pentecost in Persia

*Book Editor*: The story of Pentecost in Persia was written by Andrew D. Urshan, and was published in several parts that began in August 1916, making it the longest account of any region. I have shortened it slightly but had to include a lot in order to tell the whole story. Yet there are a few deletion dots . . . in this account.

Bro. Ursahan (1884-1967) was born in Persia and later returned as a missionary. He received the baptism of the Holy Spirit in 1908 in Chicago, was ordained in 1910 and preached in numerous countries. He became one of the pillars in the Oneness Pentecostal movement, but it appears that he was also well received within all of Pentecostalism, based on his numerous articles that appeared in the Weekly Evangel and other Pentecostal papers.

*An address given by Andrew D. Ursham on July 12, 1916, in the Persian Mission, 707 Wells St., Chicago, Il.:*

Tonight it is on my heart to tell you how the Lord began to work in Urmia, Persia. I do not know how far I will get in my story, but I will tell you the rest [later] . . . .

It is written about the righteous man, that when he falls seven times we should not rejoice, because will rise again. The enemy will not rejoice, because some foolish things have crept in among us, and if we fall seven times, yet we will arise because God is in our midst. What you will hear tonight is God in the Pentecostal movement.

**My Testimony**

In order that you should know of the glory and power of God in Persia, I must first tell you about the terrible conditions and difficulties which existed when I went there. I knew the Lord was not sending me to the Mohammedans, not to the Jews, nor the Armenians, but to my own nation which is called

Chaldeans or Assyrians of Persia. I know God sent me among them, and I knew I was not to stay there very long at this time, but was on a spying business for the Lord in the whole of Asia. I only expected to stay there for a few months, but things happened in such a way that I stayed over a year. The Lord also kept me in Russia on my way back, and gave me something I did not expect during the nine months that I spent there.

The people of the nation are called Nastorians [Nestorians], or eastern Apostolic Christians. In the plain of Urmia City there are about 60,000 Nastorians. . . . All these people had heard false things about me. Being one of the boys of the Presbyterian Mission School there, and my father being a minister, we were well known, and what made them know me even better was that the power of God had fallen upon some of their children in this country, and that our boys who were converted here, belonged to all their different denominations. We had Catholic, Plymouth Brethren, and Nastorian boys.

The people of my country heard some very fatal reports about their boys, and I was, of course, the cause of the whole trouble. I am glad I was, and I wish I were the cause of more. . . . The enemy reported to some of the fathers that their children were becoming insane; that they shook their heads and did not work any more; if they did work they gave all their money to Urshan; they went near the lake, laid down in the snow all night praying; has lost their health and were almost consumptives. . . .

In addition to all this something else happened. One of our young men got sick when he came to this country. Timothy, my brother, and myself took an interest in him, praying for his healing. He got somewhat better, and we spent $150 to send him back to Persia, seeing that he would only die in misery here. Instead of appreciating our kindness, he told many lies about us, in order to justify himself. He said he had never been sick, and that I took him all over America collecting money for myself, under pretense that it was for him. As his father was one of the most noted preachers there, people had great confidence in him. That boy and his father convinced the people that I was the worst man that ever walked on the face of the earth.

When the people think such things about you, not only that your religion is devilish, but that you are bad and cruel, how will they look upon you when you come around? My own father was in doubt about me. I knew all these things were awaiting me, but I went in the name of the Lord for my heart was right with Him, and He was with me.

**Experiences in Persia**

I left for Persia on the 14$^{th}$ of March, 1914. When I arrived there, the people looked upon me as though I were a terrible and cruel murderer. Some of my dear friends only looked at me from behind walls. . . . My father said, "Son, you will have to prove you are not what the people think of you; you must act thus and so." Mother said, "Son, be very careful in speaking of the Holy Ghost; don't mention it too much, and be careful of your praying so that the people will not believe what they have heard." . . . The devil attacked me from all sides . . .Two months

I was silenced; I only held one meeting in the street during that time, and that was for the sake of my Christian brethren who came to visit me. They came with the thought that they had better break the power of the devil, and have a meeting outside our door. . . . I could not see how He was going to work if we did not preach and hold meetings, but His voice in me said, "I will work." . . .

While I was resting the Lord inspired me to write on seven or eight different subjects. I wrote five tracts and gave them to the Protestant missionaries to publish. I knew that after I started preaching, they wouldn't print for me, so it was best to have them printed before hand. About the time the tracts were ready for distribution, God commenced to work. Glory to His name.

There was a little band of Plymouth Brethren in the village of Adda. These few brethren and sisters had a little chapel, and as they were praying there one evening, a special spirit of worship came upon them. They said afterwards that they had never had such a prayer meeting in their lives. Suddenly the power fell on one of them and he strangely shouted. The people were disturbed about it, as they had heard concerning my work. One school teacher told the man who was under the power, named Brother Andrew, to come to my village and get more information from me regarding this matter.

On Sunday morning, which was the Pentecostal holy day, according to the Eastern Christian observation, June 10, 1915, about six o'clock, I felt someone kissing my face on both cheeks. I woke up and saw that big fellow, Brother Andrew, with his face shining. I knew him and said, "What are you doing here at this time?" He said, "Get up, I want to tell you something. We were praying last night and the Spirit moved upon us. Such power came upon me that I was almost beside myself. I have come here to know if this is the baptism of the Holy Ghost."

O, beloved, I was so happy I didn't know what to do. I knew the Lord had commenced to work. That meant to me, "Get up and get busy, and go forward in the name of the Lord." Brother Andrew said to me, "Brother Urshan, let us go into the vineyard hut [to pray] and I will get my baptism." I answered, "Let us get some breakfast first." He said, "No, no, not now." . . .

We went into the vineyard hut, and he began to pray. He prayed, and prayed, and prayed. Then I prayed too. I did not know what to say, but I praised God, thinking in my heart that Andrew was not yet ready for the baptism of the Spirit. I am glad he did not know my thoughts and doubts, for suddenly, in spite of my lack of faith, Brother Andrew began to shake. He almost shook the mud hut, and he spoke powerfully in new tongues. His eyes were open and he preached in tongues. I said in my heart, "Go ahead and preach to me." He turned and preached towards the east, the west, the north, and the south. I prayed and prayed, "Go ahead, blessed Spirit of God."

The Holy Ghost preached through that young man to the whole country, signifying to me that He would rebuke the powers of darkness, and deliver His message through His witnesses all over that land. Hallelujah! Who can describe the glory of the Lord in that place? Beloved, I was overcome with wonder, amazement, and joy; I was lost in the realization of God's love to me and my country.

## Messengers of An Outpouring

Our beloved Brother Jeremiah Eshoo live about three miles from our village. He had received his baptism in the United States as you know and was praying earnestly for God to do a blessed work in Persia. I knew that he would rejoice exceedingly to know how God's power had at last fallen in his country. Overwhelmed with joy, we went to see him in his home, but we found he had gone into the fields to pray. We went to meet him, determined to gladden his heart with the knowledge that his prayer, with the prayers of all God's people for Persia, was finally answered. As we entered the field, we saw him afar off, returning. I raised my hands. Looking upon us with surprise, he also raised his hands. Brother Andrew starting running toward him, speaking in tongues. Brother Jeremiah, seeing and hearing him, was so overcome with joy that he could no longer stand on his feet; but falling on his knees and stretching his hands towards heaven, said like Simeon of old, "Now lettest Thou Thy servant go in peace, for mine eyes have seen Thy salvation." The whole of heaven seemed to be filled with music over this event.

**Baptism Brings Amazement**

We were only despised young men in a country which had been in the hands of the devil for centuries, and which was filled with superstition and darkness; but we three [were] filled with the power of God, determined to break through the obstacles and practically insurmountable difficulties which surrounded us, at any cost. It was wonderful! . . . Abraham, Jeremiah's brother, who had somewhat cooled toward the Lord, when he saw Andrew filled with the Holy Ghost, got hungry again and began earnestly to seek God anew. He was revived.

After these great blessings in Brother Jeremiah's home, we all decided to go back to my village, Abjaloo. As we went into the house, my father met us. When he looked upon us, he realized something wonderful had happened. Seeing Brother Andrew's face shining, he asked me, "Son, did Brother Andrew receive the baptism of the Holy Ghost?" I said, "Yes, father." My mother and my family heard this, and they all came into the parlor to look upon Brother Andrew. We sat together, overwhelmed with the joy of the Lord. My parents were busy staring at us. The operation of the Holy Spirit in Brother Andrew was causing his lips to tremble as an expression of joy in his soul. Sometimes he would break forth in new tongues, which caused our family still greater surprise.

While this was going on, a wealthy and noted man of the village, who knew Brother Andrew, came in to see him, not knowing what had happened. He sat still gazing on us, too, and undoubtedly saying in his heart, "What means this?" Especially as he saw his friend Andrew moved by the Holy Spirit with manifestations that are strange to the mind of the flesh. That moment the Spirit of the Lord came upon Brother Andrew. He sat up on his knees, and stretching his right hand towards that big man, his friend, said, "Why will you remain in sin? When are you going to repent?" The impression was so strong on the man that he immediately asked forgiveness and hastily left us. He then went into the street and told the people of the village what he had seen and heard, and how he felt when he saw Brother Andrew so under the power of the Spirit.

He warned the elders of the village to be careful not to speak lightly of us, telling them that we indeed had great power with the people. That man, although he is not converted, is now a great help to us in many ways, believing that we are from God, and asking the benefit of our prayers. He has also allowed his family to come to our meetings from which they have derived wonderful blessing.

In the morning before I went to pray with Brother Andrew, I had given him my promise that if he received the baptism of the Holy Spirit that day I would go back with him to his village and stay with him that night. The condition of the promise was fulfilled. He received his glorious baptism as you have heard. Now that the eventide had come, Brother Andrew, with is face shining, said to me, "Brother Urshan, God fulfilled the promise of His Spirit in me. Will you fulfill your promise of this morning?" I said, "Of course I will, but just see what a downpour of rain we are having. How can we go? We will be soaked through." "But," he said, "if we don't go now, we cannot go at all, for the night is coming." So trusting the Lord, we started in spite of the rain.

As we were going, with the rain pouring down upon us, God said to me, "What are you learning from this rain?" I answered, "I wish we might have such a spiritual outpouring." Then He said to me, "If I care for the grass and the trees, how much more do I care for precious human souls? Can you not believe that I will give you just such spiritual rain?" I said, "Lord, I believe, and I claim the promise." To my surprise, right after taking the rain as a sign of a blessed outpouring of the Spirit, the skies cleared, and the sun shone.

**The First Pentecostal Mission**

You know Persia has beautiful springs, great large rivers for irrigation. The waters flow from the mountains. The fragrance and natural beauty of that country is wonderful. We felt like happy Pilgrims in the sunshine that evening, and singing praises unto God, we entered the village called Adda. As soon as we were in the streets, the people started looking at us in astonishment. They had somehow heard that Andrew had come under what they termed "my influence."

We entered Brother Andrew's home, and not more than a few minutes elapsed before the room was packed with people. The yard outside also was filled with the crowd. They sat on the floor just like we sit in Persia, and stared first at Andrew and then at me. Looking on me they said, "That's the fellow that makes people faint. We see that he has made Andrew to become like him. Why does Andrew shake? Did Urshan give him what he had?" When we looked at them they dropped their eyes; and when we turned our eyes away they stared at us.

Seeing the crowd that had gathered, their excitement and their awe, we asked them, "What is the matter? What have you come for?" Then Brother Andrew suddenly broke out in tongues, and taking the New Testament from me, opened it at John 3. He read the story of Nicodemus; and as he read, filled with the Holy Ghost, he was stammering with the power, and his face shone. When he had finished he handed the Testament back to me, and I began to preach on the new birth. "What is the new birth? How do we know that we are born again?" While I was speaking I was praying in my heart. God said to me, "These people are seized with conviction in a powerful way, but they do not know how to confess."

They were all sitting silently on the rugs. Then the Lord led me to sing the 51st Psalm in our own tongue. As I sang this heart confession of David, I put myself in their place, and cried to God in their stead. The power of God fell on me; I could not help but weep, and as I sang and wept, the Word of God pierced the hearts of the people. Terrible screams were heard; such cries of conviction and confession, that the strongholds of Satan seemed shaken to their very foundation by the power of the Holy Ghost.

Some of the women had children in their laps. Such conviction seized them that they practically threw them aside, and cried to God for mercy. I do not remember how many were under conviction, but about six got saved with a thorough and square salvation. The meeting would have continued all night if I had allowed it to, but I said to the people, "We must now stop; don't be afraid, you will get what you want." The power fell on those that were saved, and they began to shake. The rest went home, crying to God and weeping.

These things raised terrible persecution against me. The Lord told me I had better go home and praise Him for a couple of weeks, and then when I came back I would reap the harvest. "While you are away," said the Lord, "the whole town will inquire of Brother Andrew regarding the work and his experience, and then the door will be opened to you, and the people will be ready and anxious to hear the truth." On going home I told the brethren that were praying, to come and help me. The battle was on, and God would work mightily.

After two weeks had elapsed, we went back to that town, and this is the song we sang: "Hold the Fort for I am Coming." "Hallelujah." As we sang we marched along the streets. The men, women and children came in crowds, and we began to pray. Beloved, in about four weeks the glory of God seized that town in such a way that if the devil had not hindered the people through religious men, every one of them would have been converted and filled with the Holy Ghost. The persecution became very terrible, so much so that our lives were in danger. They threatened to kill us. In fact, one of our sisters was the first martyr in this town; and yet, in spite of it all, the people came out to the meetings. About fifty were saved and received the baptism of the Holy Ghost there. Glory to Jesus! That was the first assembly.

The news and excitement spread all over Urmia, and to the government, which also opposed us bitterly. The people of Adda proposed new laws, and sent up petitions to the Russian Consul, who was over the government of the country, asking him to stop us, and forbid our preaching in the villages again. My own village people began to curse me from afar; they tried to injure my ministry by their insulting words. I took this as a sign from the Lord, that the time had come for me to go back to them and begin work there. Surely God was allowing them to be stirred up for [this] very purpose. After I had arrived home, I sent for the band of the Adda saints who had received their baptism. A number of us went to the outskirts of our village to meet and welcome them. We had a glorious time shaking hands and talking in tongues. It was wonderful; and then we marched along the streets singing the new songs which I had written in the Syriac language. We went to the home of Brother Saul, the present pastor of the Persian mission in Chicago.

After singing and praying for the whole village, and capturing it by faith for God, we partook of the dinner which my mother had prepared for all of us in our home. Then we had a meeting. Our two parlors were filled with new saints. As the meeting commenced, the power fell. The wife of our Brother Abraham shook, and called on the Lord. She got saved and baptized with the Holy Ghost while we were singing. . . . Beloved, we were there a few weeks. About thirty were saved, and about twenty-five received their baptism, one of whom was my precious mother. (August, 26, 1916)

Then the devil was stirred up in the town of Karajaloo, where Brothers Jeremiah and Abraham lived. The priests in that town had formed a mob against us which threatened us with death if we ever attempted to enter the town. In the power of the Spirit, Brother Jeremiah traced a circle on the ground, and bound the mob therein, figuratively, in the name of the Lord, saying, "You shall not move from there until the church of God is established in my town."

The people heard that we were coming, and the mob took clubs and got ready for us. Someone told us to be careful, to go into a house and not in the streets as the mob was drawing near. I answered, "I will die here," and continued to sing, "There's a Highway, Blessed Way." Soon the people heard us, and almost the whole town came. The street was too small, so Jeremiah called us to go into the hay field. Hallelujah! We went in yonder, and when I looked upon the people, I saw the "mob" standing afar off. We sang and preached.

The power of God fell upon Jeremiah's wife, and she got saved. He was so happy. People seeing Jeremiah's wife under the power, got excited; but Brother Jeremiah cried to them, "Why are you troubled about my wife? Is she not my wife? I know that she is in the best condition she can possibly be in." To make the story short, in three or four weeks about forty got their baptism, and I do not know how many got saved in this third village.

One day the terrible news reached us, "The mobs are upon you." Religious leaders were heading them against us. There was screaming in the streets and in the homes. The women, screaming, locked and bolted their doors. We went inside a home and sang together, "Though we melt in a fiery furnace, yet we will whisper to the Lord, 'Thy will be done.'" We kept singing that song. The mob came beating against the door, and the dear people said to me, "They will kill us before they touch you." I said, "Don't be frightened, you will see what the Lord will do." As the mob was trying to force the door open, something occurred which caused great confusion among them, and they began to curse and fight one another. In a short time they had all scattered and left us, and we were able to leave the town in peace. Glory to Jesus!

Often, when I was in danger of being assaulted, the women would throw themselves on their knees around me, threatening to take their own lives if I was touched, and often pulling down their hair as an appeal to our persecutors.

# Messengers of An Outpouring

## Revival at Shirrabad

One of the new converts in Shirrabad was the daughter of a Protestant minister. She was a school teacher and had been touched by Brother Andrew's wife who had just lately been wonderfully baptized. They prayed together, and this young lady got her baptism also. Then we held special meetings for young women and started a wonderful work among them. God saved and baptized about twenty-five young girls and two young men. Then we started a good school for the young girls only.

The priests of the Greek Catholic Church came together and said, "If we let that many go, he will shake the whole country." One said, "My wife is on their side;" and another said, "My daughter has gone crazy over their songs." Another said, "My deacon agrees with them more than with me," and another, "My congregation has gone after these people. If we don't do something to stop them, our churches will have to be closed and we will soon have to believe them too, and leave our ministry." They said, "We will go to the Archbishop, (in our country he has power not only in religious matters, but in government also), "and we will take our crosses and throw them down before him." (This meant the abandonment of their ministry.)

Some of the priests made a petition and sent it to the government, beseeching the governor to do something to stop us, and send me back to America. These priests said that before we came they used to have good fellowship with the people of their towns, but since we had come, there had been nothing but trouble. Now this reminds us of the words of our blessed Lord, "I came not to bring peace, but a sword," and also, "There was a division among the people because of him."

I was called before the government, and three or four brethren with me. We were commanded to be put in prison, but the Lord caused the Mohammedian chief of police to treat us with great kindness. They put us in a beautiful parlor among their guests, and served us some fine tea. The Mohammedans said to each other, "Do you know why this minister Urshan is here? He says people shouldn't get drunk, and that is why they have imprisoned him." Nothing pleases the Mohammedans more than if you oppose liquor, which to them is accursed.

So they came and slapped me on the shoulder and said, "You are alright. We will treat you well." They kept us one night, and the Lord uses us among some of the noble Mohammedans. Soon a telegram came from the American Consul, inquiring [about] their right to imprison us. They immediately loosed me, but I would not go unless they would allow my brethren to go with me, as they were imprisoned because of me. So they had to give me my brethren also. After coming out of prison, we were led to keep quiet for a couple of weeks and wait on the Lord for guidance.

## The Assembly at Gogtopa

After this the Lord led us to one of the largest and most aristocratic Assyrian towns, called Gogtopa. One night, while singing, the people broke out crying and weeping, and gave themselves to God. The glory of God fell upon us there. Over thirty got saved, and six baptized in one night. Do you see? He works, and no man can stop Him. Glory be to our great God! I thank God that during those four months He gave us about 170 converts, and filled them with the Holy Ghost and power. A great many more were converted in secret, but we only heard about them later. Glory to Jesus!

The people often thought that I had some mysterious magical power which protected me from all danger. In fact, they feared me, and never laid hands on me personally. Once I used my handkerchief to wipe the perspiration from my brow, and when I preached I sometimes stretched my hand with the handkerchief in it, towards the people. They said, therefore, that my handkerchief contained a strange and costly chemical which would cause them to faint. [It was the anointing.] Others said I hypnotized them with my eyes, so I often preached with my eyes closed. Others reported that I had a small, noiseless, American revolver which I carried about with me, and that this accounted for my fearlessness and boldness. But some believed that we truly had supernatural power, and yet for fear of the people they dared not acknowledge it.

My country had forgotten that the God of Pentecost is just the same today, and that He was stretching out His mighty arm to heal, to save, and to do mighty works in the name of His holy child Jesus, in confirmation of the everlasting Gospel, "the faith once delivered to the saints." Of course we knew the secret of these mighty revivals; we knew it was the earnest prayers and intercessions of God's Pentecostal saints all over the world for us. O, beloved, "if God is for us, who can be against us?" Glory to God! I cannot tell exactly how many got saved, but I believe that there were over two hundred, many of whom got their baptism. And then the massacres came. . . .

Almighty God did a wonderful breaking up in the face of stupendous difficulty. We sowed the seed, watered it with our tears. God sent His first and latter rain, the sunshine of His face, and the seed grew. We reaped a wonderful harvest; yes, beloved, it pays to serve our God.

O, young men and women, you have the same God. I have seen young girls like some of you interceding and agonizing for the salvation of souls in the whole world. Like the pilgrims of old, the apostles, and the prophets, some of these young people whom I have seen, walked carefully, with their eyes and hearts filled with God; singing praises unto Jesus, and pleading tearfully with souls, before their persecutors. When I see some of you here so careless, minding earthly things, fashions of dress, and the pleasures of this world, in spite of your wonderful advantages in this free country, I suffer in the spirit for you. How I pray that the Holy Spirit, which is in you, may quicken you. I wish all the Pentecostal young people in this country would have the consecration which these young people had in Persia, being dead to sin and to the world, and alive to God. It is easy for you; you are not in danger of death. You should take advantage of your privileges and get ready for missionary work by beginning at home. But no, you are going back into the world, and losing your first love. May we wake up to our divine responsibilities, and putting off all sin and all its weights, get right with God and run the race which is set before us . . .

Both Brother Jeremiah and Brother Andrew died martyr's deaths, as you will hear later; but the rest of the brethren are still holding the banner of the cross, going on in helping the established Pentecostal missions in Urmia, with three sisters who are our spirit-filled school teachers.

Beloved, these dear ones are our helpers in the vineyard of the heavenly Father there. They are poor in worldly goods, having been robbed of all they possessed during the massacres; they suffer daily persecution, and they need our continual help in prayers and support. Remember also the widows and orphans of our precious brethren who laid down their lives for the Gospel's sake. (*TWE*, Sept. 2, 1916) (Continued below:)

### The Martyred Six of Persia

When God works with apostolic power, apostolic persecution is sure to result. Following close upon the mighty signs and wonders [worked] in Jerusalem in the first century was the martyrdom of Stephen and James, and ere the second century dawned all the apostles had laid down their lives for the Gospel with the exception of John. When we stand for the full Gospel of the Lord Jesus and preach in the power of the Holy Ghost, our lives are in danger, but though we shed our blood in preaching a crucified Lord we have naught to fear for we shall be alive forevermore.

While I was in Persia I was in danger of death five times, but God preserved my life. While some of these martyrs were killed because they were faithful Christians, yet that is not the case with a large number. Some people think that the Armenians and the Assyrians were punished [the Turks slaughtered millions of them in WW1] because of their loyalty to Christ, but not so. They were punished like the Jews of old who were the people of God but they turned their backs on their God and compromised with the Gentiles, and God left them, nationally, in the hands of their enemies. Our people, the Armenians and the Persians, are suffering as nations. . . .

Now I want to tell you of the first martyr. She was a young girl about seventeen named Sophia, a Russian Catholic girl. I was not acquainted with her at all, but she came to one of our street meetings and became converted among a number of others. The following Sunday, while in her own home sitting at the dinner table, the power of God fell upon her and she began to shake and say in her own language, "Glory to Jesus." Then, looking up, she burst forth into a new tongue and glorified God. The home was a Russian Catholic and the parents of this young girl knew she had been to our meetings and said that happened because I had hypnotized her, but I wasn't there at the time. They sent for the Russian priest who came and threw water upon her, but she just lifted her hands and praised the Lord. He commenced to rebuke the devil, but she looked into his face and told him to get right with God and that he needed to pray for himself. She was filled with the glory of God and became a wonderful missionary in that place and the Lord blessed because of her faithfulness.

But she had terrible persecution in her home. They didn't want her to leave the house or attend the meetings, though she worked for God at every opportunity. She would go on the streets and speak to women and the Lord would reveal to her the hearts of the women, and in the power of the Spirit she would say to them, "This is your sin." "You have this and that in your life," and she knew that it was God as she bared the secrets of their lives. There was great confession among the women through her simple ministry and the enemy was angry at her and wanted to kill her, and he did; but she is alive forevermore.

The young girls in that village were so happy they used to go in bands in the eventime; they sang on the streets and knelt down in the fields. One night a crowd of them wee taking their evening walk; it was on a Sunday evening and they were returning from the fields, singing as they came. Near the village a little boy of eight years was instructed by the enemy to stand behind a building with a rifle. That boy was holding his gun and he said to this girl, "Shut your mouth. I will kill you." Suddenly he fired at her and the shots entered her abdomen. She lived about a week after the she was shot, and in that week many came to see her.

Although they did not believe in what God had done for her, they said her face shone like an angel's. The power of God would rest upon her, and many were brought to Jesus through her. The mother said to Sophia, "I will arrest the parents of that boy and he shall be killed," but oh how she wept and pleaded with her mother. "Mother forgive him. He didn't know what he did. The older folks taught him and they don't know what they did. Jesus was killed too." The power of God was on her until the last. She went to the heavenly world praising and glorifying God; our first martyr.

It is a very serious thing for a man to be killed under Persian rule, but because she was a Russian and the ruling government being in the hands of Russia, they didn't do anything, but instead they took a dear Brother, Andrew, a tailor by trade, and put him in prison. They held him responsible and said if he hadn't held meetings in that town the girl would not have been killed. God showed him that a terrible massacre would come upon that nation because of their unrighteousness. Three brethren who were killed later lost their lives through Mohammedans, but this sister was killed by professing Christians.

When the Russian army fled, the Turkish army came in and the Mohammedans commenced to massacre all the Persian nominal Christians. They were crying, "Holy war" in the streets, and if they could get hold of a Christian they would butcher him. The American flag was lifted up in the American mission and one of the American missionaries was a representative of the consul in another city, so he had a right to act. He unfurled the American flag and thirty thousand people found a refuge. Those who ran into this refuge were not killed by the Mohammedans, but our brethren did not go and I will tell you the reason.

The first, Brother Andrew, who was the first fruits, had taken refuge with the family of a Mohammedan friend, but he heard that many poor people were left in his village comfortless, and in great fear, and that they had nothing to eat, so his soul was stirred and he said to his wife and children, "I am going back to be with those people who are left. I will preach with them, pray [for] them and give them comfort, and if necessary I will die with them." So he left his wife and children in the home of the Mohammedan friend and went to live with those who were unfortunate.

He helped them in their work and exhorted and encouraged them that possibly God would deliver them, and if not they would stand for Jesus when the test came. The Mohammedans gave a challenge that if he took the name of Mohammed he would not be killed, but if he would be true to Jesus he would die. He told them he would stay with them and die with them. Suddenly the wild Kurds and the other Mohammedans around that village came and commenced to massacre. They took the girls and women and insulted and commenced to kill every young man, and they found our Brother Andrew in the midst of them. First they stripped him of his clothes and then they asked him about his faith. He joyfully said he was a child of God. There was another young man with him at the time, but they didn't kill him then. They thought they better go back and they got down under some leaves of the trees and prayed, and while there two Kurds came and shot them. They died joyfully. The most of the people were delivered, but he and that young man died for Jesus' sake.

I want to tell you something remarkable before that massacre took place. While in prison, God showed him all the wars that were coming to the earth. Then he commenced missionary work in his own town, to prepare the people, as it were, for the awful things that were before them. One day he suddenly said, "I am going away. After two weeks you will never see me anymore." The brethren and the sisters said, "Brother Andrew, are you going to meet Christ? Do you mean to tell us you are ready and we are not?" "I don't know," he said, "but God tells me that after two weeks I am going somewhere. You will never see me until we see each other up yonder." A number of people told me this who heard him say it, and that was two weeks before the massacre took place. God showed him he was going to be taken, and two weeks later his spirit went into paradise where the spirits of the just are waiting for the first resurrection.

The other brother who laid down his life was Jeremiah Eshoo, and a wonderfully used man of God was he. He helped me in the mission. When the trouble began many people were running away, but the poor people said, "Jeremiah, your God will deliver us. We will not run away." There were many poor women and children around him. He said to them, "Let us go to the Mohammedan village! We have friends there. We will go there and pray and see what the Lord will do." So he went to the home of a Mohammedan friend and into that home came two wild Kurds. One of the men of that village came and said to these Kurds, "Every one of these people would turn to the Mohammedans if he would let them, but he is such a religious Christian they will all be cut to pieces before they give up their religion, and furthermore," they said, "he has a good friend in America who has many gold pieces of money, and he is at the head of a religious movement, and he ought to be trained to be a Mohammedan. If he turns, he is a strong character and every one with him will turn to be a Mohammedan, so we will put him to the test."

Some of the friends hid him in a barn under the hay, but the other man knew the place and came with the Kurds and broke the door of the barn and seized

Jeremiah. They slapped him in the face and said, "Are you the head of these people?" "Will you be a Mohammedan and work for our prophet?" "Are you going to keep these people?" He didn't say anything, and they took him away, his wife and children screaming and crying. They said to him, "No give us the pocket of golden money that you have." He took his New Testament from his pocket. "Here is what is in my pocket." They were very angry at him, and said, "Do you mean that you are not going to be a Mohammedan?" He lifted up his Testament and said, "Jesus Christ is Lord and King." Some of them were on horseback and he was put in the front, and as they pointed their guns at him they said, "Are you going to be a Mohammedan?" He said nothing, and they shot him in his heart. He fell there and a sister came and put his New Testament under his head as he died. (*TWE*, Sept. 9, 1916) (Continued:)

The name of the other martyr was Elisha. He was with us in the village of Gogtapa. The people ran from that village and some held us by the coat and said, "If you run away, we will run away to the American Refugee Home. If not, we will stay here and die with you and God will take us to heaven because we died with you." We saw a number of people in the house of Brother Bob Lazar and they really meant what they said, they would stay. Our responsibility then was much more than our own life and we were perplexed to know what to do. Everybody was running away and the town was surrounded. Thousands of people were falling all around. One brother said, "We had better go. It is no use to stay. We cannot preach to Kurds and the people have gone," so we decided we would go, but Brother Elisha with this Brother Samuel said, "No, we will not go. We will stay and preach to the Kurds and then we will die." We said to him, "Brother, you had better come with us," but he refused. We each said, "God be with you," and went.

Our band thought if we could get under the American flag we would be safe. We went to a little distance when we were surrounded by the murderers. Men came on horseback with guns and spears ready to kill. We prayed and the Lord told us to run in front of the horses with our hands uplifted to heaven. This I and the brethren did, and when the horses were close up to us the men told us to get up. They asked for my overcoat and my brother Timothy's watch, which he gave them. They didn't do us any harm and seemed friendly to us; they told us if we would go in another direction we would be safe.

As we went on a little further we saw the Mohammedans destroying the people. Suddenly a man came before us, one of their religious men, his eyes filled with blood. He looked as though he would drink the blood of the Christians. As I looked at him I saluted him and said, "God's mercy be with you." Then I confessed to him the sins of our nation. I told him we were Christian people. His heart was touched; he stood and looked at me and almost wept. He said, "Young man, I am going to deliver you. I will give my life to take you safely to the American quarters. I could take thousands of dollars from the Christians, their houses are left, we could rob them, but I do not want anything. I cannot take you to safety by the regular road, it is filled with thieves, but you must follow me."

# Messengers of An Outpouring

The women with us said, "Oh Brother Andrew, he is deceiving us. He will take us off into some lonely place and kill us." I said to him, "They say you will take us into some secret place and behead us all." He swore by Mohammed and that his life should be written in his blood if he let anybody touch them. I said to the people, "Let us trust God. He will make him take us to a place of safety." That man took every one of us safely to the city, not one of us was touched, bullets flew around us but none were hurt, not a girl was harmed. Around us people were being killed, stripped naked, we saw terrible sights, dead bodies lying around, dogs eating their faces, girls taken from their fathers and mothers, wives from their husbands, but we were unharmed. Our God in whom we trusted had delivered us.

## Elisha Martyred

We left Brother Elisha and his brother in the work. While they were in that home in the evening the Kurds came killing the people they found in the village. Some of them, women and children, stayed in the house. Suddenly, the Kurds came and broke the door. They were all silent on their knees, praying. The Kurds struck a match and saw eighteen people on their knees. "Oh, what a sacrifice for Mahomet," they said. "Now we will butcher every one of them." Then Brother Samuel stood up, falling down at the feet of those Kurds, "Oh kill us, but don't touch these people." Then they asked him, "Why didn't you run away?" and he said, "We believed God and that He would put love in you so you won't kill us, and we thought we would stay here and tell you something about our faith."

When they heard that they were surprised, and one left. Another said, "Let us massacre every one of them." Then Brother Samuel said to the one who left, [sic] "Will you let me say a few words before you kill us? I will sing you a song." Our boys have a song called, "Repent, Repent, and turn to God," and he commenced to sing it with tears in his eyes, and these Kurds were greatly interested. They said, "What is your name?" "Samuel, servant of God," he replied. They looked around the room. "Well, Samuel, we will divide what is in this house; half for us and half for you; these beautiful rugs and these beds for us. Now tell these women to make us some tea."

Oh beloved, you don't know what that meant! Those Mohammedans were thirsting for the blood of Christians! Well [Samuel] asked permission from these Kurds to let these women and children go down stairs. They went down and Brother Samuel and Elisha started to make tea for them, and while they were drinking tea they asked many questions about Russia.

Night came on, and the women and children were very much afraid. They said, "Surely at night time they will butcher us." Then Brother Samuel came and said to these Kurds, "They are saying that you will massacre us all in the night time." To which they replied, "Go tell them nobody will touch you. For the sake of that New Testament in your hand you shall be saved. We can see you are honest and do not run away, so nobody will be killed." They passed the night in safety; the Christians could not sleep for fear, but the Kurds slept nicely.

In the morning the women and children were still afraid, and they said, "Tell that Kurdish officer to let us go to the city and give us a recommendation that we will not be killed." So Samuel asked him for this permission, and he said he would do it but was afraid when they got far away the other Mohammedans might kill them, as they didn't know his name and he would have no influence with them. They went through massacred towns, one after another, and the Kurds would look at them and come towards them as if to kill them and then turn back. They almost reached the city when suddenly a Mohammedan came and shot our brother Elisha, firing a bullet into his breast. Brother Samuel and fifteen of the others came in safely. Elisha died the next morning, the brethren and sisters around him singing praises to God.

**More Martyrs**

These four are martyrs, but I will tell you of two others who, though not killed, willingly laid down their lives for Jesus. One was my mother and the other a member of the Presbyterians, a teacher. She was wonderfully converted and had the baptism in the Holy Ghost. She was in the Refugee Home and the building was too small for the crowds they had there. In a room two or three yards square they would put about ten people for four months; the floors were cold and they had no rugs and no mats, scarcely any food but a little bread made by Mohammedans, and that bread was mixed with mud and plaster, so they would eat it and die. I cannot speak in a meeting of the terrible condition we were in. The beautiful hair of our women became filled with small bugs from the dirt, so they had to shave their heads. Many people were stripped by the Mohammedans while running away, their clothes being taken from them. Some people lost their children, some their wives, and others their dear ones. In two months two thousand children died. You could hardly find a baby in a mother's arms.

Then typhus fever came and hundreds died every week. These typhus cases were terrible, so contagious no man dared to come near to them. They had no care taken of them, and they just laid there and died in hundreds. My mother and that principle of the school said, "We will wash these people and care for them." And they laid hands on them and prayed and God raised them up. There were many young girls affected with this terrible sickness -- they could not eat, nothing would stay on their stomachs, and their hearts were broken because their fathers were killed. So these dear ones tried to make good food for them. My father many times warned my mother that she would not be able to resist the disease, but the doctors never came near and mother could not see them suffer -- she gave her life for these afflicted ones.

I caught the disease and for thirty-six days was in bed and finally recovered; but mother and that lady principal took the disease and never survived. They were so worn out they hardly had slept during all this time and succumbed to the disease. We prayed for them, but felt it was God's will for them to be taken, so they could be free from the murderous Mohammedans who were killing and committing such awful outrages. They sacrificed their lives for Jesus' sake, and they will have as much reward as those who were killed.

I cannot describe to you the terrible condition of our people at that time, nor the joy we, who loved the Lord, had. While the bullets were whizzing outside, inside we were singing the praises of God and people were getting the baptism in the Holy Spirit. Among all the saints there were only two who died, all the rest were healed. When I had the fever it seemed as though I would burn up. My hair all came out and my eyesight and hearing left me, but God wonderfully healed me. I cannot tell you how faithful God was to us. Those dear martyrs didn't lay down their lives in sorrow; they departed in joy.

I was disappointed five times. I was ready and was expecting to be a martyr, but God spared me. Several times they came in mobs and tried to kill me, but the power of God would fall upon me and I would sing; they would say to the other, "You do it," but they could not get anyone to strike me or shoot me. One man wanted his servant to strike me and became angry because he would not do it, but the servant said, "I cannot." It seemed as though the arm of God withheld them. Once they hired a man who was a murderer to kill me, and promised him two thousand dollars to do it. He came to the town where I lived and called the men of the village together, and my father also, and lied to them about me, saying that I went around in the villages and insulted their women. He said I had such power in my eyes that I hypnotized the girls. In this way he tried to stir up the elders so he would have them as witnesses that he had a right to kill me.

I was in another village at the time, but a man who was a sinner found out what this murderer was planning and knew that he had been a traitor to his government, whereupon he reported him and he was arrested and afterward killed. This was before the massacre. I was willing to lay down my life for the Gospel's sake, but God preserved it.

That which came to our nation and to the Armenians will come to other nations. I do not say there will be such massacres, but there will be "distress of nations." The testing days are upon us. Daniel prophesied, "Many shall be purified, and made white, and tried; but the wicked shall do wickedly, and none of the wicked shall understand; but the wise shall understand." Beloved, let us give ourselves to prayer. Oh the sad condition in Europe! Let us pray for the nations of the earth. (*TWE*, Sept. 16, 1916)

## Pentecost in Russia

### Andrew Urshan

The Latter Rain outpouring began about five years ago in Russia through our brethren who went from this country [USA] to Finland, and by German brethren in Germany, also by the Pentecostal papers in Swedish, German, and other languages which were distributed in that country.

Th Pentecostal work began in Petrograd three years ago, among the Baptists, but as it was bitterly opposed both by the Protestants and Orthodox, the few who received the baptism were obliged to leave their churches and hold meetings in secret. Sad to say, as soon as they commenced, the enemy crept in among them like angels of light, speaking in other tongues terrible devilish doctrines which opposed [what is taught in] the Bible. This caused the few saints to be discouraged, and, soon commencing to doubt their experiences, they went back to their old churches. Then as they were made to doubt further, most of them began to confess that they had received the evil spirit and they wanted rid of it.

While doubting God and dwelling in darkness, God sent us to them at this critical time. Hallelujah! God showed us their condition and we soon began in His name to explain God's dealing with us after our baptism. Many darkened eyes were opened and the news soon spread. The scattered sheep began to come back, and as they heard the sweet voice of their Good Shepherd through His servants, they commenced to weep and cry aloud to God for mercy and forgiveness, and the Lord came, reclaiming over one hundred and forty (140) backsliders. The power came in a marvelous way upon them all.

They soon learned the tricks of Satan by which he had them to doubt God, and they also learned many true ways of God's dealings with His saints after receiving the baptism. We certainly had a time of great refreshing from His hallowed presence. Praise His dear name!

There were two brethren who were specially used of God in Petrograd. Satan had them cast into prison because of their usefulness for God, as they were preaching faithfully. The war broke out and many of their converts would not take up arms, and these two precious brethren were accused for that, therefore arrested. Now they are under guard and prohibited from preaching, but they are praying and doing a work by correspondence. They said it was in answer to their prayers that God in due time sent us to Russia. They need your prayer. (*TWE*, Sept. 30, 1916)

## How the Outpouring Came to Chili, S. America

*Book Editor*: It appears, based on statements later in the article, that the pastor of this Methodist church which received an outpouring did not even have the baptism of the Holy Spirit at the the time the outpouring began in his church. But he approved, and allowed it to go on. Actual title of the original article is: *A Phenomenal Self-supporting Native Work*, by Dr. W. C. Hoover, Missionary from South America, Oak Park, Il.:

I went to Chili thirty-one years ago and was with the Methodist work for twenty years, twelve of which I spent in Iquique. Then I was transferred to Valparaiso where I worked with the Methodist Church for eight years. During this time the work grew and we had a number of revivals. We bought a large property to build a church, aided by the Bishop, and in 1908 we built a large church that would seat over fifteen hundred people.

While we were laying the foundations of this great church it seemed to me as if we were enclosing all out-doors, and I sometimes felt it was a foolish project to build such an enormous church. But every time I looked at that foundation I would say to the Lord, "Lord, You know we are building it as a man-trap to catch souls. Don't let these walls ever mock us, but fill this house to Thy glory and the people to Thy praise." I continually praised the Lord as I witnessed the construction of that building, and prayed that the Lord would never let it be an empty mockery.

At our first service in the new church, Watchnight, ushering in 1909, we had a blessed meeting. Then we observed the week of prayer at the beginning of the year, with all the evangelical churches, and in the first service we had what was unusual at that time. After reading the Scriptures at the opening, I expected one and another to lead us in prayer in turn, as we always had done, but when we knelt to pray, the whole congregation, perhaps one hundred and twenty in that meeting, burst out into simultaneous prayer for about ten minutes. It was an astonishment to us. We were praying for a revival though there wasn't anything in my remarks or my expectation to lead to such an outburst. But it was a sign to me that the Lord was waiting to bless. This occasionally repeated itself during the month of January.

One afternoon a brother who was a night watchman, came to me and said, "Pastor, I was asleep today and the Lord came and spoke to me. He said, 'Wake up. I want to tell you something.' I said, 'Yes, Lord.' Then the Lord said, 'Go and tell the pastor to gather together some of the most spiritual members of his church to pray daily, because I want to pour out My Holy Spirit and fire upon them.'" He resisted the first time and went off to sleep. Then he heard the voice again and thought he had better obey. He asked the Lord, "And may I be one of them?" And the Lord said, "Yes." He came and told me and I told him to come back the next day at five. I prayed about it, and called together Mrs. Hoover, my assistant, and one of the spiritual brethren in the church, and put the matter before them, and we all agreed that it was of God. So the five of us met daily in my study for prayer.

Then I went to the Conference of the Methodist Church, and one of these five was left in charge of the service on Sunday evening in my absence. That night he called the official brethren forward before he began, and said to them, "You and I are responsible for the condition of this church." (We had been a year without having united meetings because we had been building. I had to preach in turn in different places and, of course, it was detrimental to the highest interest of the church.)

He preached and called them to the altar. Then he dismissed the congregation and said, "We will settle this tonight if it takes all night." About thirty remained. They had an all-night of prayer and during the night some supernatural manifestations occurred; one and another had visions, and at one time all kneeling at the altar felt the Lord laying His hands upon each one of them in turn. The people received such a blessing they asked him to appoint another night of prayer which he did for the following Saturday. When I reached home my assistant said to me, "What will you do about that meeting they have appointed for Saturday?" I said, "I will attend it, but Brother M. shall lead it as he announced it." I did, and we had a blessed time.

In the morning people sat around the altar loath to leave. I was walking back and forth in front of the altar, meditating as to whether or not I had received a blessing, and was humming the hymn: "Oh! how happy are they, Who the Savior obey," when suddenly I felt my voice breaking, and I broke forth into violent weeping, but yet felt such a blessed joy and tenderness in my heart. I knelt at the altar shaking with the weeping, but all I could say was, "My Savior!" "My Savior!" in Spanish. When I got control of myself I resumed my walk and suddenly I broke out in most joyous, hearty laughter, which I could no more control than I could the weeping. After that, every now and again as I would be praying alone in my study I would be overcome with laughter.

We continued to have all-night meetings every Saturday night through March, and at Easter time we held an All-Day meeting, from 7 a. m. until 10 p. m. with intermission. In that All-Day meeting we had some supernatural manifestations. One sister laughed for an hour, and went off into a corner so as not to disturb the meeting. Another sister was overcome and sang in the Spirit. When she came to herself she said the angels had been teaching her to sing.

On the following day I visited the sick, and took the Communion to those who had not been able to attend. I visited one brother on his death-bed and in conversation with him I was pained beyond expression at the impossibility of getting his mind on heavenly things; he was completely occupied with his physical condition, doctors and medicine. When I came out of the house I was filled with pain and grief and despair. I said, "Lord, that man will die. Is he saved,?" I had a doubt in my mind about his salvation, and so I complained to the Lord and said, "But what can you expect with such a pastor?" It seemed as if it wasn't I that said it, so I prayed audibly as I walked home, "Yes, that is true. Lord destroy this pastor."

I went into the five o'clock daily prayer-meeting, and for two hours that was the burden of my prayer, "Destroy this pastor. Don't let him in any wise hinder the carrying forward of Thy work." Two days later when my assistant pastor came in to begin the day's work, we knelt to pray and I remember praying for half an hour with such liberty and delight it seemed as if I didn't want to stop, and I remember saying, "Lord, I stop now, not because I want to stop, but to give my brother a chance to talk with Thee." He began to pray, and I remember hearing him say, "Lord, we thank Thee that we are so united in this Thy work, for it is not human work." As he said that it touched me in my inner being exactly as anything exceedingly funny does, and I burst out in the most violent and hearty laughter such as it wasn't possible to contain. As I rose from my knees I sat down to converse with him, and the shouts of praise burst forth from my mouth, which seemed too small to let them out. From that time on the Lord worked remarkably.

I went to visit other churches, as I was presiding elder as well as pastor. While I was absent I dreamed that I was in a large Roman Catholic Church in Valparaiso and there was a great revival on which had broken out in a remarkably short time. People were running to and fro, and it seemed I also had part in it, and I heard a voice saying, "And the pastors of the two hundred other churches came to see how it was done." I kept that in my heart and treasured it as something that the Lord was intending to do, but I told only one or two.

In May, before I returned, the assistant pastor invited the people to the altar at the close of a sermon, and they began to pray. An old member of the church who had been a dead stick came forward and knelt down with his wife, to whom he said, "I cannot pray. I do not know what is the matter." He stood on his feet to ask the people to pray for him, and as he did this He fell as though he had been knocked down, and then prayer just poured out. He knew not where the words came from, but remembered saying, "Lord, it is right I should be on the floor. I have been so unworthy." This was a signal for wonder and comment in the church, and that man from that day on was a blessed, spiritual factor in the work, something he had never been before.

Our five o'clock meetings were now held in the church, and one evening a very large man fell to the floor in that meeting. When that big man got up, he saw fire in all directions, and was convinced that the Lord would pour out the Holy Spirit and fire upon us. That was the end of June. The third of July we had an all-night meeting and the fire fell. Four young ladies were prostrated and humbled before the Lord. One of them after being dealt with by the Lord for an hour or two, arose and said, "*The Lord is coming soon and He bids us get ready.*" The people were filled and thrilled with the Spirit; the manifestation was really indescribable.

The next day, July 4, 1909, there was a most memorable out-pouring upon the church and the Spirit of God was present in a remarkable way. In the afternoon meeting, children rose from their knees and asked pardon of their parents. We had meetings for the boys, for the girls and for the grown-up people all at the same time in different parts of the church. One after another began to speak in tongues as when they received the baptism of the Spirit [at Pentecost], and fifteen children were converted that day.

The Sunday School from that time grew in a phenomenal way. In the month of June the average attendance was something over 300, 'the month of July over 400, and in August over 500. My class alone of young men had over one hundred in actual attendance. The great church with its galleries began to be almost too small, for the attendance at the evening service went up to 1,000 people. Crowds came in from all parts and the back of the church was filled with people who stood and listened.

My dream was coming true. As the Lord blessed the work in Valparaiso, the people heard of it all over Chili. A preacher and his wife from the Alliance work in the far south came and spent a week in the church, observing all that was happening. From Concepcion, a Presbyterian pastor with two of his official members came up to see the work and spent a number of days with us. From Santiago, the Methodists came in numbers to see the work, with the consent of their pastors. So the knowledge of it began to spread and people became hungry for this baptism all over Chili.

The reporters came in to write us up, and for two or three weeks one of the daily papers had lurid headlines, telling how we gave the people a beverage we called "the blood of the Lamb" that made them fall upon the floor. They got up a criminal charge against me and the judge cited me to appear before him three or four times. The state's attorney was present on one of these occasions and the city physician on another. They treated me with all respect and did not seem to find anything which would give them any occasion to pronounce any sentence against me.

About this time the brethren of the Methodist Church began to criticize me. The Presbyterian Church also entered into the opposition. They asked me to change my methods (though they were not mine) and I told them I didn't see that I was doing anything but what I always had done, preach the Gospel, and the Lord was doing the work.

The days of trial and persecution that followed for myself and my church resulted in our both withdrawing from the Methodist Church. When I first took charge of that congregation they gave very sparingly, but I immediately began educating them along the line of giving, and that they should thereby show their gratitude for what the Lord had done for them. They increased their giving to such an extent that they paid nearly half the pastor's salary and also the running expenses of the church. When the separation occurred, the large givers, who were also most spiritual, were the most willing to go out.

Those who had given least said, "We have just built this church, how can we leave it?" The others said, "The Lord has given this church, He can give us another." The building of stone and mortar wasn't any attraction to them without the Spirit of God, and from the time we left until the present moment they have given generously and have never failed in supporting us comfortably.

When the war broke out our people began to be financially [tightened]. One of our official brethren came to me and said, "Pastor, I haven't the heart to ask people for money now." I said, "I haven't either, but I have to tell them what the Lord says." So I told them how the Lord spoke to His people through Malachi when they were robbing Him and how He said to them, "Prove Me now!" in time of poverty and of need.

I said, "Perhaps some of you are out of employment because you are robbing God; perhaps some are in need because you have not been faithful to Him." I could only tell them that the Lord's Word is sure; that it was not the quantity of money He wanted but their faithfulness. Not very long after that I wanted someone to do some work but I could find nobody out of employment, which was remarkable to me. Through all the crises of the years of the war we never failed in meeting all our obligations.

We have at least eight hundred now in our membership; received two hundred new members within a year. Just before I was taken sick in December we received one hundred, and again in July we received one hundred and nine. During all these months that I have been ill the word has been carried on by our official members. We have four whom we call local preachers and at least twenty-eight of the official board are baptized in the Spirit. Our official board is composed of thirty-three members, a number of whom are class leaders.

A number of our people have been professional rogues. In our first revival one was converted in 1909. In 1910 was the Centennial celebration of the Independence of Chili; the chief of police declared his intention of gathering in all the known rogues in the town during this celebration so that they would not be troubled along that line. This man heard of it and came to me rather affrighted, because he had done with that kind of a life. I said he should not be troubled and went with him to the secret service office. In my talk with the chief, he said, "I had occasion to observe your work last year, and although there are things I do not understand, I saw you were doing a far better work than the Anti-Alcoholic League." Then he called the man and catechized him, and turning to me he said, "I am going to make you a Christmas present." I thanked him but hadn't the remotest idea what he meant. Then he turned to this man and said, "If you continue to walk as you are now doing until Christmas (this was August) I will give this gentleman your photo and cause you to disappear from the Rogues' Gallery." So on December 3rd I got his photo. He had been converted for a year but this took him from that gallery officially.

We have now in our official board five that were really professional rogues, pick-pockets, or highwaymen, before they were converted, but you would be amazed at the gentleness and sweetness of those men after they were born again. And you could give any one of them the key to the bank, they are so trustworthy.

During the revival this year (1920) there were quite a noted thief and his wife converted. After his conversion the police followed him around and arrested him. On one occasion they took him to the detention house of the detective service, and when the brethren of the church heard of it they went and asked to have him set free. The second chief said, "Well, you had better let him go; if you do not, you will have all the church coming here to vouch for him." So they let him out. He went to Santiago and they arrested him there, for he was known as a professional thief all over Chili. He gave his testimony to his conversion before the judge and they set him free. He talks of his salvation all the time, to the authorities and everybody he can.

Since he was saved, his wife, his brother, his mother and father and a cousin have all been converted. [End of part 1. Continued below:] (*TLRE*, Jan., 1921)

## Apostolic Power Brings Apostolic Persecution

Dr. W. C. Hoover, Supt. of Pentecostal Missions in Chili

Our Pentecostal revival in Valparaiso, Chili, took such proportions and was of such a character that it became an offense to the Methodist Church, and they desired to send me home, but the revival had I been a blessing to so many people that they were rebellious at the thought of having me sent home, which was in a way sequestering me because they didn't want me there any more. So the majority of my church who had been quickened by the work of the Holy Spirit and many of whom had been converted and brought into the church through the revival, resolved to separate. They said, "When they turn you out, you can come and be our pastor." . . . So we betook ourselves to prayer.

The Lord was working in apostolic power, and we were also having a taste of apostolic persecution. Coupled with the persecution from the city, came criticism and opposition from my brethren in the ministry. The Presiding Elder of Santiago came down one day and got the American Consul who was also a Methodist, and the Presbyterian pastor, and these three, without saying a word to me, went to the Judge and talked with him about our work. They promised him that the revival should stop. The Presiding Elder then went back to Santiago and wrote me telling me what they had done, and that the Judge had refrained from sentencing me because of their promise that I would refrain from the extravagances that had been going on.

I went on with the work of the Lord just as usual. He also cabled home and wrote all sorts of charges and the Bishop wrote me a very anxious letter begging me that I would not dishonor Methodism. The work continued until Conference which was held in Valparaiso that year in the new church. We were also able to finish the parsonage that year above the church, and we entertained a good many of the brethren. The Conference continued for eight days, and they spent the entire time laboring to get charges against me in my own church, with a congregation such as they had never seen in Chili and a Sunday School of 580. The missionaries even said that they had never seen a Sunday School so perfectly under control of its leader as was ours. If I wanted quiet I just lifted the bell; didn't even strike it. They noticed it and commented upon it. They saw my large class of 100 members and still they spent their time formulating charges.

When the conduct of an elder is in question, nine elders are required to get together and pass judgment. I was an elder and they gathered together in my study criticizing me and laboring with me to get me to see as they saw. In the midst of the discussion a native preacher came to my side and said, "Brother Hoover, tell me why it is that you are so obstinate? Don't you see that all the brethren are against you and yet you do not yield a single point?" I said, "Brother, when my brethren show me fruits using the methods that they recommend that will compare with the fruits the Lord has given us here in the past year, then it will be time for me to yield to them." He remained a moment as if silenced and then said, "When you have said that there is no reply." When they had the charges formulated to present to the home Board, it occurred to me that if I were to come home I could put the matter before the Board and they would understand me.

So I said, "Well, send me home." "Will you go home?" they asked. "Yes, send me home." "Well then," they said, "we will take away the charges." I said, "No, I do not want the charges removed if they are legitimate charges." But they went into Conference and at the next session voted to remove the charges, and I was then invited up on the platform which I had not been hitherto; in fact I was not recognized officially though in my own church. But now the Bishop appointed me back to Valparaiso to prepare the place for my successor.

One of the things that caused offense to the brethren, my fellow-missionaries, was that I permitted a woman to be used who in her sinful days had been a woman of the street. She was saved in August, 1909, and her conversion was indeed wonderful. When in the Spirit, she went through the audience with her eyes closed, picking out people and telling them what was in their hearts, which those who were honest admitted was true. Many times overwhelmed with conviction they would confess in penitence. With great power she spoke and witnessed for the Lord, but the Conference objected to the prominence she had. All that year I had been learning new lessons, and I myself was not baptized in the Holy Spirit until two years after that.

My attitude toward all these new things was that of waiting and watching. I saw things that I could not quite understand but I didn't want to destroy that of which I was not perfectly sure. From the moment I promised to go home, I became very unhappy in my spirit. All that week through all the contradictions and opposition I had felt a strength and exultation and absolute rest in the Lord, but now I began to feel down-cast and perturbed, as if I had made a mistake.

So before the Bishop left the next day I told him I felt as though I should not go home. He said that I had promised, but I told him I felt as though I would be doing wrong to go. Up to this time I had always been my own presiding elder because we do not aim to have a presiding elder apart from a pastorate, but under the circumstances they named the Santiago presiding elder over me, and he came to hold his first quarterly conference. He was so autocratic in his rulings and dealings with the brethren of my official board that they felt his [extortions] were unjust.

So a few days after [the meeting] they came to me and said, "Pastor, we in Valparaiso are going to separate." (The year preceding, two congregations in Santiago had separated from the M. E. Church in a sudden, unexpected way). I begged my people not to withdraw, that they should be patient.

"No," they said, "the purpose of the Bishop is to send you home and destroy the work, and there will be nothing left. We will withdraw and then when they put you out, you can come and be our pastor." I talked the matter over with my wife and we decided to go out with them. I asked them to say nothing to anyone for a week for I wanted to put my resignation in writing so that it would not be misconstrued.

On the following Sunday after Communion I read my resignation. In the morning I had prayed, "Lord, You can show me today if what I am about to do is pleasing to You," and as we rose from prayer in the Sunday School one of the young ladies who was baptized in the Spirit arose and Mrs. Hoover told me she had a message. As soon as she was given opportunity, she said, "We are going to eat the Passover today. Let everyone see that the blood is over the door." She repeated it twice, and I took it as a wonderful answer to prayer. She knew nothing about our going out, and was speaking of the Communion as the Passover. We were preparing to go out of the church like the Israelites, and that last Communion service was a wonderful scene.

They came to the altar so filled with joy that they could not contain themselves, and two in the audience were converted. One man whom I had never before seen rose in the back part of the church, came and knelt down; then went and was reconciled to his wife and gave his heart to the Lord, afterward partaking of the Communion.

At the close of that service I read my resignation and the separation occurred, about 450 going with me, the spiritual life and fire of the church. From that time we held our meetings in small places where we formerly held class meetings, and in a little while we were able to get a little hall but it would seat only about half our people.

We were, however, able to keep together by the local preachers and myself going around to the twelve or fifteen meeting places. *From that time on the native church supported me.* Later we were able to rent a larger place, and yet that was not sufficient for our needs.

When we separated there were a few who thought we ought to obliterate all memory that we had ever been Methodists, and that we should formulate a creed for ourselves and rules of government, but I said to them that we had always flourished under Methodist polity and had been guided by the Discipline, and we hadn't deviated from its doctrines in any degree during the revival, and so I didn't see any reason for changing. We continue to be guided by the discipline, although not bound rigidly thereby, and have been saved the necessity of studying and discussing and disagreeing upon forms of expression, terms, and matters upon which we at heart were agreed.

The separation of the churches in Santiago was on this wise: . . . I counseled them to return to their churches and they made an effort to be reconciled, but the pastor refused their overtures. . . .

As soon as I separated they wrote me asking me to become their superintendent, and three others also separated and asked to come under my oversight. Thus I became the Superintendent of the Pentecostal work in Chili. . . .

We are just as Methodistic as Wesley, and how they could put us out we have no explanation, except that they would put Wesley out if he were here today. . . . The brethren form groups and preach on the street-corners, in the market-place, at the fisheries and wharves. We have been taken to the police station for preaching but we go out and do it again. They have arrested us so often and found it useless that they practically let us alone now. Mrs. Hoover was also taken to the police station once. The women go out in groups afternoons and evenings, and we have had much fruit from that kind of work. . . .

Our present church was bought in July, 1919. We spent the remaining months of the year in remodeling it, and it was dedicated at Christmas. . . .

They paid all my expenses during my illness, and are looking after our needs now during our absence. We had 1,087 in attendance when the church was dedicated, and our Sunday School attendance has run between 520 and 550. Lately I received word that it had reached 605 and they are having conversions all the time. I stand for the position that every church ought to have conversions all the time, and I am not satisfied if our church is without them. We had a dry time a few years back, and it was a time of waiting upon the Lord, in complaint, in sadness, and in humiliation, and the Lord met us. I have been ill since January, 1920, and the Official Board has carried on the work.

In June, 1920, another revival broke out, beginning by half a dozen little children dancing in the Spirit. The Spirit of God fell on those watching them, and they began to dance, too; often they were out of their consciousness. They danced with their eyes closed and moved around among others not knowing they were near, and not colliding with them. This produced a wave of conversion so that in July we received 109 probationers and 97 full members. Great crowds of people came from the outside; members of churches as well as many strangers came in to witness the strange scene. Some of those who came in were affected by the Spirit, so they began to dance, or weep, or pray. One young man who had only one foot and a crutch says he sees a light and hears beautiful music when the Spirit comes upon him and to him it appears that he dances with two feet.

I have had revivals wherever I have been. In our revival in 1909 they said, "It is Hoover. He is hypnotizing them." In this revival I was ill in bed, and it is still going on without me. It seems the Lord has sent it to show that it wasn't "Hoover," and to encourage me that if I were taken away the work would go on.

The Lord has worked miraculously in healing, and more than once money has been multiplied. Two young men were baptized in the Spirit out in one of the country towns. They were peripatetic photographers. They went into a new place to work and wrote me within about a month telling me they had a congregation of fifty, sending me their names; some had been converted and some already baptized. One of these young men, a day or two after he was baptized in the Spirit, arose one morning and was thinking of what he had to buy during the day, and that he hadn't money enough for what he wanted. As he was dressing he heard the clinking of money in his pocket. Putting in his hand he got out six or seven pesos in coin. He inquired in the house of one and another, thinking they had put money in his pocket, and they said they had not. He told me the story and believes the Lord multiplied his money. We have had other cases of the same kind.

In all the letters I received from my people they tell me that the work goes on; the revival continues. The church is crowded even on week nights and the attendance in the Sunday School continues at 600. To God he all the glory. (*TLRE*, Feb., 1921)

> *Book Editor*: The dancing is reminiscent of what happened in the Kentucky Revival 100 years before (See, *The Kentucky Revival*, by Richard McNemar)
>
> A similar article describing how Pentecost came to Chili was written in The *Latter Rain Evangel* of 1911, but this article had an additional couple of paragraphs, which I include below:

The great enemy of souls and especially of this work has done his mightiest to destroy us by bringing dreadful scandals into our midst. A couple of broken homes, a fallen girl who had been baptized (yes, two, but one reclaimed), an attempted murder and then suicide by a man who had been reclaimed from a life of crime, and who left word that he had done this because of a fall [into sin] and that he never could go back to the old life; but, blessed be God, in spite of these hindrances, the work has gone on continuously. It will not be new to anyone that sitting in judgment, spiritual pride, inconstancy, etc., have had their part in hindering. "But God!" . . . Glory to His Name!"

A number of features have appeared latterly, some of which are clearly error and have been largely corrected, while others, though causing question as difficult of solution, yet accompanied with such evident fruits of the Spirit that one may not boldly pronounce them wrong, are in practice among us.

About six months ago someone began to "bring through" those seeking the baptism of the Holy Ghost by causing them to repeat some word rapidly and persistently. I marvel where he got the idea, for he does not read English. I had seen this error referred to in Pentecostal literature, but never mentioned it as I had not imagined that it would rise spontaneously, and I had no purpose to put erroneous ideas into people's minds. It spread rapidly, though I soon was able to correct the originator, but after he had sown the seed. However, good judgment prevailed soon among the leaders in most places where it had gone, and it has practically ceased.

The teaching of interpretation, too, "Put yourself under the blood and say what comes into your mind," "Because one is in a sure place when under the blood," this, too, had some spread, but has also been mostly set aside. During a few months there were many interpreters, a considerable number of whom were after this sort, but I believe most of the interpretation now to be really Spirit given, though I could not say all.

We have been struck with the readiness with which many new converts are baptized really without any experience in the Christian life and evidently not sanctified, This causes us wonder, but we stand before our God with our hand upon our mouth, or with loud voice glorifying Him, for He hath done what He pleased. . . .

Eight or ten members of our official Board have removed with their families to other places largely with the thought of propagating the good news. This is originating some new centers, while it makes place for the training of new workers in the board. Many newly converted or newly baptized ones feel a call to go to their country and to their kindred to tell what great things the Lord has done for them and the compassion He has had for them, and thus, too, the blessed news is spreading.

In December and January, two other congregations (almost entire) retired from the Methodist Episcopal Church with their pastor. Another pastor retired without his congregation, and was assigned the care of one of the congregations in Santiago which had been without a pastor since its separation.

A Presbyterian congregation which had accepted the Pentecostal Movement and was without a pastor, on the arrival in their city of one of our official members, dissolved their organization and rallied around him, sitting at his feet, so to speak, and received the blessed news with open hearts, though it meant a destruction of old traditions and a transformation of life. The Lord is with them and is being glorified in them. . . . the great, great cause of gratitude in our hearts and on our tongues is the transformation in the lives of so many. Here, practically all are drinkers, yes, drunkards, unclean and unfaithful in the marriage relation, liars, and dishonest, until converted. Tempers between husband and wife, something intolerable, and even conversion in the past has failed to cure this. . . . [But the power of the baptism in the Spirit cures it.] (*TLRE*, July, 1911)

> *Book Editor*: The above chapters leaves out two important points of Pentecostal history, one is that over 100 people received the Baptism of the Holy Spirit at the Schearer Schoolhouse revival in 1896; which led to the founding of the Church of God. Another is the large contribution made by Maria Woodworth-Etter. We will learn more about the great part she played throughout this book.
>
> There are several more articles that could be considered historical and relating to how and when the outpouring came to an area, but I include them under the year in which they appeared.

# Chapter 4

## Pentecostal Newspapers 1906-1909

Book Editor here, several different Pentecostal papers are quoted in the following chapters. The majority of the information was taken from these papers:

*The Latter Rain Evangel*, (*TLRE*) began in Chicago at the Stone Church in 1908.

*Word and Witness*, (*WaW*) published by E. N. Bell, pre-Assembly of God paper, that ran 1912-1915. It was discontinued as the publishers felt the need was being met by *The Weekly Evangel,* an AOG paper.

*The Weekly Evangel* (*TWE*) which became *The Pentecostal Evangel* (*TPE*), the paper of the AOG. (1913-**).

With only a few articles taken from an assortment of other papers such as:

*Confidence*, in the UK began in April of 1908
*The Midnight Cry*, published by Glad Tidings Mission, New York
*The Pentecost*
*The Bridegroom's Messenger*, the paper of Aimee Semple McPherson, and a few other papers.

Only a few pages of this book were taken from *The Apostolic Faith* paper produced by Azusa Street, because there are already other books which focus entirely on Azusa Street.

Some articles had a heading at the top, but other short ones simply had *** or something like it above it, so that is what I usually put above the articles, just as it appeared. So now, the papers:–

***

In about an hour and a half, a young man was converted, sanctified, and baptized with the Holy Ghost, and spoke with tongues. He was also healed of consumption, so that when he visited the doctor he pronounced his lungs sound. He has received many tongues, also the gift of prophecy, and writing in a number of foreign languages, and has a call to a foreign field. (*The Apostolic Faith*, V. 1, No. 1)

***

Many are the prophecies spoken in unknown tongues and many the visions that God is giving concerning His soon coming. The heathen must first receive the gospel. One prophecy given in an unknown tongue was interpreted, "The time is short, and I am going to send out a large number in the Spirit of God to preach the full gospel in the power of the Spirit." (Ibid)

\*\*\*

When Pentecostal lines are struck, Pentecostal giving commences. Hundreds of dollars have been laid down for the sending of missionaries and thousands will be laid down. No collections are taken for rent, no begging for money. No man's silver or gold is coveted. The silver and gold are His own to carry on His own work. He can also publish His own papers without asking for money or subscription price. (Ibid)

\*\*\*

In the meetings, it is noticeable that while some in the rear are opposing and arguing, others are at the altar falling down under the power of God and feasting on the good things of God. The two spirits are always manifesting, but no opposition can kill, no power in earth or hell can stop God's work, while He has consecrated instruments through which to work. (Ibid)

\*\*\*

Many have received the gift of singing as well as speaking in the inspiration of the Spirit. The Lord is giving new voices, he translates old songs into new tongues, he gives the music that is being sung by the angels and has a heavenly choir all singing the same heavenly song in harmony. It is beautiful music, no instruments are needed in the meetings. (Ibid)

> *Book Editor*: There is a possibility that some mentions of the heavenly choir refer to people actually hearing angels singing and heavenly instruments, which is also a claim that was occasionally directly made.

## Evangelist T. W. McConnell's Testimony:

About 28 years ago, I went into a meeting to break it up, and the Lord broke me up. My conversion I never could doubt. I was called to preach and refused, and went on for a number of years trying to get away from the call. Finally I obeyed the Lord, and started to work for Him, but not to preach. The Lord sanctified my soul. Then I commenced to try to preach. About two years after, the Lord appeared to me in a dream. He so filled me with His Spirit that people were not able to stand up before me, for a time.

A few days after [the dream], He told me to give up my business, and make my wants known to Him, and not to man. I obeyed. The Lord supplied my every need, and was with me in revival meetings and in healing many that I prayed for. But I heard of people receiving the Holy Ghost and speaking with tongues.

I came to Los Angeles to investigate, and found it was a fact, and earnestly commenced to seek the Lord for the baptism with the Holy Ghost. And the Lord, knowing my heart, came and took possession of me and spoke with my tongue. I want to say to every person, test God and you will never deny the baptism with the Holy Ghost. (*The Apostolic Faith*, Vol. 1, No. 1)

# Messengers of An Outpouring

**Pentecostal Faith Line:**

There are a dozen or more Christian workers who are devoting their time to the salvation of souls, having been called of God from other lines of employment to devote their time in praying with the sick, preaching, working with souls at the altar, etc. We believe in the faith line for Christian workers, and no collections are taken. During the four months, meetings have been running constantly, and yet with working day and night and without purse [savings] or scrip [payment], the workers have all been kept well and provided with food and raiment.

Workers who have received calls to foreign lands are going out, the Lord providing the means with no needs being presented. The ones that give, give as the Lord speaks to them and do not want their names mentioned. It is a poor time in these last days to hoard up treasures on earth. When the Lord speaks, it is a blessing to those that obey Him, but we covet no man's gold, nor silver, nor apparel.

A sister who was called to Oakland had her faith tested as to her fare; as the time was near and she had not received it. [She must have cried out to God, or questioned Him.] That night she was caught away in the Spirit [and flown over the city] when the Lord brought her back, the words came to her, "If I can carry you around Los Angeles without a body, I can take you to Oakland without a fare." So that day she received the money. (*The Apostolic Faith*, Vol. 1, No. 1)

\*\*\*

A sister was healed of consumption when she had but a part of a lung left. She lay in a trance for three days and saw heaven and hell and unutterable things. She received the Pentecost and gift of tongues and feels called to a foreign land. (Ibid)

\*\*\*

The first time I was out of wood [to heat his house] after the Lord had shown me to trust Him [for provision], I asked the Lord for wood and the wood did not come. The Lord had shown me that I could not ask for what I already had. If there was flour in the barrel, I could not ask for flour till it was gone. I went down into the basement that morning and found hard knots that had been laid aside and had enough wood for that day. The next morning I asked the Lord for wood. The wood did not come. I picked up enough chunks and chips to do that day.

The next morning, I went to the Lord and said, "Father, there are no more chucks and chips, we are out of wood. Send the wood." I went down to the city and forgot all about it. Did not think of it until I returned home, and my daughter said, "Papa, who brought the wood?" I told her that "she need not trouble, the Lord would send it."

But she said, "Some man brought wood, who was he that you sent it by?" I thought she was joking, but she said, "Look in the box and in the basement." I went down and found a large load of wood already for the stove and just the length that we used in our stove.

I did not know for some time who brought the wood; but one day when holding a meeting in South Seattle, a man invited me home with him, and while at dinner he said, "I want to tell you something that happened to me. I was crossing the bridge with a load of wood. My wife had written out a bill of some things that we had to have, and I needed feed for my horses. I was taking this load of wood in to [trade it for] the groceries and feed. While out on the bridge and no one near me, an audible voice said behind me and just above me, 'Take this wood to McConnell.'

"I looked around me and there was no one near me. I said, 'I cannot take this wood to McConnell, I have got to have groceries and feed,' and drove on. The voice said again, 'Take this wood to T. W. McConnell.' I said, 'How can I take this wood to McConnell; I must have these groceries and feed for my horses.' And a third time the voice spoke, and so strong that it scared me, and I answered, 'Well, I will.' For I believed it was the Lord talking. There was no one about.

"I went and made inquiry, finally looked in the directory and found where you lived. I drove to the house and unloaded the wood, then drove back home as quickly as I could, loaded up some wood that I had and drove back to town, sold my wood as soon as I reached town, got my feed and groceries, and from that time I have prospered as never before." -- T. W. M. (*The Apostolic Faith*, Vol. 1, No. 1, 1906)

## 1907

**In Fort Worth, Texas:**
We have small band here. Have been meeting in private houses asking the Lord to open a door for us that no man could shut. We are praising the Lord this morning that we have a tent paid for and lights and seats secured. O, how happy I am at the prospect. Just as soon as the weather clears away, we want to begin meetings. We are expecting our God to do great things, for when I read of the wonderful work at Azusa, my heart rejoices so that I fall to my knees to thank God. We want the heavenly showers to fall on us too. We have four now waiting for the promise of the Father.

A young man, a preacher, came to see me last Tuesday. He said that a little more than four months ago he was down waiting on God for an infilling of the Holy Spirit, when after waiting on God he began to pray in language unknown to him. This came on him [again?] in a few days. He told his presiding elder, who said that was foolishness. He said that once after that he felt like letting the Lord have His way with him, but on account of discouragements he did not do so. When he came here he hunted us up, and the power all came back to him. He never had anyone to help or tell him about this great movement. -- Mrs. C. A. Roll. (*The Apostolic Faith*, April, 1907)
\*\*\*

There is a Swedish Pentecostal Mission in Los Angeles at 8th and Well streets. The power of God is falling there. The Swedish people have been among the foremost in accepting the doctrine of the baptism with the Holy Ghost and many are endued with power from on high. (Ibid)

\*\*\* Russians and Armenians in Los Angeles are seeking the baptism. The Armenians have a Pentecostal cottage meeting on Victor Street . . . Some have been baptized with the Holy Ghost. (Ibid)

## A Wonderful Baptism in England

Two years ago, a special work of grace began. The Holy Spirit came upon me with manifestations, and the old natural life was in very deed and truth crucified with Christ. And from that time, I became a crucified follower of the crucified Lord. Anointings of the Holy Spirit were continually given [to] me for service, as each need arose. It was indeed a walk in newness of life, proving the power of His resurrection.

On the last night of the old year, came the command to tarry, which was promptly carried out. The result being a further revelation of the exceeding sinfulness of sin and of His glorious holiness and love. At the end of eight days came a baptism of fire burning and consuming through my whole being as the very ashes of my old life were consumed and done away with. Love to God and man took possession of me, and I was filled to overflowing with the resurrection life of my Lord. Much time daily was spent in silent waiting before the Lord, receiving from His Holy Spirit such teaching, that what had formerly been light was translated into life for spirit, soul and body.

With two dear Pentecostal saints, I met for prayer and waiting. [This must have been a reference to the above mentioned Pentecostals, because *All Saints' Vicarage* did not receive the Holy Spirit until Dec. 2, 1907.] I saw in vision Christ on Calvary, bearing my sin. Each act of sin was laid separately upon Him and weighed Him down deeper and deeper, until beneath the awful weight of blackness and darkness of woe and anguish, His heart was broken and mine seemed to break with His. How long this lasted, I do not know; but at length, consciousness returned. The glory broke and the Holy Spirit sang through me in English a hitherto unknown song of praise and thanksgiving for the precious, precious Blood, and of glory to the Lamb upon the throne.

On the evening of our next united gathering for prayer and waiting, revelation after revelation was given of the Lamb; the glory of the Lamb, the power of the Lamb, the victory of the Lamb, the marriage of the Lamb, and the reign of the Lamb with His glorified bride. I knew from that moment that Christ Jesus was on the throne of my heart as the Lamb slain from the foundation of the world, and that His purpose was to demonstrate the Lamb life through me.

The Holy Spirit descended in clouds of glory, wave after wave of glory broke upon me. Tidal waves of resurrection life and glory surged through every organ of my body, so that I was constrained to cry aloud for everything within me shouted "Glory" and could not be silenced.

I realized that this was that which was spoken by the prophet Joel, that God had made good His promise to me, and poured upon me His Holy Spirit. Glory to His name.

When I was once more alone, the Lord spoke to me and asked if I was disappointed that the gift of tongues had not been given. Disappointed Lord![?] I have You and You can speak in every tongue. It was You I wanted -- You alone; and now You have taken full possession. He gave me to understand that tongues would soon be given. And a few days later when in prayer with two dear friends,

He gave me the gift, and the Holy Spirit sang through me in a tongue utterly unknown before. The interpretation was given, and I knew it was all about the precious Blood. Glory to the Triune God! Glory to the Lamb upon the throne. Your English sister, M. J. D. (*The Apostolic Faith*, Oct., 1907)

**Success at Laurens:**

Dear Bro. Cashwell: [of *The Bridegroom's Messenger*]

We have just closed a victorious meeting at Laurens with Bro. N. J. Holmes of the Altamont Bible Institute in charge. On arrival here we found some of the most prominent ladies of the various churches had received their Pentecost with Bible evidence, and others hungry and earnestly seeking. We also met with great opposition, the Devil had all his forces marshaled against us, but with all this, large crowds attended our meetings, the altar was full of earnest seekers for salvation and the Baptism of the Holy Ghost.

The powers of darkness were so great that for days it seemed as if we were at a standstill, people who were earnestly seeking seemed to get nowhere. All we could do is pray, and wait before God. We have never witnessed a meeting just like it before.

The Devil had many evil reports out, and some were afraid to come to the meetings for fear they would catch this speaking in tongues as they called it, but they were kindly informed it was not at all catching, and there was no danger whatever.

After we had prayed and held on to God for days the power began to fall and precious souls swept through to victory. Sinners came to the altar crying out for mercy and found pardon. One young man came to one of the Sunday afternoon meetings, and the Holy Ghost was upon us in great power, many shouting and speaking in tongues, he with others, came close by to satisfy their curiosity, he was soon stricken to the ground and crying unto God for mercy.

In about thirty minutes he arose shouting the praise of God in an unknown tongue. Glory to God for Pentecost! How I love this way! It grows more wonderful every day.

On this same afternoon, the last day of the meeting, the Holy Ghost fell on the children. One little boy, whom his mother said could not sing, rose beating time as a grown man and sang "I would not be denied," and many other songs, when the power left him he stopped, saying, "I can't sing any more."

A man in the audience said this child convinced him more than anything else. Glory to God! Through "babes and sucklings Thou hast perfected praise. Matt. 21:16. A number from the Cotton Mills received, and Watts Mill have called fro a tent-meeting, offering to pay all expenses. Glory! God will bless them for this. Some of us will go there from Greenville. Praise, God! We never know defeat after Pentecost. -- Clyde Cotton. (*TBM*, Oct. 10, 1907, page 4)

**Pentecostal Work in Florida:** (excerpt)

We were invited to Manchula, Fla., where God worked in a marvelous way. Many souls were saved, unclean spirits cried with loud voices as they came out of those possessed with them. Strong persecution arose here against us . . .

We went next to Orlando, Fla., [was] there about sixteen days. . . . Rev. S. C. Perry, pastor of the Holiness Church at Pleasant Grove, invited us to Durant, Fla. . . . Before the meeting closed seventy had received the Holy Ghost and all spoke with other tongues and magnified God. . . . Frequently six to ten people would be singing in the foreign tongues without discord. . . .

Sister F. E. Bowen, leader of the Rescue Home, has the baptism and most of the girls in the Home have been saved, sanctified, and filled with the Holy Ghost. Glory to God! It is a Pentecostal Home now. . . . -- F. M. Britton (*The Bridegroom's Messenger*, Oct. 10, 1907, page 4, col. 1)

**Victory at Coconut Grove, Fl:**

I thank God for permitting me to go to this place and preach His Word. . . . But there was great opposition to the work as the people did not have the clear understanding of the Holy Ghost. Many of the oppposers met us in the first service and God wonderfully blessed me in giving the message and those who had opposed the work came up at the close and said they had no more to say against it.. . . four of some of the best people in town, and those who cannot be doubted, received the Baptism of the Holy Ghost. Some have received the Baptism since we left . . . (*The BrideGroom's Messenger*, Dec. 1, 1907, page 1)

**Letter From China:**

Dear Brother Cashwell:

Pentecost has come to Wuchow, China. I wrote to you that the missionaries were fighting, but O, thank God, they are coming down at the feet of Jesus at last. Seven missionaries at Wuchow have received their Pentecost and about thirty Chinese which makes forty. . . . (Ibid)

**Birmingham Report:**

Pentecost has come to Birmingham to stay, as well as at two other parts of the state. . . . One saved and one filled with the Spirit in a cottage meeting in this city last night, others seeking.

Those who get the baptism of the Spirit in my meetings speak and sing in other tongues as the Spirit gives utterance . . . M. M. Pinson. (Ibid)

**From Toronto, Canada:**

My Dear Brother Cashwell:

Glad to hear that you have launched "The Bridegoom's Messenger" as a Pentecostal light-bearer. We have opened up a permanent Pentecostal Mission here in Toronto, and a door of great opportunity seems to be inviting us to enter. Have bought a fine large church and lot, and are holding forth every night except Monday and Saturday. A few have their Pentecost in this part of the city, and a number are upon their faces seeking their Pentecost. We are getting out another issue of "The Latter Rain." Praise God for the victory. In Jesus' love, J. E. Sanders. (*The Bridegroom's Messenger*, Dec. 1, 1907, page 2)

## Susie Bain's Testimony:

"Bless the Lord, O my soul; and all that is within me, bless His holy name." Two years ago, while attending a holiness campmeeting at Clearwater, Fla., God sweetly saved me, and on this last April He cleansed my heart from all sin.

Like many others, I thought I received the Holy Ghost when I was sanctified, until I attended a meeting at Durant, Fla., conducted by Brother Britton. When I saw the wonderful works of God and the mighty manifestations of His power, I was fully convinced that I did not have the Holy Ghost, so I tarried in the "upper room" until July 20th, when it seemed that the windows of heaven were opened into my soul, and the blessed Comforter came in to abide forever. Glory! Since then I have been feasting with the Lord. Pray for me that I may keep humble at the feet of Jesus ever abounding in the love of God. -- Lakeland, Fla. (*The Bridegroom's Messenger*, □ Dec. 1, 1907, page 2)

## Goteborg, Sweden:

Andrew G. Johnson writes:

God is working so wonderfully. I do praise Him for victory through the precious Blood of Christ. God is in our midst every night in mighty power. We have baptized fourteen more. Most of them had the gift of the Holy Ghost before they went down into the water.

About fifteen young men and women are ready to go out [into God's work] in the name of Jesus. Some of them are out in the work already. Pray for us. . . . (*The Household of God*, Nov., 1907)

## 1908

## A Rescue Mission Worker's Recent Experience:

Pastor W. H. Standley, of Watertown, N. Y. for fourteen years in charge of the Gospel Mission; after fourteen long months of seeking, and laboring to bring the Pentecostal truths to others, on the night of December 9th, received his definite Pentecostal baptism of the Holy Ghost, with the Bible evidence of speaking, in what seemed to be, two different languages.

I was lost in praise, and my soul was filled with love as sweet as heaven itself. All night long the love flowed in and the volume of praise flowed out. Four days afterwards, when eighteen miles away from home, God gave me the gift of [another] unknown language, which as yet, I speak at will, 1 Cor. 14:22, as a sign to the unbelieving. I am waiting on God to give me the interpretation. Some few sentences have been given.

Now after fourteen days of blessed fullness have come and gone it is deepening me more and more into God. Hunger has passed away, for He satisfies me with His abiding presence. I have some hard battles with the enemy, but He has kept me in perfect peace. I am satisfied with Him. He is making me a new man, with a new book, and a new message, and a new tongue. Glory to God! I am sure this is the new wine experience of Acts 2:13. My desire is to do His whole will, and thus glorify Him in service or suffering, as He wills.

I want, in closing, to say a few words of help to some tardy seekers. Hold right on, keep your eyes on Jesus, Hab. 2:3, last clause, will surely be fulfilled to the joy of your hungry heart. Move over on Praise avenue, stay there, He will come. -- W. H. Standley, Watertown, N. Y. (*The Bridegroom's Mess.*, Jan. 15, 1908, page 3.)

**Report from the Channel Islands:**

Dear Mr. Boddy: [letter to the *Confidence* paper]

I must thank you through Christ for the blessing I have received in reading your little book "Health in Christ." I had for many years suffered from a weak knee, that at times I could hardly walk. A friend of mine lent me your little book, and as I was reading all alone with God, I believed there and then that he had power to heal the body, as well as the soul. I began to walk in my room better, and said, Yes Lord I believe it, and went to the stairs, and the Devil said Hold on to the handrail, you are going to fall.

I told him he is a liar, and praise God, I went running down the stairs. My friends were surprised, they could hardly believe it; even some worldly relations of mine say it is wonderful. The devil tells me sometimes that it is not true; but I cling to God, and say yet I believe, help me, and [the devil] departs for a time.

Ever since you came to Jersey I have not forgotten to pray for you every morning that your books may be a blessing to all those that would read them. . . . Adelina Amy. (*Confidence*, May, 1908, page 18)

**Letter from a Nurse:**

Dear Sir,

Will you send me some more booklets, "Health in Christ."

I had a copy of "Health in Christ" sent me some time ago when very ill, and it proved to me such a help and blessing that I long for others to read it with the same result, that they may by faith through the teaching of the Holy Spirit take Jesus as their Divine Healer. Just before seeing your book, I had been under five different doctors, two of them saying I would never do any more work (Hospital Sister) so must give it all up, as I had heart trouble, also lung [problems].

So I just took it all to the Master for He knew that I consecrated my whole life to Him when I took up the work, and I did not feel it was His will for me to lay it down so quickly. Then it was the Holy Spirit gave me such faith to trust Christ that I never before thought it possible to have.

Now I am so well, and have commenced my work again with renewed energy and love for the Master. Now, instead of taking a dose of medicine when I feel tired, I take an extra five minutes at the Throne of Grace with great results. . . . W. B. M., Upper George Street, London, W. (*Confidence*, May, 1908)

**About China:**

Some months ago articles appeared in religious papers referring to the disappointment of those who had gone from their homes to distant lands after receiving their "Pentecost", and hoping to speak fluently the language of the natives. Many did not then fully realize that the gift of "Tongues" is not the gift of any known language in it entirety. We are sure that God honored their zeal, and we are sure that He has permitted them to be a blessing though not as they expected.

The Lord raised up interpreters for them, and always they reached English speaking people with their Pentecostal message, while missionaries with whom they came in contact were encouraged to seek the Baptism of the Holy Ghost. (*Confidence*, May, 1908, page 21.)

## Hong Kong China

Dear Brother in Jesus, Your card and "Counsel to Leaders" [was] received. We are glad to know you are sending them abroad. They are much needed in these days of conflict.

As to whether I know of any who have received a language, I know of no one having received a language [of the people they went to as missionaries] so as to be able to converse intelligently, or to preach in the same with the understanding, in the Pentecostal movement.

Regarding the language I have, that was given to me in Los Angeles, Cal., about two years ago. I can speak it at will, and feel the power of God in most every instance when I speak at length, and can truly bear witness to the scripture that "Speaking in tongues edifies the one speaking."

Regarding the question of an Indian language. When I was baptized with the Spirit in Los Angeles, I began speaking in tongues immediately, and a day or two after a young man, about 25 years of age, came to meeting and hearing me pray in the unknown tongue, said I was speaking things he could understand, and desired that I should pray for him. I did so, he kneeling with me, and as I prayed it seemed he was moved to desperation, and began to cry to the Lord for himself, and presently began to shout and proclaim that the Lord had saved him. During the course of these meetings he informed me that I had been speaking in several languages of India. One of them his mother tongue.

I know for some time I was saying the word, "Bengalee," and when I reached India I found myself in the Bengal Province. Their language is called Bengalee, but I never knew there was such a language before until after starting for India. However, before leaving America I noticed that the languages changed and I was talking quite a different tongue, and after reaching Calcutta I noticed another change but could not understand the words.

It would be very impossible for me to believe that these were not real languages, as they are spoken with such accuracy and entirely free from guidance by my own mind. Whether or not I was speaking an Indian language in Los Angeles does not shake my faith or even cause me anxiety. I know that God was talking through me, and what it was He knew all a out it, and that was quite enough for me. . . .

I know that some of the best men that ever lived talked in tongues, and if the devil can make a fellow talk in tongues, then God can, and if the magicians of Egypt can turn a stick into a snake, then our God has one to swallow all of them, so I am not uneasy. I am delighted with all God has done for me on this line. I supposed He would let us talk to the natives of India in their own tongue, but He did not, and as far as I can see, will not use that means by which to convert the heathen, but will employ the gifts -- such as wonderful signs of healing and other powers, that the heathen can see for themselves and know that there is no cheat to the performance. . . .

While I do not understand all there is connected with this movement; yet I see enough to know that God is pleased to work miracles among the people today in the same manner as the early saints. I know He performed a miracle on me, and have seen him do the same on many, and because the devil counterfeits, backbites, scandalizes, and misrepresents God's work, does not shake my faith, but rather confirms it in the present movement as being of God. . . .

Here in Hong Kong, we preached the word to the Chinese through an interpreter, and God has saved some, and there are about twenty-five or thirty that were baptized with the Spirit of God and spoke in other tongues, seen visions, and received interpretations, etc. . . .

Would you kindly remember us in prayer, as the opposition from some, especially the native pastors and missionaries, is very severe. The personal onslaughts of the devil are very trying at times. . . . H. G. Garr. (*Confidence*, May, 1908, *Special Supplement*)

## Testimony of Smith Wigglesworth

Dear Mr. & Mrs. Boddy,

After 7 full days of the Glorious Presence of the Glory of God resting upon me, I send you this testimony for the Glory of God. For 3 months I have been exercised [thinking deeply] about the full Pentecost. I had the clear witness of the Baptism of the Holy Spirit 14 years ago last July, and this brought a marvelous manifestation of God in special gifts to sick ones, and a constant living and seeking to bring others to Jesus. But from time to time when reading the Acts of the Apostles I always saw that the signs were not following as I am led to believe ought to be after a real Pentecost, according to Mark 16.

The desire more and more increased in my very inner soul, giving me a holy breathing cry after this clear manifestation. I have visited meetings at London, and Sunderland, and other places, but always knew they were not seeking Pentecosts. There seemed a great deal of letter, but very little of the spirit that would give the hungry and needy a Baptism of Fire such as would burn up distinctions and officiousness and appearance of Pride and evidences of social standing.

Today I am actually living in the Acts of the Apostles' time, I am speaking with new tongues, the Holy Fire of God's Presence fills me till my pen moves to the glory of God, and my whole being is filled with the Presence of the Holy Ghost. Almost am I led to believe that 20 years is not too long to wait for the Holy Anointing of God the Holy Ghost. . . . [He backtracks to before he was Baptized in the Holy Spirit, then up to it again]

On Saturday, I and a friend went on to Sunderland to wait for Pentecost at All Saints', at Mr. Boddy's Church. We had heard much about this blessed work and were encouraged, but after arriving at Sunderland [the city] found the enemy very busy discouraging believers; this did not disturb me, because I had gone with an open mind and prayed much to be clearly convinced if there was anything there that did not reveal the Glory of god that I would at once have cleared out and protested against it, but God was with me there.

But I found the full Presence and Power to restore believers and to heal the sick. My experience is that this does not take place in some kinds of meetings, the reason is that, to a great measure, they do not believe the full Gospel, and it is nothing new to me to find great leaders against the tongues, and I find that, even in these times, "they cannot enter in because of their unbelief." I praise God for Pentecost. . . .

I went to All Saints', to the Communion Service, and after this was led on to wait in the Spirit, many things taking place in the waiting-meetings that continued to bring me to a hungry feeling for Holy Righteousness. At about 11 a.m., Tuesday morning, at All Saints' Vicarage, I asked a sister to help me to the witness of the Baptism of the Holy Ghost. She laid hands on me in the presence of a brother. The fire fell and burned in me till the Holy Spirit clearly revealed absolute purity before God.

At this point she was called out of the room, and during her absence a marvelous revelation took place, my body became full of light and Holy Presence, and in the revelation I saw an empty Cross and at the same time the Jesus I loved and adored crowned in the Glory in a Reigning Position. The glorious remembrance of these moments is beyond my expression to give -- when I could not find words to express, then an irresistible Power filled me and moved my being till I found to my glorious astonishment I was speaking in other tongues clearly. After this a burning love for everybody filled my soul.

I am overjoyed in giving my testimony, praying for those that fight this truth, but I am clearly given to understand that I must come out of every unbelieving element. I am already witness of signs following. Praise Him. -- Smith Wigglesworth. (*Confidence*, Oct., 1908)

**Testimony from Bournemouth:** (A Visit to Sunderland)

Dear Mr. Boddy,

I was sorry I saw so little of you in my recent visit to Sunderland, but as I had been away from business for three weeks I thought it necessary to run away back on Friday last, and subsequent events have confirmed it as the Lord's leading.

When I was in Sunderland last May there is no doubt that the Lord gave me a great uplift, but I don't believe I was earnest enough to receive my Baptism. On the Wednesday, when the Lord so graciously gave me my heart's desire by baptizing me in the Holy Spirit, I realized the meaning of that text, "The Kingdom of Heaven suffereth violence, and the violent take it by storm." As you said to me last May, it is a combination of resting and wrestling; resting in the Lord for the blessing, and wrestling with Him and not letting Him go until you have been blessed.

Apart from the value of the laying on of hands -- and I notice that the Lord used this method of conferring the baptism on the early Christians at both Samaria and Ephesus -- it was so good to have encouragement and faith and assurance whilst I was myself pleading. I have a letter from a friend who thinks the Lord may give him his Pentecost at home, but I am urging him to go to Sunderland, as I cannot help feeling that I myself would never have got through into the tongues if I had stayed at home. I have often prayed for a vision of Jesus, and whilst I was under the power I had a dream [he was not asleep so it was a vision]. I saw Him take a goblet, from which He drank, after which He handed it to me, and I drank all its contents. It was real Communion, and I recalled His words to the sons of Zebedee. When I prayed for a vision, I expected to see the glory and majesty and pomp of Heaven; but this was just as sweet to me as anything I could have imagined beforehand, and the lesson underlying it is very significant. Glory to Jesus for the simplicity of all His ways.

For years I seem to have been in the wilderness, rejoicing, that I had left the bondage of Egypt, eating with thankfulness of the heavenly manna, drinking of the precious water from the smitten rock, but I got no further than the wilderness. I delighted in reading of all the promises of the Coming Kingdom of God, but looked for all these things beyond the Advent of our Coming Lord. I did not realize that I could be translated into the Kingdom of His dear Son right now.

There is no doubt that the supernatural crossing of the Jordan, when Joshua led the chosen people into the Promised Land, is typical of the Baptism of the Holy Spirit when Jesus leads His chosen ones into the place He has prepared for us. It is, indeed, a land flowing with milk and honey.

Since I received my baptism I have had an abiding joy, and I find myself praising God every hour I am awake; praise seems as natural as breathing. Thanks very much for sending "Confidence" . . . Stanley H. Frodsham. (*Confidence*, Nov. 1908)

## From Brother Smith Wigglesworth

My Dear Brother,

After twelve months of this blessed fullness I desire to witness to the truth of the anointing with power for service. There is an affinity and unity with the blessed Holy Spirit as never before, and a fearlessness, or a clothing with a consciousness that the source is His, and the results are His, and I am one channel only. [I am] now without fear, a vessel unto honor for the Master's sake.

Then there is the presence of the Holy Spirit abiding -- the anointing received abideth -- as it is an unction from the Holy One, thus renewing the spirit of our mind, thinking about the pure and holy things, the Epistle to the Romans being fulfilled. "Conformed to the image of His Son," growing up into Him our living Head. First it is power with God and then it is power with man. First stripped, then the clothing from above. No longer seeking our own but His. Responsibilities and results are His.

The yoke is on His shoulder; He sees to thee, O son of man. Can the Acts of the Apostles be renewed? Lord, Thou knowest. The given faith stands and says;

Let it be so and the workings are mighty. Our position is to see that we are clothed with the Spirit. The Spirit led Philip to the wilderness, and the Eunch was ready waiting. Samaria also was ready. The secret was that Philip was in the power of the Spirit. He increases when we decrease; we cannot do both and be fruitful. All the glory must be Christ's, and then it will be the same as of old -- "the sword of the Lord and Gideon."

Speaking with tongues is an external evidence that God has done something, and it is always done when the motives are pure and the life cleansed. The blood meets the poor, needy soul and it enters through the gate into the city and begins to share in divine privileges of power, of lifting burdens, of weeping with discouraged souls, of bringing health to sick and weary ones, "as He is so are we." As God dwelt in Him and did the work, now He dwells in us and teaches us by the Holy Spirit how to do the work and it is done. We are daily witnessing to the work being done.

Demons are cast out, the sick are healed, and sinners turn to Jesus. Saints are becoming more saintly. Speaking with "tongues" brings me into a deeper sense of His abiding presence; it much resembles the Shekinah glory over the Ark. The divine glory is right over me day by day. The messages [sermons] are with power; never lacking power and zeal. Of a truth God is with us. I admit that the price to pay is much, and you may have to lose as good friends as Elijah, but, praise God, there is a mantle of power just to meet your need.

David speaks in the 23$^{rd}$ Psalm of the valley of the shadow of death. It was a day in the life of David of separation. Notice that as soon as he got there the table was spread. Brothers, it will be a destruction of the flesh -- a real death -- but God has another food, another robe for you, another power, another glorious victory, but it is through the valley, where God spreads the table. He knows best what the spirit life requires, so He spreads the table.

Everywhere we go with this truth in the power of the spirit we have to deal with sin in believers. The filthy acts of the self-life have to be dealt with, and men cannot always stand the purging. I have never heard or seen God baptizing an unclean or fleshly life. There is only one life, only one way, only one thing. Reality can move the holy wind, and it is crying out for a clean heart. As the blood is applied through separation and holy surrender, the fire falls, the spirit's clothing comes on to a pure spirit. What I am, what I have been, must be lost in Him. (*Confidence*, Dec. 1908)

## The Lame Walk

I was an invalid for more than four years, pronounced incurable by physicians in New York, Hartford and Greenwich, Connecticut. The trouble was a serious chronic disease of the spine. I wore a heavy plaster cast and walked on crutches, dragging my feet, my limbs being nearly useless.

In May, 1907, I left my home in the East to become an inmate of a home for incurables in Chicago. While on an Indiana avenue [street] car in Chicago, my attention was attracted by a sign on the Stone Church. I afterwards came to the meeting where I heard teaching and testimony on Jesus the Healer.

One remark in the sermon made a deep impression upon me; it was that we should lean, not upon the arm of flesh but upon God. I realized that I was leaning upon the crutches and the cast, and that God wanted to set me free from these things.

I went back to the house where I was staying, and by the help of a Christian nurse the cast was removed. I was very weak. The misery was intense. I seemed to lose consciousness. After lying upon my bed for a time I began pleading with God through His Son to strengthen me, when I seemed to hear a faint voice saying: "Fear thou not; for I am with thee: be not dismayed; for I am thy God: I will strengthen thee; yea, I will help thee; yea, I will uphold thee with the right hand of my righteousness."

God heard my cry. The pain ceased, the spine was healed, the crutches were thrown away, and I am now walking in perfect ease, without helps of any kind.

Ever since the Lord so wondrously healed my sick body I had been seeking to know more of Him who has all power in Heaven and earth. I had been asking our dear Father why He did not give me the baptism in the Holy Spirit, for I did so enjoy seeing others about me so full of joy, that I felt my healing was only a part of what the Lord had for me.

After several months of waiting, I was told by a still, small voice to wait on the Lord more earnestly. I confess I did not seek as I should, for I had a little doubt about the speaking in tongues. I confessed this to God and received a wonderful blessing. I began to see the reality of His power and sought the baptism in the Holy Spirit in earnest.

Wednesday, September 30, I was so filled with the Spirit that I did not know what it meant. I seemed to be in tears all day, and felt very much depressed. Now I know the meaning of it all. Friday evening I felt again the power of God through my whole body. The sister who sat beside me asked me if she could help me. She went to the Lord in prayer for me. I was utterly helpless and became oblivious to my surroundings. Upon regaining my strength I found I had received the baptism in the Holy Spirit and was praising the Lord in some peculiar tongue. Glory to God! Praise His precious name! -- Dorothy E. Goodman. (*The Latter Rain Evangel*, Oct., 1908 The inaugural issue)

**Voice of the Spirit:** [interpretation of tongues]

God would have us to walk obediently after His Spirit, to obey the voice of the living God, and go forward and onward and upward into the Kingdom, because God is going to restore the Kingdom to Jesus Christ, who will reign. God wants to prepare His people so they can enter into the work of the Kingdom, that the power of the living God shalt come into the body of Jesus Christ. God is striving so hard to make 'us obedient unto His Spirit and go forward and upward, seeking to do His will, seeking to go onward and upward.

God is calling His people from the East and the West, and North and South to go forward and upward, and Jesus will perfect the body which He will present to the Father without spot or wrinkle. God will exalt Jesus the Christ and exalt His Kingdom far above all kingdoms. God will lift His people up and glorify His name. God is going on to victory whether you go or not. God will set aside any one who will not obey His Spirit and will not obey the voice of the living God. God wants you to go forward each one in his own place, marching as soldiers trained for the battle. He wants to train you every moment of the time so He can use you, that the power of the living God may rest upon you. Go forward in His name. Jesus wants us to do these things. (*TLRE*, Oct., 1908)

## Miracles of Salvation, Healing, Provision and Protection
(Biography of Pundita Ramabai 1858-1922)

I am so glad to have this opportunity, which I believe the Lord gave, to tell you about this beautiful sister of ours, the beloved Ramabai. How God has led that woman! He has made her so dear to the people's hearts. I wish she were here tonight instead of me. You could see by her face that she has the spirit of Jesus. Every time I think of Ramabai I praise God for what He has done for her.

She has passed right into death. She is crucified with Christ, so that the life she now lives, she lives by faith in the Son of God. She knows what it is to be nailed to the cross, with Jesus, and the resurrection life of Jesus is shining in her moment by moment. That little woman of India, I believe, is showing to the world what the Lord Jesus Christ can do through one fully surrendered, fully yielded, wholly consecrated servant of His.

Pundita Ramabai is a Brahmin. That is the very highest caste in India. She had a remarkable father. He was a learned reformer, and gave his daughter a good education. Her mother was married when she was nine years old. Oh, it is awful to be married when one is so young. This woman was married to a man of forty, and she became a beautiful mother of a beautiful family.

The youngest child born of this marriage was Pundita Ramabai. All went well until Ramabai was growing up into womanhood, and then one of those awful famines came. . . . The price of food went up about seven times higher than it should have been, and starvation was staring them in the face. They had to begin to sell their jewelry, their clothing, and their furniture. They sold everything in order to get bread to keep them alive.

One day the father said, "We will go and die in the jungle, and hide our shame." Ramabai told me she saw her father becoming weaker every day. He became totally blind. One day he said, "My strength is gone; I can go no further." He gave his blessing to his wife and children, and said to her, "Farewell, Ramabai, my youngest darling; be good, Ramabai, and love God." You people are thinking he was a Christian. He was not. He had never heard of our God or of Jesus Christ. He only knew among the millions of gods of India there must be one Supreme Being, and Ramabai said, "I will, father. I will be good, and I will love God." . . .

Kamabai said, "We got the largest garment we owned and wrapped that around the body of our dear father. My brother, my sister and I carried him out and buried him in a portion of ground he had purchased. We returned to the jungle to find our mother slowly dying of fever. One day I said, "Let me go, mother, and try to get you some food," so she went off with her heart breaking.

## Messengers of An Outpouring

She knocked at a door and a woman came, and she said, "I could not say one word. Instead the tears ran down my cheeks, [and] the blood rushed from my nose." The woman said, "What is the matter? What do you want?" And she said with almost superhuman effort, "My mother is dying!" The woman gave her a little piece of coarse, dark, hard bread that some of you people would hardly throw to your dogs. Ramabai could not say, "Thank you," but hastened back to the jungle, and said, "Mother, I have food. Try to eat it and live," but the famine sore mouth was there. Every time she tried to open her mouth the corners would crack and bleed, and Ramabai's precious mother died of hunger in that awful famine, and they buried her by the side of her husband. The sister too died, and Ramabai and her brother were left alone.

They had no friendly door open to them. At night the brother would find a little sandy lace where the rivers had gone dry, and he would scrape out a little hollow, grave-like bed, just as deep as his strength would allow, and into that grave his little sister would crawl, and he would scrape the sand over her body. She had no warm clothing, she had no blanket, she had no pillow. He made himself a little grave by her side, and into that he crawled. Ramabai is quite hard of hearing from that exposure, and she has been in delicate health ever since.

She told me she has often gone and scratched in the dirt of the street to get a little bit of last year's grain, rice or wheat to eat. She said, "I have often taken last year's fruit and swallowed the stone and the skin. Do you wonder that I was seized with most acute indigestion?" When she was twenty-two years of age she was married to a pleader [lawyer or law clerk]. After she was married nine-teen months, her husband was taken sick with cholera and died. Now Ramabai was a widow of India.

Do you know what that means? The most pitiful object on God's earth is a widow in India. Everybody hates and curses her. Not only was she a widow, but she had in her arms a helpless babe three months old, and that babe was a girl. Do any of you understand that girls are unwelcome at birth, unloved in youth! unhonored as wives, and unmourned at death? The Hindu treats his cows better than his wife. When his cow is sick he gives her proper food and cares for her, but when the wife is sick he puts her into an outbuilding and leaves her to die. And Ramabai said, "Oh, the widows of India! Something must be done for them," and so she started a school.

That school has gone through bitter persecution. She did not start her school until something beautiful came into her life. She went to England, and while there she came in contact with some dear, holy women. God has had in every generation women of prayer, women of holy lives ... Ramabai said these women lived like the teaching in that book. "They are pure and holy and unselfish. Oh, would to God I could be like that!" These holy women left an impression on that life that lasts until this day. Do you want to be a power for God? Let your every day life, your conduct, tell not only in meeting, but in the kitchen and in the shop.

So Ramabai came to see there was a power in the name of Jesus, and a power in this blessed overcoming life, and she sought it, and God heard her. She gave up worshiping her idols and became a true Christian. This has meant more to India than we shall ever know.

She came to America, and then returned to India where she started her school when thirty years of age. God was with her and God alone kept her. The Brahmins said, "We will not have this school." They persecuted and hindered in every possible way, but this is one of the proofs that God is in it. The school that Ramabai started has grown from two to two thousand. Isn't that the Lord's doings? Oh, it is, and it is marvelous in our eyes! She bought a house in Poona. She had fifteen girls. She went to one of those campmeetings in India, and heard of this beautiful truth, the deepening of the spiritual life. She began to seek the Lord for this deeper blessing. After six weeks God sent her some more holy servants of His that led her into these deep truths.

God gave her fifteen conversions in her family, just after this experience. . . .

In a few months there was another famine coming. God said, "Go into the central province and gather up the little famine orphans." She said, I have only eighty- seven cents. That won't take me very far, but if You want me to go, send me some money." Off she went into the central province, and there at the station she met a lady in white. This lady said, "God said to me this morning, 'Go to the railway station and I will show you what to do.' Where are you going Ramabai?" "Going to gather some famine orphans," and the sister said, "Praise the Lord, He means I am to go too." So these two women gathered the children . . .

How could she put two hundred and twenty-five girls in a house that only holds a hundred? God went before her again. Oh, it is beautiful to watch His leading. The people in America sent thousands of dollars, and she bought a farm of two hundred and seventeen acres. This is her farm at Kedgaon. She built a barn and into that barn she gathered the little orphans, and then she dug wells. . . .

All the wells in that district were dry; the rain did not come, and the people were praying that God would look upon Ramabai and send the water into her wells. Now I want to tell you a miracle. Every night for six weeks those nine wells were empty, and every morning those girls went praying, hoping, believing, fearing at times, but in answer to prayer there was just enough water to satisfy nineteen hundred thirsty mouths. . . .

Hundreds of people in India said, "Did you hear they have water in Mukti?" That is the name of her mission. It means "Salvation," and it is salvation for spirit, soul, and body. They came by hundreds to the gate, bringing their little cups, and said, "Ramabai, is it true that you have a God that can send water into your wells?" And she said, "Yes, I have a living God who makes the clouds and who makes the springs in the earth, He knows where to send the water." She gave these dying people water from her wells, and as they gathered by the gate she preached to them the blessed gospel, and told them of Him who said, "If any man thirst let him come unto me and drink." These heathen said, "If that is the kind of God Ramabai has, He is the living God; there is no god around Mukti that has sent water into any other wells." . . .

She built a great church that would hold four thousand people. They frequently have a congregation of two thousand. Right over the entrance gates she built a tower, which she called her prayer-tower. Into that prayer-tower two of her workers go every hour of the twenty-four, not just in the day-time, but every hour, and they pray for every need of Mukti. Ramabai herself rises every night at midnight, and spends an hour, from twelve to one, in that prayer-tower.

Let me tell you of a few things she has prayed for. She wanted a woman who would come and be her bible teacher, one who understood the scriptures thoroughly, and He called out Minnie F. Abrams, who was used of God in teaching this blessed truth you love so much, and who was a successful missionary in India. She came to Ramabai and said, "Ramabai, God distinctly said to me, 'Go to Mukti,' and I do not know what it means, but I had to come." Ramabai said, "Praise God, we have prayed for you for seven years," and Minnie F. Abrams has been working there ever since.

Upon Minnie F. Abrams the Holy Spirit was poured out. She thought she had the baptism of the Spirit before, but the last four years Minnie F. Abrams has been baptized again and again. She has been filled with the Holy Spirit until she has spoken in tongues. She has sung a hymn of praise to the triune Jehovah in Hebrew, and she knows no Hebrew. Minnie F. Abrams has been wakened in the middle of the night so filled with the fire of the Holy Spirit she could hardly contain herself.

Ramabai has prayed out [into the mission field] twenty of these earnest, Christian women. She gives them no salary. She has not a penny. How could she promise salary? She said to me when she came to my home in Windsor, Nova Scotia, "People think I am a very rich lady, that I have great wealth, but the truth is I have nothing but my bible and a few clothes." She has the God of the bible, a God who owns all the gold mines and the diamond mines, and because she trusts in Him, He sends her the money.

Do you know the beautiful text she lives on hour after hour? A friend in England felt led of the Holy Spirit to send Ramabai this text, it is in the form of a bank check. "My God shall supply all your need according to His riches in glory by Christ Jesus." Phil. 4:19. And so day by day she takes that beautiful check up to the big Banker and tells Him it is His word, and has His signature on it, and she tells Him her need for each day and claims the promise. . . .

Ramabai has to pray for six hundred dollars a week. Even then she cannot afford to give them so much as rice. It costs too much. If you had nothing to eat today but rice you would feel pretty hungry, and yet Ramabai cannot even afford rice. She gives them the cheapest food, the jowari and barjeri. They never drink coffee or tea, only water.

Could you make one hundred and eleven jackets out of ninety yards of cotton? I have never met an English person or any American who could, but Pundita Ramabai could, and she did.

A few years ago she prayed for some time for a very big thing. She wanted a lot of churns and other things for her dairy. She prayed God would send them to her, and they came. Then another time she said, "If only I had a printing press where I could print testaments, and the gospels and tracts." She prayed for them and God heard that prayer, and sent her the printing press and the type. She sends out from Mukti thousands upon thousands of those beautiful books that tell about God's mighty works....

Some years ago Ramabai's girls came to her and said, "Ramabai, it is so cold in the morning, our blankets are so thin, they are nothing more than rags." She said, "Girls, where do I get my blankets? You must pray for blankets." They did pray. Class after class began to pray for blankets.

They sent word, "We are praying for blankets." She taught them what it means to pray and get an answer; that they must be obedient, must meet the conditions. You and I cannot get answers to prayer unless we are keeping the conditions. God doesn't answer prayer unless we obey Him. We must abide in Him and His word must abide in us. So Ramabai taught these girls if they wanted blankets they must obey the Lord, they must live holy lives; they must do right to each other and put sin out of their lives, and God would answer their prayers.

One day she went on the platform and said. "Girls, how many of you have prayed for blankets? I have just received this letter. I will read it to you:"

Dear Ramabai:

I was praying the other day and I got such a vision of Jesus. I never saw him so wonderful. His love seemed to fill me until my heart overflowed. Oh He was so precious to me! He filled me with His glory. And I said, Lord let me do something to show Thee how I love Thee.

That is love, isn't it, when you want to do something to prove it? So the Lord took her at her word and said, "Send Pundita Ramabai six hundred pounds." That was $3,000. This dear woman had a draft written out to pay Ramabai six hundred pounds sterling. Ramabai has never been able to write and thank that sister. She signed herself, "One of His." I could show you the entry in one of Ramabai's [account] books....

In this church in India they are seeing God do wonderful things. Talk about healings! These girls get healings every day. They know what it is to pray the prayer of faith that saves the sick. They have had demons cast out. They have had visions of Jesus. They have seen the very heavens on fire with the promises of God. Numbers of them have seen in letters of fire, "Jesus is coming soon," written in the heavens. Oh doesn't it make you feel glad that He is coming? I feel so happy when I think of it. The last letter I got from Ramabai, began, "Dear Sister, Jesus is coming soon."

These girls know what it is to wait in prayer and get the baptism in the Holy Ghost. They have prayed whole nights before going out to those raging, raving, idolatrous people. A hundred of her girls were in the city of Pandharpur, the worst city in India in some respects. They took their stand before the heathen and began to sing of the precious blood of Jesus that cleanses from all sin.

As they were witnessing one day, a man took a brick and struck the eye of one of these dear girls, and she said, "Oh, I shall be blind." The pain for a minute was awful. Then she said, "the Holy Spirit seemed to well up in me, and He gave me such a prayer for that man. I said, 'Oh Father, forgive him, he knew not what he did.' Jesus healed my eye that minute, and let them see there was a living Christ." Then the heathen said she was a god.

Another day a man threw a live scorpion right among our girls. They have bare feet and the scorpion's sting is intensely painful. They said, "We will stop their preaching," and our girls as they saw the scorpion wriggling along said, "We know what the promise is, if we call on the name of Jesus it shall not hurt us." These girls stood in the all-victorious name of Jesus, and they were not stung by the scorpion. . . . Miss Abrams is worn out, and other workers have had to leave for a rest, and there is our dear Ramabai all alone. . . . Pray for us all. (*TLRE*, Nov., 1908)

*Book Editor*: This reminds me of the stories of the orphan boys in China of the same era that was written about by the missionary H. A. Baker, in his book, *Visions Beyond the Veil*.

## What God is Doing in South Africa
### John G. Lake

I feel that we are but reaping the result of the prayers of a multitude of precious saints of God, whose prayers have gone before, and have followed us night -and day. At the Missionary Training Home, Alliance, Ohio, the entire school spent one hundred and twenty days and nights in continuous prayer for missions.

I have felt that from the day my foot touched African soil, I passed under an anointing of God hitherto unknown by me. God promised me in a message from heaven the second night I was in Africa, that Salvation should flow as a tide, and the healing of our God as a mighty river, and verily it is so. I have a pile of testimonies of marvelous healings in answer to the prayers of the congregation such as I have never seen before anywhere, in the same period of time.

In my personal work it has not been my experience as in former times to preach conviction for sin upon people by long and hard effort. The Spirit of Cod has already convicted them. On Thursday last I visited three homes; fourteen persons were converted, and four instantly healed, one of them a woman that had a tumor of twenty pounds weight.

Under this new anointing that came upon me as I reached South Africa, I have been enabled to take hold of God with a living faith that I never before possessed in the same degree. We have ceased to ask people before praying for them, whether they are Christians. We have simply accepted the commission as given in Luke 9:1-6 and Mark 11:22-26, and have assumed that when Jesus spoke these words He spoke them to the disciples and not to the people.

Seventy-five percent out of every hundred who come are healed. To lay your hands on a woman with dropsy, with legs as large as a big stove pipe, and see them diminish and become natural while you pray has been the experience of the past week, a Hebrew at that.

To see a tumor of twenty pounds burst and run off as you pray is another manifestation of the power of God.

This week I have seen the blind receive their sight, the deaf hear, and the paralyzed walk. One day my wife and I prayed for a girl who was paralyzed for seven years. She immediately rose and walked two hundred feet. The following day Brother Tom and I prayed for a woman who had not stood on her feet for nine years. She immediately rose and walked. Mrs. Dr. Davey of Vryheid, writes me that she has seen one hundred people healed in a day in that place.

As the first member of our Board of Trustees the Lord gave us a Mr. Schumann, the editor of the Transvaaler, an independent secular Dutch paper with a weekly circulation of 5,000. One time in his life he had been an ordained Dutch preacher, but became a notorious drunkard, demon possessed and unable to control himself. The demons were cast out, God saved him, and he at once resumed his place as editor of the Transvaaler, and there has been added to the paper a four-page religious supplement, entirely devoted to this work.

Praise God, He is moving! Another is the Rev. van de Wal, at one time a very influential Dutch Reformed preacher in South Africa and the head of the Dutch Reformed College at Capetown. He had been a drunkard for ten years. God saved him. He is a strong preacher of the precious blood that has delivered him.

Rev. von Marle, a Hollander who never had a conversion under his ministry, but since he has been baptized in the Holy Spirit, conversions occur in every meeting. Some of the most marvelous healings occur under this man's ministry.

God has given us a wonderful boldness of faith such as I never knew before. To illustrate, last Sunday night a hypnotist who had a patient with what he called extreme rheumatism, brought her to the meeting. He sat on the front seat with a hard-looking crowd of followers. He gives performances at the theatres, but had not been able to help this girl at all; she was a great sufferer.

I told her to come up on the platform which she did with assistance, and asked her to point out the hypnotist to me. I showed the people that hypnotism was not just the exercise of a natural faculty, but a natural faculty energized by Satan, just as a baptized child of God is energized by the Holy Spirit; that Satan hypnotizes, but Jesus heals. He laughed at this.

I went on to emphasize "Greater is He that is in you, than he that is in the world." We prayed for the young woman. She was instantly delivered from all suffering. I told her to walk. She walked about the platform praising God.

Then I said to the hypnotist, "In the name of the Son of God you'll hypnotize no more," and leaning over the front of the platform commanded the demon in Jesus' name to come out of him. I said, "Hypnotize now, if you can." He said, "Do you mean to tell me I can't?" He worked at it all night, but accomplished nothing. Early in the morning he came to my home, and said, "This thing is my bread and butter, I have engagements at the theatres," and wanted me to give him back the power to hypnotize.

We finally had prayer together. He left under great conviction for sin, but had not yielded to God. Johannesburg, Sept. 12, 1908. (*TLRE*, Nov., 1908)

> *Book Editor*: Some people might say that he did wrong by casting the demon out of someone who was not saved, but Apostle Paul did the same to the girl who was following him who was saying, "These men are servants of the Most High God, who are telling you the way to be saved" (Acts 16:17).

\*\*\*

A man who was a Jew and had heard of the baptism in the Holy Spirit and speaking in tongues, expressed himself as desirous of seeing a young girl, whom he knew, when the power of God was especially upon her. He said he didn't believe it, but was curious to hear some one speak in tongues. One day while this young girl was in travail for souls he came into her home. We do not doubt the Lord brought him. The girl was perfectly oblivious to her surroundings and did not recognize him, but as he came into the room she raised up and pointed to heaven. The Jew came over to her to listen, and he became perfectly white in the face, and said, "My God, I understand what she is talking about." Part of the time she was praying for him, then she sang a psalm. She told him that his Messiah had come, and unless he accepted Jesus he would be lost. He said she spoke in the Slavonic language. (*TLRE*, Nov., 1908)

\*\*\*

During the Convention some people who were in the city met a poor woman on the street, and upon questioning her they found she was seeking some one to pray with her. They took her into the home where they were staying. She. told them her father was an infidel, her husband a spiritualist, and that she was sinful and wanted God. While in prayer, the Holy Spirit spoke in the unknown tongue with the interpretation commanding the evil spirits to come out of her. She was wonderfully delivered. She wept for joy that she had found salvation through Jesus and that God was her Father. She came into that home heavy with her burden of sin, and left it with a heart lightened by the love of Jesus. (Ibid)

## A Helpful Vision, In a Sculptor's Studio [Main part]

I have had many lessons in the days that are passed. One day I was thinking about the wonderful things God had done, and I thought how good God was, He was with us all the time. But God said to me, "That is not Jesus; it is only His works." God wants us to glorify Jesus Himself.

He doesn't want us to be on dress parade, showing off His gifts, but to live the life of Jesus, to glorify His name by doing the works that He did, or letting Him work through us. When we bear the fruit of the Spirit, and the gifts of the Spirit are manifested, we glorify God the Father and exalt Jesus Christ, because people know there is a real Christ in us. It is so blessed to have the Spirit poured out into our beings, His temples! Oh what a wonderful thing it is to converse with Jesus Christ, to talk with the Master, to eat of the Bread of Life. He will give you the fresh bread, the fresh manna every day.

Oh that men would praise the Lord, and magnify His holy Name! Get down low at His feet. Get down where He can speak to you. Put away the things of the flesh, the things of men, and magnify the name of Jesus Christ, for in Him only have ye life. If you eat the body and drink the blood of Jesus Christ, you have life within yourselves. You have to eat the Word. Let the Spirit of God reveal the word to you. Let Him make known the mysteries of God. Then you will have life within yourselves. . . .

I think God would have me tell what He gave me this morning. I was in sweet communion with Jesus, and He closed me in with Himself. He was so precious. After communing with Him a long time, it seemed to me I was taken out of the spirit of communion and placed in a sculptor's studio, where I saw a block of marble that had the semblance of a man. The sculptor had chiseled it into the form of a man, but it was still very crude. There was nothing very beautiful about it. It was very dark gray. I said, "Lord, what does this mean?" but I got no answer.

At first I saw only the marble, but as I looked down at the foot of the statue I saw a man working at the feet, chiseling the little fine lines in this marble. At first I did not recognize Him as Jesus, for it was He. I saw only the sculptor as Mary in the garden saw only the gardener. Suddenly the Sculptor took the chisel and put it right on the shoulder. There seemed to be a little raised part there that needed to be removed, and a little chip flew off. I said to myself, "Methinks that looks very much like the chip people carry on their shoulders, that they are very sensitive about; their own opinions which they like to have people touch that they may have something to talk about."

Back to the feet the Sculptor went. He was chiseling little fine lines into the lower part of this marble. I watched the process and I thought, why doesn't He work on the face and bring out its beauty? He kept on working at the feet, drawing the lines and marking them, and chiseling out the marble, and I saw the dust of the marble fly away. Then He who was kneeling arose, and I saw it was Jesus. He took a bowl and poured something over this marble, and I said, "Oh, the blood! the blood!! Now it will be beautiful and white." It was so gray before. But to my surprise there were gray spots and marks in it yet, and I said, "Why is that, Lord?" And He said, "You have to come for, the cleansing blood every day." *That which the blood touched was perfectly white*. It is a continuous process getting under the blood every day.

Then He took some more off the shoulder, that sensitive point. He wants us to get all the sensitiveness out of us, get all our opinions out, and let Jesus have His way. Just let Jesus be glorified in this place. He said we were in His studio and He wanted us to get away from doctrines and opinions, to Himself.

Then He put the bowl down and resumed work upon the feet. I wondered why He was not working upon the face of the image, and I said, "Why is it, blessed Master, you are not working on the face?" It seemed as if the feet were not of so much consequence, but He said, "I want the feet prepared with the messages of the gospel of peace, to go forth in my vineyard. They must fit the sandals." Then He brought to me this verse:

"How beautiful upon the mountains are the feet of him that bringeth good tidings, that publisheth peace?"

I said, "Isn't it precious that the Master would want our feet to be just such shape that they fit the gospel of peace? Every time He took a chip off the shoulder He put His finger in the precious blood and touched the spot and healed it. He wants to heal every sore-spot with His blood, as He takes out of us what He doesn't want there.

Every time He took the chisel He reached the hand into the bowl with the blood, and made it smooth and white, gently, oh so gently He touched the marble. I never can forget how tender He was! I said, "Lord, why is it you do not bring out the beauty of the face?" And He said, "That can only come through the inward graces. While I am working on the outside, I am dwelling within the temple, and out of it shall come that which will beautify the face and make it blessed." He said, "My people have been too much on dress parade. *They have been parading my gifts, and I want them to get down where they will have the inward graces, and grow up having the image of Jesus in their face*s."

He said He wanted to make these garments to suit Himself, and that people should not fasten their eyes upon the garments they wore [speaking spiritually].

He said He had called this Convention to take off many chips, and many times He used the chisel on that shoulder. Many times He put the chisel on me. He said we were not yet in the clay to be molded; we were marble, so hard He had to use a chisel on us, and He wanted to get us where we would be pliable, where He could mold us according to His image. I never shall forget the tenderness of the touch of His chisel.

As the blood flowed over the figure, there were some places that remained gray, and the Sculptor with His pierced hands applied the blood to them especially, and they became white. The heart out of which the blood flowed was filled with compassion, and He wants us to have the same love that was in Him.

After the vision passed, I asked Him what He wanted me to read. He gave me the 5th of Matthew:

"Blessed are the poor in spirit: For theirs is the kingdom of heaven. Blessed are the meek; For they shall inherit the earth."

Those "Blesseds" were the inward graces that made us like Jesus in the face. Oh it was wonderful that He taught me that beautiful lesson about Jesus not being on dress parade. He said, "Let your dress be a meek and quiet spirit, and in Him shall be your rest and confidence."

The Lord told me that the reason I did not recognize Him was because He came, oftentimes, in the hand of my brother whom He sent to me. God wants us to get away from demonstrations, to Jesus Christ. I was wondering why my joy was waning; I did not have the joy in the demonstrations I had. I found the secret of joy was in Jesus Christ, and in Him alone. Jesus wants to use the gifts in His own way, but He doesn't want us to parade them.

[At this time, the Holy Spirit interrupted the woman speaking and spoke through tongues and interpretation of tongues, to those in the church:]

**Voice of the Spirit:** [tongues interpreted]

> The Lord thy God would have thee obey His holy word, to walk in His way, to do that which is pleasing in His sight, to exalt His Son, magnify the name of Jesus. God created you in His own image, to glorify Jesus in the temple which He created. God would have you seek His face in all things, seek His holy counsel. Walk lowly and humbly at His feet, willing to be crucified, willing to pay the price, willing to give up all for Jesus, exhibiting His love and power,

getting away from the trifling things of this world; exhibiting the love and power and liberty that there is in Christ Jesus. Glorify ye your King and praise His holy Name.

[She continued speaking:]

Jesus is hovering over this place, and He will manifest Himself if we hold Him up . . . May God keep us low at the cross where we can know His will, and where the cleansing goes on and on, and on. His word says, "cleanseth you;" that means continually under the precious blood.

May God magnify and glorify Himself in this people, and keep us always under the blood. -- Mrs. Elma Jaques, at the Convention, Oct. 23. (*TLRE*, Nov., 1908)

**Jesus the Way, the Truth and the Life:** (excerpt)

Noise is not power. Physical manifestations are not power. Our seminaries think they have to manufacture ministers having oratorical and intellectual power, but it is the power of the Holy Spirit we need.

Some say, what is the use in speaking in tongues? The Word says, the speaking in tongues first edifies the speaker, and oh brethren, when we get so near God that He can control every muscle of our being, our tongue, too, and just let the heavenly message flow through us, it is like rivers of water flowing from the throne of God, and you feel you are lifted and brought into the very presence of God.

I remember the morning He took hold of me. As I awoke my whole being was under the control of Jesus, and for an hour I praised Him with all my heart in my mother tongue, and then when I began to speak in the unknown tongue, I just praised God that He could do such a thing for a worm of the dust. There was such a filling, such a flooding of God. It was immersion; wave after wave flowed over me and through me. . . . .

I saw the utility of speaking in tongues beautifully illustrated in Pueblo [Colorado], a city of sixty thousand people. Over twenty languages are spoken there at the Bessemer Iron Works. There were Poles, and Russians, and Slavs and Jews, Chinese and Japanese; in fact, there were twenty nationalities, and they would stand on the street before the big mills and listen as the missionaries stood there and sang, and some of them would speak in tongues. There were little groups of Russians here and there. A sister came up to a group of Greeks, and she said, "Lord, let me speak in the Greek language," and a beautiful language flowed off in a message to them, and they said they understood her. I never saw the beauty of it as I did there. And some of them would come into the mission and cry to God for mercy.

One night while we were in the South, a girl spoke in an unknown tongue, and she wondered why she could not speak in English. The Lord took her English from her. Finally after speaking for about ten minutes she sat down. When we gave the altar call, a poor Mexican came [to the front], and he said, "Oh I sinner. I Catholic, that woman spoke in Spanish, God said I a sinner, I must be saved." That man gave his heart to God. -- Gilbert E. Farr, at the Convention Oct. 20. (*TLRE*, Nov. 1908)

## Confirming the Word by Signs Following

F. F. Bosworth

While in South Bend [Indiana] where we had been holding meetings for several months, Brother Fockler and I were clearly led of the Lord to leave South Bend to come to Plymouth, a beautiful little city of about five thousand. How I praise Him that not only will He "direct our path" but that even "the steps of a good man are ordered of the Lord."

I am asking Him to bring me into such blessed and intimate fellowship with Himself, that whether by a vision, a dream, an angel, or by the direct Voice of the Holy Spirit and the Word, which is best of all, I may get His orders for every step. I worship Him that the "exceeding greatness of His power" is "to usward who believe," and that "He is able to do exceeding abundantly above all that we ask or think." I can ask and think of Him opening my spiritual ears to hear His voice, and "enlightening the eyes of my understanding" to know "what is the riches of the glory of His inheritance in the saints," and cause my soul to "delight itself in fatness"; in fact to heal every deformity of my soul. Praise His Holy Name!

We obeyed the leading of the Spirit and pitched our tent in Plymouth in the latter part of June. Brother Fockler remained here about five weeks, when Miss Jean Campbell was led of God to come. When she left He clearly led Miss Edith Baugh and Miss Bernice Lee to come from New York City.

Realizing that "we wrestle not against flesh and blood. . . . but against the rulers of the darkness of this world, against wicked spirits in the heavenlies," during the early part of these meetings God put upon me a great burden of prayer to plead the blood of Jesus and pray that He would send a stream of His power upon the city which would penetrate through the darkness and drive back the spiritual foes, so that He might work. Late one night as I thus prayed, God gave me a beautiful vision. I saw plainly a stream of the most intensely white light, reaching as high as I could see and widening as it came down covering the city. In this light I could see multitudes of the Heavenly Host both coming and going, while just outside this cone-shaped light, on either side, was the most intense darkness. We prayed that God would expel from the city the wicked spirits which stir up the people to fight God's work, and thus far we have had little opposition.

Not only in the tent and in the hall, but also in the large street meetings, even while teaching the deeper truths of divine healing and the baptism in the Holy Spirit, there has been the most respectful attention. We have never taught the people to expect anything more than the glory and power of the Lord and the "unknown tongue" to accompany the immersing in the Holy Spirit, so there has never been the slightest tendency towards fanaticism or extremes from the beginning, and nothing has occurred that has not been edifying.

When the meetings began, God led us to work for the salvation of the unsaved, rather than teaching His deeper truths, and many gave themselves to Him, something so unheard of in this place for years that thus we gained the good-will of many of the people. Then when we began teaching them regarding the Latter

Rain Baptism in the Holy Spirit, it seemed to be accepted by nearly all who came to the meetings.

In almost every service God confirms His Word by causing some one to speak in other tongues, and also to interpret the words thus spoken. Both the unknown tongue and the interpretations have been identified by some in the audience. They have heard the gospel "in their own tongue wherein they were born." Miss Campbell has been understood several times as the Spirit has spoken through her in the unknown tongue.

Last Friday night we conducted a service in LaPaz, Indiana, in the United Brethren church. God gave us a blessed service, and as Miss Lee was speaking the precious Holy Spirit spoke through her in German, every word of which was understood by a German lady in the audience. It was the first time she had ever heard anyone speak in the unknown tongue. The lady, although a Christian, became deeply convicted, and a great longing came into her heart for a deeper experience. That night as she retired, she was unable to sleep. She arose and knelt by the side of her bed, and as she yielded herself fully to God, the room which was so dark that she could not see her hand before her face, became perfectly light so she could see all the objects in the room. The glory of God filled her soul, and as she continued to praise Him, the room was lit up by His presence again and again. In the morning she came to the hotel where we were stopping, and with tears of joy told her wonderful experience, and how she had understood every word spoken in the unknown tongue. She remembered nearly all the message which began with the twenty-third Psalm and ended by saying that He had called the speaker to deliver the message which was on the subject of the "Latter Rain" and the imminent Coming of Jesus.

We praise Him for giving this sign in the very first meeting. We had services there again Monday and Tuesday evenings, and the people are insisting that the meetings continue. The minister took a seat in the congregation, and said, "go ahead, I want to keep out of the way." He is now seeking the baptism.

In regard to the meetings here, many have been saved, demons have been cast out in the Name of Jesus, others have been wonderfully and instantly healed in answer to the "prayer of faith," while God's hungry ones are being baptized in the Holy Spirit and fire, and are speaking in other tongues in according with Acts 2:4. Fire, seen with the natural eye, has fallen upon some at the time they have been immersed in the Holy Spirit. One night in the tent a large ball of fire came into the tent and fell upon the head of a brother who came that day from Mishawaka to seek for the baptism in the Holy Spirit. At the very instant the ball of fire fell upon him, he magnified God with a loud voice, and in a language which he had never learned, while the audience looked on in amazement and in tears. He found the Lord in a cottage meeting in Mishawaka while we were holding services there.

Last week a sister living here who has been earnestly seeking for the enduement of power, who over and over again has received wonderful anointings when her soul would be flooded with the glory of God, was awakened by the Spirit at three o'clock in the morning, and saw what seemed like a half bushel of "tongues of fire" falling right into her face and all over her body. Her soul was so flooded with the power and glory of God that she arose and praised Him until morning.

One night a few weeks ago, while the people were standing for dismissal, God pressed me to urge them to much closet prayer, and while I was speaking His Spirit fell on me in greater power than I had ever before experienced, and spoke in a loud voice in another language, which He interpreted through one of the other workers. While the Spirit yet spake through me, the power of God fell upon a sister from LaPaz exactly as He did upon the household of Cornelius Acts 10:44-46. Instantly she began to address the audience with a loud voice, speaking a beautiful message which was also interpreted by the sister on the platform. We knew God had baptized her "for we all heard her speak in tongues and magnify God." The glory of God that accompanied her mighty baptism in the Spirit so blinded her that she could see nothing until she was through speaking.

Soon after coming here, three of us united in prayer one evening asking God to deliver a man from the insane asylum. For years he had been possessed by a demon and had to be kept in the Logansport Asylum. God heard our cry that evening and in a few days we had the joy of seeing him come into the tent with his mother. This was five months ago and he is still out and working.

The tent which easily seated three hundred was at times too small, people coming by train from South Bend, Mishawaka, and other nearby towns; some drove by team as far as twenty-two miles.

We are taking no collections and it is beautiful to see God supply us day by day out of an unseen store-house. How sweet to live like the sparrows.

In closing will say that I take no credit for anything which God has done here, and only give the above facts that He may be glorified. (*TLRE*, Dec., 1908)

\*\*\*

A lady from Springfield, Il., was visiting in Chicago. In the home where she was visiting a woman received the baptism in the Holy Spirit and began to speak in the unknown tongue. She walked over to the visitor, who was a stranger to her, put her arm around her, and talked to her a long while in the unknown tongue, then left the room. When she was gone, someone asked the visitor if she understood her, and she said: "Why, of course, I did, she was talking Latin." She said she told her about heaven and what we must do to get there. The woman whom God used does not know Latin. (*TLRE*, Dec., 1908)

## An Inspiring Night's Service: (excerpt)

While we were singing "I need Thee every hour," the one sitting at the instrument struck up a strain of heavenly music, the Holy Spirit guiding the fingers into a harmonious accompaniment.

Strain after strain of inspired music floated out over the audience. It was the wooing of the Spirit drawing us to God and filling our hearts with worship and deepest adoration to Him who purchased for us the right to enter into the Holy of Holies.

In the harmony of the Spirit we were led into the beautiful chorus of worship,

"Oh come let us adore Him,
Oh come let us adore Him,
Oh come let us adore Him,
Christ the Lord."

As we sang the last line, the Spirit again took up the strain in the unknown tongue in a beautiful, impromptu melody, the song carrying the voice far above the natural range [this is another example of the Heavenly choir].

It seemed as though in Spirit we soared up to the very gates of heaven, then back to earth again, as we took up the refrain, "For He alone is worthy! For He alone is worthy! For He alone is worthy! Christ the Lord." The singing in the unknown tongue and the refrain alternated many times, as the Spirit led, until the whole room was filled with the presence and glory of God.

While the Spirit of God never lifted, the meeting took a different turn and linked the supernatural with the practical, the heights of glory with the daily cares and crosses, showing us that the joys of the world to come would only be attained by our helping to alleviate the sorrows of a sin-cursed world, and by pointing the lost to the One who is mighty to save.

The Spirit led a sister to tell of a dream which God gave her to deepen her love for the unsaved:

## A Remarkable Dream

### Mrs. Eugene Nix

I pray that God will impress you tonight as He impressed me last night, with the seriousness of being a Christian, especially in these days. Last night when it came time for me to retire I could not sleep. I was troubled in spirit. I lay down, but was restless. I arose and walked the floor.

Finally I became quiet, and God began to bring to my mind relatives and near friends to whom I had never said a word about the coming of Jesus. I said, "Lord, they would never listen to me." He said, "You have never even sent them THE LATTER RAIN EVANGEL." I said, "Lord, they wouldn't read it."

Just then I seemed to go to sleep and had either a dream or a vision, I don't know what it was. In spirit I was in the home of one who was very dear to me. I think the Lord wanted to show me the condition of the ungodly world and that I had not prayed as much as I should have for the unsaved.

This home that I saw was filled with people. Two men seemed to be contending for power. They were the only ones at first who were fighting, and every time they hit each other the blood would flow. Gradually all in the room were drawn into the fight, until there was terrible confusion there. They were screaming and groaning and wailing. The air was so stifling I could not stand it.

I said, "This is no place for me," and went down stairs to get a wrap, thinking I would go out. There was a man and his wife in the room below. He said to me, "What is the matter upstairs?" I said I didn't know. They said, "We are going up." The thought came to me I might be a help to a very dear one that was there, and

## Messengers of An Outpouring

I started to go along. The screams and the groans continued, never stopped for a minute. The blood was running down the steps and covered everything. As I started up the stairs something seemed to stop me. God said, "IT IS TOO -LATE, THE DOOR IS SHUT. YOU CANNOT GO."

While I stood on the steps the wall became transparent and I could see into the room. They lay on the floor in all positions, wounded from head to foot. Their screechings and their groanings I shall never forget. They have been with me all day, and I hope they will continue to ring in my ears, until I fully realize my responsibility to my fellow-men. All the messages from the Holy Spirit, and all the glory I have ever had never gave me the desire to see sinners saved as this has.

When I awoke it seemed as though my very flesh quivered from the fear and the awfulness of the scene. God said to me, "This is the tribulation." Then I said, "Lord I will send them the EVANGEL or do anything you want me to do." Jesus came to this earth from His home in glory, and we know nothing of what it meant to Him. He spilled His blood for us and we cannot sit down and sing ourselves away to everlasting bliss. We have to do something for Him. It will not be without regret even to go with Jesus in the rapture if we have not done our duty and tried to save others.

As I was writing postal cards the other day inviting some people to come to the services, God stopped me and said, "You haven't prayed. It will do no good unless you pray." Then He asked me if I believed Him. He told me I had better send half the number and pray than to send what I was sending and not trust Him to bless them. He showed me that it was useless to do work for Him *unless we believed and looked to Him in faith for results*. I said, "Oh God, I will do anything if only I can be saved from the blood of these people."

I often thought God was not just to allow people to suffer in this way. Then He gave me this illustration: If you were on a ship and the captain came to you and said, "Now here is a broad plank, you can go down this way but it is bound to sink. It is broad, you can take your friends with you and have a good time, but it will go down. Here is another plank. It is narrow, you will have to go alone, you are sure to get to land, but you can take no one with you."

Then God said to me, "Could they go to the captain of that ship, and say that he was unjust?" He had already told them and pointed out the two ways, just what God is doing through His word. He shows us the two ways, the broad and the narrow, and He permits us to choose.

I hope God will put in all our hearts what He has put in mine today. Messages in tongues cannot do it, ecstasy and glory cannot do it. God has put into my heart today a love for sinners, and by His help I will pray until they are won into the Kingdom. We all have dear ones. God showed me that I should take one person on my heart, if I could only pray for one, but to pray and believe until that one was brought to Him. Jesus' blood was shed for them as well as for us. I never felt so honored in my life as I have today, to think that Jesus saved me, but I am saved because someone told me of Jesus, and we too must tell others.

We all look forward to the coming of Christ as a wonderful victory for us. It will be, but how will it be for us to be taken up with Him, and know that our loved

## 1909

**The Lord for the Body:**
In a report of the convention at Elim House, Rochester, N. Y., a worker from Holland testified to the healing power of the Lord, saying that he had been healed of consumption, of weakness of the eyes, and had perfect healing of his teeth, after they had gone into decay. Praise God for that testimony. Not many have taken victory over decayed teeth, but since they are a part of the body, He will show us this too. (*The Bridegroom's Messenger*, March 1, 1909)

## The First One to Speak in Tongues:
[as it was then believed in 1909]
Miss Agnes Ozman

In the fall of 1900 I went to a Bible School in Topeka, Kansas. We studied the Word and had much prayer, not only in the school and in our rooms, but also in the Prayer Tower, where a constant vigil of prayer was kept up day and night.

At this school I had many feasts with the Master, while I sought to make a full surrender to God.

Much time was given to meditating upon His Word and in praying for the whole world. A mission was conducted in the down-town district, cottage meetings were held, and house to house visitation carried on. The school was conducted on faith lines for we trusted the Lord to supply all our needs, which He bountifully did.

We were urged to seek for and to receive the promised baptism in the Holy Spirit. Our hearts became very hungry for his enduement. We prayed earnestly and also fasted, as the Lord laid it upon us. During the last days of 1900 we had a special season of waiting before God, and He gave us blessed times of refreshing. Indeed, about three weeks before this, while three of us girls were in prayer, I spoke three words in another tongue. While I did not understand this manifestation then as I do now, yet it was a very precious and sacred experience, and was treasured up in our hearts. Not feeling satisfied with the above experience and having a great burden within which I knew God could relieve, I decided, Jan. 1, 1901, to obey the Word and have hands laid upon me and prayer offered that I might receive the baptism in the Spirit. As this was done, I began to speak in an unknown tongue. Afterwards I saw my experience was somewhat similar to that in Ephesus, Acts 19:6.

After this I attended the mission with others and offered prayer, beginning in English, and then the Lord spoke through me, finishing the prayer in another tongue. One man who heard understood the language. It was very blessed to know that it was intelligible. This manifestation attracted much attention for it was new, and I was the first one to speak in tongues in these last days. How I longed for the people to behold Christ, and that through me, God might glorify

Himself! We searched the Word for light on the subject of speaking in tongues. I was surprised to find so much in the New Testament on that subject. When heaven's glory filled my soul, so that I spoke in tongues, I urged upon others *not to seek for tongues but for the baptism in the Holy Spirit.*

On January 3rd some thirteen others spoke in tongues during a time of waiting upon God. Other gifts were also manifested. "All these worketh the one and the same spirit, dividing to each one severally, even as he will." 1 Cor. 12:11.

Our school home was carried on by each one doing a portion of the work, and sometimes friction and disobedience was manifested, but during this visitation from heaven there were blessed unity and love. The glory of God was wonderful! Praise be to God the glory abides to this day.

A continual feast is in my soul as I feed on the Word and pour out my soul in prayer, both in the known and in the unknown tongue for the lost. As I speak in tongues, my soul is blessed and lifted up as in I Cor. 14:4, and I wish that all might so speak. My heart is burdened for the church and I would that more were prophesying or preaching. Since "there are diversities of workings but the same God" we do need to urge upon His children to be surrendered to Him so He may have more channels through whom to work. "We are witnesses of these things; and so is the Holy Spirit whom God hath given to them that obey Him." Acts 3:32.

Some time ago I tried but failed to have an article printed which I wrote calling attention to what I am sure God showed me was error. The article maintained that tongues was not the only evidence of the Spirit's Baptism. When that article was refused I was much tempted by Satan, but God again graciously showed me He had revealed it to me, and satisfied my heart in praying that He might reveal this truth to others who would spread it abroad.

For awhile after the baptism I got into spiritual darkness, because I did as I see so many others are doing in these days, rested and reveled in tongues and other demonstrations instead of resting alone in God.

My power to speak in tongues has not been lessened by giving up the errors which have become attached to this work, but instead it has increased. For all His blessings I praise Him.

I am looking for the blessed hope and appearing of the glory of the great God and our Savior Jesus Christ. (*TLRE*, Jan., 1909)

**Tumor and Peritonitis Healed:**

I was an invalid for more than three years and pronounced incurable by many physicians. My trouble was a tumor that had been growing for three years. I suffered agony, day after day; was not able to do my own work and was in bed half the time. I had grown very weak and thin, and was not able to wear any tight clothes.

The last doctor I had told me that unless I had an operation I would not live long, and that it would lead to something else, which it did this summer. I was taken down with peritonitis and was sick in bed for two months. I sent for Dr. Curtis and he said I couldn't live a week unless I had an operation. He gave me up in June, so I knew of nothing to do but pray. I sent for Mr. Piper to pray for me. He came to my house Monday afternoon, the day after the doctor gave me up to die.

I was suffering dreadfully with pain. He told me to believe that God would heal me and I gave myself to Him to do with me as He saw fit. Praise God, He heard our cry. The third day after I was prayed for, I could sit up in bed, and the swelling began to decrease. In a week I could walk around the house. I continued praying to God and grew better all the time. I am now in perfect health. The tumor has gone and my size is normal. I can do all my work.

I thank God for His goodness. I now know He is willing to help every one that asks in faith. -- Mrs. Rosy Carroll, Chicago. (*TLRE*, Jan., 1909)

**Healed of Ovarian Tumor:**
Two years ago two physicians pronounced my trouble an ovarian tumor, and said there was no help for me but to submit to a surgical operation, and that immediately.

My husband and I talked the matter over; I have always been opposed to surgical operations, and I finally decided that if I must die, I would die with my body whole. About this time, through the influence of a dear friend in Chicago, I began praying to God to heal me. Both my friend and my husband united with me in prayer.

In July, 1907, while visiting in Chicago I was prayed for at the Stone Church, and while I cannot say I was instantly healed, yet I have been improving and steadily ever since, and no evidences of the tumor remain.

I have taken no medicine nor consulted any physician since July, 1907, and I am able to do practically all my own housework. It is a pleasure to me, instead of a burden as was the little work I was able to do two years ago. A number of years ago I entrusted my spirit to the care and keeping of our Heavenly Father, and now I am trusting my body to the same kind and watchful care.

When the physician told me I could not live without an operation it was a severe blow to me, and the future looked very dark, but our faith in God's love and power finally triumphed through Jesus Christ, and I give Him the glory and praise for the health and other blessings that I now enjoy. -- Mrs. L. N. Medsker, Fort Wayne, Ind. (*TLRE*, Jan., 1909)

**Himself Took Our Infirmities and Bare Our Sicknesses:**
About five years ago I was taken with swelling of my limbs. They pained me greatly. I could not walk up and down stairs without almost shrieking with pain. My feet and limbs felt as if I was walking through ice-water.

Someone told me if I went to the Wesley hospital I would surely be healed, as there was a man there who was a specialist in my trouble. I went there twice a week and received no help whatever. They said it was rheumatism [arthritis] and varicose veins.

I sold my flat [apartment] and went to St. Paul, thinking if I should go to my old physician he could help me. When I told him my trouble he shrugged his shoulders and said; "Well, we can perform an operation, but I would not advise it at your age." They wanted to take some of the cords out of my limbs.

I was broken-hearted because I could find no relief. I came back to this city and heard that Christian Science was doing a great work, so I went to their meetings twice a week. I got their book and studied it, but didn't get any help at all in that way.

A sister came to my home to visit one of my roomers, and I told her of my condition. She said, "Go down to the Stone Church, I know you will be healed." I said I didn't believe it, I had been around so much and had given up hope. She said it wouldn't hurt me, and I should go with her. So I went one afternoon, and as soon as I entered the room it seemed as though I could feel the very presence of Jesus. I never went into a church in my life where I felt that God was so in the work. If ever I prayed in faith in my life I did that afternoon, and I knew I was going to be healed. All my doubts disappeared.

The pastor said to me, "Do you believe that God will heal you?" I almost yelled the answer, such a feeling of lightness came over me, it seemed as if the whole room was lit up with the glory of God. After prayer he said, "Now get up and walk!" I walked across the room, the pain was all gone, and I have never felt it since. I was healed in a moment. I had supposed that if I ever did get well it would be gradual, but it was all done at once, and I am just as well today and a great deal happier than I ever was in my life. Before I went there to services things used to worry me and make me unhappy, but that is all gone.

I have also been a great sufferer from neuralgia, have had it for twenty years; but God has also healed me of that. I can go to Him and He hears my prayer, for which I praise Him. -- Mrs. M. L. Blancher, Chicago. (*TLRE*, Feb., 1909)

**Atrophied Optic Nerve, Spinal Trouble, and Gastritis Healed:**

I praise God for victory through the blood of Jesus, and what He has done for me in the past four months. Until July, 1908, I had never had any deeper experience than conversion, but at that time while attending some special meetings held in this place, I received light on the full Gospel.

I had been an invalid for over three years and could find no relief through the best physicians. I had a complication of diseases, gastric ulceration of the stomach and other internal trouble; also spinal and head trouble. I was confined to my bed at least one-third of the time. I was pronounced incurable without an operation and had given up all hope of ever being healed. At the same time I had atrophy of the optic nerve and was almost blind. I had been told by some of the very best specialists that my case was hopeless and in two years I would be totally blind.

During these meetings I learned that our blessed Savior had made provision in His precious atonement to heal our bodies as well as to save us from sin. Prayer was offered for me with the laying on of hands, and my body was instantly healed. I have been perfectly well ever since. Later on, two sisters prayed for my eyes and anointed them that they might be healed. My sight was perfectly restored. I am now able to read my Bible without glasses, where before I had to wear the strongest of double-vision lenses, and could scarcely see with these. Praise His Holy Name for such a healing!

The same night my body was healed, God sanctified me and set me apart for His service. After my heart had been cleansed and I had been anointed by the Holy Spirit as a witness to my sanctification, the Lord gave me a deeper hunger and thirst for more of His life, and the baptism in the Holy Spirit in all its fullness. I felt the need of more power in prayer and more love for lost souls; a greater need for His Word and a deeper death to self.

On the 24th of September, 1908, I opened my heart and the Holy Spirit came in and took possession. Oh, such rest and peace! Such joy! Such heavenly, divine sweetness filled my soul! Rivers of living water flowed through me. Volume after volume of love and power seemed to take full possession of body, soul, and spirit.

In visions too beautiful and too sacred to describe, I traveled all over the missionary fields of India, China, Japan, Sweden, Africa, and Jerusalem, with my precious Savior. As I rose to go home from the meeting, the Holy Spirit spoke through me in another tongue for at least an hour. He also gave me the interpretation which was an exhortation to preach the Gospel to every creature; that Jesus was coming soon and we must work while it was day.

I am praising Him continually for the real evidences of this Pentecostal baptism, not only of speaking and singing in tongues, but for the enduement of power to glorify Jesus and witness for Him, and for the unspeakable joy I have in worshipping Him. How my heart goes out in prayer and intercession for lost souls and a perishing world! My heart is overflowing with love for poor, fallen humanity. I want to keep low at His feet and "walk worthy of the vocation wherewith He has called me." My only desire is that I may be dead to self, and that Christ shall live in me. -- Mrs. J. C. Ament, Tulsa, Ok. (*TLRE*, Feb. 1909)

**Some Manifestations of the Spirit Thirty-five Years Ago:**
Beloved, I feel I have a little message to deliver tonight. God has wonderfully blessed me directly and indirectly, through the Latter Rain Movement, and yet I have had more or less of it for a number of years. I remember the first time I was permitted to hear the voice of "tongues." It was thirty-five years ago and was in connection with other verities of the restored Gospel.

The question came to me in regard to water baptism, when [I was] a boy, "How shall I be baptized?" I found that the only "historical" baptism was trine, or triune baptism, and so I sought a dear good man of God -- the very man whom I had heard speak in tongues -- to baptize me. My baptism was "into the Name of the Father, and into the Name of the Son, and into the Name of the Holy Ghost." I was not baptized into the "Amen," but into the Name of the Triune God.

In connection with this same work, God was doing some wonderful things. A woman who was one of a band of disciples who worshiped God in Spirit and in Truth had smashed her elbow. I must use that word because that was what it was, literally. She smashed it completely. She sent for the elders of the church according to St. James 5:14-15. They prayed for her, and while praying they heard the bones snap together. One of the ministers who was present gave me the testimony, as also did the sister. The next day, to the wonder of all her neighbors, she did her washing, and her arm was well as long as she lived. Many other cases happened round about me, in the same town. . . . C. E. Preston, Shelbyville, Ill. Former Rector in the Episcopal Church. (Ibid)

## The Lord's Healing
### Lessons learned before healing came

*Book Editor*: This book contains several articles by Miss Elizabeth Sisson. Born in 1843, she was converted at age 20 in a Congregational church, then joined the Holiness movement. After working as a faith-supported Gospel worker for several years, she went to India as a missionary for the American Board of Commissioners for Foreign Missions, but later gave up her salary to become a faith-missionary.

Then she worked at Bethshan Healing home in London for a few years. She returned to the US in 1887, and held meetings and taught in a small office in Chicago with Elizabeth Baker. She also spoke at Christian and Missionary Alliance churches and conventions.

Then Miss Sisson became co-editor of *Triumphs of Faith* magazine from May 1889-1890, with Carrie Judd Montgomery. Then she worked with Maria Woodworth for a short time before going to New London, Connecticut, where she taught locally. She worked with healing evangelist Finis Yoakum in Los Angeles in 1901-2, then started her own mission.

In 1908 she began to travel and speak once again, after joining the Pentecostal movement. She also wrote some 140 articles for several different Pentecostal newspapers, and wrote several books and tracts. In 1915 she worked with F.F. Bosworth in Dallas for four months. She became an ordained minister with the Assembly of God in 1917, at age 74. She lived with her sisters in New London until her death in 1934 at age 91.

*One moment unable to turn in bed, expected to pass away in any one of the violent hemorrhages that almost choked me, sinking in death-weakness --- the next, walking the floor strong in the strength which God supplies through His beloved son!*

It was the 1st of August, 1908, that in St. Andrews, Scotland, whither I had gone to join other Christian workers in a gospel campaign, I was seized with a very heavy cold, aggravating an asthmatic tendency, which in those days always hung about me. For six weeks the cold deepened daily in consequence of being in a very raw cold climate, without the possibility of fire [heat] day or night. Soon I had developed a most fearful form of bronchial asthma with heart failure, and for weeks was unable to lie down or recline in a chair, the pulsation was so great in the whole body from the action of the heart.

Spiritually, I was much blessed and quickened in faith for my body, just before I was taken ill and was holding in God for full deliverance for two forms of chronic suffering, namely growths in the head, inducing a very acute catarrh, which in turn caused an asthmatic condition with extreme sensitiveness to every atmospheric change. Rom. 16:20: "God . . . shall bruise Satan under your feet shortly," had been made very precious to me. With it came marvelous [great] buffetings of the enemy. It was very difficult to pray or get light from God.

Occasionally He would burst through the intense darkness with a great illumination, as after I had given up thought of response to a call to Bombay for Pentecostal service, and said, "Thy will be done" to sickness instead, He gave me the whole of Ps. 18, with its promised answer to prayer, mighty power of God in deliverance, use of His delivered one, among the heathen. But as soon as His immediate presence was withdrawn, the hosts of the enemy closed in darker than ever upon me.

The light of the Word seemed literally swallowed up, in the torture of the sleepless nights and days. "This is your hour, and the power of darkness" was much of the time my one text. Later, God came again with I Isa. 54:11-17. Oh! the wealth of love, with which He said; "Oh thou afflicted, tempest-tossed and not comforted," and the power with which He said, "Behold, I will lay thy stones with fair colors," etc., down to the end of the chapter. I thought then I was to be immediately healed.

As the days became weeks, I could not understand the dealings of the Lord with me. The awful spiritual darkness increased. I seemed [to be] the tramping ground for demon hosts. The enemy hissed into my soul, how I had failed God and got off His ground, else I would be healed; or, taking another tack, how God had failed me, and broken all His promises. How He only mocked me, etc. I felt the malice of Satan would like to foreclose on my body, because God had by me proclaimed our privilege of "tarrying till Jesus comes," in a little tract by that name.

One of the darkest mornings, I had fallen into a little doze. I had no regular sleep -- but when sheer exhausted [I] caught five or eight minutes by dropping my head upon a table in front of me, and was wakened with Ps. 105:19, powerfully impressed upon me; "The word of the Lord tried him." -- (This had been the peculiar thrust of the devil that God's word had promised so much, but nothing materialized) -- "until the time of His word came," I saw as never before that there might be a time quantity in the promises of God.

I waited for morning light and my Bible that I might review the story of Joseph to which the Psalm referred. How truly it was "the word of the Lord," that tried him, as he was standing on the promises! It was this that got him into trouble when his brother sold him. It was this that thrust him into prison from Potiphar's house which prison was a university course in the school of God. We learn of "two full years" that he meditated there upon the fulfillment of "all the sheaves bowing down" to his sheaf, "sun, moon and stars" bowing down to the star Joseph, and the outcome of all was months lengthening into years (there may have been four or five of them for aught we know), as a criminal in an Egyptian dungeon!

Yes, the word of the Lord tried him and it seemed to be full intention of the Lord that His word should try Joseph. Could the lesson have been otherwise learned? Could the fine soul-qualities have been otherwise brought about? Could the faith and the patience over which God triumphantly declares "His bow abode in strength" (Gen. 49:24) have else developed? But the word of the Lord only tried him till the time of His word came -- then how everything changed? "The king sent and loosed him" and with me it was much the same. The King of kings sent and loosed me. But the time was not yet; I had lessons to learn, and though there was a glorious illumination that morning, I continued in my prison-house of pain and sank even lower.

One morning while suffering from frightful heart action [palpitations] the room was filled with brethren and sisters; some had come to see me die, but most to pray me through to health. Finally they sang the victory, and I was able gaspingly to join the chorus, and after hours of distress suddenly the heart became normal, we all praised the Lord, I was well. They left rejoicing. A few hours after other forms of illness set in, my head was again under water. Acute gastritis [stomach ulcer].

Through force of circumstances I had been carried more dead than alive from St. Andrews to Dunfermline, and thence to Edinburgh, and here the Lord began to talk to me of crossing the Atlantic. At first I could not make sure of His voice, and the journey look appalling. I could not walk across my bed chamber, nor dress, nor recline in a chair, nor lie in bed. The journey from Edinburgh to Liverpool alone was too formidable; from thence to steamer, the wide stretch of ocean -- the fatigue of the New York landing, then the rail to Connecticut [her home] alone. My whole never force was now exhausted [sic]. I could not contemplate it. But my Heavenly Father seemed to fairly coax me to it. In answer to prayer He gave courage and wonderfully helped me to pack, write, etc., and make all necessary arrangements. In fact, from the time that, leaning on His arm, I consented to go, there was continued marked improvement in health.

I sailed October 1st, having been unable for many days to take solid food. The increased suffering from nutriment was such, that on the 6th of October, I resolved to swallow no more till I reached home, where I arrived Oct. 10th. Among other things said to me by the Lord before leaving Edinburgh was; "You shall have a nice room to yourself on the steamer." I thought -- "Yes, when they see how ill I am, they will take me into the ship's hospital." But no! When about half over the voyage, the captain had an interview with me, and although I was a second class passenger in a room with three others, he gave me a first class left-over state room all to myself! We had a smooth passage and many mercies.

As soon as I reached home came the reaction from all the strain of the voyage. I fell into a bed from which I never arose till healed by the Lord the morning of Nov. 16. I only attempted liquid food, but nothing would stay on the stomach, and while various parties were recommending what they thought I could retain, a physician who had made a specialty of sick-diet was asked simply to give advice on food. The doctor consented to come for that purpose only. In a few days I had failed very rapidly -- took nothing but granulated ice -- and often for days together could not bear even that, and was living on air forced down my throat with two fans. Then, to ease the awful sufferings, a little medicine was given. I was too ill to know to care. Thus, the doctor was soon in two or three times a day.

Terrible hemorrhages caused by the gathering and breaking of ulcers in the stomach, would be preceded by most frightful sufferings all through the body. "Nerve storms," I called them. *The hemorrhages were so violent, the blood almost choked me as it poured from my throat, and so great was my exhaustion, that sometimes they would have to pick the great clots from my mouth and throat.* After every hemorrhage I would sink so low that they looked for me to pass away. With joy I hailed these times of exhaustion, thinking I was about to be admitted to the open presence of my Lord. The joy of the thought was great, for though I felt I was such a disappointment to God and to myself, in that I had failed to rise above illness into His Divine Life, and failed to give Him in myself, one for translation [ready for the Rapture], yet He made me constantly know how dear I was to Him, because of the blood on me, and how full was my acceptance with Him through that blood. I longed to meet His love and see His smile.

One night after profuse hemorrhages from both the throat and the bowels, (and, as I afterwards learned, while they were watching for the end) I seemed to slip the body, and be borne away into space. Oh, how much it meant to leave the tortured frame behind, and like a bird on glad wings, to be floating in the upper air! We rose high up above the earth, for I realized that "underneath were the everlasting arms." On these I rested as a bird upon wing. As we sped on, we passed far above a great city, in the full swing of civil celebration. Grand illuminations, bands of music, phalanx of soldiers; as we passed by, I thought "How feeble all this to the light of the glory of God, the heavenly music, the angelic hosts I shall soon be among! Then on and on we went, far out in outer darkness. We seemed to be passing with incredible speed through a night of limitless space, impenetrable gloom, but like a babe nestling in the dark, in the warm arms of motherlove, I only reveled in the Spirit-comfort of the God-arms that bore me on. Whether this was vision, dream, or the fancies of a sick brain, I know not, but toward morning I found myself again in the sick chamber, the bed, the tortured body -- but this I do know, there was a spiritual joy in God from that hour on, of which the enemy was never able to rob me.

As I woke to consciousness, I whispered to my sister, what had transpired, and mournfully added, "I never expected to come back here." *It was a terrible disappointment, and to bear this new phase of God's will I had to cry for fresh grace.* Thus, again and again, I sank so low only to revive measurably, till it seemed to me, I could not die (and no wonder! so many holding on by faith for my healing as I afterwards learned). I felt like old King Saul (2 Sam. 50:9), though I dared not pray his prayer, "Stand upon me and slay me," but against every inclination was helped to cry "Thy will be done."

Shall I ever forget the 15th of Nov., 1908! That was the darkest day my life had ever seen. "Life was too strong in me, it must take a long pining sickness to exhaust this remaining strength." "How could we afford this length of dying?" so my mind ran on. My sisters were already exhausted with the care of me. As I said to the doctor, we were working in a rule of subtraction -- "kill for to save one." I was sure there would be some terrible breakdown if they had to care for me much longer. Then there was the expense, physician, trained nurse, etc. How could all this go on? It came to me, the free ward of a hospital would reduce expenses and relieve the family. I might be till spring wasting unto death, but I found there was no courage to leave the little home nest. So all that blue day I was crying to God for courage, but it was a struggle! I would think God had helped me all over to point, then all at once everything in me would recoil, and the battle would have to be fought all over, and the victory regained.

All this went on till after midnight, when the Lord approached me with the suggestion, *"You are like Hagar crying and dying by the side of the well."* I had been contemplating all winter to die in. [?] He showed it was only a moment to be healed! How clear He made it, that *"Christ, the deep, sweet well of love," as a Fountain of Healing was right by the side of every sick one*, and, as with her, it was only to turn and live (Gen. 21:15-19). Then the accuser of the brethren came in big, with all his showing of what I was, and what I was not; that at this juncture healing was never for me, etc., etc. God applied with mighty power "By grace are ye saved, through faith, and that not of yourselves, it is the gift of God." Eph. 2:8. Grace -- "free, full unmerited favor," a provision all outside of me, coming to me the Christmas gifts to the children, because of the love of the giver.

"Through faith! through faith!" says the enemy, "You have got to take it and you have no faith." Within I could see nothing, without I could see everything, such richness of provision in Jesus. Then came the word with God-power "Through faith *and not of yourselves*, it is the gift of God." I ceased to resist the thought of healing and cried; "Oh, God, give that faith which is the gift of God." the spiritual atmosphere was moment by moment warming [getting better]. No wonder. One of my sisters was in another room on her face before God, crying for Him to break through and bring deliverance.

In many towns, aye, in many countries, Faith in God's children was holding on for His victory in my healing; and as near as we could figure it, at the very hour when the power of darkness was broken in my bedchamber, a precious brother in the Lord, a cook in a hotel, there in the early morning, making out his rolls for breakfast, and who had all along, had an assurance of my healing, was energized to cry with agony, *"Lord help, Lord help."* He said that was all the prayer he offered, as the vision of me came before him, but oh, the power that resisted his believing! The conflict for a time was terrible, but thank God, he got the victory.

My dear sister got the victory ere she rose from her knees, and the spiritual atmosphere was so clearing that this poor weakling, in the jaws of death, was getting the victory. "Hallelujah, what a Savior!" As my sister came into my room I felt her quickened spirit, and she felt mine, though neither knew of the spiritual exercises of the other. I asked her to sing some hymns, and we spoke of the mercy and might of God. Then Acts 3:6 came into my mind with great force, "In the name of Jesus of Nazareth rise up and walk." Again the enemy came tremendously. "That is Satan quoting scripture to you. Don't follow that wild impulse. You may succeed in pulling yourself up by your will power, but the consequences of further and more terrible illness, and far more trouble to the family, will ensue," etc., etc.

Spiritually, everything grew black around me, as I cried to God to protect me from Satan, to take away the voice if it was his, or to intensify it, if it were God's. He made me know without a doubt that God was speaking. My heart cried, "Lord, I will, I will, if it costs me my life to do it," for my whole nature gathered now into a spirit of obedience, and what cared I for the consequences. The devil said, "If you stir it will kill you." (This was true enough in the natural, the doctor did not allow them to raise me for fear of causing vomiting and then hemorrhage.) I thought, "What do I care if it does kill me, I will obey God." Then it occurred to me how impossible it would be for the family to let me "obey," and all my prayer was, "Lord, prepare them."

Just then another sister came in bringing my morning mail, which they daily opened and read me as much as they thought best, when I was not too ill to hear. Now she read from a sister in Winnipeg -- Mrs. Lockhart -- to whom they had written to pray for me. She replied she was not surprised with their letter, though she knew nothing of my return to this country, but while I was yet in Scotland, God had revealed to her in the spirit that I was very ill, and put upon her a great burden for me. Now she sent a handkerchief, that had been prayed over, and asked us to lay it on the diseased part, and wrote what assurance God had given her of my healing. Oh, that letter! I knew God was breaking my way to speak and act by that letter. It was but finished, when my sister who had been assured of deliverance before God that morning took the handkerchief, and laid it on me, and bowed in prayer. I was only waiting for the "amen" of her prayer, till I should obey Acts 3:6.

"Yes," I burst out, "God says 'in the name of Jesus of Nazareth, rise up and walk,' bring my underclothes, stockings, slippers, wrapper." The one sister turned white as death, and fled the room. I called again for my clothes. They had been laid aside all the long weeks of my illness and the sister who had since been sent for to see me die, did not know where to find them, so she followed the other saying, "Bring her clothes." "Belle, I dare not," was the trembling reply.

Who would in the natural? (And God had intimated nothing of His will to this one.) However my clothes were found and as my sister began to put them on [me], I sat in the bed and drew on one stocking, then as I put out my foot to walk my whole being gathered in the word "In the NAME of the Lord Jesus," I never seemed to put my foot on the floor, but right in the Name; *in the Name*; IN THE NAME, and in His Name *each foot fell*, till I had walked to a chair.

Mentally I saw Peter walking the waves on the word of Jesus ("Come,") and like Peter I was safe, while I did not look around, but walked in the Name, (Oh, had not my prayer for "that faith which was the gift of God" been answered?) The joy of obedience -- and faith comes in obedience -- filled my soul. I cried, Sing the chorus:

> "Come, come and His bidding obey;
> Come, come and believing you'll say
> Jesus hath healed me, praise Him today!
> Jesus hath taken my misery away."

# Messengers of An Outpouring

As my sister sang I joined in with a full clear voice, and over and over again, we made it ring. The other members of the family came in, half happy, half frightened, but now the color was coming to my face, and the appearance of healing. Oh, the joy of that hour, as I believed, and then felt, I was healed of the Lord. And grace had been given me, even poor me, to obey Him! Then came the whisper "Walk in the other room." Two of them took hold of me as I started. But they said, "How strong she walks!" emaciated skeleton though I was. When I took the chair in the second room I began to feel warm currents of life from the soles of my feet to the top of my head and finger tips. (In bed I had three water bags to keep me warm!) Oh, it was delicious, the God-life flowing in! Wave after wave coursed through my being.

Next suggestion to "call for solid food." The devil withstood here and tried to put a great care upon me, but it came, "Well people can eat solid food and I am well, *"the healed of the Lord.*"" So I called for the solid food and ate it and have gone on eating everything ever since. Nothing hurts me. It seems as if my stomach was bomb proof. We went round the house that resurrection day and many days after, crying "God is great in Zion." Hallelujah, what a Savior! Oh, the enrichment that has come through this illness and healing! Oh, the lessons learned! They cannot all be put on paper.

Previous to my illness I was distressed before God for the shallowness of my compassion for the sick and had prayed for deepening at that point, also that I might know the fellowship of His sufferings and conformity to his death, as I had never experienced. A blessed measure of answer has come to these prayers -- though I need much more. Then the reality of the Satanic battle against God's life in the bodies of His people has been opened up to me.

Also the beautiful truth of the unity of Christ's body, the members prevailing for, and holding on with one another. When in the beginning of my illness a telegram asking prayer for me went from St. Andrews to a meeting at Dunfermline, seven in succession got in tongues the answer "Victory," "Healing," etc. And from that on in different places, children of God were exercised in prayer for me. Two friends, missionaries to Africa for many years, were then in Vermont, and not having heard from me in months, were greatly burdened in prayer in my behalf, feeling in the spirit that I was ill, then God gave them the assurance of His victory at the very time I was healed. Cases like this could be multiplied. We are coming upon a time in the Lord's battle, *when we need each other's prayers*. Christ will thus both demonstrate and increase the unity of His body. "Ye-also helping together by prayer for us, that for the gift upon us, by the means of many persons, thanks may be given by many on our behalf" (2 Cor. 1:11).

But more than all was I taught the all of God and nothingness of the creature, especially this creature, during the long discipline of those painful months. "I was brought low and the Lord helped me" (Ps. 116:6), and He will help and heal any "low one" who will let his whole case go into God's hands, and in simplicity rest in Him, to do all. "He shall save him that hath low eyes." (Job 22:29 marg.) God waits to be all, when we are ready to be nothing.

Hallelujah! So often one sitting at our dining table, looking at me quotes "There they made Him a Supper, Martha served, but Lazarus who had been dead, whom He raised from the dead, was one of them that sat at the table." I am glad His grace has made a Lazarus of me, and I feel His resurrection life flowing through my veins. Oh, that every sick one would let the God of Lazarus raise them. (*TLRE*, April, 1909)

## A Gospel Worker's Dream

"If any man's work abide, which he hath built thereupon, he shall receive a reward. If any man's work shall be burned, he shall suffer loss; but he himself shall be saved, yet so as by fire." -- 1 Cor. 3:10-15.

I sat down in an arm chair, wearied with my work. My toil had been severe and protracted. Many were seeking Christ, and many had found Him. As for myself, I was joyous in my work. My brethren were united; my sermons and exhortations were evidently telling on my hearers and my church was crowded.

Tired with my work, I soon lost myself in a sort of half-forgotten state. Suddenly a stranger entered the room, without any preliminary "tap" or "come in." He carried measures, chemical agents, and implements [with him], which gave him a very strange appearance.

The stranger came toward me, and, extending his hand, said: "How is your zeal?"

I supposed that the query was to be for my health, but was [expecting to be] pleased to hear his final word, for I was quite well pleased with my zeal, and doubted not the stranger would smile when he should know its proportions.

Instantly, I conceived of it as "physical quantity" and putting my hand to my bosom, brought it forth and presented it to him for inspection. He took it, and placing it in his scale, weighed it carefully. I heard him say, "One hundred pounds [in weight]."

I could scarce express an audible note of satisfaction; but I caught his earnest look as he noted down the weight; and I saw at once that he had drawn no final conclusion, but was intent on pushing his investigation. He broke the mass to atoms, put it into his crucible, and put the crucible into the fire. When the mass was fused, he took it out and set it to cool. It congealed in cooling, and when [dumped] out on the hearth exhibited a series of layers or strata, which all, at the touch of the hammer, fell apart, and were severally tested and weighed; the stranger making [detailed] notes as the process went on. When he had finished he presented the notes to me, and he gave me a look of mingled sorrow and compassion, as without a word, except, "May God save you!" [then] he left the room.

The notes read as follows:

ANALYSIS OF THE ZEAL OF JUNIUS: A Candidate for a Crown of Glory.

Total Weight of Zeal: 100 lbs:
Chemical analysis shows:
Bigotry ..........................11 Parts

| | | |
|---|---|---|
| Personal Ambitions ............22 | " | Wood, |
| Love of Praise ...................19 | " | Hay, |
| Pride of Denomination ........15 | " | and |
| Pride of Talent ..................14 | " | Stubble, |
| Love of Authority ..............12 | " | (1 Cor. 3:10-16) |
| Love of God .....................4 | " | Pure |
| Love of Man ....................3 | " | Zeal |

I had become troubled at the peculiar manner of the stranger, and especially at his parting look; but when I looked at the figures, my heart sank like lead.

I made a mental effort to dispute the correctness of the record. But I was startled into a more honest mood by an audible sigh from the stranger, who had paused in the hall. I cried out, "Lord, save me!" and knelt at my chair, with the paper in my hand, my eyes fixed upon it. At once it became a mirror, and I saw my heart reflected in it. The record was true. I saw it! I felt! I confessed! I deplored it! And besought God to save me from myself, with many tears. With a loud cry of anguish I awoke.

I had once prayed to be saved from hell, but prayer to be saved from myself now was immeasurably more fervent; nor did I rest or pause till the refining fire came down and went through my heart, searching, probing, melting, burning, filling all its chambers with light, and [dedicating] my whole heart to God.

When the toils of my pilgrimage shall be an end, I shall kneel in heaven, at the feet of the Alchemist and bless Him for the revelation of that day. (*TLRE*, May, 1909)

\*\*\*

Take an attitude of Contentment with the way God made you; and with the way He may choose to lead you and deal with you. (Ibid)

\*\*\*

Never go by supernatural impressions alone (the devil is supernatural); try the spirit that leads you, whether it be of God, by the concurrent testimony of God's revealed will in the Scriptures. (Ibid)

## They Were All With One Accord in One Place

Convention report, by Miss Bernice C. Lee, Chicago

Weeks before the opening of the Convention the children of God in the Stone Church as well as many of His faithful ones elsewhere, were upon their faces pleading with the Father for the Spirit's presence and blessing. God especially laid the spirit of intercession upon a little band who met every morning for the definite purpose of praying that God might have His way.

These days of preparation were days of blessing, and the cry that went up from hungry hearts was, "Search me, oh God, and know my heart; try me and know my thoughts, and see if there be any wicked way in me." Earnest heart searching is sure to bring God and heaven very near, and when the Convention opened on May 13th, it found eager hearts waiting to see the face of God and hear His voice.

From the very beginning the earnest prayers for unity were answered, and as His children gathered from many places throughout the States -- from far and near, they greeted one another in Jesus' Name and all felt that He was standing in the midst. There was special cause for thanksgiving because of the blessed spirit of unity which prevailed more than ever before in the Pentecostal work in Chicago.

God sent dear Brother and Sister Myland, and Brother Robbins, of Columbus, Ohio, to be with us, whom He used as special channels through which to pour His truth and blessing. Upon the first evening volumes of joyous praise burst from the lips of those whom God had brought together a fitting beginning for the days that were to follow. Jesus was lifted up, His precious blood honored, and the Holy Spirit began His mighty movings in our midst.

The "Red -(blood-sprinkled) Key" that unlocked the Convention was "for the Lord Jesus Christ's-sake and the love of the Spirit -- and as the days came and went these thoughts deepened in our lives.

Announcements were made for three meetings a day, and beginning at nine o'clock these oftentimes merged themselves into one long grand time of waiting before God, intermingled with prayer, praise, reading of the Word, and precious messages from different ones of His children, as the Spirit led.

Between the afternoon and evening sessions the people gathered for lunch, during which time there was a drawing together and a relating of blessings received during the day. Frequently songs burst from the lips of one and another, which were caught up and sung heartily and in the spirit, as they ate not only of the food which satisfied the physical body, but feasted with Him who was so abundantly supplying the spiritual food as well.

Many "camped" before Jehovah, tarrying for the "promise of the Father," and were abundantly blessed. One day in particular the Spirit hovered very low and a dear sister, a Christian worker who had been passing through many deep trials was blessedly baptized in Holy Spirit and spoke in other tongues; another sister who had been tarrying before Him broke out in the language of the Spirit, praising and blessing God.

The morning sessions were especially blessed and helpful. As the people gathered in the prayer-room, it was not with the thought of listening to man, but with the Psalmist many could say, "My soul wait thou only upon God; my expectation is from Him." Sometimes the Spirit called to prayer, and the voice of the people crying out to God was "as the voice of many waters." After seasons such as these the hearts of all were refreshed and strengthened, and many of His children had precious victory. Many times the noon hour would pass by, and 2:30, the time for the afternoon service frequently found some still before Him, either in praise or silently waiting before God.

There was no program and the afternoon meetings were varied. At times the Spirit called to prayer and again the Lord would lay a message upon the heart of some one which caused much searching of hearts. The close of the service nearly always found the people upon their faces before God, with the prayer: "Less of self and more of Thee!" The singing in the Spirit, both in the English and the unknown tongue was a precious feature of the meetings. One afternoon while on our knees the spirit of worship fell on the people and at least twenty burst forth in heavenly chorus which filled the house.

At the close of every meeting there were inquiries from hungry seekers after God, hearts crying out from their very depths. The old Stone Church often heard the cry of the distressed and the song of triumph as the midnight hour approached. One dear sister to whom God had given a wonderful baptism three years ago, but who had gone into utter darkness because of disobedience, was graciously reclaimed in the midnight hour and baptized anew as she tarried with one or two of God's humblest. She had been led to pray that a revival might start in these Convention days that would last until Jesus comes, and as the meetings drew to a close she found herself asking the Lord about that prayer she felt He had led her to utter, when He so sweetly said to her: "Hasn't the revival started in your heart to continue until Jesus comes?" The joy in her soul was her answer.

Between the meetings could be heard the joyous bursts of "This is like heaven to me" and truly God walked and talked with His people. As we drew near to the tenth day, there seemed to be an expectancy in the hearts of the people, and while nothing was said many felt the meetings were to continue. This impression deepened when, as we neared the end of the ten days, God definitely led some of His workers from distant points; Brother and Sister Hebden of Toronto were especially impressed of the Spirit to come to Chicago, not knowing that a Convention was in session, and [also] aged Sister Mossman with two of her associates from Los Angeles. Another evidence that it was the will of God that the meetings continue, was the coming of Miss Minnie Abrams, who has been connected for eleven years with the work of Pandita Ramabai among the Child-Widows of India. She brought us many precious lessons from God's Word and from her experience as a missionary among the people of India.

God especially used this sister in bringing to us precious lessons along the line of the crucified life. As she spoke we realized that we were listening to one whom God had wonderfully taught and who had gone deep with Him in her own experience, having consecrated her life to the foreign mission field when but eleven years old. God enabled her to show not only the need of giving all to Him, but also the sweetness of such a consecration and of the blessing that floods the life that is wholly yielded to God.

The Convention continued until twenty-five days had passed; days of exhortation, of heart-searching, probing, consecration, emptying and dying as many of us had never known. It seemed as though the Lord was calling for a deeper death to self, and a fuller abandonment to Him than we had ever made, so that He could use us to the praise of His glory.

The shouts of praise are good, the bursts of enthusiasm in the midst of such a gathering are refreshing, but when a soul out of love to God, in humility and quietness yields himself wholly to Him for time and eternity, then God is pleased, the angels rejoice, and all heaven sings the song of victory.

And so it was that many who came, scarcely knowing why (but God knew) were led to consecrate as never before, and as the thought was borne in upon their hearts both by the Spirit directly and through His servants, of the shortness of time, they were enabled to lay all upon the altar, giving their lives as a willing sacrifice, to be used wherever the great Husbandman deemed best.

The crowning day of the Feast was the Anniversary of Pentecost, and from early morning until near the midnight hour the glory of God overshadowed us. At the close of an inspired message in the afternoon, the Spirit speaking through a humble handmaiden made a heart-searching appeal for the money and lives of the people, which met with a hearty response, and we must believe that the Father's heart was made glad as two young lives offered themselves for His work in India; it seemed impossible to dismiss the meeting, and while the people came and went the Spirit never lifted.

On the following Sunday the Spirit again called for laborers, and offerings, and about twenty responded, offering themselves definitely for God's work, more especially the foreign field.

The most marked characteristic of the twenty-five days spent before God was the emphasis laid upon the study of His Word, and as the Spirit drove home the great importance of feeding upon the Word and becoming established therein, a divine conviction of this great need seized every heart and we were constrained to vow to God we would give more earnest study to His Word.

A number were healed in the Name of the Lord Jesus, at the Divine Healing meetings, and at other times as the Spirit moved. One day in particular as the Word was going forth in power, faith reached the climax in two lives, and while they were sitting in their seats they were healed.

And so the twenty-five days have passed into history, but who shall say they are ended? In the plan of God we believe the work He has brought in our hearts will continue until Jesus comes, and the blessing and victory and unity shall never cease.

Praise God for what has been!
Praise God for what shall be!
And unto Him-be the kingdom,
the power and the glory forever! (*TLRE*, June, 1909)

**Rejected for Speaking on Tongues:**

Almost one year ago I came [to Oblong, Il.] from Colorado Springs, where we Pentecostal people were having such blessed meetings. I found very few sanctified people here and none that believe in the baptism of the Holy Ghost. I began praying that God would give me wisdom, knowledge, and above all, love. 1 Cor. 13. He hears and answers prayer, praise Him!

He led me to attend a holiness camp meeting on July 11th. How He blessed me and took supreme control of my tongue. But while I was being so blessed, others (God pity them) were calling me the devil. When they made the call for all to come to the altar I stepped forward with the rest. I began to pray. God knew it took His power in such a place, so He talked German through me. The preacher took me by the arm and walked me out of the tent. The Lord was giving me the interpretation and gave me English long enough to tell him if he would let me I would interpret what I said. But he would not.

Then the Lord took my tongue again and talked the rest of the way out of the tent. Praise God for victory in my soul! This incident brought to light that there were two others present that had received their baptism and also revealed that there were others who were hungry for the experience. O pray for us that God will have His way with us and we will be able by His power to open Pentecostal meetings. May God burden some soul to come and teach the whole Bible. You remember praying for my husband for consumption. Praise Him! He is much better and still gaining. . . . (Mrs. M. E. H.) (*The Pentecost*, Aug., 1909)

## Telling the Lord's Secrets

*Book Editor*: This is one of the few teaching articles which I have decided to include because it is on such an unusual, unknown subject. The closest thing I have ever heard to this subject, was teaching the opposite from what this article shows. As I was reading it I felt that I had found a chunk of gold.

Daniel Awrey, Hong Kong; at the Chicago Convention, Oct. 23, 1909:–

In Psalm 24:14 we read. "The secret of the Lord is with them that fear Him." There are some things that the Lord puts into our hearts that He considers as secret, and just as sure as we give away His secret, that which was shown so clearly to us does not come to pass.

Sometimes the Lord gives us an assurance about some matter, and as we talk about it and tell it out, the assurance weakens and the circumstance does not come to pass; then we are humiliated and God is not glorified.

We might look at the Word along this line. We find in Matt. 8:4, 9:30 and Mark 9:23 almost the same words falling from the lips of Jesus, where He said to different persons, "See thou tell no man." There is a deep meaning in those words of Jesus.

True they went out and told it contrary to the Master's instructions, just as many people do today; we are just as human as they were. When the Lord shows us something we feel so good over it we have to tell it, but what has often been the consequence? We find that many things we have told do not come to pass.

The very meaning of the word "secret" is an understanding between two persons, and just as quickly as you tell a third person, it is no longer a secret. People say to you, "I want to tell you a secret," and just as soon as it is told it ceases to be a secret. The Lord has some things that He regards as secrets. In Romans 14:22 we read. "Hast thou faith. have it to thyself before God."

We might turn to Judges 16:17, 18, and find where Samson gave away the secret of his power. The Word says, "He told her all his heart," and later on we read, "And he wist not that the Lord was departed from him." What caused the Lord to depart? giving away that deep secret that neither his wife nor anyone else should have known.

In Nehemiah 2:12 we read, "Neither told I any man what God hath put in my heart to do at Jerusalem." He didn't tell it out, and you know how successful he was. Nehemiah built the walls of Jerusalem, and carried out all the things which God had secretly put into his heart. In Daniel 7:28 we read, "But I kept the matter in my heart." He kept in his heart that which God revealed to him.

In Luke 2:19 we read, "But Mary kept all these things and pondered them in her heart;" also in the fifty-first verse, "But His mother kept all these sayings in her heart." These passages go to show that God has His secrets which He entrusts to His children. [*Book Editor*: She did not say to anyone, "An angel told me I will have a son." Would she have become the mother of Jesus if she had told?]

Many persons have wondered why things which they felt sure the Lord had revealed to them did not come to pass; some things, for example, of the nature of prophecies. This giving away the secrets does not mean that we should not testify to the goodness of God after He has done some good things for us, but, as nearly as I can understand it, it applies more especially to assurances that our prayers are to be answered. When the Holy Spirit helps us to intercede at the throne of grace, and the Lord gives us the assurance that there will be an answer to that prayer, and we tell that we have the assurance, it seldom comes to pass.

Of all the cases brought to my notice, especially in the last three years, I do not know of a single one where the assurance which had been given was verified after it had been told. Oh, how puzzling that has been to us; we have felt in our own hearts that the Lord certainly spoke to us in a way that we could not possibly doubt, and yet it did not come to pass.

I remember the first time I lost out on that line. It was in the matter of trusting the Lord for our temporal needs. We used to get into many tight places. This time in particular as I prayed I got such a sweet promise and very sweet assurance from the Lord that He was going to provide for us. My wife was bothered and worried because of our close condition, and I thought I would encourage her, so I said to her, "I have the assurance the Lord is going to answer prayer and give us the needed money today," but it didn't come, and I was almost afraid she would lose confidence in me.

Many times we think we will encourage people by telling them what God tells us, and we have failure on our hands because we give away His secret. I told her I had the assurance from God, but the day passed and we didn't get anything, and it distressed me. Some of these things we can explain away, but others we cannot. When people are not healed but die instead, some explain the failure of their assurance by trying to spiritualize it, or try with their human wisdom to explain it away, but it is never satisfactorily explained. How this whole matter has puzzled me! Two or three times right along the line of money matters I told of my assurance from the Lord, and I never received anything. This failure caused me to look into the difficulty.

At first I thought that as we told these things the devil heard it and hindered, but soon I saw that *we failed God*, and it seems the Lord does not hold Himself responsible to answer the prayer after we give away the secret which He committed to us. The assurance the Lord gives you is a kind of contract He enters into with you, and when you break your side of the contract, God is free, and evidently feels under no obligation to fulfill His part. You may try to make yourself believe and try to force matters, but all to no effect. If that prayer is answered at all you will have to pray through to victory again.

Many people have said to me, "The Spirit has whispered in my heart, 'Keep this to yourself,' but I didn't do it and I have lost all by telling it." I have met these people all around the world; everywhere I have been there have been enough failures to enable them to see the cause when I have explained to them as the Lord has shown me.

The very [morning] I gave this teaching in Los Angeles a request was brought to the evening meeting to pray for a little girl who had broken her arm; they called for prayer and the Spirit of prayer was mightily poured out upon that meeting. I really believe in my heart God wanted to work a miracle, but soon a sister jumped up (she hadn't been in the morning meeting) and said, "I have the perfect assurance in my heart that that child is healed." The remark caused me to groan in spirit. Then another said, "I have the witness of the Spirit, too, that she is healed," and they all rejoiced. In my heart I prayed, "Oh, God, give us some sense and some wisdom." I hoped this might be an exception, but not so; the child wasn't healed at all. Her wrist was bent nearly at a right-angle; that is not a healed wrist.

These failures when people say they have the assurance have caused many to wonder and lose confidence, and some try to do like the Christian Scientists, believe they have nothing the matter with them because they had received the assurance in their hearts that they were healed. They say, "God told me I was healed, and I will believe I am healed anyhow;" but in many cases the failure was in telling the secret that God intended them to keep in their hearts.

At another meeting in Los Angeles a brother arose and said, "I have received the assurance in my heart that I am going to be baptized in the Holy Spirit today." Well, he wasn't baptized; didn't receive the baptism for months afterwards. A day or two later he spoke to me personally and asked me to pray for him. I said, "Brother, I believe you made a mistake the other day in telling your assurance," and he said, "I felt it down deep in my soul the minute I had told it," but he didn't know the reason.

This instruction is so necessary for those who are used as intercessors; for those whom God has called to minister in the prayer-life; that they should keep the secrets the Lord has spoken into their hearts. Many times the Holy Spirit intercedes in us and through us and gives us the assurance that He will answer, and we tell it out, thinking we will encourage others, but generally there is lurking within a conscious or unconscious pride in the fact that God has revealed these things to us, and we take the glory that belongs to Him.

We like to say after a thing has come to pass, "I told you so," and when we speak of the assurance which God has given us, it is a satisfaction to us and feeds our spiritual pride. With many, this may be unconscious, but it is there, nevertheless. Oh, how many people have lost blessing because of this, and how the work has been hindered in many places! Often God has revealed to people whom the Spirit has burdened for a certain work, or a certain convention that He was going to manifest Himself and pour out His Spirit, and then they have told the people, and God didn't do it at all. They failed God and He wouldn't keep His promise. This is a very serious matter; one person giving away the real secret of the Lord could stem the whole tide of power at a convention. This undoubtedly is the reason more prayers are not answered. People spend days on their faces before God in prayer, and then through lack of wisdom or knowledge, by a few words, their efforts are lost. Sometimes it requires real self-control to keep still, and a real dying out to self, but we get victory by overcoming this desire to tell, which in a great measure exalts ourselves instead of Jesus.

You know one man in the Bible on another line actually brought defeat to a whole army, and one person by giving away the secrets of the Lord may cause a series of meetings to fail right on our hands. I have seen it more than once. Years ago in the country we were holding some meetings, and one day a person came in from the woods, his face just shining with the very glory of God, and he said, "I have the assurance in my heart that these people are going to get saved tonight." Not a soul was touched.

Sometimes they were almost discouraged, and didn't know what to think. They said, "I thought surely God told me that; it was the same feeling of assurance that I had when my sins were forgiven." It puzzled them when it failed to come true, and shook the faith of others. They feel you are not a safe person to trust in when you tell things that do not come to pass. Just because we have not known these simple things we have many times brought disaster and failure on God's work. God forgives us, that is true, but His work suffers.

I remember one time God showed me there was to be a certain number of people saved at a certain meeting and I just believed it with all my soul, and I thought I had better tell it, because if I told it afterwards they wouldn't believe I had the assurance. So I told it, but it didn't come to pass. I tried to fix it up and say that maybe the results would follow afterwards; that was before I understood this truth. I believed it with all my heart, but it failed.

When I was coming through India there were two baptized missionaries, praying for the sick child of one of them, and as they prayed God gave the one a wonderful assurance that the child was going to be healed and raised up, but it died the same day. It shocked them so much they didn't know what to do; they almost felt like separating one from another because of that misunderstanding. "Why," one said, "how can I believe in what God says if I cannot believe He gave me that assurance?" But the trouble was, she had failed to keep God's secret.

When I came through Edinburg, Scotland, they were praying for a sick sister; they sent out word to all the missions and much prayer was offered up for the sick one; the missions sent word back. "We have the assurance that the sister will be healed and raised up," but she died, and they were so shocked, and wondered what could be the solution of it all. When I came there giving this little teaching they were delighted out of measure. When one fails God like that, we have to pray and sometimes fast in order to get sweet communion again.

I know it makes us very happy to get assurances of victory from God, and we just feel we must tell it, but just as sure as we do, it will fail right on our hands.

There are ways and times we may express ourselves without giving away what God really speaks into our hearts, but, friends, by the help of God keep sacred that with which He entrusts you.

Sometimes we think if we do not tell it beforehand people will not believe God gave us the assurance, but that doesn't matter; we don't even need to tell them that we have had the assurance at all. If our lives are hid with Christ in God and He gets the glory, it doesn't matter whether anybody ever knows we even prayed. It is almost impossible to speak of our prayers and of the assurance that God gives us that He will answer prayer without taking some of the glory to ourselves. Can't we afford to wait until the day of rewards to get recompensed? "The Father which seeth in secret Himself shall recompense thee."

People don't need to know that God uses me to pray anyone through into victory, either for spiritual or physical blessing. I believe the less we tell the more God will use us. Give Him all the glory, the blessing is from Him. The less we make remarks about the Lord using us the more answers we will get. Sometimes it is almost necessary to say some things, but the secret we need to learn is to tell it in such a way that people will see that Jesus did it all, and not speak of ourselves. These instances are enough to show you the principle that underlies this subject. May the Lord write it on our hearts in such a way that we will not lose blessing by giving away that which He entrusts to us.

This teaching is so necessary along the line of God supplying our needs financially, on the line of salvation of souls, and in the matter of revivals and in regard to healings; on every line it seems we would get more answers to prayer if we didn't so often fail in our part of the contract.

When I went through St. Louis last year I was in an All-Day Meeting, and in the morning I gave this teaching; in the afternoon a great many more came and I felt impressed to talk on the same line again. I didn't want to do it, and had quite a struggle about it, but finally decided I would, and the very person who I thought would not receive it was the first person to stand up and relate some experience along this line. She said: "This is the first time in my life I have understood some things." She told us that she, with others, prayed for her husband right through to victory, and all three of them felt God had under-taken and given them the assurance that her husband was going to be saved.

Time went on, a year or two went by and he wasn't saved, and she felt burdened again and called several more of her friends together; they prayed and laid before God the promise, and they said, "We are going to believe," and they were almost lifted out of themselves, they had such assurance of victory, and she went home and took the candle and went in to look at her husband to see if he wasn't really saved, but he wasn't. After awhile circumstances were such that she prayed through herself and got the assurance; she had no occasion to tell anyone, and he became saved, and has been saved ever since; and she said this was the first time in her life that she understood the matter. She said, "We just felt that God gave us such assurance that we could not possibly doubt it, because it was the same Spirit that told us everything else we ever got from God, but it failed, and we wondered about it."

When you tell the secrets God has put into your heart you may force matters all you can, but God doesn't answer. He doesn't seemingly undertake the case at all; and you can pray and try to believe all you want but there is no answer. On the other hand there are some things the devil may do his utmost to hinder, but with God's secret hid in our hearts, we can go right on to victory.

It is a great hindrance to God's work when we fail in this way, for people will soon call us false prophets. May the precious Spirit of God teach us. You will have to watch carefully because sometimes you will feel so happy you will think you just have to tell it, but you must not tell anybody. Little things that I have told only to my wife have failed, but I have learned how to cherish the Lord's secret. Sometimes when the children were sick she almost thought I didn't care; I had the assurance that God had undertaken the case, and yet I could not say anything about it. Don't give away your assurance, don't talk about it. Keep it in your heart, under the blood, and then just sit back and see the Lord work.

Many people fail in their healings right along this line. They think when they get the assurance the healing is settled, and they talk about it, and it fails on their hands, even after they have had a wonderful touch from the Lord.

May the Lord by His Holy Spirit open up the Scriptures along these lines, and make them real to us. Are you going to do your best and not fail God? Are you going to be willing to pray without telling people about it? And when you have faith to the answer, have it to yourself?

Last fall when God told me to take a trip around the world without any money it almost staggered me. It looked like a big thing, but in my heart I said, "He is able," and then He dropped this Scripture into my heart, "My God shall supply all your needs according to His riches in glory by Christ Jesus." Just think of it, "His riches." No wonder I went all around the world and didn't have to flounder anywhere for money or take up collections, or ask anybody for anything. But I kept God's secret hid in my heart.

The Lord did not send me on this trip as a test to my faith, but I believe to give this and other practical teaching [as he went], and it was quite new in many places. They saw there was something that was causing failure among God's children, and as God led me to point out these failures they were glad to give even without my saying anything about money.

Beloved, keep God's secrets and, like Mary, ponder them in your heart, and verily, they shall come to pass. (*TLRE*, Nov., 1909)

> *Book Editor*: Daniel Awrey was born in Canada (Feb. 10, 1869- Dec. 3, 1913), his family moved to Minnesota as a teen. He became a Holiness preacher, then a missionary to India, Hong Kong, South America, and traveled around the world 3 times. He died in Africa. Full biographies of him are available online, the best is found in the *Assembly of God Heritage,* Jan. 2000. When Daniel left on his trip around the world to teach about not telling the Lord's secrets, he had 28 cents in his pocket, but because the people were so thankful to have the teaching that they gave generously without him having to ask for a cent. Later, while in Africa he wrote to report on his work there before he died:

Dearly beloved in the Lord,

Peace be to thee in Jesus' name.

I left New York September 16th, arriving at Cape Palmas October 10th, stopping over in Monrovia over night, and spoke to a large congregation in the Apostolic Faith Church there.

After one nights' stay at Cape Palmas I came in a sailboat, about 25 miles, to Garraway. Here I remained over two Sundays at the M. E. Mission. I gave some teaching, the leader stating that she received enough good from it to pay for my entire trip to Africa.

I started for the bush, first in a canoe up a river, and then afoot with a hammock carried on the heads of two natives, wading through the waters and crossing on the back of a stalwart native, then perched on his shoulders. Thus we crossed the streams. One river we crossed on a log under water. One misstep would land us all in the foaming river. This was all new experience for me in mission fields.

The second day I arrived at Newaka in Barobo and met my brother, J. M. L. Harrow, and received a royal welcome.

I was quite surprised to see the great work that has been done in the last five years in the Pentecostal work in the bush country. They have five stations, and have built about thirty houses and a nice church 24 by 36 feet in size. After stopping here a week I went to another station where Sisters Hisey and Boddy have charge. It is at this station that Sisters Harrow and Scutt are buried.

I started for another meeting in another tribe and reached Dorobo, where Sister Mendenhall has charge. It is here Sister Lee is buried. I was attacked with fever and remained here. Was sick for several days.

On November 15th about one hundred gathered for a convention at this station, and God was with us in power. Some were saved and some were filled with the Spirit and spoke in other tongues. We ordained five natives to preach the Gospel, and three of them to baptize, and truly these brethren are worthy of support. Any draft sent to J. M. L. Harrow, Cape Palmas, Liberia, W. Africa, will be faithfully used for the glory of God.

Two of the missionaries who have been here five years will leave for a rest in the homeland, and these native brethren will carry the Gospel to those who never heard the name of Jesus.

At the convention a goodly number were baptized in water. The king of the tribe gave us a bullock for a present.

The last night of the meeting the Lord baptized an old woman in the Spirit, and she spake in tongues. She had recently come from heathenism, and was yet unclothed. This astonished the congregation, for she knew no book, and had been only a quarrelsome old heathen woman. Some got up and confessed they thought she had no business to be baptized in water that day, but now they saw their mistake and praised God He was no respecter of persons, and we all left the convention encouraged to win old and young alike. -- Daniel Awrey. (*Confidence*, Feb. 1914 p. 36)

## Healed of Arsenic Poisoning:

August 25, 1892, occurred my second healing, after I had been located in Cleveland, Ohio, one year. I continued two years in the Methodist church after my first healing, but the Lord led me out because of the pressure, though it came about in a very sweet way and with no reflection on anyone.

Our first Convention at Beulah Park, Cleveland, was held in a large tent. God did a marvelous work of healing there, the blind received sight, the lame were made to walk, consumption and cancer were healed; it was a marvelous time of healing. We have been at Beulah Park Conventions for nineteen years, but none has ever surpassed the first one in healings.

A little weekly paper was being published in Collinwood, the editor of which came down and interviewed me. I told him plainly all about it; he went back and published the facts in his paper, and said, "This is all right; this is according to the Gospel." But the people around Beulah Park became very bitter, and made great threats as to what they would do.

I went to the store to pay my bill, as we were about to move back into the city. I agreed to watch the car my people took at the lower end of the line and get on the same one. I was standing in the grocery where I paid the last bill, reading my mail, when a young man said, "Reverend you must be hungry, won't you have a banana or two?" They often gave us something like that when we paid the bill. It was about twelve o'clock; I noticed they were soft at the end, but bananas are frequently like that. I thanked him; I was very hungry, and I ate them rather rapidly; the car was coming and I got on.

Before I got half way into the city, which was about eight miles from our starting point, I was deathly sick. Everything began to look strange to me; perspiration came out on my body, and the Lord confirmed me in the belief that I had been poisoned. It was about half past two o'clock when I reached home, and I grew worse and worse until after supper, when I began to have convulsions, which continued until eleven o'clock.

Then they sent to our weekly meeting, which was in progress, for my elders to come and pray for me. Elder Brown was not there; the other elder came, but he was fearful, he could not pray the prayer of faith. He thought they had to locate this trouble, so he sent to the drugstore for some lobelia, but said he, "If he knows anything about it, he won't take it." As they brought it to me I rallied out of one of those convulsive strains, and I remember as I looked up I saw his face and knew him; I seemed to know my wife was there also.

I said, "What is this?" "Just a little something to quiet you." I said, "Don't give me that; it always pays to wait on God." Immediately I went off in to another convulsion, and as I rallied out of it, the thought, "It pays to wait on God," came back to me, and with that I began to see light, and I said, "Lord, is this your time for me? If you want to take me home take me quickly."

I saw Jesus come up to the foot of the bed with His hands up, and I thought, of course, He had come to take me. My eyes were not open. It was a spiritual vision I had of Him, and I said in my soul, "Oh, blessed Lord, take me quickly."

He put up His hands and waved me back, saying, "I have not come but for victory."

That was the first vision I ever had of the Lord. "Thanks be unto God who giveth us the victory through our Lord Jesus Christ." I Corinthians 15:57. I went off into worse convulsions after that. My brother-in-law would get up into the bed and hold me. The poisonous substance poured out of me at every avenue; a chemical analysis afterwards revealed that I had been poisoned by arsenic. I was completely delivered.

They laid me on a bed in another room, and early in the morning my parishioners came to see me. I could not lift one of my little fingers, I was so weak and exhausted, but the life of God was thrilling my mortal body, glory to His name! [He made a full recovery!] D. Wesley Myland. (*TLRE*, Nov. 1909)

**The Lord Reigneth!:** (excerpt)

Think you that the people who gathered together in that insignificant Bible-school in Topeka, Kansas insignificant from the standpoint of the world-or the people that gathered in the old barn at Azusa street, Los Angeles, think you they were special favorites? I tell you nay.

Why, then, did they speak in tongues? The time had arrived for the exercise of the sovereignty of God! Why did He choose them rather than hundreds of other people just as earnest, just as godly and sincere as they? This is one reason: they had no reputation to lose; they were simple folk; they did not care anything about what others thought of them; they were willing to be used of God in any way that He wanted and were not ashamed of it, whereas if God had chosen others, although just as faithful and loyal to Him, their reputation would have hindered them in letting it become known, and they would have been tempted to hide the new experience under a bushel.

Today, as in the Master's day, the common people accept these things gladly, for every new (old) idea finds its best soil in common clay. They were praying for rain all over the world, but since it was time for the "latter rain" God sent the latter rain, and that differs from ordinary rain in some particulars; it all makes wet and all feels good, and it all makes the grass to grow, but the latter rain differs from ordinary rain, as I have just been showing.

Now we are in the period of the latter rain, but let us not put ourselves on a pinnacle. The generation of Israelites that were set free from bondage were no better than all those who had lived and died under all the hardships of Egyptian slavery. The Jews who lived in the days of John the Baptist and of Jesus were not any better than the Jews who lived before that time. These received the larger blessings, not because of their superior goodness, but because the door of God's sovereignty hinged upon those respective generations. They deserved no credit for the display of God's sovereignty nor did the people that lived in the succeeding generations deserve any censure because they moved on in the even tenor of their way.

Neither do we deserve any credit for having these latter rain blessings thrust upon us, for it is the Lord's doings. The people that are receiving these blessings today are not any more zealous for God than tens of thousands of others. Some of you who have been baptized --I wonder whether you wouldn't flinch if you had to go through what the martyrs did. I wonder what some of you would do if you faced the rack or the stake. I tell you again, we deserve no credit for these blessings because we are living in the time when they are due. Let us get a broad view of it. I thank God for this idea of His sovereignty, for it just fills and thrills my spirit, my soul and my body. I rejoice in God that I am permitted to live in this time of the latter rain. I do not deserve any credit for it, neither do you. This time the door of God's sovereignty hinges upon this our generation. Praise God for the marvelous privilege of these days and bow *before the majesty of His almighty sovereignty*. . . .

Therefore, I say again, in the Name of Jehovah-God, let us not take any credit to ourselves for any manifestation or any experience, or exalt ourselves as superior to our ancestors, for He is doing it all; we have reached the time in the economy of God when these things must be accomplished. . . .

How, but on the theory of God's sovereignty, can you account for the strange places and strange times in which some people have been baptized? Some who have waited for months and even years, and who are just about ready to give up, have suddenly received the blessing. I know of several cases where people have been awakened out of their sleep speaking in other tongues. Some people who went away from the Rochester convention last summer, disappointed that they had not received the baptism, were awakened in their bed in a hotel, praising God in other tongues; others have been baptized on boats, still others on street cars.

Therefore, with your eye fixed upon the pole-star of your faith, move on, not discouraged, for the promise is, "water upon him that is thirsty," and "floods upon the dry ground."

Another way in which God is manifesting His sovereignty is the fact that He is picking people up everywhere, out of all nations and out of all denominations. During the Alliance (Ohio) Camp Meeting I had the pleasure of listening to Vicar A. A. Boddy of All Souls' Parish, Sunderland, England. Just imagine a Vicar of the Church of England speaking in other tongues! I found him a beloved brother. God is going to make the people baptized by one spirit come into one body; I do not say one denomination, the Lord deliver us from any more denominations. The trouble is that some of the people in this Movement are already trying to make it a denomination by driving a peg God never intended to have driven. God's sovereign hand has reached out and taken in some Methodists, some Presbyterians, Congregationalists, Baptists, and a hundred other denominations in this, His Pentecostal sweep of the earth.

Are you grieving, as I have sometimes in the past, because of the lack of unity in the Movement? Practically all other movements have headed up in one man who forged the theology for the whole body, and the people united under his banner by accepting the dogma of his theology. Not so this time. Men and women from all parts of the world, holding totally opposite views on many points of doctrine, have been baptized by one Spirit, and it requires some time to have all these baptized into one unified, sympathetic body.

Today it is expected that an ultra-Calvinist shall live in harmony with an ultra-Arminian, because each is baptized in the Holy Spirit. Jesus baptizes the Arminian and the Calvinist; He baptizes the man who insists upon single immersion in water, and another who says water baptism must be by triune immersion; He baptizes the Methodist who believes in infant baptism and the Quaker who doesn't believe in water baptism at all.

But because He baptizes in the Holy Spirit men holding these opposite views is no argument that any or all of these varied opinions are right for He baptizes men, not doctrines. By and by the doctrines, too, will be baptized, and then we shall begin to see eye to eye.

When we are tempted to complain about the lack of unity just remember the "shell" that is sticking to each of us. God is doing a marvelous thing in reaching down into every denomination, and reaching down into the slums where there is no denomination, and baptizing His disciples. What else could so effectually break down bigotry than the fact that God is bigger than our denominational difference? Thus there is left little or no room for one set of people to exalt themselves over another. With all our previous opinions and prejudices it is remarkable that we get along as peaceably as we do.

If we had been as bad as our ancestors we would have been figuratively scratching each others' eyes out. They met in convention and fought and abused each other over the word "filioque," whether the Holy Spirit proceeds from the Father alone or from the Father and the Son. Be careful lest we do as foolishly over our differences. Let us, for His sake, leave some room for God to manifest His infinity through His sovereignty by giving the experiences and manifestations to His children as He wills and cease trying to bring every soul to the standard, whether high or low, of our own experience. . . . William Hamner Piper, in The Stone Church, Chicago, July 4, 1909 (*TLRE*, Dec., 1909)

> *Book Editor*: *Filioque* is a Latin term added to the original Nicene Creed, to indicate that the Holy Spirit proceeds from both the Father and the Son (as opposed to the Eastern churches which believe the Spirit proceeds from the Father alone). It has been the subject of great controversy between Eastern and Western Christianity.

## Chapter 5

## 1910

**A Potato Miracle**

Dear Mr. Boddy,

The following is the account you asked me to write for you of the miracle the Lord worked for us during a time of great testing in the Home [likely an orphanage or missionary resting place].

One Monday I was told there were barely sufficient potatoes left for the next day's dinner, and on going down myself to the cellar to see, found it was only too true. We prayed about it as we do about everything and asked the Lord to supply the need, which He did, not by sending us more, but by making those last till the following Thursday week. Day by day as we went down for potatoes there were sufficient for the day's need. Praise God! the days of His miracle-working are not past. In many ways too numerous to mention has the Lord increased the food provided. When serving out what seemed a short supply there has always been enough and often some to spare.

We write this that God may be glorified, and the faith of His children strengthened, as ours has been in our Almighty Father. -- M. C. Scott.(*Confidence*, April, 1910, page 90)

\*\*\*

The first Pentecostal Conference of this kind in Great Britain began in All Saints' Church. Sunderland was the place in Great Britain where God began first to pout out His Spirit with the gracious Sign of the Tongues, and the work is getting purer and deeper all the time.

While there are dangers, there are mightier blessings. Fears within and fightings without 'were not unknown to the Apostles, and we must stand firm amid similar experiences.

We know that through this blessing souls are being saved and Jesus is being glorified. If sections of the religious world are against us, we know that God is for us. Best of all, God is with us.

We have to admit that, in the case of unsanctified people, there is a danger of putting the Tongues forward too prominently. Possibly we at Sunderland may inadvertently have done so at first, but it seemed as if God had to do a new thing to awaken the sleepers, sleeping so heavily before the Day Star rises.

We were spoken against, written against, shut out and banned, but we have continued to this day, and do not intend to go back. Pentecost, as at the beginning, a Baptism of the Holy Ghost as they received at Czesarea and at Ephesus; this is what we expect, and some of us can be satisfied with nothing less. (*Confidence*, May, 1910 page 104)

## Raised from the Dead

*From the pen of Pastor Humburg of Mülheim [Germany] . . . The following is a translation made by Brother Arthur Bootn-Clibborn:*

In June, last year, our Sister W. was wonderfully healed of tubercular consumption of the lungs, and received the Baptism of the Holy Ghost, with the scriptural sign of Tongues. The great power of voice with which she sang in Tongues showed that the Lord had done a complete work in her body, as well as in her spirit.

However, on Good Friday, a hitherto unknown power fell suddenly upon her. She felt it to be the power of death which was seeking to obtain the mastery of her body, and noticed how it commenced at the feet, and how the lifelessness proceeded upwards. Darkness and great fear overcame her. She noticed that her faith to withstand these powers had not increased. The Lord showed her that this was a case of wrestling against the powers of darkness described in Eph. 6. She distinctly felt as if a cold hand had touched her heart and sought to grasp it and make it stand still. Some brethren and sisters hastened to her help in prayer. Suddenly, before their fervent, persevering supplications, the powers of darkness gave way, and Jesus became visible to one sister in a wonderful light, and said to her, "My child, trust Me, I have given thee strength."

All of us who were present with her realized the blessed presence of the Lord, and soon there rose up to the Lord much praise and thanksgiving, also "in other tongues," with psalms and hymns and spiritual songs. Then we all went home late at night, powerfully quickened by the Lord. The two Easter days were spent by our sister in stillness, and in the power of the Lord, but with an ever-increasing longing to be soon at home with Him, and behold Him face to face.

On Tuesday, the third Easter day, came the removal of the family to another house. In the evening she went early to bed in her new home. She hardly laid down when she noticed that something wonderful commenced to take place within her. She describes it thus:

"Lying quite still, looking up to the Lord, all the events of my life began to pass rapidly, as in a dream, before my inward view, and I realized how blessed and holy it was to know that all my sins had been forgiven, and that He had loosed me from everything of earth. After a "Hallelujah," I received the distinct consciousness that now my spirit would depart from the body. I felt some throbbings of the heart, then convulsive movements in the neighborhood of the heart, and then it stood still.

"I distinctly noticed how the last breath left my life, and how my spirit left my body to ascend to its Lord. Blessedly happy and ravished was my soul before Him, my beloved Lord, and it was now as if I lived on by the breath of His mouth. Ever fresh streams of life and power went out from Him, and I was permitted to receive them into myself, and was thus received into His life."

Our Brother, Emil Humburg, continues the narrative thus: --

While Sister W. was thus with the Lord, a brother and four sisters remained in fervent prayer before the Lord. Before 11 o'clock at night two sisters came to fetch me. Before they left to come, my mother-in-law (who lives in the same house) [the writer is apparently related to the girl who died; perhaps he was married to a sister], who had seen all the signs of death upon Sister W., said to them: "Children, it is useless, you can see it is all over," for she thought that now that death had stepped in, there was nothing more to be done. Notwithstanding this, the others cried all the more to the Lord.

When I arrived with the sisters at the bedside of the deceased, I took her left hand from the chest where it lay, and it fell down lifelessly at the side. I felt for the pulse, there was none, there was also no breath, the lower jaw hung down, and the body was cold. Then we prayed on fervently, each independently, but the heavens seemed as brass, and shut up. We said to the Lord: "Thou hast conquered even death!" and realized that looking into it was according Heb. 12:2, we might count upon His power.

Suddenly the heavens opened above us, and there was given to us great joy in believing. While we continued thus, each for himself or herself, praying fervently and praising God for this joy in believing, I received the inward summons to command death to give way. I did so, though tremblingly, but hardly had I spoken than there fell upon me a power of doubt such as I have never experienced. However, the Lord showed me at once that this came from the enemy.

Then I uttered a second time the command, "In the Name of Jesus, death, let go!" and behold, at the same instant Sister W. breathed deeply, and said with this first returning breath, "Jesus, Hallelujah!" Overcome by the power and presence of God, we all sank down and praised Him long into the night. After the "Hallelujah," Sister W. commenced to worship God in New Tongues.

The first words of "Prophecy" which came from her lips were these, "Rejoice and exult, for I have done great things; go and proclaim what you have seen and experienced, I have taken away the power of death."

Never have I felt the power of the presence of the Lord in so humbling and yet at the same time so uplifting and overpowering a degree. Sister W. had remained thus 2.5 hours with the Lord, in this "fallen asleep" condition. It is also very characteristic that thus "present with the Lord" and at rest, she suddenly noticed that the Lord breathed upon; her powerfully and in a special way, and thus, giving her a new life, caused her spirit to be re-united with her body for further life on earth for Him. This return to life could also take place only when the Lord had given us all full faith in its possibility, and we acted in accordance therewith.

Sister W. said, "My this which the Lord in His great grace has done unto me, serve this purpose-- that He shall be honoured and glorified, and may He be able to give all the confidence of faith, that He can do everything and that all things are possible to them that believe." May we all permit Him to give us hunger and thirst for His glory, and to be led of Him alone, and thus honour Him in worship and service and in burning love, winning souls for the Lamb. Hallelujah!

The circumstance is also remarkable that already a month before this experience, the Lord had prepared us for it, having suddenly, in a prayer-meeting where about 1,000 were present, given this message through a sanctified sister: "My servants will, before long, raise the dead." As this message came, there fell upon me a sort of holy horror, whereupon I foolishly groaned with myself; "Then, O Lord, permit that I may not be present."

Yet now our hearts are filled with praise and thanksgiving, and with a much greater assurance of faith in our blessed Lord. His beloved Name-- Jesus the Christ, is becoming daily more great and "transfigured." To cling to Him in a perfected faith, with Him to love, to live, and to suffer, shall be our only desire, till we shall see Him face to face. Hallelujah, glory to the Lamb!

P.S.-- This "sign" has become known in the whole neighborhood, and has brought much serious reflection to many. I think we shall shortly see and experience greater things than this. A clergyman friend from England writes: "I was in Sister W.'s company at Mulheim . . . She is about 22 years of age, very fair, sweet disposition. She loves her Lord. She told me how the Lord breathed upon her. He was all glorious brightness; too light to look upon or to distinguish any feature." (*Confidence*, July, 1910)

**Australia, A Young Man's Baptism:**

I am writing from Ballarat to you, to tell you how graciously the dear Lord has Baptized me with the Holy Ghost . . . [1909] My mother had told me that she had always expected God to pour out His Spirit and Power in some way that it would be the means of a great revival among God's dear children.

I went to a prayer meeting with my mother on the following Monday after I had come home. This Pentecostal meeting was the first which I had ever been in; all the people present were perfect strangers to me. . . . It was glorious to see them worshiping in the Spirit. I at once sought God to baptize me with the blessed Holy Ghost, and praise His name! it was lovely when I felt the power of God come into this poor heart and body, and shake me from head to foot. Then I started to praise God in my own tongue, when all at once, there seemed to me as if there was a mighty rushing wind, and I was filled with the Holy Ghost, and began to speak in new tongues, and magnify God.

Dear brother, I never had such joy and peace before, although I was a sort of a Christian two years previous to this, thinking that as long as I went to Church and Sunday School, and lived a good moral life, it was all that the Lord required of me; but no, I see that there are higher heights and deeper depths of which I know nothing. Since then the Lord and the Holy Ghost have been leading me into all truths . . . I do believe His coming for His saints will soon take place, for I have had interpretations, some of which are: "I am coming soon." "Get ready, for My time is short." "Hold fast, for I am coming soon."

Your paper, "Confidence," has been the means of blessing many. At present, we are holding meetings in cottages, but in Melbourne (which is near Ballarat) meetings are being held in a large Pentecostal Hall, which is packed nearly every night. On the opening night twelve souls were saved, three of whom were drunkards. An atheist, acting under the cloak of Christianity, was exposed and expelled from the hall.

The work out here is very young, but there is wonderful healing going on. Several demons have been cast out in the name of the Lord. I myself have been wonderfully healed of Catarrh of the nose, of two or three years' standing, and many things the Lord has given me victories in, and I have had many wonderful visions.

The Lord has led me to speak to Chinamen in their tongue, and they have understood; it has all been about Jesus. . . . I am sixteen years of age, and I am determined to go on with the Lord. Edgar Roy Krygger, Victoria, Australia. (*Confidence*, July, 1910)

**Spoke the Zulu Language:**
A missionary from South Africa while in this country was attending some Pentecostal meetings in Indianapolis. While in South Africa he had learned the Zulu language, and had been praying that he would hear someone speak, in the power of the Spirit, in the Zulu language.

One afternoon while a meeting was in progress a man arose and talked at great length with no edification. After speaking for nearly an hour, a sister stood and said two words in an unknown tongue, twice, without interpretation.

Immediately the missionary was on his feet to interpret them. It was the Zulu language, and the words meant "Be quiet." He was so overjoyed that the Lord had answered his prayer that he did not at the time realize the significance of the words, and that it was a message to the speaker to cease from talking. (*TLRE*, Jan., 1910)

## Echoes From the Jungles of India

(Some Pentecostal Experiences)

In the month of June, 1906, in California, I first heard of the present day Pentecost and Pentecostal mission in Los Angeles. The first reports I heard of the work were false and came from the enemy, but in spite of their being false my interest was very much aroused. I had been longing for nearly ten years, during my sanctified life, for still deeper things, and for more of God, and I was quite anxious to go down to the city of Los Angeles and see for myself. I was living twenty-five miles from the city, and went there the following month, July.

I was impressed with the presence of God at the Azusa St. Mission, yet I was much puzzled and could not understand the speaking in tongues. I was wonderfully worked upon after I returned home and was much in prayer. The Holy Spirit made it clear, and led me into His truth about the matter. I waited upon God; my soul was crying and longing for the fullness of Pentecost, because it was quite plain to me now that this was that for which I had longed for nearly ten years. Oh, that seeking hearts would not stop short of waiting upon God in earnest, and not be confused by the opinions of man!

## Messengers of An Outpouring

On the 13th of September that same year I was determined to go to Los Angeles and wait there until I should be baptized in the Holy Spirit. I arrived there on the 15th and resolved to wait at the old Azusa Mission for the "promise of the Father." At four P. M., I was kneeling at the seekers' bench, waiting upon God, and felt convinced He would meet my need that very afternoon. I began to talk to God in this wise; "Oh, Lord, search me through and through with Thy light." At once the Spirit said to me. "Thy heart is right, but thy head is crooked." God will speak very clearly to every honest and humble soul if he will only hear His voice. Then I said, "Oh God. if my head is crooked, You set it right in Jesus' name. Take out all the rubbish of preconceived ideas and opinions, whether my own, or some one else's," and I meant it.

Then I seemed to be in a vision for a few moments, looking at myself as I was kneeling there. I saw another Being standing over me, and pulling out of my head, as it were, a lot of stuff which had no doubt been hindering me in the past.

When this process was finished I felt the need of God's melting power so keenly that I cried out from the depths of my soul. "Oh Lord, melt me, melt me down, down to nothing." At once I seemed to be again in a vision for a few moments, and looking at myself kneeling there, I noticed I was melting down until I was about the size of a grasshopper. Then I cried to God that I felt I was ready for almost anything.

Right here I must say that about this time the Holy Spirit spoke most beautifully in Hindustani, through a brother close to me, and when I opened my eyes to see who was speaking, I was convinced at a glance that the Holy Spirit was really speaking through His children in clear languages. Satan had bothered me so much in the past in regard to this, because up to this day I had never understood a word, but I had learned the Hindustani language in India, and I understood it very distinctly. Oh, how my heart went up to God in praises!

At this time I felt quite ready for the Holy Ghost to come in His fullness, and at once I felt a trembling all through my being. I was rendered entirely inactive, yet I was very keenly conscious of everything; the room was crowded, and there were about forty people seeking God, but I was dealing entirely with God alone. Next I felt a wonderful sensation going all through me like as if beautiful, pure water was being poured into me until I was so filled I cried out to God to enlarge the capacity. Then I realized most keenly that the power of God came upon my head like balls of fire, and it went all through me, down to my feet, hallelujah to the Lamb forever! I realized that another Person had come into my being to stay; my jaws began to move and out of my lips came words of a language utterly unknown to me. The Holy Spirit had come in and was speaking Himself.

The whole process took less time than I can tell it, and through it all I was perfectly conscious of everything that was going on, yet aside from my crying to God for the full baptism, I had nothing to do with the whole matter; it was entirely the work and operation of the Holy Spirit. Oh, beloved reader, if you are still a seeker for the full baptism, wait upon God; don't question or argue, but wait in humility, and remember that if you want to be fully "endued" with the "power from on high," you must first be fully "subdued" by the power of the Holy Spirit, and I dare say that after we are baptized with the Holy Spirit, we can only keep endued with power as long as we keep subdued. Oh, to be nothing, nothing, and Christ Jesus to be all in all.

The Lord God of the harvest field called us again to dark India, and we arrived at Bombay, February 28, 1908. Since that time we have been ministering to many, carrying the blessed Pentecostal truths to the missionary and the benighted heathen. God has been with us in great blessing. We have been much tested along temporal lines, but we praise God it is good to trust Him for soul and body.

We are now ministering to the poor neglected jungle tribes in South India. These people have almost no caste, are very poor and are very much neglected by all missions because of the fear of wild beasts and serpents in these jungles. But our Jesus died for these poor souls as much as for us, and I am sure God will hold His people responsible if we do not take them the Gospel.... (*TLRE*, April, 1910)

**Warning:**
We wish to again warn the people of God against having anything to do with the matter of organization, which is being urged by a few would-be leaders here and there. Last year an attempt was made to form what they pleased to call the Pentecostal Missionary Union. God's people protested against this organization in no uncertain voice. At our convention in Chicago, last September, about seven hundred Pentecostal people, representing twenty-five states of this Union, rose in solemn protest against this movement.

We sent copies of the resolutions to Mr. Lupton and others, composing what they were pleased to call the executive council, and Seeley D. Kinne of St. Louis, who was the strongest man in it, came out. Different others have come out of their own accord. I understand that others from different parts of the country also protested against this movement. Little attention, however, was paid to these things by the real promoter of this scheme, and notices have been sent out stating that they will attempt to further develop the scheme this year at Alliance, Ohio.

We cannot recognize the authority of this one man, who is not even in charge of a congregation, to call such a meeting. We will give the organization no recognition if formed.... Every Pentecostal Mission in Chicago is against this thing ...

Other men in different parts of the country are trying to organize the work on different lines, and the brethren are writing to us expressing their regrets that such should be the case. People of God in every land, pay no attention to these men, and above all do not help them in carrying out their plans, as by so doing you will become in a measure responsible for the irreparable damage that will be done, and the division that will unavoidably result.

The great majority of God's people do not want another sect organized, but want to remain free, and they will do so whether these little sects are formed or not. We believe God wants His people to be untied and to meet together and discuss any problem which may arise at any time, but as a council or convention, and not as a sect.... God is able to solve the missionary and all other problems connected with His work, and only He can do it, anyway, so we had best let Him work it out. (*Pentecostal Testimony*, (W. H. Durham), Vol. 1, No. 5,7-1, 1910, p. 9)

## Our Foreign Missionaries:

The last missionaries going out from us were Mr. and Mrs. R. J. Semple and Miss Phoebe Holmes, who left us last winter and are now situated in Hong Kong, China, which will be their field of labor for the present or till the Lord leads them elsewhere.

Mr. B. Berntsen and family and some other workers are located at Cheng Ting Fu, Chili, North China. Brother George Hanson and family are at Shanghai, China. Miss Jennie Mishler is in Santa Isabella, Porto Rico.

These are all strictly faith missionaries, and are worthy of the support of Pentecostal people. We also contribute to the support of Brother A. H. Post, who is now in Egypt and to Pandita Ramabai in India. We are in sympathy with every genuine faith missionary on the face of the whole earth. . . . (Ibid, page 10-11)

## The Work in Columbus, Ohio:

Brother T. A. Lee, who has for some time been laboring in Columbus, Ohio, writes that they are having wonderful meetings there. About fifty have been saved and about forty have received the Holy Ghost and spoken in tongues. He has baptized thirty-seven in water and the work is still going on. There are seekers at the altar in nearly every service and their little mission is crowded to the doors every night, with crowds on the outside who cannot get in. We rejoice with our dear brother for the success he is having in the Work of the Lord. (Ibid, page 11)

## A Prophetic Message

(Given by Mrs. R. J. Semple, in Belfast, Ireland, while en route to China.)

The voice of the Lord came unto me, saying, "Lift up thine eyes that I may show thee my plan concerning thee. Give me thine ears, that I may speak unto thee concerning the preaching of my gospel." And I said unto Him, "Yea, Lord, not mine eyes and my ears only turn I unto Thee, but my whole soul, my whole being longeth to hear Thy voice."

Straightway mine eyes were opened and I beheld a Book of Light and wisdom. Its pages were written in letters of fire, and the words thereof were words of power and glory; making death and life; and giving bondage and freedom; making deep wounds, and also giving healing; giving great hunger, and also satisfying the hungry soul; causing great sorrow, yet giving great joy; telling of endless bliss and glory; causing great drought and thirst throughout the earth, yet giving showers and rivers of living water and bread unto the nations thereof.

But, I beheld that as the light of the Book shone forth dispelling gloom and darkness, giving light unto the world, there came those clad in priestly robes and ministerial attire. Each one held in his had a scroll and was writing thereon with a pen, and the name of the pen was "The Wisdom of Man." I beheld the writing; it was the wisdom of man, the thoughts and theories of men. When they had ceased to write I saw them take with them page by page the Book of Light and life, so that the light thereof was obscured, as the word of man obscured the word of God.

Then saw I that they brought great stones and mortar and built a wall about the Book [of Light], and my heart was sore within me, for I beheld the nations groping in darkness, searching for the light that was hidden with the Book [of Light]. Then cried I unto the Lord, "How long, how long shall this be? Shall thy mercy endure forever, O Jehovah?"

But straightway lifting up my eyes, I beheld a messenger of righteousness, and his inner garments were the garments of humility. His face shone with Heavenly light, while within his hand he held a flaming sword.

And I beheld that as he advanced he came unto the Book whose pages had been covered, and wielding the flaming sword, he severed page by page the writing of man which had obscured the pages of light and power of life, so that they were again revealed unto the blinded nations. The wall of stone and mortar he overthrew, so that again the rivers and life-giving waters flowed into the regions around about. Give ear, therefore, and harken unto the voice of God, and let him that hath understanding, understand aright.

And the Lord spoke unto me, saying, "The Book which thou seest is the word of the living, the eternal God. The burning words thereof are the words of the Lord Jehovah who liveth and reigneth with power. The writing which obscured is the dark and foolish sayings and theories of the unbelieving and false church. But behold, even as thou sawest the messenger of light come forth, even so have I chosen and ordained thee, that thou shouldest go forth, and clear away the debris and contamination, with which they have covered and obscured the light of My Word. I have chosen thee and called thee by name that thou should speak unto My people. Look not upon the pages that contain the theories of men, but upon the burning, flaming words of My Word as revealed and illuminated by the Holy Spirit which I have given unto you."

And again I beheld the messenger of God holding aloft the word of power. The nations looked upon it, and where the light of its pages shone forth upon the earth, it dispelled the gloom and darkness and shed forth the light of day.

"Even so hold thou My Word unto those whereunto I shall send thee. For I, even I, shall break the fetters that bind. I, even I, shall give liberty unto those in bondage, and light unto those in darkness through thee if thou shalt be as clay in my hands." (*Pentecostal Testimony*, July 1, 1910, page 12)

> *Book Editor*: It is my opinion that the vision was for more people than just the person who saw it, but to many that were to follow throughout the history of the Pentecostal movement.

## Pentecost in Holland
### G. R. Polman, Amsterdam

Grace, mercy and peace be multiplied to you. We do not know how to begin to give an account of the many blessings the Lord is bestowing upon us. Indeed, we can say with David, "Bless the Lord O my soul, and forget not all His benefits."

# Messengers of An Outpouring

Two years ago my dear wife received the baptism in the Holy Spirit with the sign of tongues. It was wonderful to see the overflowing joy, the power of testimony, the love in her for Jesus; her whole life was changed. All this made me very hungry for the same baptism. This outpouring of the power from on high brought a great change in our Mission; the Christians became awakened, pride and self-righteousness were discovered, hidden sins revealed, and a revival started right in our midst.

After a thorough cleansing and heart-searching the streams of living water began to flow; sinners were saved, the sick were healed, great hunger came into souls, and our little hall was packed every evening with a hungry gathering.

On the 4$^{th}$ of June, 1908, while in Sunderland at the Pentecostal Conference, I myself received the baptism in the Holy Spirit while dear Pastor and Mrs. Boddy laid hands on me. A great joy and power came into my life, and I could well understand 1 Cor. 14:2. Praise Him, the Blessed Lamb.

There was great joy in the dear little mission in Amsterdam that their evangelist had received the baptism in the Holy Spirit with the gift of tongues. How we longed to see each other again, and the hunger deepened more and more. After a month floods of God's rain came; one after another was baptized in the Holy Spirit with the sign of tongues.

Since that time about two hundred have received the baptism in the Holy Spirit in Holland. Glory to Jesus, He is still doing great things in our midst; He gave wonderful prophecies, interpretations, visions, tongues and healings. But the best of all, the dear people are more and more hungry for holiness and a deeper life with Christ.

God has graciously kept us from mistakes which have occurred in other countries, and I believe the best way to avoid them is to stick close to the Word of God and lead the people deeper into the death of self. Of course, there are still many imperfections, but we open our hearts for every blessing God has for us, and close our hearts from everything which has not its foundation on the Word of God.

It is also wonderful to see the change among young men and women. Their only aim now is to glorify Jesus, and you ought to hear the dear boys from fifteen to eighteen years old, pray. They are very earnest, and so kind and loving to each other, with a great desire to please God.

Our meetings are full of spiritual power, and our Pentecostal people are growing in the knowledge of Jesus and His precious Word. We have four Bible-classes every week, two for young people, and two for adults. One Bible-class is held with those only who are looking forward to becoming missionaries; about twenty-five young men and women attend the class.

We send out a free paper, "Spade Regan" (Latter Rain), 4,000 copies every [issue]. Many are sent to South Africa and also to America, Germany and other parts of the world. In the beginning of this year we had the privilege of having a visit from a few German pastors and evangelists. They came to see the things God was doing in our midst, and returned with great hunger. Many others came, and now a great awakening has come to Germany. In some assemblies many have been baptized and the fire is spreading. Praise God for the latter rain.

The spiritual life has deepened in the hearts of our people. The sixth and eighth chapters of Romans have become realities in our lives, but Pentecost cannot come as long as we are in the seventh chapter. When we have passed Calvary the Holy Spirit can come and fill the cleansed temple with His glory. The Holy Spirit throws such a light on the finished work of Jesus at the cross; the blood and the Holy Spirit work together and make us ready for the rapture. Hallelujah!

We hardly know where to end in telling of the blessing brought in the lives of old and young. We cannot do otherwise than humble ourselves in the dust for the great, unaccountable work the Pentecostal blessing has brought into our lives. The persecution is great and the devil is stirred mightily here in Holland, but "if God is for us, who is against us?" and "who shall separate us from the love of Christ?"

Pray for us, dear brother, and have your dear assembly pray for us. We thank you very much for sending of your very good paper. How wonderful that the Holy Spirit has put such a band of love around the Pentecostal people. It is Jesus! yes, all the way it is Jesus! (*TLRE,* Feb, 1910)

## My God Shall Supply All Your Needs
### Miss Marie Burgess

In the few years that I have spent in mission work in New York City, God has manifested Himself to me as a kind and loving Heavenly Father ever mindful of my smallest need. Some remarkable instances of His providential leading are to be a precious memory and have strengthened my faith and trust in the living God who inclines His ear to the cry of His children and answers the prayer of the heart.

Several years ago I was invited over to Flushing, Long Island, to spend the day. I didn't have a cent of money, not even [trolley] car fare but I went with some friends from the meeting the night before, and they paid my fare over. The next day I had to come back to New York City in time for an engagement which I had at six o'clock in the evening, and in order to do this I had to leave there at five o'clock; my friends would not be coming over to the evening meeting at the Mission until seven.

As I put on my things I happened to think I hadn't a cent of money in my pocket-book. I went aside and prayed, and said, "Now, Lord, You know I haven't any money; for Jesus' sake remind Mr. A. to give me some." There wasn't any one else over there whom I could think of who would give me any, and I kept asking God to put it into his heart.

We started off for the car. On the way he showed me through his storage-rooms, but I wasn't thinking about the storage-rooms; I was thinking about that money I needed. As we reached the place where I was to take the car I was wondering what I should do. Satan said, "Borrow a quarter," but another voice whispered to me, "My God shall supply your need." I said, "Yes, Lord, I am on business for You; You have promised but it doesn't look like Mr. A. is going to give me any money, and here comes the car."

# Messengers of An Outpouring

I stood for a moment not knowing just what to do; the Spirit said to me, "You preach, 'My God shall supply all your needs,' and you say you never borrow. Why don't you step out on the promise and prove it?" I said, "Hallelujah, I will prove You, this time, Lord, if I only ride a block," [they would make her get off if she did not have the fare] and I stepped on the car.

As I did so, a great peace and joy came into my soul, that I had really stepped out on God's word. The fare to New York City is thirteen cents. As I walked into the car I saw an old minister that had been to our Mission many times, and he motioned to me to come over and sit with him. As I went over and sat down, I said to myself, "Oh, glory to God, I know where my fare is coming from now." He paid my fare; then as we got to the ferry the devil says, "You don't know whether he has any money or not; you can't step on the boat."

But I said, "Lord, I can trust You; I think I could walk on water and trust You." The devil couldn't disturb me. I went on the boat and Brother C. paid my fare, and I said, "Brother C. you don't know what a blessing you have been to me," and I told him my story and the struggle I had had in my heart to obey God and prove Him; how God had him on that car to pay my fare, and what a sweet blessing it had been to test His promises and prove them true.

Then he began to weep and said, "Let me tell you my part of that story. I was eating supper and wanted to drink a second up of tea, but felt so hurried I could not; something kept telling me to get up and go. My wife said, 'What are you going for now? You don't need to go now, it is only five o'clock, but something kept telling me to go. So I took my overcoat over my arm and started down the street, running to get that car (he is an old man seventy-eight years of age). I saw the car coming a block away and ran down the hill to catch it, and when I got on I said to myself, 'C., you are a fool; you act as though this is the only car going to New York tonight.'" Then he told me that if he had obeyed God at the first he would not have had to run, but he waited to reason it out, and almost spoiled God's plan.

When I reached home that night there was a letter waiting for me with a ten-dollar bill in it. Brother A. also gave me two dollars that same evening when he came to the Mission, but the Lord didn't let him give it to me that day, as He wanted to teach me that sweet lesson of real trust. I saw God's hand in it; I had my eyes on Mr. A. that day, expecting him to help me instead of God. If I had borrowed a quarter from him, I would have lost that beautiful lesson.

On another occasion I had ten dollars given to me. As I started out to the Mission that night the rain was just pouring down. My clothing became soaked through and through, and when I reached home I said, "I wonder if the Lord doesn't want me to take that ten dollars and buy a rain-coat." Then I saw other places where it really ought to be used, and I said, "No, I guess I won't use it for that, because there will be other needs very soon." It wasn't especially needed that day, but would be very soon, and I thought I'd better hold on to the ten dollars.

The next day I had to go out to Flushing, and it was still raining; I thought, "Well, now I am one of the Lord's children, He has promised to supply our needs, and I really do need a rain-coat; if I go away out there in the rain I will become sick." So I went aside in my closet and prayed, and said, "Lord, did you really give me this ten dollars for a rain-coat? If you did I will trust you for the other needs when they come; I know they are not here [yet], but I was just trying to save that money." And I just felt the Lord say to me, "Yes, you can trust Me, for I will supply your every need." Then I said, "I will go then and get a rain-coat," and I felt an assurance that the Lord was really going to let me have it.

I went down town and went to several different stores; I was looking for a store that would give me [a] discount, but I found I couldn't get a rain-coat for ten dollars; fifteen was the cheapest. It came to me that I could borrow five dollars at home, but the Spirit said, "You know what a lesson you had on that one time." "No," I said, "I will not borrow."

I was just then passing a store which had signs up all over its windows, "Anniversary Sale," and I went in. As I went in I saw a brother who attended the Mission fixing the electric cash boxes; he was in his working clothes, and pride said to me, "You wouldn't go to speak to him in his working clothes!" I realized it was Satan talking to me and I rebuked him in Jesus' Name, and walked up to the brother and touched him on the shoulder. He shook hands with me and then all that feeling of pride left me -- that feeling that didn't want me to shake hands with a man in his working clothes before the people in the store.

I got victory over that, told him I never knew he was working there and mentioned the fact that I was looking for a rain-coat. He said he would introduce me to one of the ladies, who would wait on me. So I walked down the store with him in his working clothes, all the feeling of pride gone; usually I would have hated to walk through the store under such circumstances. He took me over to a saleslady and said, "Show this lady some rain-coats; she is a friend of mine." He stood there while I tried them on; they were having a sale on them. Pride stepped up again; I wished he would go; I didn't want to ask [in front of] him if they gave discount; I didn't want him to know I didn't have enough money to pay for the coat, and wanted to ask the clerk about a further discount, although they were selling them at a reduction.

He wouldn't go, and so I had to ask about the discount. He said, "Do you like the coat, Miss Burgess?" "Yes," I said, "I think it beautiful." "Well," he said to the clerk, "Miss Mary, just wrap it and charge it to me." That embarrassed me and I remonstrated with him. I didn't know what the clerk might think.

Then he began to tell right before the clerk about his sick wife; how that in the preceding January, when she was dying in the hospital, he had come to the Mission in despair -- I can remember him yet; he came and wanted to know why God hadn't answered prayer for the healing of his wife, and said to us at the time, "You say the Lord heals. Why doesn't He heal my wife?" He was almost beside himself in grief. I answered, "He will heal her, and we will go to prayer right now for her." So we gathered around the platform and prayed definitely for her, and he promised the Lord on his knees that if his wife was healed he would give an offering to the Mission. She was healed that day as we prayed, and he told this story in the presence of the saleslady and he said, "This twenty-one-dollar coat I give as an offering to the Lord, and that is not all; I will make a special offering to the

Mission besides in thanksgiving to God for blessing upon my wife, for she was perfectly healed that day."

She had been in the insane department of the hospital, her mind having left her. So I not only had the rain coat, but I had the ten dollars in my pocket-book besides for the special need that was coming. As I went home that day it seemed I was walking on air, for the Lord had led me to the right place and given me such a beautiful rain-coat.

Another instance of God's love and providence was in connection with my room rent. The rent for the month of August was due on a Monday and the Saturday night before I hadn't a cent towards it. As a rule, I had the money for my room, which was eight dollars, before it was due. I generally received money at the Mission on Saturday night from some one, but on this particular Saturday night I didn't get any, and I went home feeling rather discouraged, and said, "Why, Lord, I don't understand this at all; I didn't get a cent of money. You know I need ten dollars, and I never get money on Sunday." I got on my face and prayed, but could get no assurance because I was worrying instead of trusting, trying to figure out where it would come from; I could get no peace.

Finally, after praying and agonizing, the Lord seemed to say to me, "Rest, child, rest." I said, "Lord, I don't see how I can rest, for the rent isn't paid; I can never stand it not to have my rent paid promptly." He said, "It is not time for the rent until Monday morning." I always liked to have it on Saturday, a little before it was really due. I prayed until two o'clock Saturday night, when the Spirit of God told me [again] to rest, and I said, "Lord, I will rest it with You; there is no use in my crying and weeping over this thing; I cannot bring it that way." And when I began to say in my heart that I knew God would supply, I was delivered from fear and unrest and a great peace came into my soul. I told Him I would trust Him if Monday morning came and I didn't have a cent.

On Sunday afternoon a brother came into our Mission who had never been there before. He came to me and said, "Are you Miss Burgess?" I said, "Yes." He said, "I have hunted and hunted for your Mission, and something seemed to say to me that you were Miss Burgess." We had a blessed service in Glad Tidings Hall that day, and when the altar call was given he came to the altar, knelt down and wept as though his heart would break. As I was going out between the services to get a little lunch, he got up off his knees, came to me and said, "The Lord has spoken to me. I feel He wants me to give you a little money. Is it all right? Will you accept?" "Well," I said, "that is the way Father has of supplying my needs; He speaks to the hearts of His children and when they are obedient, my needs are supplied."

"Well," he said, "thank God. I had never met you before, didn't know how you would take it, but on my knees I cold not get away from the impression, so I will give you just what the Lord told me," and he opened his pocket-book and gave me ten dollars. When I saw that ten dollars I said, "Lord, You were true to Your Word," and I told him how God had used him.

To me, it is a greater blessing to have your ear open to listen to God speaking, to have your heart open so that God can use you to answer prayer, as that brother had whom I had never seen before, than to receive the money. A number of times I have been impressed to help others, and I found upon yielding to the impression that they had been praying for help. -- Mrs. Marie Burgess Brown. (*TLRE*, Feb, 1910.)

**A Remarkable Case of Healing: (At Glad Tidings Mission)** [Miss Burgess]

A woman who had a very peculiar disease came to New York to be treated by a specialist. Her bones were very brittle and some of them had broken without cause [osteoporosis]; her ribs had been broken several times, and one of her shoulder blades also. Two of the broken ribs had never knit together. She could not sit up without a brace, and was suffering continually the most untold agony. The cords in her neck and face would swell up at times because of the great pain. They were always trying some specialist, and she came to New York to be treated by the last one she had heard of. After going to him a week, she got no better. He told her where to get a new brace and thought that might help her.

Going on the [trolley] car to this man's office she went by our Mission and saw the sign, "Jesus Saves, Sanctifies and Heals," and said to her daughter, who was with her, "I wonder if I went there if I could get healing; I don't believe this doctor is going to do me any good." She was a nominal Christian. Her daughter said, "That Mission is not far from our house! I have heard about Miss Burgess." [The woman's daughter must have lived in New York.]

So the next night her daughter brought her to the Mission; she brought rubber cushions with her, for she couldn't sit on an ordinary chair. When I came in she told me about her case and asked if she could get healed. I told her that God wanted such cases as hers. We had a brief service, prayed for her and anointed her according to James 5:14, and she was instantly healed. She didn't understand why we talked in tongues, but thought we were all Swedes and said, "If that is a Swedish Mission, they have something down there."

She hadn't been able to sleep for two years without taking some opiate, but promised God she would drop everything and trust Him absolutely. She felt rather afraid it might come back and hesitated about taking off the brace, but when she went home she obeyed, and slept like a child. Her whole being was touched by the real, living power of God. In this one week with the specialist she had spent three hundred and forty dollars, but God touched her in one night and made her perfectly whole. (*TLRE*, Feb, 1910)

## Jottings From the Mountains of Tennessee

(A Vision of the Blood)

At the June Convention at Elim, Rochester, I was set apart for the ministry. I felt a call then to come South and work among the poor mountain whites, but God did not open the way until the end of November, when He sent me a fine outfit of clothes, and other necessary articles, together with my car-fare.

I am located at the foot of the Cumberland Range of mountains, of which Old Smoky Mountain is the highest, being 4,944 feet high. I have had two trips through the mountains on foot, walking more than one hundred and fifty miles over very rough roads. When my feet became sore God healed them right on the way, in answer to my cry. He has also given me victory over indigestion caused by the mountain diet, and over rheumatism contracted from sleeping in damp beds, etc. If I wasn't trusting God for my body, I would have been out of commission long ago. He is daily showing me what He means when He says; "My grace is sufficient."

I have had a few little prayer meetings, some school-house services, and entered into the homes of this people, and eighteen souls were gathered from the highways and hedges. All praise be to Jesus!

I bought a pony for one hundred and fifteen dollars, on the installment plan, but don't get the pony until I pay the last installment. God has sent me forty dollars of this, and a new bridle and saddle-bags and as soon as the balance comes I expect to make some evangelistic trips into North Carolina. It is a needy, barren field.

I found an old gentleman on his death-bed on my last trip, prayed with him, and he cried earnestly to God for salvation. I sat up with him several nights, helped dig the grave for his burial, and preached the funeral sermon to about one hundred and fifty mountain people. This one bit of service was well worth the trip south. I believe sometime in the future God will send me to a foreign field (Africa). I am getting practical training along all lines now, and this is better than much theology.

I held a Christmas-Day service at the County poor-house; drove five miles through mud and sleet. My congregation consisted of the halt, the maimed, the blind and all sorts of unfortunates. I told them of Jesus and His love; four were saved, and an old lady reclaimed, and everybody wept. It was the spirit of God that did it. One woman had never heard the Gospel and wept all through the service; at the close she fell on her knees without an invitation, crying, "God be merciful to me a sinner."

I gave out some little Testaments to such as could read. One poor woman wanted one; the manager said, "She can't read," but she looked at me so wistfully, saying, "I can mammy it, anyhow," meaning "I can treasure it." I gave her one, and she wept, saying, "Nobody can ever make me forget you ever."

The manager said with tears in his eyes; "I have asked many preachers and circuit riders to come here and have a service, but none has ever come."

As I was praying this morning [and] thinking about the value of the blood of Jesus, God gave me a vision. I saw myself covered with the merits of the blood, and it was like a canopy of impenetrable steel, like armor on a battle-ship. It seemed transparent and I saw demons trying to get through, but they could only look through. Then I saw an open place around the side, but lo! a wall of solid rock [covered it], and this scripture was brought to me, "He shall be a wall of fire round about thee."

I also thought of Job when Satan said to God, "You have put a hedge around him." Then I seemed to see other evil spirits coming with haste; some were labeled discouragement, and various kinds of names in temptation; lastly I saw Christ, and as the evil spirits bore down with the temptations, I saw Jesus nailed to the cross, and He said, "I bore them all." Praise God! -- Herman E. Tower. (*TLRE,* Feb. 1910.)

**Notes:**
God is continuing to bless the ministry of *The [Latter Rain] Evangel*. Interesting word comes from a sister in Arlington, N.J., who received her baptism while reading a copy of The Evangel. Her husband had for many years experienced the blessing of sanctification and thought he had all God had to offer him, but when he saw his wife receive the baptism he saw there was also more in store for him, and he sought and obtained this pearl of great price. A brother, realizing the change in their lives became hungry for God's fullness, and as he sought, God baptized him. May God continue to add to this chain of three. (*TLRE,* May, 1910)

## The Power of Pentecost in Indianapolis

It has been some time since any report has been published in any paper telling of God's dealings with the saints at Indianapolis. Since the last report the work has gone forward with leaps and bounds. The Sunday attendance was so large that we were compelled to move into larger quarters, and we are now located in an upper room over No. 9 North New Jersey St., where seating capacity will accommodate from about six to seven hundred people.

Several months ago the Lord sent Brother John Stroup to us from Ohio, and blessed his ministry among us. He is now in Pennsylvania, where the Lord is marvelously working. Our missionary interest has been greatly revived and the work is gaining ground constantly. Brother Howard A. Goss and wife from Texas spent a few days with us recently and were also of much blessing to us. About the first of March we had the pleasure of hearing Sister Abrams speak on the revival in India. On the following day a young brother, George Carriger, of St. Louis, left us expecting to go to New Zealand. Others of our mission are preparing for South America, Africa, India, China, and Iceland, and expect to leave before long for their different fields.

One thing which the Indianapolis work has stood very strongly for, has been the evangelization of the foreign fields. We believe this interest and enthusiasm in foreign missions has been largely the cause of success in the work. From its very inception it has been deeply interested in the heathen, and we now have one representative in India, one in South Africa, two in China, and one in Egypt.

We have proved the truth of the scripture, which says; "The Lord loveth a cheerful giver." Only recently about $1500 was given to send forth more workers, and that, too, from an assembly composed for the most part of ordinary, common, working people. As a result of this liberality God has blessed exceeding abundantly above all we have asked or thought.

A few months ago a young Japanese, Yoshio Tanimoto by name, came into the assembly. He is the son of a wealthy wine merchant of Hiroshima, Japan, who sent him to this country several years ago to acquire a business education. He had not been here long before he was convicted of sin and was converted. He determined to become a missionary and carry the Gospel to his own people in

Japan. This resulted in the withdrawal of his father's support financially. Nothing daunted, the young brother pressed on to know Christ. He obtained the experience of sanctification. Some months ago, while kneeling at the altar in our mission waiting on the Lord to know whether or not this Pentecostal baptism was scriptural and for him, he heard a brother at his side pray in the Japanese language. It was so convincing to him and he felt the Lord so fully back of the prayer that he began to seek for himself and in a few weeks, after tarrying before the Lord nearly all night, he was baptized, speaking in other tongues and praising God.

Being, like most of his race, reticent and undemonstrative, his testimony has had great weight and when it was announced that he would give his experience one Sunday night, the large hall was crowded to hear him, and we had a very stirring missionary service. Later, one of our number, a young woman, was called to go to Japan. God has led in each detail and in a very remarkable and definite manner supplied her with an experienced woman companion, and several Sundays ago we had a farewell service for these two sisters, who are now on their way to the "Flowery Kingdom," the little Japanese brother accompanying them.

God has greatly blessed in the work among the young people who number somewhere between forty and fifty, many of whom have been baptized [in the Holy Spirit]. The young man who is in South Africa was one of the number. Others are called to different fields and some are doing effective evangelistic work in and around Indianapolis and still farther away.

The Wednesday night service at the mission is conducted by the young people, and on Saturday night of each week there is a prayer meeting in some home, where they meet to wait on the Lord. Some of our young people have been baptized this winter in these tarrying meetings. At one of them a young woman was present who had never heard anyone speak in tongues. Her sister questioned a little as to what the effect might be if she should hear some one speak in tongues during the evening, but when they were leaving the house this young woman expressed her deep appreciation of the service, saying she felt God was there and there was something real and satisfying about that kind of religion. She also said that she had heard one of the young girls pray in Latin, and she understood what was said. Both the young women are hungry for the baptism and the joy, praise and spirit of worship that it brings.

During a testimony service some time ago, one of the young girls gave a long message in German, with interpretation following. She had never learned the language. It was done wholly by the Holy Spirit, and the message was full of praise and adoration. When she had finished, a young German girl, who had only been attending for about a week, arose and said, "I want to say something. From the first I have not doubted God's power in speaking in tongues, but if I were an unbeliever I should have to be convinced tonight, for I heard Sister Alice speak in my own language and understood her, and her interpretation was correct." This produced a decided effect upon the sinner in the back part of the hall and everyone felt a spirit of deep conviction settling down upon them through this bible "sign to unbelievers." . . . Zella H. Reynolds, J. Rosewell Flower. (*TLRE,* May, 1910)

**The Homestead Pa. Campmeeting:** [excerpt]

One who was present at the Homestead campmeeting gives us the following report:

"It would have been difficult to find a more earnest band of believers than those who assembled in the hills of Pennsylvania near Homestead, in Pentecostal campmeeting from July 8 to 25. They came, some for hundreds of miles, hungry hearts seeking after God . . .

"The one thing that seemed to burden the hearts of many workers was the fact that most of the Pentecostal workers today had slipped back into the natural; many, after a mighty infilling of the Holy Ghost, found themselves not walking in the Spirit, as at the first, but according to human understanding and human wisdom. The Holy Spirit had come in mighty power and transformed the lives and preaching of many, but for some reason instead of waiting to deliver a message only under the illumination of the Holy Spirit, the ministry had gone back to old methods and old ways. Instead of the Holy Spirit using the instrument, it was the instrument using the Holy Spirit. Emphasis was again and again laid upon the fact that when the Holy Spirit comes in He takes us out of the natural into the supernatural; out of the human into the divine, and this is the place of power." (*TLRE*, Aug., 1910)

**Notes:**

Recently the Lord graciously visited us at the Stone Church with a very deep wave of spiritual blessing and power. It began on July 4th; when the world and many Christian professors were running after pleasure, some of our hungry people were in a meeting seeking God. Two or three received the blessing of sanctification on that day, and in one week the holy fire had spread in our midst until at least twenty were sanctified, eight saved, two delivered from stubborn demon possession, and four baptized in the Holy Spirit and spoke in tongues, all glory to the Name of Jesus. (*TLRE*, Aug., 1910)

## Testimony of a Baptist Minister

### Alvin L. Branch, Colon, Mich.

Hungering to attain to the best that God has in the way of equipment for His servants, both to live well-pleasing to Him in all things and to be fruitful in every good work, led me to welcome the glad news that some of His people were receiving real Bible experience in the baptism in the Holy Spirit.

I had long been convinced that none of God's promises to His church had been withdrawn by Him, and none of the New Testament commandments had ceased to become binding upon His followers, and that the command to "Tarry ye until" was still as much in force as when it was spoken. The still small voice within would not be silenced by the words of this world's wisdom which declared that apostolic experiences especially speaking in other tongues and the healing of the sick were intended only for apostolic times.

I prayed earnestly that God would baptize me in the Holy Spirit, and then tried hard to believe that because I had asked what was according to His will I therefore must have it and must just believe and go ahead, taking it for granted that the prayer was answered.

Time and again when souls were converted in some of our regular or special meetings I was almost convinced that God had answered the prayer, notwithstanding the unsatisfied heart hunger, but God opened up the way for me to go to Chicago, and while there the blessed Comforter came into this temple, which seemed to me more like a hut, unworthy of such a Heavenly Guest, and used these lips to talk with Father in a language, the words of which I did not understand, but I unmistakably understood the sweet consciousness of His abiding Presence.

This has never left me; neither have I been induced to do or say things ridiculous, absurd or unseemly, as some of my friends feared. It has not made me a blazing light in the religious world, but enabled me to live in the realm of the Ninety-first Psalm. It deepens the passion to win men to Jesus Christ, and brightens the hope of His coming.

My subsequent experience makes plain to me the absurdity of the position of many opposers of the work, who describe it as "ecstatic," "rhapsodical emotionalism." Almost without exception in my daily talks with Jesus now, when the burden of prayer be- comes real, I find myself praying in another tongue. There may be a feeling of joy or pain, or there may be no more emotion than in ordinary conversation. There is a vivid reality to prayer unknown before.

The preparation of the Sunday messages is not a burdensome "getting up a sermon," but a waiting upon God to hear His voice and then, perhaps, like a flash, the whole plan or outline comes before me, and the only difficulty comes in compressing the whole message into the thirty or forty minutes allotted for the sermon.

The blessed Word is so much more a vitalizing force both in myself and in the flock over whom the Holy Spirit hath made me overseer. Many of the dear brethren feared that I had gone into fanaticism, but when after a long time they do not discover irrational traits or outbursts, some are convinced that it is of God, and are hungering to know more of God in their lives.

The accompanying hymn, "Looking Up to Jesus," [an original song] was given me in another tongue one Sunday morning when I was waiting for the message. Two weeks later, under similar circumstances, the interpretation was given.

The most blessed thing in this world is to live in the center of the will of God. It is the vestibule of heaven. (*TLRE,* Aug., 1910)

### *** Looking Up to Jesus ***

I'm just waiting for the fire that shall burn away the dross,
That shall burn up all my passions as I nail them to the cross;
That shall take away the pride and every worldly thing,
As I'm looking up to Jesus and crown Him as my King.

Chorus
Oh, I'm looking up to Jesus and would Jesus only see,

And I'm trusting in His merit because He died for me.

I am looking up to Jesus to fulfill my every need;
There's a promise of His fullness in the Word which is the seed,
That when sown in the hearts, will surely bring release,
And fill those hearts with God's own perfect love and peace.

I am looking unto Jesus to take away the sin,
That for many years has burdened, cursed the life within,
I know His power is able to cleanse away the dross.
And I'm looking unto Jesus as He hung upon the cross.

I am looking up to Jesus as He sits upon the throne,
And gives me sweet assurance that I am His very own.
My eyes are fixed on Jesus, and in His blessed face
I see that He forgives me and saves me by His grace.

I am looking up to Jesus and His hand outstretched I see,
As He points me to the nations that dwell beyond the sea.
As He bids me go to them with the precious Bread of Life.
And tell them of the Savior, the wondrous Prince of Life.

I am looking up to Jesus for the all-sufficient grace
That will come to those who trust Him to fit them for the place
That He has chosen for them in this dark world of sin,
As they keep their eyes on Jesus and crown Him King within.

I am looking up to Jesus for the strength I need each day,
For the wisdom that shall guide me along the narrow way
That leads me up to glory where angel hosts sing praise
To the wondrous King of Glory as they look upon His face.

I am looking up to Jesus and the pains of earth seem small
In the glory of His presence I soon forget them all.
And the grief that comes like arrows, very soon gives place
To the joy that comes like sunshine as I look upon His face. (Ibid)

**A Note of Praise:**
Let me sound abroad the praises of the Lord for His wondrous grace in preparing the company of missionaries and providing the money for their going forth to India.

We were delayed in sailing because the berths in ships sailing from London to Bombay were all filled. We have now taken passage to sail from New York, Oct. 22nd, and we are due in Bombay Nov. 24th.

Our party so far consists of Miss Phinette K. Bristol and Miss Grace Dempster, both of Monrovia, Calif., Miss Minnie L. Houck, N.Y., Miss Lillie E. Doll, Jersey City, N.J., Miss Blanche Cunningham, of Richmand, Ind., and myself. Until we sail my address will be . . .

We expect to open up a work in a wholly unevangelized field. We are having a conveyance made for village work, in one of the Mission Industrial Schools of India, which will shade us from the fierce rays of the sun by day, and can be made into a bed at night. The Lord who has provided the money for this will also provide for the oxen to draw it, the servant to drive them, and the fodder to feed them.

At this early date we cannot give details, but we shall keep the readers of The Evangel posted . . . Minnie F. Abrams. (*TLRE,* Oct. 1910)

**The Stone Church:** [Which produced *The Latter Rain Evangel*]

God's blessing has been with us continually at The Stone Church. We have not had great cloud-bursts of "latter-rain" neither have we had a drought, but there has been a steady stream of living water flowing from the Fountain Head, and the stream has given spiritual life and power to many.

Intercession and soul-travail will bring forth spiritual children, and when people are willing to pour out their lives, souls will be born into the kingdom of God.

On account of the cool weather the work of our Gospel wagon has been closed for the summer. Our workers have had great joy in carrying the Gospel message into the highways of this great city. It has been a privilege to preach to the crowds that have gathered; sometimes as many as five hundred have stood for an hour and listened with respectful attention as the blessed salvation which Jesus brought has been fearlessly proclaimed, night after night, and not a few times have a number held up their hands for prayer, and said with tears streaming down their faces, "Pray for me." We have sowed bountifully and are trusting God to give us a rich harvest this fall and winter.

Some who had seriously backslidden have been brought back to God. One man coming into the city with such hatred in his heart that he was determined to commit murder, dropped into our service and was so deeply convicted by the Spirit that he confessed the crime he had contemplated and found forgiveness and pardon at the foot of the cross.

Satan is waging a fierce conflict along many lines; some who have been seriously tempted to commit suicide and others who have been possessed with evil spirits of various kinds have been delivered; one who had a demon of blasphemy and could scarcely resist blaspheming God, was set free through the power of the blood of Jesus.

At the Wednesday afternoon Divine Healing meetings many witness to the fact that Jesus is the Healer today. One man recently testified that he was healed of a tumor of the brain, of a serious nature, his mother having died of a similar affliction. (*TLRE,* Oct. 1910)

# Chapter 6

# 1911

**A Vision:**

[Pastor Friemel, from Germany at the convention in Sunderland:] The Pastor's address was an earnest exhortation to implicit faith in God, and moved the gathering to great enthusiasm.

Just before he was asked on the previous Saturday to speak, he said he saw a vision. The heavens opened, and he saw one of the angels of God breathe upon the earth. It just looked like a small cloud, and then it poured out brilliant rays. He asked the Lord the meaning, and He replied: "I have now given the order that the Heavenly messenger is to come down to My children who have open hearts, I will pour My heavenly rays upon them." (*Confidence*, June, 1911, page 124)

## A Testimony by Mrs. Marie Burgess Brown:

"And it shall come to pass in the last days, saith God, I will pour out my Spirit upon all flesh, and your sons and your daughters shall prophesy, and your young men shall see visions, and your old me shall dream dreams. And on my servants and on my hand-maidens I will pour out, in those days, of my Spirit, and they shall prophesy. (Acts 2:17-18)

Praise God that his prophecy of Joel is being fulfilled today and the Holy Spirit is again being poured out upon us as it was upon the disciples on the day of Pentecost. And just as the multitudes at that time were amazed and in doubt, saying: "What meanth this?" And others mocking said, "They are filled with new wine." So it is today -- the churches and people for the most part have rejected His visitation. Some have even dared to call His work the workings of Satan. But, dear children of God, I beg of you in Jesus' name to not let that old deceiver deceive you any longer, for truly "this is that" which was spoken by the prophet Joel, for I speak as one who has for over four years proved it to be from God. Hallelujah.

I was a young girl who loved the pleasures of this old world, dancing, card-playing, theater-going, etc. And to the sorrow of my dear Christian parents and sisters, I would follow the world and live in its pleasures, though many times under deep conviction for sin, knowing I was on the road to hell.

And thus in the year 1899 the blessed Master came to me in a dream. I dreamed I was dying, and just before me was the awful pit of hell, and I saw it so dark and deep, and where I was soon to go. I then began to cry to Jesus to save me from this awful fate. He came and stood at the end of my cot and said, "Wilt thou forsake all and follow me?" And I said, "Yes Lord, all." And as I did He reached forth that pierced hand and took mine, and as I arose I awoke, but it was so real and is even today.

Right there I gave my all to Him and promised Him I would do all I could to tell a lost world what the pierced hands and feet and side would save them from -- an awful hell. There was joy in that home next morning when I told my dream, and what I had done. That my life was now consecrated to Him. After a few months I went to a Bible training school to prepare myself to work in the master's vineyard -- anywhere.

I spent over two years there, and then expected to go to the foreign field, but for some reason was hindered and so I worked as a home missionary for a few years. Then I began to feel there was a lack in my equipment somewhere, and knowing my education was limited, felt that must be my need. So I went back to school. Had one year in the preparatory, but before the next year was quite finished I was called home on account of sickness, and this kept me from returning.

After some time I sought a position [job] and then for several years I labored, and it was at the counter demonstrating this world's goods that my Master found me [again].

It was in 1906 at the beginning of this blessed outpouring of the Holy Spirit that He put such a hunger in my heart to know Him better. I had heard of this outpouring of the Spirit, but was warned against it -- said to be the work of the devil and so I did not go near the meetings where this precious truth was being taught till one day a desire came over me to just see how the devil did his work in the lives of God's people, and so I went to a meeting and to my great surprise found it not at all as reported, but God [was] there in power.

However, fearing it might be the work of the devil, for in the last days he is to deceive, if possible, even the very elect, thought I would not say anything till I had gone again. I did so and Oh! how my poor thirsty soul drank from the living fountain that night. He was there, my Master, with that pierced hand that had lifted me from the pit of hell many years before. [He] Came to the meeting that night with a message for me, "Thou hast left thy first love," and I knew it was true, and said, "Yes Lord, I have, forgive me." And again that hand took mine and said, "Follow thou me." I obeyed and He led me to a waiting room, where I stayed till the promise of the Father was given me. (The baptism of the Holy Spirit and fire.) During these days of waiting He became very precious to me and one day I received a most blessed anointing of the Holy Spirit and it was so different from anything I had ever experienced that I thought it must be my baptism and thus I labeled it. Some hearing me say it corrected me, but I still kept thinking that I knew what I had, even if I had not spoken in tongues.

## Pentecostal Newspapers

In searching the word of God I found I had not what the disciples had when they received their baptism and it created a deeper hunger in my heart for all He had for me. And on the third day of waiting (tarrying) He came as He came to them in that upper room. He did not make me a Peter or a John, but just a witness, and for five hours He filled and flooded my whole being.

Then He opened my eyes to see the great need of this dark world. It seemed as if I went from one foreign field to another [in a vision] and in each field He would pray through me in the language of that people. I knew it not -- but He did. There seemed to be great stone walls about each field and I could hear them cry for Jesus, and as the Holy Spirit would begin to pray in the language of each field, I could see the walls begin to crumble and fall.

How this cry touched my heart, as every cry of the Holy Spirit will, and I said, "Lord, send me, send me," that those who want Jesus may find Him.

I felt this was my call renewed and left all to follow Him. You see that promise was for me. "And on my servants and on my hand-maidens, I will pour out, in those days, of my Spirit and they shall prophesy." So I went out then as His servant to labor for Him -- first at home, then to fields about there, and in January, 1907, He brought me to New York City to witness here for Him and to tell His dear children that He is soon to return and that we must all have on the wedding garments and the vessels filled with oil and lamps trimmed and burning, for truly many have lights gone out and many are going out. He has given the call. "Behold the Bridegroom cometh," and if we shall go to meet Him, we must now get ready.

I never expected He would keep me here in this city so long, but my delight is only in His will, in His way, in His place. On May 5, 1907, "Glad Tidings Hall" was opened and God gave us as a token of His opening the door– a precious soul, one that had not drawn a sober breath for over four years -- the hallways and streets was all the home he had, but such our Great Redeemer came to save and this brother is with us, a new man in Christ Jesus, today. Many others have found Him and many have received the baptism of the Holy Spirit according to Acts 2. . . .

There is nothing in all the world that could take from me this wonderful experience with my Lord. Though all should fail and fall from their experience, I can truly say mine is real. And He is more real today than ever – yes, while now writing He is speaking through me in tongues and praising my Lord. Glory be to Him for ever and ever.

I want to add before closing my testimony that as the dear Lord sent His disciples out by twos, that a year ago He gave me a dear helper, one who has had many years of training in the battle's front, and has a stronger force for Him in "Glad Tidings Hall." And this dear child of God is my companion . . . (*The Midnight Cry*, March-April, 1911)

> *Book Editor*: Miss Burgess (1880-1971) founded *Glad Tidings Mission*, married Robert Brown in Oct. 1909, who she met at the mission. It later became *Glad Tidings Tabernacle*, a prominent Pentecostal church which they both pastored; and published *The Midnight Cry* newspaper. He died in 1948 and she continued as sole pastor. She did not go onto the mission-field, but her church sent missionaries to the places she saw in her vision.

**A Message in the Spirit:**

My people are not humble. Oh! That they would hear my voice. They think they are humble, but they are not. My people have failed to obey my commandments and hence the Continual Message, humble yourselves. The bleating of the sheep I hear; like Saul you have held back in order to Sacrifice. You have saved the king of pride in your heart; my heart is longing for a people that will hearken and obey my voice and my word. Oh! I must have a people to work through. Get down. I want to do mighty things through you. But you are not willing to go my way. My way is the way of humility. My people have proud hearts and high looks. Humble yourselves. I made the sacrifice of the Cross for you that you might be one through my precious blood. Even as I and my Father are one. But you are not willing to be one with one another. I am calling a people that are willing to be anything for me. The time is short; I am coming soon. Oh! Church of God, awake. He calleth for thee. Put on your armour. Gird your loins. The day is almost gone. (Given by Sister Yates) (*The Midnight Cry*, March-April, 1911)

\*\*\*

The Lord has shown us very clearly that the Spirit and the Word agree; that it is only truth without a compromise that He will bless. Therefore we have taken a stand against any vision, revelation, or manifestation which cannot be plumblined by the Word of God. (Ibid)

\*\*\*

The Lord has visited us in an unusual way in the mission of late. For over two months a weight of glory seems to continually rest upon us. Thirty-one souls have been baptized in the Holy Ghost, and spake with other tongues as the Spirit gave them utterance. Today if you will hear His voice harden not your hearts. (Ibid)

## A Remarkable Dream
### Mrs. L. E. Eames, Oneieda, New York

I will relate the dream as it came to me, but it will be impossible for me to describe it [exactly] as I saw it. This dream was given me while very ill in the hospital, five days after an operation. The next night it was repeated in every detail.

The day before the operation and the next morning I prayed constantly for the Lord to restore me to health again if He had anything for me to do for Him; I was ready to go if there wasn't anything, but my constant prayer was that He would let me try once more. Five days [later] He gave me this wonderful dream.

I was carried back to the time I was converted, at nineteen years of age. All the past between that time and now seemed blotted out. At the little village church they had been holding evangelistic meetings for several weeks, and a great number had been converted.

I saw a great, long, white road beginning at the church and running perfectly straight up into the heavens. At the end of this road I could just see great mammoth gates. The road was very wide and crowded with people. I saw all those who were converted at the time I was, and I remembered them all. There were also crowds of others I had never seen before.

It seemed that the purpose of all was to reach the gates, and I also thought only of that one thing. The road was so beautiful and smooth, it seemed to me there wouldn't be any trouble in making the journey. I said over and over to myself, "The road is so smooth and I am getting along so nicely that it won't be hard at all to reach the gates." After I had traveled awhile I noticed some attraction at the right side of the road, and a great many looked to see what it was and crowded off the road to find out. In the rush I was crowded off with the others. I tried to hold back and didn't want to stop, but it was in vain; I was crowded off with the others.

I found myself in a large entrance which opened into a large place, something like an amphitheatre, where there were all manner of amusements going on. Yes, everything from a dance hall to a pool room. I could see a play going on, the characters on the stage, the curtain and the boxes at the side. In another direction I could see people playing cards, laughing and drinking. All seemed to be having a good time, but oh, so restless!

Some looked so tired and nervous, and I said to myself, "I must get out of this place. I didn't want to come here, and I must get back on the road again. I shall be away behind the others and be delayed in reaching the gates." I had to push and crowd my way out. I had difficulty in getting out of that place, but I finally succeeded. After I had gotten back on the road again something seemed to turn me around, and as I looked back a flash of light circled over the entrance spelling the word, "AMUSEMENTS" in large letters.

I started again on my journey, and said I wouldn't let anything stop me again. I tried to walk fast, but somehow I didn't get along as easily as I did before. I could look up the road and see the people who were with me before I stopped, so far ahead. I thought I would try hard to catch up with them, but the road was harder to travel, and I saw it would be useless to try, they were so far ahead. I was so sorry I had been stopped, and was more determined than ever to press on. The road was quite a little rough, so I couldn't get along very fast, but I thought perhaps it would get smoother farther on, which it seemed to do.

I was making good headway, when all at once there was some commotion on the other side of the road, and the first thing I knew I was crowded off from the road again. Everyone didn't stop to look, but there were a great many who did, and they seemed to be those who were around me, and I couldn't help myself. No one spoke a word. Everybody seemed so intent with only the one object in view – reaching the gates. As far as I could see ahead, there was a solid mass of people, and back of me they were so packed they were beyond number. I had struggled hard to keep on the road but I found it was impossible in the awful crowd. The people didn't want to stop, it seemed, but just to look and see what all the commotion was about.

There was a large entrance like the other one, but the place was more like a village. There were stores and sales going on, and people rushing against each other; everywhere there were people selling something. I saw all kinds of markets, and a street something like a midway. Men were in wagons, selling real estate, with signs tacked up, and all were in a mad rush. Everybody acted as though everything must be done at once. I made up my mind to get out at once, for I knew I was losing much time and would be delayed again in reaching the gates. After pushing and crowding, I again succeeded in reaching the main road. I had the same impression to turn around, and as I looked and wondered that same flash of light circled over the entrance, spelling in large letters of fire the word "BUSINESS."

I felt dreadful because I had stopped, for I could see those who had been with me before I was crowded off, far up the road. The road was harder than ever now to travel; there were deep ruts and bumps along my way, and it seemed almost impossible for me to make any time.

Still I kept plodding, more than ever determined not to give up. The old friends who had started with me, but had not stopped, were nearly to the gates. I thought I would get into the middle of the road so it would not be so easy to get crowded off again. After a time the road seemed to travel better and I felt encouraged, for I kept saying over to myself, "I shall reach the gates before long."

While in that contented frame of mind, I began hearing something like the wail or moaning of the wind. First it sounded like that, then it became louder and seemed coming nearer. After a little I could hear plainly these words as of thousands of voices calling in the distance, "Open those gates." I had noticed as the road seemed to ascend there was a large wall on each side of the road that led to the heavenly gates, and large iron gates about a quarter of a mile apart, on each side. Each one had a great iron bar for a latch. Louder and louder came the call, "Open the gates;" it seemed to fairly shake the walls, and the wail of it was terrible.

The road traveled so smoothly now I made up my mind I wouldn't look aside no matter what happened, so I kept straight ahead for a long time, but the cry seemed so heartrending and so full of suffering I could not stand it any longer.

All at once the thought of myself and reaching the goal was swept away, and I turned and looked, and what I saw I shall never forget, neither can words describe it. Some great calamity had come upon the world; it was covered with a dim, red light, and it seemed it was being destroyed. As far as I could see there was nothing but a surging mass of humanity fleeing toward this road to escape death. It was the most horrible sight that one could imagine and seemed to paralyze me for a moment as I saw the awful horror-stricken faces, eyes bulging, arms out-stretched, people rushing over each other pulling their hair in their agony. I looked at everyone near me to see if anyone would help save those people, for it was perfectly plain to me they were fleeing to this road for safety as they were facing death. I flew to the nearest gate, and forgot everything else in my desire to open that gate.

I tried hard to move the bolt, but found it impossible, so I called as loud as I could, "Won't someone help me open the gate?" Three or four hurried to help me, and after tugging with all our strength for awhile, the large iron bar slipped up in the socket and the gate was pushed open by the awful crowd. In the rush I was jammed between the gate and the wall so that I could hardly breathe. I worked my way out and tried to get back into the road again, but I was hurt so I had no strength and sank down. There seemed to be no end to the awful crowd as they came surging in. I succeeded in holding myself up by supporting myself against the wall, and as I stood there watching those suffering, struggling people, the question came to me as before. What is the meaning of this? What has happened? And that same flash of light circled over the top of the gate spelling in letters of "INDIFFERENCE."

Oh, how that word burned into my soul! I understood everything at that moment, and began calling to the people, "Oh, will some one go back and open the other gates? What will become of those poor people who are calling so far down the road for someone to open the gates?" I called several times, but no one paid any attention, and then I seemed to understand it was impossible to go back, for the road was so crowded all had to go straight ahead. I moaned over and over to myself with remorse for those poor lost people. "If I had only looked before." I couldn't bear the sorrow it caused me and I sank down by the side of the road. Then it seemed I was lying on my bed, and my room was there by the side of the road at the gate. I was so ill I couldn't continue my journey up the road to the heavenly gates.

I understood it all, so I began to pray, and called with a loud voice [still in the dream], "Take me now, dear Lord, the struggle is too hard." I uttered the same call three times, then a voice said to me in plain words, "You cannot go now!" This was repeated four times, then the voice said, "There is somebody coming up the road that won't hold out; something you will say or do will help them on, and you will reach the gates." That voice I shall never forget; it seemed to sink into my very soul. It is impossible to convey to anyone the sound of that voice or the way it impressed me. It was a heavy, musical voice, firm, but tender and gentile. As the voice spoke these words to me I awoke in tears. (*TLRE*, Aug., 1911)

## How God Led Me to Pentecost
### Sarah E. Keatley

I was born and raised near Norfolk, Va. My father and only brother died in the Southern Army [U.S. Civil War] and my mother being left in destitute circumstances, my three sisters and myself were obliged to go out into the world and earn our own living.

After a time I became engaged to be married to a gentleman, a widower with four children. His former wife was a Catholic and he had promised her to bring the children up in that faith and as I had no religion he asked me if I would learn the Catholic religion so that I could bring them up as he had promised their mother. I respected him for being faithful to the promise he had made his wife and told him I was willing to become a Catholic.

He then proposed to send me at his own expense to a Catholic institution in Boston, where I would be free from the influence of all my friends and be instructed in the Catholic faith. I consented and he went to a Catholic priest in Norfolk and got an order from him admitting me to the institution. I now see the hand of the Lord in this as I was a young giddy girl with no thought of God or religion, but would rather dance than eat; and the Lord took this way to get me away from my young companions and turn my thoughts toward Him.

## Messengers of An Outpouring

I made the journey to Boston by boat and became acquainted with a Christian lady on board who invited me to come and see her at her home in Boston. I did not tell her where I was going or for what purpose. At this institution I tried to learn the Catholic religion for eight weeks. When I prayed to the Virgin it seemed like throwing a ball against a wall, it bounced back and I always finished by praying to Jesus, and it seemed as if He heard me. At the end of that time I made up my mind there was nothing in the Catholic religion for me and that I would get away from the institution, but that I would not stop seeking the Lord.

When I told the Catholic sister who had charge of me that I was going to leave she said I could not get out without the permission of the priest in Norfolk. I told her if she did not let me go I would jump out the window. She then said, "Keep still, and I will see what I can do." She went to the Sister who had charge of the wash house at the rear and told her if she saw me coming out to turn her back to me and not see me go out. She did so and I left my extra clothing and went out after sunset and found myself a stranger alone on the streets of Boston.

I remembered the lady I had met on the boat and thought I would try and find her. But I had neglected to take her address and only remembered her name and that she lived in East Boston. I saw a policeman and asked him to direct me to East Boston, and then I prayed that the Lord would lead me to this lady's house. By this time it was getting dark. I started to turn into two different houses but had the feeling "this is not the place." Then I came to a row of about twenty houses all alike. I turned into one of these houses and something seemed to say, "This is the place," and it was, for when I rang the bell the lady I had met on the boat came to the door.

When she recognized me she said, "I am so glad you have come, my husband has gone on sea voyage and I am alone." I went in and felt so thankful to find a friend I could confide in and I wept as I opened my heart and told her all that I came to Boston for. She pressed me to stay with her, but I told her I was not going to marry the man who sent me there and I would get a position. All I knew how to do was plain sewing but in two days I found a position in the family of a Baptist minister.

When his wife engaged me she asked me what church I attended. I said, "The Catholic." She said, "That is all right if you are a good Catholic." I said, "I am not a good Catholic." They were very kind to me but never invited me to their church nor said anything to me on the subject of religion, yet all this time I was praying and seeking the Lord. I believed in a change of heart and nothing else would satisfy me. Whenever I had spare time I went to my room and prayed. After a time I learned that revival meetings were being held at Mr. Pentecost's church nearby, and I went one night, and was the first who rose for prayer at the close; and I kept on seeking the Lord in my room.

About two weeks after that one evening sitting with the family in the room I became lost to everything about me and arose and going to my room fell on my knees and told the Lord that I would never get off my knees till He had saved my soul. I asked Him to show me my sins, as He saw them, and when they rose up before me like a mountain, I drew back and said, "Lord, I don't want You to forgive me; my sins are so great. I do not deserve it. If I had known I was such a sinner I would not have asked You."

When I said that, the burden rolled away and peace filled my soul. I arose and went down stairs where there was a room full of company, the tears streaming from my eyes and said, "Let us pray," and we all prayed one by one. When we came to the seventeen-year-old daughter she prayed, "Jesus have mercy upon me," and about two weeks from that time she was converted.

After I was converted I went back to the church where I rose for prayers and testified. Then Mr. Pentecost said, "I remember that lady. The night she stood up for prayer I was so impressed and burdened for her salvation that I went home and told my wife I had to pray for her."

I went on serving the Lord about twenty years and then there came a trouble in my life, and I lost my first love; I remained in that state for about eight years, but being a Baptist I did not know I was backslidden. All these eight years I was hungry for God, but did not know that it was Himself that I wanted.

After a very severe sickness I [and husband moved], upon the advice of the doctors, to Los Angeles, where I united with the Memorial Baptist church but my heart was still unsatisfied. About this time I heard of some consecrated colored people who were holding meetings on Azusa street. I knew that the colored people in the South, where I had lived, had more religion than the white people and I thought I might get help there.

The first time I went [there] the Lord spoke to my heart and said, "This is of God." The second time I went an aged Christian in his testimony told his experience in sanctification and the power of the blood to cleanse from all sin. Then the Lord spoke to me again and said, "That is for you," and the tears rolled down my cheeks. I arose and went home and commenced to pray for sanctification.

Then the Lord spoke out in an audible voice and said, "You are a backslider." These words broke me all to pieces. I said, "Lord, I did not know it, but take me back. I am no more worthy to be called Thy son but make me as one of Thy hired servants." In about two weeks the Lord did take me back and really made a fest for me and put the ring on my finger and a robe on me, and then I went to praying for sanctification.

I was to have my husband's relatives, who like himself were infidels, at a Thanksgiving dinner; and about two weeks before the time I felt that as I had backslidden once, I must have more strength, and I told the Lord if he would sanctify me before Thanksgiving I would testify before these unbelievers to what He had done for me. The day before Thanksgiving I was in the kitchen singing, "Jesus' blood covers me," and the Lord spoke to my heart and said, "Go and pray." I said, "Yes, Lord, I am glad I have got to a place where I can pray" and I went and He sanctified me and filled me with joy and holy laughter. Next day as I had promised, I testified and prayed before my guests and when I finished they all said, "Amen."

From that time I commenced waiting on the Lord for the baptism with the Holy Ghost. My husband saw the change sanctification made in me and he said, "That's all right, but you have got enough now. Don't seek anything more or you will go crazy." After I was sanctified till I was baptized, every time I went to pray I saw Jesus on the cross with the crown of thorns. In any prayer I always told the Lord I was waiting for Him to baptize me when He saw I was ready, and I knew He would do it.

On the 22nd of February, 1907, I retired early, desiring to be alone with the Lord and He commenced working on my body. One of my limbs had been broken in two places and always trouble me. He took my hands and grasping my limb at each place where it had been broken, shook it more violently than I am able to shake it myself. Since then I have had no pain in that limb. Then He worked on every part of my body like a physical sculpture and made me all over new. I had kidney trouble and stomach trouble, which He perfectly healed. I said, "Lord, how long are you going to work on my body?" He answered, "Till 12 o'clock." I so feared to interrupt His work that I said, "Lord, when you have finished turn me on my right side." He did so and just then the clock struck twelve.

I was so conscious of His presence and so happy I did not sleep at all, but seemed to be in heaven all night. The next day through a severe trial my joy departed and a cloud settled upon me so that I thought I had lost all my blessing. I wept and mourned before the Lord all that night. I could eat no breakfast and as soon as my husband was gone I locked the door, went into my kitchen and throwing myself on my knees, I told the Lord I would follow Him whether He ever restored the joy or not, and if He sent me to hell I would go there praying. When I said that the cloud lifted, the joy returned and I said, "Praise God, praise God!"

Then the Holy Spirit spoke in an audible voice, saying, "Praise Jesus. He is standing right here with a perfect language for you." So I began to praise Jesus and broke out in another tongue; a clear, distinct language; I also sang. One song was made up of different passages of Scripture joined together so that they rhymed. The oft-repeated chorus was, "Jesus is coming soon." I seemed to be before a congregation and the Lord told me, "I am going to use you to bring this message to you, and you, and you," pointing my finger in three different directions. I talked and sang for about three hours. Then I went to a neighbor's and continued praising the Lord in tongues and singing for an hour and a half longer. Later I went down to Azusa mission and kept singing and talking in tongues till four o'clock.

Since then God's power has kept me; I have sown the seed and seen the fruits. First, I began to pray for my husband and God saved him. Then I sent to my neighbor and prayed for her husband and the Lord saved him. He also saved several other neighbors. Later He sanctified my husband and baptized him with the Holy Spirit and he spoke in the Chinese language. I gave Him our home and He sanctified it and has sent many here for help, and has saved and sanctified and baptized many in it. I want God to have all the glory. That is the reason I write this testimony that all may know what God is able to do. -- Sarah E. Keatley, L. A. (*TLRE*, Nov., 1911)

> *Book Editor*: In 1916 an updated version of this testimony appeared in *The Weekly Evangel*, with details that apparently took place after 1911, as follows:

Since then He sent me to China, and there Sister Dean and I started the mission in which she now is. God gave her the management, and me the prayer. I could not speak the language, but God gave me such a ministry in prayer that I saw many of the Chinese saved, and since that time they have been baptized in the Spirit. God gave me a native preacher, and I supported him. I am still interested in China. (*TWE*, May, 5, 1916)

> *Book Editor*: In this updated version of the testimony there is no mention of "sanctification," which was once believed by many Christians, especially those in the Holiness movement, but the Pentecostal denominations rejected it as a second work of grace and said you get sanctified when you get born again.

## That Big Black Bear
Miss Elizabeth Sisson, New London, Con.

It was the hour of morning worship in a home in Winnipeg, where the writer was a guest during the closing days of a campaign for God, in that city. Several persons knowing it was one of the last days of her stay, had, unknown to each other, come to that hour of worship. Thus, as we gathered around the Holy Word, we were surprised to find ourselves quite a company.

After singing and the Word, as we knelt together before the Lord, the power of the Holy Ghost fell upon the waiting group. Several were prostrated under the slaying might of God, among them our hostess, Mrs. D. When the power was lifted in measure from us and we rose to our feet, and the visitors were about to leave, Sister D. said,

"Oh, I have had such a vision! It is something about Miss Sisson. I do not know whether it is about her personally, or in connection with her work. I saw her prostrate on the ground; in air over her, in the act of springing upon her in terrible rage, was Satan in the form of a big black bear. While I held my breath, a bright light shone around everything. Then I lifted my eyes and saw the light proceeded from a *glorious Person* above the big black bear. It was Jesus! His arms were extended. His strong, benign countenance was beaming upon His prostrate child, and under His power and outstretched arms. Satan was paralyzed; ready to pounce, but he could not touch her."

Being thus forewarned and forearmed, to walk softly before the Lord and look out for what was coming -- the devil's attack and Christ's deliverance -- our little company separated. The plan for the few remaining days in the city was: a young lady coming in her carriage that morning to take me to her home for [a] meeting that night, the following day carried to another house where I might pack my trunk, etc., then to leave by train the next day for the Atlantic Coast. In the mid-afternoon, in a very swift, terrific thunder storm, came my young friend, wet to the skin, and she so delicate! Bright sunshine when she started from home, the swift shower had caught her half-way, so she pressed on. To return with her just then was impossible, but in the afternoon when the sun had come out, with "clear shining after rain," we thought to go.

# Messengers of An Outpouring

Now Winnipeg has a peculiar, sticky, greasy soil. Walking in its mud will rot the leather from your shoes, and it is so slippery that to put your foot upon it when wet, is to fall. It is so greasy that whatever garment it touches is ruined; therefore, ladies avoid walking in it during, or shortly after a rain; but as we are going in the carriage this objection was not thought of. In the evening my young friend, Miss G., having been seated in the [seat] -- she had but one limb which was supplemented by a crutch -- I, the writer, a bundle of loose wraps, etc., in one hand and umbrella in the other, essayed to pass by Miss G., crutch and all, and land myself on the other side of the carriage.

But as I put my foot upon its step, and threw the other limb beyond her, to take my seat, somehow my foot touched mud on the carriage step. I slipped and fell backward, and with such force that my umbrella having caught the rung of a wheel in my descent, snapped in two places. With great power I struck on a mud-covered wagon [drive-]way of sharp cobble stones! I remember as I went down, feeling a delicious, soft-sinking, as of going into a feather bed, my whole body was relaxed, my arms spread out, and I touched the entire length of my spine, the back of my hair and hat in the watery mud. I had no [grip] on myself whatever, and felt like so much pancake batter poured out on the pan. I did not long enjoy the soft-sinking luxury, for the second thought was, "Oh, my clothes! Everything ruined by this mud and I day after tomorrow to travel east!"

Now God in my long faith-life in His service ("Freely ye have received, freely give") had always "according to the riches of His glory in Christ Jesus" supplied "*all* my need," but as my need frequently required as now but one suit of clothes at a time, there came the haunting thought, "These are ruined! What are you going to travel in?" But quicker came the Divine suggestion, "Take joyfully the spoiling of your goods;" thus the gutter became my closet as I cried, "Lord, I do by Thy grace. I will be glad that everything I've got is ruined."

Busily occupied with getting this victory, and His help and joyfulness coming into me so fast, I did not realize what an ominous silence there was all about me, till at length Brother D. broke the stillness, saying in very subdued tones, "Sister Sisson, where are you hurt?" Everything was so delicious now, even the ruining of all my wearing apparel, that laughingly I replied, "Why, I am not hurt anywhere! Hallelujah!" Oh, what suspense this relieved! For seeing the violence of my fall and the perfect stillness that followed all three of them had concluded I was dead and they feared to break the silence. Now they and I alike saw what a wonderful deliverance this had been! I was so spread upon the cobble-stones, it was with great difficulty my six-foot stalwart friend could turn me over on one side till I could get some [grip] on myself to help him help me rise.

I was determined I would say nothing of my clothes when the Lord had saved my life, so, reeking with mud, I took my place in the carriage, and as we lingered rejoicing, Sister D. put her head in the carriage saying, "That was the big black bear that I saw."

Driving to my friend's house they soon had the bedraggled garments off me, and wiped and hung around the stove for drying. A young man of the family took away my three-piece umbrella for mending, and by the next morning all the clothes were dried, and *not a spot on them*; my black silk outer jacket a particular marvel, as that eating soil was specially hard on silk goods. My umbrella was mended stronger than at first, and I was not allowed to know even the bill. Of all the accident, nothing was left but the rich blessing that the Lord had worked for and in me, and upon the bystanders. "In everything enriched by Him."

But the big black bear was henceforth to me a parable of the spiritual dealings of the Lord with me, and all His own. Jesus always stands with outspread arms in benediction over us; always with that smile of infinite love and infinite power. However much Satan, the big black bear, may try to play pranks with us, through the incidents, accidents (?) and providence of our lives, Jesus is right over him in His paralyzing power of deliverance for us, and the devil cannot touch us.

Beforehand God has told us, "All things are of God," "All things are for your sake;" to you who love God, "All things work together for good," "Giving thanks always for all things," "Behold I have given you power over all the power of the enemy;" "All things are yours . . . things present . . . things to come . . all are yours."

It is evermore ours to raise the shout, "Thanks be unto God which giveth us the victory." We are "more than conquerors through Him that loved us," and who "always causeth us to triumph in Christ." Hallelujah! (*TLRE*, Oct., 1911)

## Reminiscences of a Faith Life #1
### Miss Elizabeth Sisson

In order to face the real problems of a faith life on the mission field, I cut free from my salary while in India, and voluntarily launched away on God for material supply. I was seeking then to lead some convicted Hindoos to Jesus, which meant for them a very literal forsaking all -- caste (which involved social standing), property, wife, business prospects, etc. They were young college students; two or three of them were in an agony of conviction. While I quoted to them, "Seek ye first the kingdom of God and His righteousness, and all these things shall be added to you," the Holy Spirit whispered within me, "Blaze the way for them yourself." We know how that is done in untrackable American forests. Thus I cut away.

I was then a missionary of the A. B. C. F. M., and God made the first steppings of faith for finances so easy. On every hand wonderful supply. No testings. Soon after my health failed, and dwelling far, far, in the interior among the dear Indian idolators, He made it necessary [for] me to go to Bombay and then on to America. However, it all ran so smoothly; almost before I realized need, it was met. Thus I came to England and America with a glad shout of the faithfulness of my Jehovah-Jireh.

Soon after reaching New London, Connecticut, much better in health, I met an old friend, a clergyman, who was deeply stirred for a life of entire sanctification, but who declared it could not be lived by the clergy, since to keep the experience (he had blessedly touched it once), one must preach it, and to preach it was to endanger one's safety in his charge and bring upon him a hostile attitude from his brother clergy. "What of that?" said I, "We cannot give up our friendship with

God for place, or for friendship of man. The price is too great to pay -- a stunted and dwarfed soul for eternity." "Yes, but you do not appreciate the situation; no church, no salary, and a wife and three babes to support!"

I insisted it was safe to trust God and obey, regardless of consequences. There was to be a convention in his church in the late Autumn, "Would I come up and bring my fuller Gospel?" "Yes, God willing." So things rested. However, when the convention dates were sent me and an invitation to Vermont -- for the first time since my "faith-life" commenced I was lacking money. I could not write my friend that God had failed me after so vigorously urging him to trust God; moreover, I was persuaded that God wanted me there and would send me. Through the few intervening days I watched every mail -- no money.

Then came a letter from a dear brother, G. M., in Putnam, Connecticut, which was on my line of travel to Vermont, but a very short distance on the way. "Would I come to Putnam and have meetings for several days?" This was a rich man who had a Gospel Hall. Oh yes, I saw the way out! In service in Putnam somebody would be moved to give me the money for my railroad ticket. I went with bounding steps to Putnam, though when I had bought my ticket I had only a few cents left. God opened the way to several of the churches as well as the Gospel Hall. At the close of each service people crowded around and thanked me, but *no money*. New experience to me, but God was withholding them from giving; He was teaching me something.

I had a well-to-do unconverted uncle whom I called on at a stopover en route. Frequently before this whenever I met him he put a little money in my hand, I expected it now. A pleasant call, no money. When I left God showed me that mine might be called a faith-life if my eye was upon Him only, but if my eye was upon man, it was little better than religious [beggar], whatever I called it. God would save me from expecting from man, thus only could I be clean unto God.

It was Sunday night and we had returned from the last meeting. I was to start Monday at four a.m. for Vermont. It was arranged that I was to be called at three a.m., then breakfast and be driven by my host to the train. So I bade the family good-by that night; as I did so, the old lady of the family pressed a bill into my hand. "Ah," thought I, "here comes my railroad fare," but on reaching my room I found it was but $1; very interesting, but not much to the purchase for a $12 or $15 journey by rail and coach.

Now for two days God had been talking to me so tenderly of "taking no thought for the morrow," "your heavenly Father knoweth," "much more value than many sparrows," etc., but as I stood in that room that night with that one cold dollar in my hand, how the devil got after me. "What are you going to do tomorrow when you go to the ticket office window?" "What will you say to the clerk?" "A dollar and four cents for a ticket to Vermont!" "No, you will turn around and say to your brother, G.M., 'I haven't the money for the ticket.'" "Oh yes, he will give it to you, he is rich." "But what will become of your faith-life?" "Stumping the world a religious pauper."

I knew it was Satan talking. I cried, "Now, Father, Thou has said, 'Take no thought for the morrow,' and if this command is obeyed Thou must take thoughts out of me or I shall not sleep tonight." I rose from my knees and went to my couch. Wonder of wonders! I never knew when my head touched the pillow. I was awakened from my refreshing, babe-like sleep by a sharp knock at the door; "Three o'clock Miss Sisson." Of all the miracles that followed I count this dreamless repose the greatest. I hurriedly dressed and went to my breakfast. The devil tried to start some of the questions of the night before, but his power was broken. God had too deeply poised me in Himself for them to touch me. What a God we have!

After the meal which was thoroughly enjoyed, Brother M. said, "We must have a word of prayer." On our knees a great rush of the quickening power of God (as he afterwards told me) came on him, "Lord," he said, "she does not ask for money, she asks for workers, but Lord, give her hundreds of dollars for the work." As he prayed the assurance dropped from heaven into my breast that it would be so, though I had only one dollar and four cents toward my railroad ticket. My soul was exultant, a very real God was dealing with me and I knew it. Without even any allusion whatever to money in all my public work (or private life), in the next six months I forwarded to the India field for God's work more than a thousand dollars; no doubt God's answer to that dear man's prayer.

The sleigh came to the door and we drove the mile to the train. Too early, ticket master not there. As we sat and talked of the things of the kingdom, my friend said, "Let me see, you go through Worcester on your route, and have to wait there for an hour. I have a pass as far as Worcester, you can buy your ticket there and save a little." So it came to pass I never saw the face of that ticket-master at the little Putnam station. How the devil likes to lift up [boogeymen] before the trusting child of God! Now he said, "You have never been to Worcester in your life before and know no one there; worse for you to be left penniless there than here." Enlargement and deliverance however had begun to arise within and without, and my soul was settled in a deep sweet peace.

Brother M. stood talking with me as the train pulled out and we said our goodbyes. I was en route to Northern Vermont with a pass to Worcester, $1.04 in my pocket, serene peace in my soul. Hallelujah! What a Savior!

We had not run far when the train backed into the station. My friend rushed in and said breathlessly, "As the train moved out God spoke to me, 'You ought to have given my child some money.' It was just then so hard for me to get hold of ready money, and charities had been curtailed, but I cried, Lord if you want me to give, send the train back. It began to back immediately, and here is the money." No time for more, the whistle blew and he was off, but he had left in my hand a roll of bills -- I counted, it was $50.

A course in a theological seminary could not have given me the equipment for that convention which I had in this venture on God, and the revelation of His power, bounty and love, which came to me in this straight place. God knows how to train His souls, and often thinks as man-made institutions do not.

This testimony of our delivering God when written back to my friend G. M., set him shouting and adoring Infinite Goodness.

    "Didn't my Lord deliver Daniel?
    And why not every man?" (*TLRE*, Nov., 1911)

## Messengers of An Outpouring

# Reminiscences of a Faith Life #2
### Miss E. Sisson

Returning to this country from years of service abroad, I found that my two sisters, energized by the same Holy Spirit who had sent me out to preach a free gospel, had, one after the the other, gone out into the Lord's work so extensively that it had caused the renunciation of their salaries as public school teachers and sent them pushing into any open doors in real aggressive Gospel service.

But *aggressive* work for the Lord often means for the fervent but indigent child of God, "without purse or scrip," and many hardships. Thus it came to pass that when they came home from their frequent raids, without money and threadbare, mother, who was already suffering the loss in the family of their salaries, drew on the tiny sum she had in the bank and clothed them, only to see them start out afresh and repeat the process. Hence it came to pass on my return to America in looking over circumstances, I found all family resources gone, only the little home left and the next imperative step, a mortgage. It was easy to figure how soon that would swallow up the house and then the almshouse [a house for poor people] for my aged mother, unless I venture on some remunerative business-life whereby I could support her and keep up the little home. Oh, what pressure I came under!

On the one hand my call to Gospel work, the most distinct thing in my Christian life and from the time of it there had always settled upon me a "woe is me if I preach not the Gospel;" and on the other, a tremendous push to go to money-making for the needs of my invalid parent and also for the house-mother sister who cared for her. Oh, how strong the voice was -- "You have talents (it has never been proved), you could make money if you gave yourself to it. Circumstances of your family demand it. Remember, 'If any provide not for his own, and *especially for those of his own house*, he hath denied the faith and is worse than an infidel.'"

I could not for a time discern which of these two pulls was the Lord's; both equally intense. The one I had known was the Lord's and had proved it in following, but the other commended itself to my judgment and practical common sense as now God's voice in charge of circumstances; then, too, it had (or seemed to have) the authority of scripture. The more I reasoned in the matter, the more confused I became and I could not abate the force of either demand. Then came a lonely day when apart with God and strong crying and tears, I went over the thing again and besought the Lord to show me what was right.

Must I neglect the family and go forward in Gospel work, or would it be true to God to turn to some money-getting scheme for their sakes? "Lord, You know, 'He that provides not for his own is worse than an infidel and hath denied the faith," I groaned. At last broke a Voice in upon my turbulent heart, "All right, provide for your family." "Ah, Lord, may I, must I leave preaching the Gospel for the support of my family?" I exclaimed, half pleased, half terrified. "Yes, provide for your family *in the faith*," came back to me. "In the faith?" I could not seem to catch the meaning. "Yes, in the faith. Have you not gone forth without purse or scrip these many years trusting Me? Have I not cared for you? Lacked ye anything when I sent you without purse or scrip?" "No, Lord." "Then, in the same faith, now provide for your family. You trusted Me to take care of you as you went forth at My bidding with a free Gospel. Have I failed you? I am the Lord of the whole earth, the gold and the silver are Mine and the cattle upon a thousand hills. Is it not as easy for Me to provide for four (just then there was returned from India an invalid missionary sister and her adopted Indian little girl) as for one? And you have trusted Me for one, will you from hence-forth trust Me for four? Will you thus provide for your family in the faith?"

Then my Lord and I entered into covenant, and let me here say, to the praise of His faithfulness, that never has He in the over thirty years since, failed me once. I have been [stingy] in my faith toward Him, both for my personal supply and the supply for the family and thus I have limited His power toward us, for He says, "According to your faith be it unto you." I look back to see that both I and the family might have had very, very much more from the hand of His bounty had I always remembered,

> Thou art coming to a King,
> With thee large petitions bring.

Halting though I have been toward Him, inexpressibly tender has been my faith-life with the Lord, and a great factor in letting me into the depth, power and riches of His promises on every line.

> They that trust Him wholly
> Find Him wholly true.

The road into His heart is plank after plank, Trust, Trust, Trust. One of the most beautiful things in that faith-life was the way God honored, all the days of her after life, [sic] my dear old mother, who held her breath from murmur, when first one then the other of her daughters had withdrawn from their salaried work, for soul seeking, and she drew bit by bit her little all from the bank to stock their slender wardrobes, and renew them for campaigns when they had come home empty-handed and ragged from their "meetings." . . .

The mortgage never came on "the little brown house under the hill" (as one of our friends had lovingly christened it). No mortgage during all my mother's long illness and many other experiences, and the house continues to shelter us and has become in this hour of hours of the world's crisis, literally, "a house of prayer for all nations." (*TLRE*, Dec., 1911)

# Chapter 7

# 1912

**Mass Pentecostal Convention:** of the Full Gospel Assemblies of Eastern Ontario; June 20th to 30th. Ottawa Canada. . . .

This convention is a united campaign of the Full Gospel Assemblies of Eastern Ontario, and promises to be the largest and best of its kind ever held in this part of the country.

Pastor W. H. Durham, of Los Angeles, Cal., will be in charge, assisted by a large staff of Pentecostal workers from the United States and Canada.

Meals and lodgings provided on the *free-will* offering plan. This will not bar the poor, and will give those who are able the privilege of helping to bear the financial burden. Dining room on the grounds. Cots provided free, but those who desire such, must provide their own bedding. (*Pentecostal Testimony*, Vol. 2, No. 2, 1912)

**The Outpouring of The Spirit in Los Angeles:**

In the last issue of *Pentecostal Testimony*, a brief report was given of the revival here in Los Angeles, and of the miraculous healing of Dr. Sykes and of Brother Easley being raised from the dead. Since that time the power of God has continued to fall, and real miracles of healing have been [worked] in our midst, in the presence of hundreds of people.

During this revival of about ten weeks, over one hundred have received the baptism in the Holy Spirit. We have seen very few meetings since the outpouring of the Spirit, where the power of God has been manifested as it was during this revival. Sunday, May 5$^{th}$, was a day long to be remembered. The power of God fell in the prayer room throughout the entire day. Many were prostrated on the floor, and ten came through to their baptism, a number of these had been saved during the day. Night after night the power of God continued to fall. One night in the early part of the meeting a Roman Catholic came rushing to the altar, and wept his way through to God. The Spirit almost immediately fell upon him and he came through speaking in other tongues. On Friday night, two weeks ago, the Lord completely took possession of the meeting, the power and glory of God filled the place, and two received the baptism in their seats.

On Sunday, June 30th, Brother Miller, of Highland Park, Los Angeles, came to the mission on crutches. He stated he had not walked without the aid of crutches in five months. He was suffering from chronic rheumatism and was beyond the reach of medical aid. As he was anointed and prayed for, God instantly healed him. He testified at the evening meeting to full deliverance, walking, and leaping and praising God.

Last Sunday, July 21st, a man came into the meeting with tuberculosis of the hips. He could scarcely walk, even with the aid of crutches, and was suffering intense pain. The meeting was already in progress when he came forward to be prayed for. God touched him and he walked off, leaving his crutches on the platform. This miracle was performed in the presence of hundreds of people. He testified that when he was anointed all pain left him. He lives at Watts, Cal.

Another remarkable healing was the case of a man named Jeo. Costa, East Ninth Place, Los Angeles, Cal. He was an Italian and a member of the Roman Catholic Church. He had been in bed for the past eight months and was paralyzed. As he was prayed for, God healed and he is well and working today.

The hall on the corner of 7th and Los Angeles streets, which seats over five hundred, is crowded on Sundays. The attendance has been gradually increasing, and the work in general was never in better shape than it is now. We know that God will continue to work as long as his people will humble their hearts and seek his face. (*Pentecostal Testimony*, Vol. 2, No. 2, 1912)

## Conversion of A Chinese Woman:

Dear Sister Sexton;

We feel to write this brief account of the conversion of a very old Chinese woman which seems to us a miracle, considering her age and environments. How she came to hear is not the marvel by any means, but her faith.

It seems that some of her relatives had attended the mission, and hearing us pray for people who were sick, told "Au-Pau," who was afflicted with chronic stomach trouble. She came in one day very cautiously and made us know she wanted to be prayed for, which some of the sisters in the house immediately did. She arose and thanking those who had prayed for her, was about to leave, when our Bible woman told her she must not worship idols, and must ask God to cleanse her heart, repent, believe and be baptized. She assented to all that was told her . . .

To our astonishment, early one morning about one week later, she came with a bundle of clothes under her arms and said she wanted to be baptized. We said, "Au-Pau" (Grandma), "are you saved? Do you really believe in Jesus?" She said, "Yes, Tinboo (the Lord) has healed me and I want to be baptized. I believe in Him." "Yes, but," we told her, "your heart must be cleansed and then you can be baptized; and, besides, Au-Pau, you have an old dirty, nasty pipe there with you. Christians don't smoke."

"Ah," she said with surprise, "you can have my pipe; I'll not smoke any more." So, urging her to pray earnestly, quit burning "joss sticks" to her idols and not be "singe her hair" any more (which she had done, hoping to drive evil spirits away from her), we told her to come back again and we would see about baptizing her, as we wanted to be sure of her conversion.

Perhaps in three days more she came in. This time [she was] another woman. She had a most wonderful experience to tell us, how something came all over her like water and beginning at her head had come on down her body, washing it all clean, as it went, and making her heart very happy. She would stop and thank God every few minutes, as she was telling her experience. She said she had cooked her rice with the sticks she had bought to worship the idols, burnt her tobacco and really and truly she believed in the true God.

You may be sure it was a real, delightful privilege to baptize this precious old soul, seventy-eight years old. She put up her hands while we were standing in the water, and kept saying over and over, "Praise God, thank God," until we could hardly put her under the water.... Do you wonder that she comes to visit us two, three, and four times a week, bringing little presents, such as fruits, eggs, etc.... (*The Bridegroom's Messenger*, March 16, 1912)

## Reminiscences of a Faith Life #3
### Miss Eliz. Sisson

That was a severe winter in the state of Maine. God had sent me with others into Gospel service in the backwoods were "the ways of Zion mourned" and even the schoolhouses had not been opened for Christian work for years.

God poured out His Spirit and [did a] work there, backsliders reclaimed, souls saved, sick ones healed. After the revival was over and workers scattering, God showed me He wanted me to stay on among the people for a while "as a nurse cherishes her children," for they were "as sheep having no shepherd." But when the weeks passed into months and still I had no liberty to leave, and had to refuse other calls which came to me, and there was and could be no money in this thing, the devil set in with heavy temptations:

"You know that mother and the little family at home are dependent on what you send them. You know these poor dear farmer-folk have no idea that you need money; if they give you food and shelter while you stay they feel they are doing uncommon well (for they never gave to the Lord until they were quickened); even [if] they desire to give you money, they have none. A silver dollar is big as a cart-wheel here, they only trade in barter, etc."

You understand how the devil can put a blue atmosphere around one. Day by day it was, "What has your mother and the family got to eat? For you know they will not go into debt. Why don't you get up and go somewhere? You have calls. You must consider your family. It is all nonsense to wait here for a 'leading' to go. You may stay here all the rest of your life, etc."

Day by day Satan was nagging me, yet no release from the Lord to quit the little flock, and I telling Him I would rather die than miss His will, to hold me steady in the center of it.

Thus things went on for nearly three months when came a letter from an old friend (Mrs. Green) whom I had not even thought of for many months. It must have been the Lord put me at that time in her mind and my mother of whom she knew little, and of whom her mother knew less. Mrs. Green did not know where I was, but the letter was forwarded. In it this Mrs. Minnie Green wrote:

"The enclosed will explain itself, as I read it, there was a whisper in my heart; 'This is from Miss Sisson's mother;' to test the voice, I read the letter to my own mother, Mrs. Fisher, and as I read mother said: 'Minnie, that is for Miss Sisson's mother.'" [sic]

Why should the thought of my mother come into Mrs. Fisher's mind; a party in whom she had hitherto taken no interest? It was God! Mrs. Green resumed: "I have sent the check to your home, [this] letter, which explains, to you." Turning to the thus introduced document I found it was from a Christian physician to Mrs. Green. He said, "Many years ago our mutual friend, Mrs. H., was kind to me as a young medical student, she saw that I was working my way through college but scantly, and was poorly nourished. She offered me money; I refused to take it, seeing no way of repaying. She urged it upon me as the Lord's money, saying if in after years the Lord gave me to pay it, good; if not, it was all right. It was given unto Him."

The letter went on, "She died some fifteen years ago. I had never been able to replace the money, but in later years God has much prospered me and I have had the joy of frequent moneys [to] put in His work, but somehow I longed that the original sum should be handed [to] Mrs. Huges. The next best thing was to give it to you, dear Mrs. Green, her most intimate friend, whom I have known for years as a dispenser of charities, and ask you to give it for her."

Thus came the $40 which covered those sharp, sharp months. God had taken care! Satan was again proved a liar. I seemed to hear the Lord saying, "Will you ever doubt Me again? Do you not see that I can cause tombstones to spurt gold if necessary to provide for My own? But I can never, never break My promises."

In writing off the circumstances to the friend who had been God's instrument at this time for my deliverance, that her faith also might be quickened in the knowledge of His faithfulness, she replied, "Can the grave praise Thee?" But it does! "Hallelujah."

"Seek ye *first* (every hour, every minute, in every circumstance) the kingdom of God and His righteousness and all these things (what ye shall eat, what ye shall drink, wherewithall ye shall be clothed) SHALL be added unto you." "For your heavenly Father knows what things ye have need of before ye ask Him." (*TLRE*, Jan., 1912)

## Reminiscences of a Faith Life #4
### Miss Eliz. Sisson

In the provident of God, time came when He had led me as a worker to Bethsham, the first house of the Lord's healing opened in Great Britain. Faith for finances had here a closer testing than in America, for few in those days understood going out in Christian work [which meant] looking to God alone for financial supply. It was generally understood if people were engaged in independent religious work, that they had a private income to enable them to do so. I stood between two precious Christian workers, each with their personal income. It was my joy there to stand, and never make a want known to the human, and demonstrate the faithfulness of God to supply.

On one occasion, called to go north to Bristol-- a friend whose home was Bristol had promised to meet me at the train the day before the meeting, and journey with me. It was nothing to me to find when I counted my little money, that I had only tram fares to the railroad station, and ticket money to Bristol, nothing for return. I had proved God too often on these lines to fear. Thus, gaily the next morning I sallied forth to the railroad station, bought [the] ticket, and (according to American custom) sat down in waiting room for my friend to pick me up.

As the clock neared the moment of departure, she had not appeared. I saw the train on the track getting up steam, and thought, "Why, she is running it very close!" I dared not move lest I might miss her, but kept my eyes on the two doors, and the one by which she should enter to find me, and the other from which I saw the train just ready to move out. I did not know that until afterward that she (according to English custom) stood on the platform by the train, waiting every moment for me to keep my appointment and join her, and only as the train move did she jump on.

As I saw it move out, I realized I had lost the train, and no money even to pay tram fares back to the city. I lifted my heart to God and it came to me to go to ticket office and ask them to take back my ticket. They did so and this enabled me to get back to Bethshan, but with an appointment for meeting [the] next day staring me in [the] face, and but little more money than enough to pay trams back to the station; none for ticket, and I must rise very early in the cold winter morning to make it, so that I could hold my meeting that evening. It was all an impossibility unless I told one of my fellow-workers. How strong the temptation! Yet why had God put me in this house but for (among other reasons) to witness His faithfulness to His faith-workers? No! I could not open my mouth.

Then the accuser of the brethren, who is always on hand when there is a trial, began to tell me, "There is something wrong in you or you would not be left in the lurch this way. God has never thus deserted you before," etc. Down on my knees I began to call on God, and with strong crying and tears, to show me what was wrong and help me get right. In the midst of my tumult came suddenly a voice, oh, so clear, "Go up in the room you occupied last year, and look in your old writing desk." Had I stopped to reason I would have said, "Why, that room has been emptied and cleaned from thirty to forty times in this over a year" (for guests did not usually remain with us over a week), but I sprang to my feet and went up and looked in a closet and found in it the old broken-down desk, discarded when I changed rooms and left [it] to be carried away as rubbish.

I opened it now with trembling hands, and found in an inner drawer, all open to the public, a precious sovereign ($5.00 gold piece). As I looked at it I thought, "Surely, God has just dropped this in here from heaven!" You had better believe I had both a spiritual and providential anointing for my Bristol meeting next day! What a glad service it was, and with what joy I could talk of Him. The spirit independent of all but God, and so dependent upon Him, with which one walks with God for finances!

It was a year later that the mystery of the gold piece was solved. Then I had a letter from a distant foreign mission field in which the writer said, "Forgive me for putting so indelicate a question, but some two years ago when passing through London and Bethshan, I was in your room and dropped a sovereign in your writing desk. I have often been charged by the enemy with folly for this, and told you never got it, likely some housemaid found and appropriated it," etc.

Well, she might in all that time! How many new maids, coming and going, we had had in that long year, in which the rubbishy piece of broken-down furniture stood, unremoved, unlocked, in that closet! But God! The consecrated moneys of His precious missionary-child were all too dear to Him, as also the need of His other little one. He sacredly guarded the treasure, and fitted the gift and the need together in His own wonderful way. "His Name shall be called Wonderful!" And when the missionary friend added, "Did you ever find it?" the story came out, which made the double delight of giver and receiver, who alike saw Him. (*TLRE*, Feb., 1912)

## Witnessing for Jesus in the Southland

(Feb. 27, 1912)

God is working in a wonderful way in Texas and Oklahoma. There are many hindrances and many scoffers in these last days, but God is calling out a people for His name, in spite of all difficulties.

The Christmas convention at Houston, Texas, which lasted fourteen days, was a most blessed time with the Lord. Several states were represented. It was a real melting-time before the Lord. Faults were confessed, restitution was made, consecrations were renewed and lives were deepened in many ways. A long dinner table that seated about forty people, was often filled three and four times, and meals were provided free for all those who desired them. The table was bountifully filled with good things from day to day, and the Lord wonderfully supplied all the needs, and when the convention closed, there were several baskets and boxes of provisions left over, which were given to the poor.

The power and presence of God was felt by all present in a marvelous way. Quite a number received the baptism in the Holy Ghost and fire; some were sanctified and reclaimed, and several ordained for the Lord's work. God wonderfully manifested His glory and power at every service, and an indescribably sweet spirit of love and unity pervaded the tabernacle during the entire convention. People from several different nationalities were in attendance and united their praises with ours to God for His goodness and mercy to us during the year 1911.

On Christmas Day, a band of Mexicans from a nearby village, all filled with the Holy Ghost, came to the convention. It was wonderfully encouraging to hear them praising the Lord. Frequently when some of these foreigners attempted to testify in their broken English, the Holy Spirit would literally flood their soul with glory until all attempts to testify were impossible, and the Lord would manifest His love and tenderness through these dear, illiterate people in such a marvelous way as to let the people see and feel the presence of the Lord about them, rather than to attempt to tell it, through lips of clay. And oh, the humility and the gratitude and the intensity of their worship! The true spirit of worship manifested by these dark-skinned children of the plains, often put us to shame.

As the several different nationalities knelt around the altar, and our voices united in sending up volumes and volumes of praise and thanksgiving to our God, all color, caste and nationality were forgotten and completely obliterated in the oceans and oceans of glory that filled the tabernacle and the sweet abiding presence of our Lord. Several times, as we stood with uplifted arms, singing and praising God, He would pour out His blessing upon us in such marvelous showers, until it seemed the Rapture would surely follow. Several expressed a feeling or a sense of drawing-upward in their soul at these times, and we felt several times the translation [Rapture] was very near.

God gave us some blessed messages and revelations. The main thought that God seemed to impress upon His children was, "The Lord is at the door." Almost every service God gave us a message to this effect through tongues and interpretation, and warned us that "very soon, quick and wonderful changes were to take place upon the earth."

Two fallen women were taken from the jail, and wonderfully saved and baptized in the Holy Spirit the same day. One of these was in attendance at the convention almost every service, and oh, it was wonderful to hear her pray. The spirit of prayer would come upon her, and with all the intensity of her soul, she would cry out, "People, I'm on fire, I'm on fire;" and looking at her, we could see her literally covered with a visible glow of red and purple, completely enveloping her body.

In the afternoon meeting as with holy boldness she testified how God had found her wandering and homeless on the streets of Houston, and had saved her from a life of sin and shame, numbers of great, big strong men who knew her and had been her companions in sin, stood there and cried like babies. Her testimony melted the hearts of hundreds of people.

In Dallas, Texas there is a constant revival [at the F. F. Bosworth tent]. The power of God has been falling at almost every service for months and months. Nine people received the baptism of the Holy Ghost in one service recently. On Sunday night, a United Brethren preacher, who was pastor of a church in another city, dropped into the meeting, and God wonderfully baptized him in the Holy Spirit.

Another Sunday night, two girls who had started to the moving-picture show but found it closed, stumbled upon the meeting, and while hearing the testimonies, one of them silently prayed that the Lord would save her that night. During the service, God wonderfully saved, sanctified and baptized her [in the Holy Spirit] as she sat in her seat, and she jumped up shouting and praising the Lord in other tongues. It was the first time she was ever in a Pentecostal meeting.

In Wichita Falls, Texas there has been a blessed outpouring of the Holy Spirit during the past few months. A sweet spirit of unity of the different denominations prevailed in the meetings at this place that we haven't seen anywhere else. Sometimes, Christians from seven and eight different denominations, could be seen working around the altar, praying sinners through to God. The Salvation Army people came to our meetings every night after their meetings were closed, and the Lord has baptized every member of the Army at this place with the Holy Ghost and fire, with the exception of the Captain, and he is seeking it very earnestly.

A Free Methodist preacher received the baptism; also a Nazarene preacher, pastor of a church at that place. For years, he contended, like a great many other holiness people, that he received the baptism of the Holy Ghost and fire when he received his sanctification, but one day, as he was tarrying before God and praying, the Lord showed him that he had not received the baptism according to Acts 2:4, and that it was for him, if he would only seek it. He sought and God wonderfully baptized him. Shortly afterwards, about thirty members of the Nazarene church were also baptized in the Holy Ghost and fire. Truly, God is no respecter of persons. He is calling out a Bride for Christ from among all creeds and all denominations and all nationalities.

In Oklahoma City, Oklahoma the power of God is falling. Praise His name! There are three Pentecostal Missions here and the Lord is blessing in all of them. In one mission recently, fifteen were baptized in one week. On Monday night of last week, a sister preached on the "Latter Rain" falling in these last days, and when the altar call was given, the Lord gave us a literal shower of the latter rain. Five people received the baptism, and several others were prostrated under the power for hours, and the glory of God filled the hall. Souls came to the altar and got what they wanted from God with scarcely no effort whatever. People passing by, on the outside and hearing the wonderful shouts and praises going up to God, would come in to see what was happening.

God has been working wonderfully in my own family since I came South last August. . . . After about three weeks, papa, who had been a member of the Baptist church for fifteen years, came to the altar and got saved. The next week he received a definite work of sanctification, and a little later, the baptism in the Holy Ghost, and oh, how thankful he is and how grateful to God. . . .

One of my sisters who had become dissatisfied with the Baptist church had joined the Roman Catholic church; she had taken her first communion only a short time before any arrival and was going to the priest for confession. I kept praying and witnessing and in less than a month, God wonderfully saved her soul, and the glory of God came down and enveloped her entire body for more than two hours. Oh, it was wonderful, and a few weeks later she was baptized in the Holy Spirit. Another sister there, who had never heard anything about the latter rain was wonderfully saved and baptized in the Holy Spirit and is now telling the story to others. Both of these young ladies were saved from lives of folly, theatregoing, parties, and such like, and now they devote their time to visiting the sick, and the needy. . . .

Aside from saving five of my relatives He has also saved and baptized a large number of my friends and acquaintances, for which I praise and magnify His Holy name forever. . . .

The enemy is also working in quite a number of places, because he knows his time is short. He is doing his very best to try to get God's children to wrangling among themselves over three works of grace, organization, or something else, but

I praise the Lord for the "little flock," a band of faithful people who are pressing forward, and holding up Jesus Christ and Him crucified to this dying world . . . -- Maude M. Delaney, Oklahoma City (*TLRE*, April, 1912)

**China:**

The eyes of the world are on China, looking with intense interest at each step taken by that great empire, and the Christian world is praying that the change in the government will mean a break in the gross darkness that has hung over China's millions for centuries.

A Chinese paper commenting on the protection that has been granted to the lives and property of the people, says it is no doubt due to the "leaven of Christianity which has had its effect on the hearts of the Chinese."

The new leaders are in strong sympathy with the missionaries. Yuan Shi Kai protected them during the Boxer troubles, and his children were educated by an English Congregational missionary. Dr. Sun Yat Sen is the son of a Chinese Evangelist, and is himself a Christian. In a recent interview he said, "Our greatest hope for China is in the Bible and education."

One hundred years ago only one city, Canton, was open to foreign residents; now the entire empire is open. But who will go to carry the Gospel? . . .

George Hanson, writing from Shanghai, in rejoicing in the change being brought about by the war, says that the new leaders are professing Christians, and thinks it will mean a more open door for the Gospel. He writes that as soon as the war is over and some one comes to take charge of the Mission in Shanghai, they are going to the far west, to Szechuan. . . . (*TLRE*, April, 1912)

## Pulling Up the Tares

I had a boy who was full-blooded and warm-hearted, but while wife and I slept the enemy sowed tares -- tobacco and whiskey. He was the brightest boy we had of our seven, but he had commenced coming in at twelve o'clock at night, our precious Donald boy. One night wife and I were walking out on the Santa Fe road, and I said, "Wife, I do not know what to do; my heart is breaking." "Well," she said, "from your talk today about committing things to Him and the Holy Ghost, I think we had better turn Donald over to the Holy Ghost."

"Oh, wife," I said, "if I take my strong hands off Donald, what would happen?" And she just looked up to me with her loving eyes, and said, "Isn't he going to hell as fast as he can?" "Yes," I said, "with all my strong hands on him." We got down in the starlit night and said, "Father, you take Donald, tares and all. We have tried to force him to church, and tried to force him to quit tobacco and quit liquor, and yet Father, the old tares grow bigger than the good seed. Take him;" and we gave him to the Lord forever, and went back into the parlor, and for the first time in ten years we were without a burden. The care of the boy was gone. "Oh," she said, "my heart is so light. I feel Donald is in the heart of Jesus. I see now the truth of the Scriptures. We have been trying to pull up the tares, and we have pulled up the wheat, too." We sat there talking, and directly I heard a step. Wife said, "That is Donald's step. Do you reckon he has heard?" "No, no; we have turned him over to the Holy Ghost."

That great big, blue-eyed boy came in; I will never forget how broad his shoulders were. He had made a living for us when we were all down. That boy came in there and threw his arms around his mother's neck, and said, "Mother, I have quit; Papa, I have quit," and we knew he had quit. I said, "Son, sit down between us and tell us about it." He said, "I was going up into the clubroom about an hour ago, and as I was going up those back steps into that gambling-room, a voice said, 'Your father and mother have turned you over to the Holy Ghost,' and Papa, Mama, I want to tell you as long as you were praying for me I was all right, but since you have turned me over to the Holy Ghost I knew something would happen, and just walked up there and threw that old cigar away and said, 'Boys, goodbye!' 'Oh, Yoakum,' they said, 'where are you going? Are you getting weak-kneed?' 'Take my name off your books; what is my bill?'"

They told him $7.50. "What are you going to do?" they said. He said, "I heard something tell me my father and mother had turned me into the hands of the Holy Ghost, and I'm going to quit you all." Just that moment he got tired of digging up the old tares, he quit.

My brother, don't you try to dig up the tares. God says right plainly the devil sows the tares and you cannot dig them up. The Holy Ghost will burn them up without a smell of fire on their garments. . . .

I was in debt three thousand dollars and didn't know what to do. I found I could put my debts, just like the rest of my sins, on Jesus, and I laid them on the altar. A man said, "Doctor, you in debt?" "No, sir." "What did you do with them?" "God took them." "Well, did you have to pay them?" "No; God pays them." "Who is God's agent?" "I am God's steward, but I am not responsible." God is.

No more creditors closing in; they have to close in on God. Before six months I had the whole thing paid. The whole debt was paid because I trusted Him. I became a faithful steward. I didn't go around and root up the tares. I told everyone of my creditors [that] I had turned them over to God, and they said He was a pretty good Master. If you have been having tares sowed in the field, don't try to dig them up any more, but let the Holy Ghost attend to them. Dr. F. E. Yoakum, in the Stone Church, June 29, 1911. (*TLRE*, May, 1912)

## Snares in the Path of the Christian Worker; God's Leading and the Result [excerpt]

Just yesterday I read a letter that came from a person who left this country some time ago, supposing that he really heard the voice of God to go to the foreign field as a missionary because God gave him some supernatural experiences. He apparently felt quite convinced that he was intended [to be] a missionary in a certain field, but the note of that letter was failure; he felt he wasn't in his right place, nothing had been accomplished and he wished he was back in America. As I read that it filled my heart with sadness, and I said to myself, "Another one who mistook his own spiritual ambition for the voice of God," and because of that failure money wasted, time gone, nothing accomplished, and Satan rejoicing, no doubt.

Now, while we can always find this condition of people being led about by wrong voices when they are thrown open to spiritual impressions, we must remember that the voice of God does speak to His children today; but unless we have been salted by fire there may be somewhere in our anatomy some little opening that will give opportunity for voices and leadings and operations that are not of God. Demons will come and speak as angels of light. One of the signs of the times is that in [the] last days seducing spirits will come forth.

Now, what are seducing spirits? They are not spirits that come in bombast, so vile and vicious that the weakest child would discern their origin, but they are subtle, alluring, seducing -- the very word explains it -- leading us on into the mistaken path, into an unsafe attitude; the seducing spirit comes as an angel of light, not in sinful ways, but the door that opens gives them entrance in through the desire of the soul to do something great for God. That is how he gets in oftentimes.

You say, "Isn't it right to have a desire to do something for God?" Ah! we must watch and pray. The desire to accomplish something is not down there at the cross, not in the place of suffering, but where we will get a name, and where we will, as we say, bring great glory to Jesus and His kingdom. Let us beware! That is the channel through which these seductive spirits enter, and when they have once entered, they are the hardest kind to expel. Those upon whom they fasten themselves are driven about by all kinds of leadings, all sorts of voices; Christ Himself, and even God the Father comes down and [supposedly] speaks through them at times, and I believe that the blocking of God's precious operations has been largely accomplished through the operation of seductive spirits in hearts that have a desire to do something for God. . . .

The apostles came down and laid their hands on them, and you know the story of how they were baptized with the Holy Ghost. Philip is taken up out of that glorious revival and told to go down to the desert. The Word of God says he harkened and he went. He heard the voice of that Messenger that spoke to him. God at divers times and in divers ways speaks to His people. He spoke through His messenger into the inner ear of Philip and Philip heard and obeyed God. He left that glorious revival. He didn't sit down and say, "This is a good field; things are going on well here and it seems to me that must be the voice of the evil one that is trying to get me out of here."

Listen! It is generally safe that it is the Lord's voice when it leads us to a crucified condition. Preachers all realize this, I am sure. We have all felt that we wished the Lord would lead us to a large audience where sinners would just fall on their faces and wonderful things would be accomplished, and thought surely that would be of God, and it would be failure to be led away into the line of sacrifice. But when the Lord speaks as He did to Philip, "Go down from this revival to the desert," He has a work for us to do there. . . . Philip is caught away, after this errand for the Lord, and is found in some other town.

When the Lord led me up to Milwaukee a few years ago I was asked by several people to send reports to different papers concerning the work of God in that city, and as I was considering it and praying about it, one night at a late hour after the Lord had blessed in a miraculous way, the Lord spoke to me. It was after midnight, and I heard the voice of the Lord just as plainly as if it had been my wife by my side. He said, "Remember David's sin." I said, "What?" And He said again, "Remember David's sin." I said, "What sin, Lord?" remembering that he had been guilty of more than one. And the Lord said, "His sin of numbering Israel." Then I refreshed my memory by turning to the Scripture and reading it, and as the Spirit of the Lord moved upon my heart I went to my knees, and I said, "Yes, Lord, I understand. I won't number the people." And I tell you frankly I don't know how many have been converted, or healed, or baptized in the Holy Spirit, or how many I have baptized in water.

God revealed to me clearly that night the force of David's sin. When David numbered the people it gave him a confidence in numbers, and they based their strength in their numbers instead of in the unseen power of God. The Lord also showed me in this connection that when we number the converts, number the healings, number the baptisms, immediately, in a subtle way, spiritual pride and self-confidence creeps in, and we begin, unconsciously at first, to rest in that. "We are getting results; we have had one hundred baptisms," and we begin to think God has chosen us in a special way, and it will react upon us as it did on David and on Israel. [Then] We become spiritually stagnant and suddenly wake up to find we are out of power with God. He doesn't answer by fire. Then there are no converts, no healings, no manifestation of the presence of God. What is to be done in that case? Get down before God in deep contrition and confess that we have had spiritual pride, and He will restore us.

I have been asked to tell a little incident of God's leading for His glory, and I want to do it in all humility, realizing that the power was God's and I only a very weak instrument. First of all, a sister who lives in this city was wonderfully saved through the planting of the Word in Milwaukee.... one day this little branch that didn't know much about theology (she knew God saved her and healed her, but that was about all), heard the voice of the Lord speaking to her, calling her by name and saying, "Marie, go over across the street to that woman who is dying with blood-poisoning and pray for her." She was [working] about her kitchen, and drew back, and said, "Oh, no, not me. I never did anything like that," and she sought to go about her work, but the Spirit of God came to her again and said, "Go across the street and pray for that woman."

Before she scarcely knew what she was doing, she threw on her wraps and was down the stairs and across the street, kneeling by the bedside of that dying woman and praying, and that woman on Ashland avenue was instantly healed. A live branch getting its life from the Vine and bearing fruit!

The live branch kept on working and one day we were called down to help fight a battle for the Lord and this live branch said to me, "Brother Fockler, wouldn't you like to have a meeting at that house on Ashland avenue?" I said, "Sure, you arrange for it." I didn't know what kind of a place it was; the woman I knew had a very nice home and I rather thought this would be the same, but when I got there the Lord gave me a lesson on the crucified, the laid-down life.

Instead of finding things so very pleasant and a big house full of people waiting, as I expected it would be and as I desired it to be, there was nobody but the woman that had been healed and her daughter and husband, and, I think, one other woman beside myself and the live branch. My first thought was, "I wonder what this means?" But I was very happy in God and believed He had some purpose in it.

We did what the Lord led us to do and dismissed about ten o'clock. I supposed they would ask me to stay all night. I hadn't any place to go. Oh, children, it is the crucified life, there where you have to die whether you want to or not. The home was small and there was no bed to offer me, so I thought I would go over to my brother-in-law's and stay all night.

As I walked down the street I thought it was pretty late to go over there, they might be in bed, so I just stepped into a place that had a telephone nearby and thought I would try to get my brother-in-law by phone before taking that long trip. As I was looking for the phone number, a voice, which I afterwards found to be the Lord's, spoke to me and said, "Don't call up Frank, but call up the Brethren-in-Christ Mission over on Halsted street."

I hadn't been there for over two years, and it was so late I began, like Moses, to make excuses, "Oh, it is so late. I don't want to go there and ask for a bed," and I continued looking for my brother-in-law's number. Again the voice of God said, "Call up the Brethren-in-Christ Mission." I then took it as from the Lord, and called them up. A strange voice answered the phone and asked who I was. I said, "I am Mr. Fockler from Milwaukee." She asked me to wait a minute and the lady in charge of the mission came to the phone, and said, "Are you Brother Fockler? Where are you?" I told her I was over on Ashland avenue. She said, "Come over here as quickly as you can. You are needed here." I said, "What is the matter?" "Oh, never mind, just come." I went.

As I entered the place there seemed to be considerable commotion and excitement, and she told me the story of how one of their workers had gone violently insane that afternoon, and she also told me of how this dear girl had been found a number of months before in a hospital. Before that she had been operated on fourteen times. There wasn't much of her left, only a shell [at that time]. These dear workers preached Christ to her, she listened to them, gave heed to the preaching, and was converted in the hospital and likewise healed. Then she became so grateful and that she asked the lady in charge of the Mission whether she could not work with them in the Mission, and felt the Lord wanted her to. Her father and mother, living on the north side, were opposed to it, but she was of age and felt free to follow the Lord's leading.

After she had been there a few months, one day something spoke to her and said, "You are going blind." She thought it was the Lord who spoke to her. I doubted it and doubt it still. I think it was a form of seducing spirit, and yet it worked out to the glory of God. From the time she heard that voice her sight began to fail, and the Sunday night previous to my coming there on Tuesday she asked the lady in charge whether she could not lead the Young People's meeting. The lady told her as she had been pretty weak in body she didn't think it would be best unless God had specially given her a message. But she felt the Lord had given her the message and was allowed opportunity to give it.

When she was almost through the light began to recede and the faces of everyone in front of her faded from her view and everything was dark. She became stone blind, and yet the Spirit of God was using the voice as she stood there and she finished her message. We do not need eyes to talk, you know. She continued for ten minutes, with great power, they told me, until she was through, and then, remembering where the lady in charge of the Mission sat, called her by name and told her she could not see. The lady came and took her by the hand.

The next day she was totally blind, and word was sent to her people and their hearts were filled with sorrow, of course. The father went immediately to the hospital where she had been operated on before, to see the specialist, and he said he was not surprised, that her nerves had been so lacerated and destroyed that there was very little hope that she would ever seen again. The mother came on Monday and visited the daughter, which moved on the girl's nervous condition considerably. Afterwards the father came down and insisted she must go with him to the hospital, but she had promised God when He raised her up before, that she would be forever through with doctors and operations, but now the father was bringing pressure to bear and insisting she must go to the hospital, and under that strain soon after the father went away she became a raving maniac, and that day until eleven o'clock at night those five sisters were there with her.

There is only one man there, the caretaker of the place, and there seemed to be no victory and they were about to send the man for help when the Lord led me to ring the telephone and they called me over. As I saw her there, fighting the doctors and the knives, I looked to the Lord, and then it all seemed very clear to me, for this purpose I was there, and for this purpose I had been to the other place earlier in the evening, and we went to prayer. In less than fifteen minutes God gave a complete victory, the girl's mind was perfectly restored.

We all retired in the course of half an hour, and she slept. In the morning when I awoke the Spirit of the Lord came to me again and said, "But that girl is blind." And I said, "Well, I can't restore her sight." Then the Lord said, "Pray for her this morning." I went down stairs, had my breakfast; they were about to have prayer in the other room and invited me there, but I said, "No, the Lord said I was to pray with the girl that was blind," and I went into the room where she was, and Jesus restored her sight. The light seemed to hurt her eyes at first, and as she shaded her eyes she said, "Oh, I see." I called one of the sisters to come up to the bed and she at once recognized her and called her by name; she threw her arms around her neck and they rejoiced together. The light hurt her eyes, and I told her to be perfectly quiet for a few days, that the optical nerve was very weak, and just ten days from the time she went stone blind she was able to see perfectly without the light hurting her eyes.

Now, the key-note of this story is that before God can use us He often leads us down; He humiliates us; He leads us to go the way that crucifies us. He took me down when He took me over to that little meeting of three, in that humble home before He could use me in bringing deliverance to His afflicted child. -- C. B. Fockler, at convention, May 25, 1912. (*TLRE*, July, 1912)

## I Will Guide Thee With Mine Eye
## (Heeding the Voice of God):

We read in Psalm 32:8, "I will instruct thee and teach thee in the way which thou shalt go: I will guide thee with Mine eye."

I am just beginning to realize what it means to be guided by the Lord. I have known what it means to be guided by people for many, many years, but it has only been of recent years that I have known anything of being guided by the Lord, and it is indeed most precious to be guided by Him.

I feel led to speak of a little instance of His guidance about six weeks before the Convention. I feel that the telling of it will inspire new hope, new courage, and new faith in God.

One day during a service in this room while some one was preaching from this platform, I seemed to have a vision which came in the way of a warning. I looked up to the ceiling and I saw this place shaken, the pillars tumbling and the walls tottering. I seemed to be lost to all my surroundings for the time, but I aroused myself and said inwardly, "There isn't anything the matter with this church." Again as I seemed to lose myself I had the same experience, and something said to me, "At the time of the big meetings in the convention, these things will occur."

I went home and tried to shake the matter off. I said to myself, "This is Satan talking to me," and I prayed about it and asked the Lord to make it clear if this was His warning. I knew the people would naturally think because I was a woman I would be inclined to be whimsical and have all sorts of notions, and I was severely tempted. I prayed to God that if it was His warning voice He would make it plain or if it was Satan it should be removed. It became more intensified. I spoke to someone about it, and she thought the Lord had spoken to me, and at any rate it wouldn't do any harm to have the building inspected.

Finally, as some of you know, I felt led to call a meeting with some of the men of the church, and this was a very hard thing to do. I was tempted deeply while going through this interview. I shall never forget that little meeting. It seemed to me there was an amused expression on their faces, and I felt I was utterly foolish before their wisdom. They finally consented to have the church examined by competent inspectors, and when we had the next meeting there was an entirely different look on their faces.

It had been found on examination that the church was not at all safe. The walls had spread seven inches on each side, and with the constant vibration of the street cars together with the vibration from the organ there might be a collapse at any time, and with a large crowd in our upstairs auditorium the danger was very great.

We felt it was a matter not to be talked about, but the building had to be strengthened before the convention. We got the landlord working at it with his inspector and he put in these six large pillars and the tie-rods upstairs. It didn't seem possible to get it done before the convention, but the Lord helped us. . . . in His wonderful goodness and infinite mercy He gave me that vision, and oh, what a lesson I got through listening to His voice. . . . I thank God that He enabled me to hear the warning bell. . . . Let us keep our spiritual sense of hearing keen so we will not fail to hear Him at all times. -- Mrs. Lydia M. Piper, Stone Church. (*TLRE*, July, 1912)

**Pentecostal Outpouring in Dallas, Texas:**
The glory of God continues to rest upon His work in Dallas. There has been a continuous revival since February 2$^{nd}$, 1911, and I believe the revival can never stop unless the saints begin to backslide and neglect to ask and believe for the things God wants to do.

I will mention only what the Lord did during the month of June, 1912. The last Sunday in June I baptized eighteen in the lake at Oak Lawn Park. Two Sundays before, fourteen were baptized at the same place. This makes thirty-two baptized in water during June, each one of whom had first received the Pentecostal baptism according to Acts 2:4. God was with us in power and the candidates were greatly blessed in their souls while obeying God in baptism. Nearly forty received the precious baptism in the Spirit during June, three of the number being ministers of the Gospel.

Pastor G. W. Miller, thirty-five years a Methodist preacher and missionary to the Mexicans, a real soul-winner, heard the voice of the Lord telling him to come to Dallas and seek the baptism in the Holy Spirit. God also spoke to Mrs. W. L. McCartney, a Holiness preacher living at Forney, Texas, and told her to come to the Dallas meetings. They both obeyed and both received their baptism at the same time at the altar Sunday night June 23$^{rd}$. The Methodist preacher lives at Falfurrias, Texas. God has used him in establishing six Mexican missions down on the Rio Grande and he said, "It is just like going home to go back to these people." All were converted under his ministry.

In this assembly at Falfurrias there are one hundred and thirty adult Mexican Christians and their children. Their Spirit-baptized pastor is now ready to begin work at once, teaching all these converts to obey Christ's last command and receive the Pentecostal baptism. He believes all in these different missions will accept the truth. He preaches fluently in Spanish. Who can tell what this may mean for Mexico, now bound by Catholicism?

The night before these two preachers were baptized, a lady residing in Dallas was wonderfully converted through a vision which God gave her in the night. She found our tent the next day and received the Pentecostal baptism that night. . . .

God also worked several miracles of healing in June. One was a Baptist lady with rheumatism over her entire body. She had "many physicians" and had not done a day's work in four years, was unable to raise her hands to comb her hair in two years, had to be turned in bed all this time and helped to rise when she was well enough to get up. She was instantly and perfectly healed in the presence of the audience at the tent Tuesday night, June 11$^{th}$. She could raise her hands straight above her head and walk perfectly without the slightest symptom of the disease. She worked hard all the next day and every day since. A Catholic lady was instantly healed of the same disease a few nights ago. . . .

Sunday night we arranged seats for two hundred people outside the tent and even then many had to stand. Our other tent was also filled. God continues to show His power as last month and every night people are "getting through."

I want to say in closing, for the benefit of any who are disposed to limit the Lord's working, that almost all who kneel at the altar for salvation receive also the baptism in the Holy Spirit and speak in tongues before arising from their knees. These that the Lord thus puts through make our best workers.

May the Lord continue to bless His children everywhere. -- F. F. Bosworth. (*TLRE*, Aug., 1912) [The revival continued for several years. Sister Etter was there about 5 months in 1912.]

Birdsall and Bosworth in Dallas

## In the Hands of the Potter
### Leila M. Conway, Hurlock, Maryland

"Ye are My witnesses, saith the Lord." In the summer of 1907 when I heard a prominent and well known evangelist publicly denounce what he called the "tongue movement" -- my first intelligence of its existence -- I inwardly sided with him, although refraining from taking an open stand. This was at a holiness campmeeting. By the following winter, judging from what I had learned, chiefly through holiness papers, I was fully persuaded that this "movement" was a delusion and was ready to unite with others in opposing it and crying it down as one of the most grievous fanaticisms of the day. However, before I could get my first public opportunity, God graciously and marvelously interposed.

One evening in January, soon after I had retired for the night, He drew near. I knew Him -- my Lord and my Redeemer; "Do not take part with others in pronouncing this 'new thing' a delusion. For the place that thou dost think to tread upon is holy ground."

Oh! the tender emphasis upon the "holy." It revealed to me that Jesus was somehow to be found in this reproached "movement" and that I had already to some extent been lifting up my hand against Him. I was dumb with astonishment. A great thankfulness began to well up in my heart for His intervention while the glad tears coursed down my cheeks. I heard Him say, "Seek and obtain," and then He was gone. From that moment as best I knew how, I began to seek, though *what* I scarcely knew, my information having been so one-sided and prejudiced; and, furthermore, holy men and women had taught me that there was no further blessing to seek beyond "sanctification," they likewise calling that "the enducment for service," "the baptism in the Spirit" and "Pentecost."

But I felt I must not be disobedient to the heavenly vision. On the strength of that revelation alone I must press through to what He had called me to obtain. And right there I would sound a note to His praise. When about to lag or grow weary He would invariably draw near to cheer me and draw me on (Canticles 1:4) [Song of Solomon], giving the assurance that I would yet receive, so that ofttimes on my knees I found myself rejoicing and praising Him for what He was going to do. Wonderful God! "Like as a father pitieth his children so the Lord pitieth them that fear Him."

More than two years passed by without my seeming even to get within sight of the goal, but early in the spring of 1910 the Lord let me know my long wait was drawing to a close. He sent to my Maryland home a letter from a brother and sister in New Hampshire telling me of a Latter Rain Campmeeting to be held that summer. This brother and sister were entire strangers and had gotten hold of my name and address by the merest chance as it seemed, but I knew it was not so. I beheld the hand of God focusing matters for me and my heart beat high with praise. A few weeks later an open letter in *The Way of Faith* did more than any other one thing in bringing me light on the Latter Rain Movement.

It appeared that a missionary, under the pressure of adverse denominational influences, was about to retract her favorable attitude toward these Pentecostal manifestations and the writer of this letter set before the wavering one a tender plea of entreaty in words that I knew could never have originated from human wisdom or understanding. The Spirit of the Father speaking through the lines brought me to my knees in prayer before Him. My soul now came to wait upon God with almost unbroken continuity.

When there remained but a few days before my departure for the campmeeting the though of the criticism I would encounter from friends began to come before me. Would it not be better for me to obtain the blessing I sought before going from home? With strong pleading and agonizing I pressed my suit night and day. Finally I thought of the promise of 1 John 5:14-15, through which I had often received blessing from God. In my secret closet I went over the words with Him: "If we ask anything according to His will, He hears us; and if we know that He hears us, whatsoever we ask, we know that we have the petitions that we desired of Him." I had assuredly asked according to His will, and I knew that He heard -- therefore I had the baptism.

Taking the stand of having received by faith I went to the campmeeting and testified that I had received the baptism. This, I found, did not meet the views of the workers and indeed, as I afterwards came to see, there was along with my real receiving by faith a subtle form of self-love and pride, an endeavor to avoid the shame of the cross in the reproach that the speaking in tongues might bring. This had to be done away with and God used one of the workers to bring it about.

During an early morning service when we were bowed at the altar in prayer I, too, prayed, thanking God for the baptism which I had received through faith in His Word, whereupon this brother exclaimed, "If Sister Conway persists in saying she has the baptism she will finally be lost and drop into hell." "No, you will not," said the Spirit within me; but at the same time under the power of that rebuke and while the brother was still speaking the words, I felt a wilting and shriveling up within such as you see on the flower in the scorching rays of the noonday sun or when held near the blaze of a fire. This -- not the words -- convinced me there was something amiss in me, something lacking. It took the strong rebuke of the brother to break down my spiritual pride and I feel that God permitted him to speak as he did in order that something more might be accomplished in me.

The revelation was like a thunderbolt out of a clear sky, so shocked and amazed was I. God had begun to tear me down that He might build me up, to slay me that He might make me alive. I had fallen on Christ the Living Stone to be broken in heart, in intellect, in will and in body, until every part of my being became pliable in the hands of the Potter. There is a world of meaning in Psalm 51:17, which says "the sacrifices of God are a broken and contrite spirit." Some of us have substituted other sacrifices and failed to obtain what we sought from God.

But, though I knew that wilting and shriveling up to be none other than the working of God, the enemy was present to tempt me. "Do not remain here a day longer but pack up and leave the camp ground at once," he whispered. "They have not treated you with common courtesy, but have as good as said you are professing a lie, when you know you would sooner have died." "Get thee behind me Satan," I cried. "If what these workers say is true, surely I ought to thank God and them for delivering me from deception, and if not true why should I care what they say? I am here to go through with God, and here I will stay until His time comes for me to go away."

This was no small victory over the powers of darkness but by no means did it dispel the perplexity and mystery settling down on me as a pall. Did it mean I had been claiming something I did not have when 1 John 5:14 was so explicit, and must I acknowledge it all a mistake and begin to seek over again? The tears fell like rain.

Some time before this the people had left the altar and I was alone with my thoughts. Rising from my knees I went in haste to the tent where the workers were assembled and bursting in on them I sobbed out, "Oh, won't you pray for me and help me to get right with God?" Instantly all were on their knees. How they prayed! But I was too absorbed with my grief to take much notice of what they said. "I don't know what else to do, nor what to pray," wailed I. For if ever a human being had "come to the end of the rope" I was that one.

"You do not need to pray any more," said one of the workers, "nor do any more than you have done." Not to pray? It put a still more puzzling aspect on the situation, "No, just quietly wait until He sends the manifestation of the Spirit."

In the tumult and distress of my mind I found it well-nigh impossible to cease from my pleading cries to God; but the prayers of His saints at last prevailed and by degrees I came into a state of outward calm. My sufferings in spirit from one o'clock until six p.m. of that day are indescribable. It was a literal fulfillment of the latter clause in Matt. 27:46, a complete hiding away of the face of God, something I had never known before. My anguish of soul brought forth the cry, "Where, oh where is God?" "He is right here," replied one of the workers. This assurance brought a measure of comfort, for to my senses He had seemed clear removed from the earth and it was good to know He was still present.

They had been telling me not to do anything save to wait and praise God; but with the spirit of heaviness upon me, rather than the spirit of praise, one can conceive what it cost to do this even with the lips, and how for some time it was no more than a form of praise.

Somewhere between the hours of six and seven I began to feel a lifting of terrible darkness and a most vivid consciousness of the returning presence of my Lord. Hope sprang up anew in my breast, mourning was turned into joy. I had in the meanwhile noted that these men and women of God had at no time denied my claim on 1 John 5:14-15, to the baptism, but only insisted that I tarry and wait for the *manifestation*. Light began to break. About an hour later I heard the voice of the Lord telling me to go out to the evening service. I rose from the floor where I had lain prostrate through all the long hours of the afternoon and went into the auditorium where already the service was in progress. I had no more than taken my seat when there dropped into my heart the assurance, sure and strong, that I would receive the manifest fullness of the Spirit's presence that night. Hallelujah! "Though He tarry, yet wait; for He will surely come" (Hab. 2:3).

Some one has said that there is a time to stop praying and begin praising, to stop asking and begin receiving. I knew that this time had come for me. Most eager expectation of my Lord, who was now on the way, was kindled within as I lay there in the straw those hours praising and awaiting His coming.

Then the Spirit began to take me through a series of questions: "If your unbelieving mother and family were here in the congregation looking on and thinking you had gone stark mad, could you still lie here?" "Yes, oh yes!" cried I, shuddering at the mere thought of missing the goal to which I had almost attained. "The pastor and people of your church and neighborhood will lose their confidence in you and say: 'Sister C---? Well, of all things! She is the last person we would think of to be so led astray by that fanaticism.'"

I watched the ignominy, slander, persecution, ill-name, trials, following one after the other in panoramic array, saw my aristocratic relatives and Christian friends leave me till the last had gone; then, turning to the Spirit, I replied: "I will go forth therefore unto Him without the camp, bearing His reproach."

"Only a few weeks ago the one whom you hold dearest was saying he had watched you amid the false teachings and deceptions around you and had rejoiced to see you stand true to Christ through them all as a needle to the pole. He is one of the number who, with all good conscience, honestly believes this so-called 'tongue-movement' has originated from the pit and is the climax of deception. What if he should leave you?"

It took me some time to answer this question. I had counted him a friend that would never forsake though all others should fail. In a sense more real than words can depict, I felt myself made as the filth and offscouring of the earth -- undergoing a stripping process -- that Christ might be made my "all in all." "Naked, poor, despised, forsaken," came to me with all of its force through this, the last stroke. But the suffering was turned into joy most exquisite as I beheld that Jesus had gone this way before me and was only opening up the lone, lone path that He had trod and saying, oh, so tenderly, "Can you walk therein?"

[With] The last question of the Spirit answered, the preparation was now complete as "when the day of Pentecost was fully come" (Acts 2:1). I first began to feel my body being taken up by a power altogether outside my own volition or control. A violent shaking and waves of electricity passed over me from head to foot making even my finger tips to tingle -- a literal fulfillment of His promise, "I will pour out of My Spirit." Then the fire fell! Under its burning both with and without (which continued in a mild gentle manner for several days afterward), I was constrained to cry out, "I shall burn up! I shall burn up!" "Did you not pray for Him to baptize you with the Holy Ghost and fire?" said someone near; then I remembered my prayer and said, "Hallelujah!"

There then came what to me was the most precious and most sacred manifestation of them all, the memory of it is in my soul to stay through all time and eternity. I became aware of a distinct physical dealing of the Lord. The clutch of a human hand could not have been more real than was the grasp of that Divine Hand on my heart -- probing, tightening -- under the mighty grip of which I lost my breath a time or more, while across my mind there flashed the consciousness of the bliss it would be to die under that Hand! God, meanwhile, letting me know it was for the purpose of getting out the root of unbelief far down in my heart.

I was amazed at the revelation, for I had firmly believed myself possessing more than an ordinary degree of faith. Through that searching illumination, laying bare the innermost recesses of my being, I saw my faith did not measure up to the grain of mustard seed spoken of by Jesus in Matt. 7:20. Oh, the different way in which God looks upon things!

I was next brought to drink in of [sic] the Spirit (1 Cor. 1:12-13) and to speak in other tongues, sensing, oh, so clearly, that the "foolishness" and "weakness" of God (1 Cor. 1:25) was being manifested through me before a scorning and unbelieving world. Jesus was hid away from the sight of men by reason of His lowliness, "a root out of dry ground; no form nor comeliness; no beauty that we should desire Him," in the light of which I could now see how it was that "His own received Him not" (John 1:11).

Ah, beloved, in the eternity to come it will be revealed that the Jews were no more ignorant of their "day of visitation" than are some of us. It was revealed to me that subtle pride and a self-life that does not want to be put to the death is at the bottom of our resistance. We do not see because we do not want to see; we do not know because we do not want to know. Those who have taken a stand against "this miserable tongue movement," as one of our good, eminent ministers terms it, are some day going to awaken to the fact that the despised and lowly Jesus has been here in our midst and they knew Him not.

Oh, to get humble and teachable before God so that He can get us to "all the way" as in song and testimony we have often said that we would do, even though it terminates in our crucifixion with Christ, being "made a spectacle unto the world and to angels and to men;" but oh, bless His dear name, He that loses his life shall have it multiplied back to him in the proportion that results from a grain of wheat falling into the ground, "And if it die it bringeth forth much fruit." Hallelujah!

There was given me a revelation of the Father and the Son far transcending what I had known before and which it had not entered into my heart to conceive of. My soul was lost in wonder at the condescension of God, yet filled with a joy unspeakable; a little foretaste of the experience that will be ours when we are caught up to be forever with the Lord in the glory of His immediate presence. It was heaven!

This precious "latter rain" outpouring of the Spirit by no means conflicts with any of God's works toward us in the past. The writer once heard certain workers say that their past association with the Holiness Union was a mistake, though scores of men and women in that throng knew of the time when these heralds of full salvation went proclaiming a Savior that saves to the uttermost, God attending their ministry in great power. Oh, to be wise, beloved! The Holy Ghost has ever been in the world since His descent in that "upper room;" but from what we sometimes hear it would seem as if He has been away and is just returned.

Neither can we overlook the "differences of administrations" and "diversities of operations" by which He has worked in by-gone years and centuries; "but all these worketh the one and the self-same Spirit."

And now that God is pouring out the "latter rain" in the closing days of this Gospel dispensation we may know it will correspond to the "former rain" given in the inauguration of this present dispensation, so that the one who receives the Holy Ghost in these "last days" may expect to speak in other tongues -- the distinguishing evidence of the "former" and "latter" rain -- as did the disciples on the day of Pentecost. There are exceptional instances on record but I am led to believe the "sign" (tongues) more particularly belongs to these periods.

From the understanding that comes to me I do not see wherein God would have us formulate this precious "latter rain" into a doctrine or even to speak of it as a "movement." I see in this recent outpouring of the Spirit an indication of the near return of Jesus and an end of the present order of things, a ripening of the "first fruits" of the harvest for Christ at His coming.

O, sleeping virgin, do not slumber longer! For only they that love His appearing, with the "first fruits" out from among the dead will be "caught up" to meet the descending Lord. "And so shall we ever be with the Lord." (*TLRE*, Oct., 1912)

# Messengers of An Outpouring

## The Finnish Gold Story:

*The miraculous is still being worked in the earth today. Though higher criticism has tried to rule out of the Word of God the multiplying of the loaves and fishes and of the widow's cruse of oil, it has failed. Even in this Twentieth Century God is still proving Himself to be a God that "does wondrous things" (Ps. 86:10), and here and there in the world miraculous events are witnessing to His power.*

*Away off in an obscure village in Finland we find in this day the multiplying of the widow's mite through the power of prayer -- true prayer in the Holy Spirit. When S. D. Gordon was in Stockholm he heard of how a poor woman in Finland, in building a little chapel, was called upon to pay an unjust lumber bill that she had not the money to meet. . . . In due time the same Hand that multiplied the money guided him to the little village and he preached in the very church that had been built by the multiplied money. She had been postmisstress for more than twenty years -- a position which, in Finland, is practically equal to being in charge of a government bank -- and has been accustomed to counting money. The following is the story as given by Mr. Gordon in his book, "The Quiet Time."* [This book cannot be found online in any form.] *We reprint it through the courtesy of the publishers, Fleming H. Revell & Co.:* —

While the building was going up, there came a bill for lumber which had been bought and received. But the amount was larger than it should have been. With the bill came a peremptory letter demanding immediate payment, and threatening legal action. The bill was for seven hundred and fifty-one Finnish marks (about $150), being twenty-seven dollars more than the right amount. The common commercial custom of the country provides for long credit. The amount was unjust, the usual time payment was not given, and legal proceedings threatened. This was a wholly unexpected and distressing complication.

She was troubled to know what to do about the unjust increase in the bill. The difference of one hundred and thirty marks was a serious one in the condition of the chapel funds, and the great difficulty experienced in getting funds. She could refuse to pay, and go to law, but that meant endless trouble, and additional expense; and, further, she could not feel free in her heart about engaging in a lawsuit over the Lord's work. The words of Matthew 5:40 came repeatedly to mind. Finally she decided to pay the full amount if she must, but only under strong protest against the injustice. It greatly strengthened her afterwards in praying for the money that she was acting in the spirit of the Master's teaching.

The chapel funds were made up wholly of free-will offerings by the people attending the services. The people are very poor; the funds were very low. Our friend stood quite alone in the responsibility. There had been much opposition among the church people to the chapel being built. It was a time of sore stress of soul. She cried to God, and there came to her a great quiet peace, that seemed to brood over her. Then she commenced praying for the money. This was May of 1908. The legal action, if taken, would give her until October.

Then followed a never-to-be-forgotten time of tireless effort, constant disappointment, unceasing prayer, sore stress of spirit and yet a strangely quiet peace, -- all intermingled. Every effort to get the money, either by gift or by borrowing was entirely fruitless. There seemed only a stone wall at every turn. There was criticism, reproach, and even sneers, but very little money. Her difficulty became known in the little community, and was freely discussed, especially by those opposed to the chapel, who said that now it must be sold to pay this debt.

Still, she prayed. In her words, "The prayer lamp burned day and night." It was a time of great searching of heart and sore strain in her spirit. The final time of payment drew near. Now something must be done. The law officer or sheriff was a friendly man, but, of course, must do his duty. A last effort, involving a journey to a near-by town, proved unavailing. The man she hoped to see was abroad; his wife thought she ought not to have begun building till she had the money. As she returned on the train her spirit was in the deepest concern and yet there was that strange sense of peace that would not leave.

That was a wondrous time on the train. The brooding presence of Jesus seemed so near as she quietly sat thinking while the train noisily hurried on. Her soul was drawn out in prayer to an unusual extent. In her dire extremity she cast herself upon God. Then there came into her mind something she had thought of all during the building of the chapel. But now it seemed to have a new meaning. Her mind was turned to the time in the desert when the loaves and fishes were multiplied. Then this prayer seemed given to her that God would touch her slender chapel funds and do as in the desert-- make them sufficient for the need.

On her return home as soon as she could get time from her work, she went to the drawer to get the little box where the chapel funds were kept. She had counted the money before that last journey, and found she had just three hundred and fifty marks ($70). Now she took the box out to the sitting room. She had on hand ninety marks ($18) of her own personal money. This she added to the Lord's money and poured all out on the table. It was at the noon hour. The post-office which was in one part of the dwelling, was closed. She was quite alone.

She bowed in prayer over the table, spreading her hands out over the little heap of money, and prayed that God would indeed do as she believed He was leading her to ask. In simple childlike language she said; "Lord Jesus, bless Thy money as Thou did the loaves in the wilderness. I will put my loaves, too, in Thy hands, and do Thou let them with Thine meet this need; let this money cover the amount of this bill." So she remained a little in prayer.

Then she counted one hundred marks ($20), and put it in a little heap by itself, then a second hundred, and a third, and so on, until there were seven such heaps of one hundred each, and a smaller heap of fifty-one marks. And she noticed that there was now much gold, though there had not been much gold in the box. This brought to her mind the words of Isaiah 60:17, "For brass I will bring gold, and for iron I will bring silver, and for wood brass, and for stones iron."

With a great awe filling her being, she fell upon her knees, thanking the Lord Jesus; then she rose and carefully counted again. Again she placed her hands upon the money, praising Jesus, whose presence seemed very real, and again she prayed that the money might remain until she could pay the law officer.

We went with her as she unlocked the drawer in which she always kept the Lord's treasure-box, and reverently handled the plain little wooden box. No one looking at the big business-like bunch of keys, which she always carried in her pocket and watching her unlocking the various drawers for papers and record books, and carefully locking each again, could have any doubt about that box being locked securely where no hand but hers could get at it.

Then she saw the sheriff, or law officer, and told him that now he could come, for she had the money. He couldn't believe her, knowing well her struggles, and asked where she got it. In her simple, quiet way she said the Lord had sent it. Two days later he said he would call on the morrow to collect the amount of the bill.

That day, when free from the post-office duties, and quite alone, she took the box, and spread the money out again. Now, she felt an impulse to put her own ninety marks in a little heap by itself before counting the rest. She obeyed this impulse. Again she spread her hands over the money and prayed and praised; again she counted, and an additional touch of God's power was revealed-- there was the full sum of seven hundred and fifty-one marks without her own scant, hard-earned and hard-saved money.

With heart too full for words she fell upon her knees, praising the Lord again and again. She understood better now what the Master was doing; she had freely given all her own reserve, but He would make the funds enough without her own slender store. Again she prayed that the money remain until the collector came.

The next day he came. She had him sit at the opposite side of the table while she told him her story. He was much moved. Then she did as before, poured the money out of the box, quietly prayed and praised over it, then counted it out to the man. Now some few silver coins were left over, after the bill was paid, though she had put her won money aside. She had often prayed that little Lord's treasure-box might never be quite empty, and that prayer was now being remembered. The collector was greatly moved, and drew five marks from his pocket saying, "I want to put a little to this wonderful money."

So the money was paid and the legal receipt duly made out. Then our friend wrote a note to be sent with the money to the lumber dealer. It said that the amount of the bill was unjust, as he knew, and was not being paid under strong protest, but in accordance with the spirit of love in the words of the Savior in Matthew 5:40. So a bit of witnessing went with the gold. . . .

The teaching of this simple, startling story is very plain. And earnestly do I ask that no editorial shears shall ever part this paragraph and what follows from the story itself. The teaching is *not* that we are to ask God to multiply our money in this way; or, even that we may do so. If ever again He leads some trusting child of His to do something of this same sort, that one will recognize His leading without needing to depend on such an incident as this, and will recognize it better yet as the results come. This same thing may not occur again in a generation, or in many generations. . . . This came in a sore emergency. It was an emergency transaction.

The simple teaching of the experience for us is this: God never fails any one who depends upon Him. He never disappoints. His Word never fails. True prayer guided by the Holy Spirit, bathed in the spirit of sacrifice [and faith], never fails, and cannot. . . .

There's a further bit of a living sermon here. It is this: true prayer is put into our hearts by the Holy Spirit. The yearnings of our hearts after God, and for loved ones, and for special needs, are simply echoed yearnings. They are God's heart. . . . As we walked over the little chapel with our quiet friend, questioning, listening, thinking, it became clear and then clearer that this story we had come for was only one chapter in a story. It was a sort of climax chapter; those going before were of the same sort, all leading up to this climax. It was a long story running through a number of years-- a story of longing, of struggle, of steady, patient fighting against difficulties of every imaginable sort, of most stubborn resistance to all her plannings . . . (*TLRE*, Nov., 1912)

**News Notes: New Castle, Texas:**

Our meeting, held by Brother W. H. Lyon and band, has just closed. It was a hard battle, but, praise the Lord, it left the saints in good order. Praise God for cleanness and for sifting out the chaff. Fifteen souls were saved and eight received the Spirit in baptismal power. Great interest was manifested. The meeting closed with six still seeking the baptism. Pray that God will help them to press their way through, as we see the time has come when people must press the battle to the very gates, regardless of every obstacle, to get the full victory.

Bless God for victory in this place. One year ago an attempt was made to hold a meeting here and preach the full gospel, and some heathen-like people tried to mob the man of God, and though God did not permit it, these people thought they had things going their way, but God has had His way, and the true gospel has been preached here. Bless the name of the Lord forever. He did it all. The devil roared, howled, threatened, and lied, but God exposed him and he lost the battle. . . . -- Nora McKnight. (*WaW*, Aug., 1912)

[Many of the mob people in those early days were actually professing Christians, some Catholic and even Baptists.]

## GLORY AND UNITY at the EUREKA SPRINGS CAMP!

The annual inter-state convention or encampment of the Churches of God in Christ of the Apostolic Faith people met on schedule time at Eureka Springs, Arkansas, July 10, and closed with joy on July 21. The attendance far surpassed that of one year ago at the same place. The entertainment committee, headed by Brother John H. James, of Kansas, had their hands full in providing tents and rooms. One night, after everything was full up, a delegation of about 40 filed in during the preaching service. Again and again they came until about 500 were in attendance. About 300 or over camped on the grounds.

Without any collections for this purpose, voluntary offerings were placed in a free-will offering box, sufficient to feed daily the whole multitude at the free tables.

A Baptist brother in attendance as a visitor said he never, in all his life, saw anything like it, and, too, without any collections. The secret was God controlled the hearts of His grateful people, and caused them to give joyfully of His substance which He entrusted in their hands as His stewards. . . .

Well, it is generally thought when a climax like this Monday night, has been reached in a meeting that the best of the feast is over, and that the meeting will peter out at the end. So next day it did seem to ebb, and the writer himself feared the rule might prove true in this meeting; but the tide began to rise again. On Friday night, all unexpected, the glory of God burst in upon us, and the power of God fell until the slain of the Lord were many around the altar. Souls were saved, others came through with glorious baptism . . .

The very best wine was reserved for Sunday, the last day of the feast. After a short address there was a sermon on the Church the body of Christ, and how one gets into it. . . . Then the Spirit of God took complete control of the meeting, enforcing the lesson on Holiness. The Spirit declared [through tongues and interpretation] God wanted a church without spot or wrinkle, that He was now calling for such to be the Bride of His Son.

The Spirit, in no uncertain tones, let it be known that God demanded of His people to be clean, pure and holy in all things. As the Spirit held up the standard of what God's great heart of love wanted His people to be, a sense of conviction for their shortage and for lowering God's standard on divorce, and some other things in the past, seized the people.

The Spirit of God in intercession interceded for the people until there were many wails and sobs in the souls of men. Suddenly the Spirit burst through to victory. The people were assured God had heard, and His people were forgiven and accepted in the Beloved! Amid the joy of it all the Spirit began again to enforce the lesson of Holiness in such a way that it is hoped His saints will never forget it as long as they live.

Though the audience was held for about four hours, the workings of God were so grand, so solemn, so awe-inspiring, withal so glorious that the saints were still loath to leave the sacred and glorious spot even after dismissed. . . . On Every hand the saints could be heard, after the meeting closed, thanking God they were permitted to attend. [No author given.] (*WaW*, Aug., 1912)

## Trip to the Southwest

I left home June 27, stopped off three nights with brethren Williamson and Todd, in Memphis, Tenn. The Lord was blessing the people there. From there to Little Rock, Ark. two nights. Not much work among the white people, but quite a work among the colored folks. . . .

I went to Dallas, Texas. Brethren Bosworth and Birdsall are in charge of the work there. A revival has been on there for about eighteen months. God is doing a new thing for these days in Dallas. They have with them Mrs. M. B. Woodworth-Etter, who has had the baptism in the spirit over twenty years. She is being used of the Lord in a wonderful way, in bringing sinners to Christ, in healing the sick, and getting believers filled with the Holy Ghost.

I saw a deaf and dumb lady healed and filled with the Spirit. She was, I suppose, 40 years old and had never heard or spoken until she was delivered. It was the most wonderful thing to have ever witnessed. A number of others had been delivered in the meeting of the same trouble. There was a woman brought in on a cot, (she was a poor sin-stricken, half-paralyzed spiritualistic medium). She was prayed for, and the demons commanded in Jesus' name to leave her, and then commanded to get up, and she did arise and ran up and down the altar in front of the congregation with uplifted hands, praising God; left her cot and went on her way rejoicing!

A big fat sinner near me broke down and cried, and said, "God is living and doing business! Who can doubt it?" Sister Etter had just prayed for his consumptive wife, who was brought in on a cot. God saved her and took away all suffering and she stood on her feet and praised God. She had not been on her feet in seventeen months.

A lady blind received her sight at the altar in answer to prayer. And many others were healed the two nights I was there. . . .

Now what God is doing in Dallas, Fort Worth, and a number of other places, He will do everywhere, if people will humble themselves, pray through, believe the Bible and press the battle. Yours in the battle for the Master. -- M. M. Pinson. (*WaW*, Aug., 1912)

## The Good of Speaking With Tongues:

It has come to pass today that some professing to believe on the Lord do not welcome what He promised to them that believe, and some are so prejudiced as to condemn as evil and nothing but evil to receive in Christian experience what He promised! Pity indeed!

He said, "These signs shall follow them that believe: In my name they shall cast out devils (demons); they shall speak with new tongues," (Mark 16:17).

Notice two things here. First, that Jesus refers to this miraculous speaking in tongues as one of the Christian "Signs." Second, that this sign of tongues is promised to follow them that "Believe."

All sane people know that not one promise in the whole Bible, conditioned on faith, can possibly be fulfilled in any one until after this person believes; yet the people will declare they do not believe this promise of speaking with another tongue is for today, because they have never received it. Their declaration of unbelief explains why.

Note this does not say these signs will follow the "Apostles," yet they are not shut out, if they will "believe." So they did not get this sign because they were "apostles," but because they "believed." Then it followed them. Why can we not "believe" as well as they? Certainly every saved man knows we can believe today, for he was saved by faith in Christ.

1. Tongues, then, are a sign of faith-- not the only sign, but one of them. This is one of the benefits. He who speaks in other tongues "as the Spirit of God gives utterance" has an additional sign or witness from God that he is a true believer on Jesus Christ. Christ's promises are verified, in him.

2. Another benefit is that they are the sign that the gift of the Holy Spirit has been poured out upon the speaker. Luke, the inspired writer of Acts, declares the Jewish believers knew the Gentiles as well as they had the gift of the Holy Ghost poured out upon them; "For they heard them speak with tongues," Acts 10:45-46.

3. Through the speaking in tongues the Spirit bears witness to Jesus that he is at the right hand of God the Father. Paul says the Spirit is shed forth or poured out "through Jesus Christ." Titus 3:6. Jesus said when the Spirit came he would "testify," (Jn 15:25). On the day of Pentecost this was fulfilled through the speaking in tongues, for the people heard these believers filled with the Holy Ghost speak in "tongues the wonderful works of God" through Christ. For Peter declared, "He hath shed forth this which ye now see and hear" (Acts 2:11-33).

Every time, then, the Spirit is poured out and causes them [to be] filled with Him to speak in tongues, we know that Jesus is still on the mediatorial throne in glory, for the Spirit is "testifying" of his "wonderful works."

4. Speaking in tongues is a benefit to the believer in talking to God, for by tongues he "speaketh 'unto God," (I Cor. 14:2). Anything that enables one to talk to God is of great benefit.

5. It is good to speak in tongues because the speaker "edifieth himself" (14:4). Whatever will edify or build up the believer in his spiritual life like this is good.

6. Prophesying is counted a gift of great value to the church for "edification, exhortation and comfort," (14:3) and Peter said the talking in tongues on the day of Pentecost was the "prophesying" spoken of by Joel, and when this prophesying is turned into English through the companion gift of interpretation, it "edifies the church" in the same way as prophesying in our own tongue does. Greater is he that prophesieth than he that speaks with tongues, "except he interpret, that the church may receive edifying" (14:5). Note this is the only benefit dependent upon interpretation.

7. Paul says, "If I pray in a tongue my spirit prayeth" (14:4). Through the use of tongues we can worship and pray to God. Great good!

8. God says through "other tongues and other lips will I speak unto this people; yet for all that they will not hear me, saith the Lord," (14:21). Then Paul concluded from this saying of the Lord that tongues are for a "sign . . . to them that believe not." So, then, tongues are one of God's signs whereby he miraculously speaks to unbelievers. Many have, to the knowledge of the writer by this means, been turned to God and saved. Yet, for all that, "some will not hear me, saith the Lord." Reader, are you one that has such an evil heart of unbelief that despite all God's miraculous talking to you through "other tongues and other lips" ye will not still believe? The Lord in mercy pity the doomed soul!

These eight benefits, right from the Word, ought to satisfy anyone, who will take the Word of God on anything, that tongues are a benefit, both to the believer who speaks, and to the church. There are misuses of tongues, as well as good uses; and when a congregation is "baptized in one Spirit into the body" (1 Cor. 13:13) as was the Corinthian church, and has reached the same stage of development in the use of tongues this church had when Paul addressed this letter to them, then, but not until then, should they be governed strictly by the rules laid down by Paul in this 14th chapter of Corinthians.

Yet we never sought tongues nor fought tongues, and never tell others to seek tongues, as some falsely claim we do. Seek Jesus Christ to baptize you with the Spirit, and the result will be that you will be "filled with the Holy Ghost and begin to speak with tongues," for "God is no respecter of persons." -- Editor. (*WaW*, Aug., 1912)

**Oakland, Cal.:**
We have just closed a most successful campaign of 10 days in this place, 47 receiving the Holy Ghost. On Sunday Sept. 8, the power of God fell in a way I have never seen during this latter outpouring of the Spirit. Fifteen on this one day were baptized in the Spirit and came through speaking in other tongues as in Acts 2:4. (*WaW*, Oct., 1912)

## Revival Fires From Heaven Still Burning

In our last issue there were blessed reports of souls being saved in many places, and the Spirit of God falling from Heaven on newborn babes in Christ, so that hundreds altogether were baptized in the Spirit, all at once speaking in "other tongues as the Spirit gave utterance" (Acts 2:4) exactly as on the day [of] Pentecost. We praise the "God of all grace" that the Spirit is still falling in power and glory. Read below and see.

**Cleburne, Texas**: The papers came [multiple copies of Word and Witness], and I believe it is the best paper we ever had. It did my soul good and I love to hand out such good news to others. It has been a great blessing to our work here.

Since leaving Burleson, God has blessed us every day, but the devil has contested every inch of the ground and sorely tried us in many ways. One day a request came not to preach so loud as a child in a home nearby was having convulsions. We stopped and went to see it. At the very hour of prayer for it that night its jaws were opened for the first time in two weeks. He had been fed only through a straw for two weeks. The power of God has rested on the work ever since, bless God's holy name! Several have received the baptism in the Spirit and some have been coming from other towns to the meetings. A holiness brother came, saw the light and went to seeking God. The Lord showed him he was a backslider. He got up and confessed it, and God saved him right there. He went to the altar that night and Christ gloriously poured out the Spirit upon him. . . .

**Canton, Ill**: Sunday afternoon among other saints a young man came 28 miles to our home to seek the baptism in the Spirit. We had a refreshing time and are holding on to God since coming here from Des Moines for Canton and Peoria, that God may pour out the Latter Rain in these two places.

The other day upon request, we went to a home to pray for the insane daughter. God heard and healed her, and she has since gone to visit God's people in Pentecostal missions in Chicago. Praise God. -- Alfred Pascoe.

**Earle, Ark.**: Brother Johnston helped us in a meeting here for thirteen days, and 4 were baptized in water, 2 baptized in the Spirit and 14 saved. At Earle the church is set in order. W. H. Copeland.

**Hot Springs, Ark**: Saints refreshed, sinners saved, backsliders reclaimed and 10 baptized in the Spirit. -- H. A. Goss.

**Golden Gate, Il**: Saints refreshed by the good news, and a blessed camp near Vienna, Ill., in which souls were saved, the sick wonderfully healed, demons cast out, the Lord gave prophecy and interpretation of tongues and baptized believers in the Spirit. -- E. F. Cunningham.

**Princeton, Mo.**: Meetings for five months nearly every night. Last Friday 6 saved and 3 of the same baptized in the Spirit. Between 50-60 have received the baptism. Looking for the revival to continue all winter. -- W. Y. Howell.

**Pickering, La.**: A number saved and 33 recently received the baptism with the Spirit. -- Maude Herrin.

**Broken Arrow, Okla.**: The good meeting in which Bro. M. M. Pinson helped still goes on here. For the last three nights 16 have received the baptism. The town and county stirred as never before. -- W.H. Pope.

**Jackson, Tenn.**: The devil mad, saints shouting and getting victory. The good work goes on. Two received the baptism last Sunday. -- J. C. Brickey.

**Stuttgart, Ark.**: Four received the baptism and 6 saved. Power falling as never before here. House running over last Sunday night. -- Della Cook.

**Houston Heights, Tex.**: Separated from Parham and God is blessing. Bro. A. P. Collins preached for us last Sunday; night service a wonderful one, the Spirit of the Lord manifested as never witnessed by me before. -- J. C. Dowling. The withdrawal of the Parhamites left a unity that God can consistently bless and he is doing it. -- W. F. Caruthers.

**Fairland, Tex.**: The power of the Lord is still falling in Fairland. In a cottage prayer meeting Wednesday night 4 received the baptism, speaking in tongues the wonderful word of God. One who had been almost blind with sore eyes, came through speaking and healed. A dog bitten by a snake and dying was prayed for by owner and healed. . . .

A man who had used tobacco 45 years, and who was miserable without it and who made his family and children miserable when without, has had all desire for it taken away. A sister who had been using snuff and tobacco 25 years was delivered by the power of God. She says, "It never troubles me now." Others who had tried to quit in themselves are now praising God for taking all desire for it away. (It will stay away forever, if they will never touch it again; but if they begin to fool with it again, it will come back, and it will be like rooting up a mountain ever to get delivered again. I have seen it and know. -- Editor.)

**Benton, Ark.**: -- We praise God for our new tabernacle. Four baptized in the Spirit, 15 in water and 24 saved. New seekers almost every night. -- H. E. Reed.

**Necessity, Texas**: I went from Lusk Camp where God did a blessed work for all that country to Necessity, 35 miles south. The last eight days 22 received the baptism in the Spirit, and many sinners were saved. I have never seen such power since I met with Pentecostal people. How I praise God for his wonderful works in these last days! -- O. W. Edwards.

**Cardwell, Mo.**: God is still pouring out his Spirit here. Over 200 have received the Spirit as in Acts 2:4 and about 300 have been saved. God puts his seal on every service. -- Jesse N. Goff. (*WaW*, Oct., 1912)

## Pentecostal Newspapers

### GOD'S MIGHTY POWER, Dallas, Texas:

[Bosworth, Birdsall, Etter].

Dear Brother in Christ:

God is still wonderfully displaying His power in Dallas, bearing witness to the preaching of the gospel "both with signs and wonders, and divers miracles and gifts of the Holy Ghost." Throngs pack the large tent at every service, many of them coming from 100 to 2000 miles [sic], bringing their sick. Letters are pouring in from all the United States and Canada, as many as 40 in a day, inquiring and requesting prayer for healing.

A most remarkable demonstration of God's power in the meetings is the mighty slaying power. On August 31$^{st}$, God came in mighty slaying power, when 21 men and women, like Saul, were struck down, as in the days of Finney and other great revivals. This slaying power has continued in every service since, making the tent look like a real battle-field, for "the slain of the Lord are many." Sinners fall and are shown their awful condition and need, and arise with shining faces and their burden gone. Some fall miles from the tent.

A more pathetic scene perhaps was never witnessed than that recently when three deaf mutes, all strangers to each other, met in the service, kissed, wept and shouted and praised God for perhaps 20 minutes, because all three in one night were saved and healed of deaf mutism. Many miracles have been performed during the past week, by the mighty power of God. All kinds of so-called incurable diseases are being healed. Many of them deaf and dumb, even those born so.

A man came several hundred miles, suffering with three broken ribs, caused by a fall. When hands were laid upon him with the prayer of faith, immediately the soreness left, and the broken ribs, the ends of which had turned inward, came into place and knitted together spontaneously; and although a few minutes before he flinched from the pain when Sister Etter laid her hands upon his side, after healing he could pound upon these ribs with his hands -- the healing was perfect!

A full-blood Choctaw Indian woman came from Okla., a great sufferer for 38 years, with a running sore on her foot, caused by a cow stepping on it 38 years ago. It was a mass of proud flesh and the odor almost unbearable. She was kept awake nights, and could not bear the weight of the covers on this foot. By the laying on of hands, God instantly took away all pain, and the foot is now healing up.

A man was brought 130 miles, who was in bed 6 months with tuberculosis of the lungs. Eight physicians in his home town had said his right lung was destroyed, and he had a bad abscess in that side. When he tried to walk, he would smother and fall. He was healed in the first service, and could breathe into both lungs without pain, and could strike those parts without pain. Was greatly blessed in spirit at the same time.

A lady in Dallas brought her five-year-old child, who from birth had suffered from kidney trouble so it could not be taken away from home, and it was instantly and perfectly healed, and the mother saved and baptized in the Spirit for good measure!

A lady was brought on a cot from Oklahoma, very low with typhoid malaria and hemorrhages of the bowels. In the first service, before the preaching, by the laying on of hands, was instantly healed, and walked and leaped and shouted, and continued to do so every night during several days' stay in Dallas.

We give the above as a few samples from among the many God has so wonderfully healed in these meetings. Another remarkable feature of the Dallas meeting is the readiness with which sinners flock to the altar, being convicted by the display of God's healing power. Last Sunday Bro. Bosworth in the presence of a great crowd, baptized 39 more in water and the power of God was present in a mighty way. Many have received the baptism in the Holy Spirit during the past two months; 8 received the baptism on last Saturday night, 12 one Sunday. There have been as many as 50 baptized in the Holy Spirit in one week. For two months the mighty power and presence of God has been present in these services in a marvelous way.

Will the saints everywhere join us in prayer that this wave might sweep around the world? This is God's time! We feel the coming of Jesus is very near.

**Visions**: -- "Where there is no vision, the people perish." (Prov. 29:18). A dear minister, who has sounded the gospel 45 years, and a great student of the scriptures, came to meeting, was struck down by the power of God, wonderfully baptized in the Holy Spirit saw the Spirit in the form of a dove, with wings outstretched, over his head. God has given him some of the most wonderful visions we have ever heard of in modern times: also some remarkable revelations.

Last Sunday morning he was carried away in the Spirit, like the Apostle John, and beheld the Holy City, the New Jerusalem, coming down from God out of Heaven, prepared as a bride adorned for her husband, all exactly as described in the Bible in the book of Revelation. He said: "I saw the innumerable company of Angels, singing around the throne, and was permitted to join in the song." (We heard him singing in tongues at the time he was in the Spirit).

Another time, he had a vision of the scientists of the world and the prophets of the Old Testament. The scientists were saying, "This world is 91,000 years old." But the prophets of God twice answered emphatically, "This world is only 6,000 years old." God showed the brother that we are on the eve of the Millenium or the $7^{th}$ day of 1,000 years, which is the day of peace and rest.

Another time God gave him a vision of a large ship, and it came right up to the tent, and great numbers of God's children, robed in white, got aboard and sailed away to meet Jesus in the air, while those who were left behind were dressed in black. He said, "As the children of God sailed away in the air, the sun went out and the moon and stars were dark, and oh, the cries and shrieks and agonies of those that were left upon the earth! It was awful!

After a while we came back with Jesus, and I saw the dead and slain and the wounded upon the earth! There were a few people left alive still, but oh, the darkness, and distress of those that were then upon the earth. This vision of the ship coming has been seen by two different persons.

Several persons have seen a ball of fire hovering over the large tent, and several times hosts of angels have been seen just above the audience, reaching out beyond the tent in every direction.... Maude M. Delaney. (*WaW*, Oct. 1912)

**Notice About Parham:**

Charles F. Parham, who is claiming to be head and leader of the Apostolic Faith Movement, has long since been repudiated. He has refused to "hear the church" and we are obeying the command of Christ, the Head of the church by letting him be unto us as a "heathen and publican." We are sorry it is so, but until he repents and confesses his sins, we cannot obey God and do otherwise. Let all Pentecostal and Apostolic Faith people of the churches of God take notice and be not misled by his claims. (*WaW*, Oct. 1912)

## North Missouri and Iowa Camps Victorious

The first meeting was held in Ottumwa, Iowa, Aug. 21$^{st}$ to Sept. 1$^{st}$. There was not much victory for several days, but when the saints humbled themselves before the Lord He came in power and glory. Pentecost fell on the first Sunday night. The next night God visited the meeting with a mighty sweep of glory and power, giving various manifestations of the Spirit. Four received the Spirit that night. Each day following the Lord had something new and fresh for His people. The last day the meeting was wonderful. Thousands of people from the city were in attendance, especially for the baptismal service in the afternoon.

From Ottumwa we went direct to Princeton to the camp for North Missouri. This meeting opened with wonderful victory right from the start, and increased in power to a climax on Thursday in the divine healing meeting. Many were healed and several remarkable cases. About half a dozen old people had their sight restored to them. One man was healed of lobomotor ataxia, who before could walk only by being supported. God instantly and completely healed him.

Mother Hicks of Mercer, Mo., more than 20 years ago fell and dislocated her ankle. She was compelled to wear an electric stocking for eighteen years to support it. But when she was converted and baptized in the Spirit two years ago, she was healed. But last year just before the campmeeting, she fell, again dislocating this same ankle. The foot was pressed clear to one side, the ankle completely dislocated. Suffering was intense. By the time two workers got there to pray for her the ankle had swollen fully twice its natural size, and already great portions of clotted blood had gathered, making the ankle black and blue.

As the workers laid on hands, praying in the name of Jesus, the Lord Himself set the foot. They felt the ankle go back into joint and the swelling disappeared right before their eyes. The blue and black and the pain left and she was perfectly healed. She sat up, stood upon the foot without pain: then walked on it, then ran and jumped on it without pain. Hallelujah to out God! Mother Hicks is quite a large woman, weighing perhaps 180 pounds and about 55 years old. It was an increased joy to see her come up again this year praising God with shining face and to know assuredly that the work was perfectly done....

On Monday, the 16$^{th}$, bands were separated for the field. Monday night was a saints' meeting. A number of workers were ordained to the ministry, and Communion observed, at the close of which the Lord spoke to us by interpretation, directing us to leave the tabernacle shouting His praises. The saints obeyed, and He met us with such a manifestation of glory as we have never seen in any meeting.

The attendance at the N. Missouri camp was far greater than last year, requiring 55 more sleeping tents this year than last to accommodate the people.

Brethren Scott, Hicks, Baker and their wives were separated for work in Egypt. They expect to sail in November. Since in Texas the Lord in a most certain way called out Bro. Willam D. Grier and wife to go to India. It will require from $1,500 to $1,700 to put these workers in these two fields. Egypt and India are crying for the Bread of Life. Will you help send them? . . . Daniel C. O. Opperman, Tyler, Texas. (*WaW*, Oct., 1912)

## God Visiting Kansas [and other places]

Since last report we have been having blessed times. The camp in Topeka, Kansas was a blessed one. God's power was manifest in many ways. A remarkable prophecy was given one night, stating someone in the meeting would die soon, and that Jesus was coming very soon, oh so soon! And urged the people to get ready, get ready. This was given at 11 o'clock at night and by 2:15 the same night a woman had suddenly died and lay a corpse on the camp ground. She seemed in the best of health, was shouting and praising God two hours before in the meeting. This caused quite a stir of excitement in Topeka. If part of the prophecy was so quickly fulfilled, may we not expect the other about His coming also to come to pass soon?

On our way south we found many, many hungry people. Some places, bankers, merchants and all alike came to our street meetings, and the officers invited us right on the side walks to preach. Streets just blockaded with people, men and women weeping on the streets under conviction.

**Pleasant Grove, Okla.**: In a ten days meeting at this place God wonderfully manifested His power; 23 were saved and 24 baptized in the Holy Ghost.

Wonders at Davenport. We held meetings 15 days in this town. A banker let us have free of rent a large brick building right on Main Street for our meeting. The first night, while we were preaching on divine healing, a man instantly fell to the floor as dead. All supposed it death of heart failure. Several tried in vain to cause him to stir.

We stopped preaching and commanded him in the name of Jesus to arise. He at once arose and walked around, causing a great stir. Some ran out of doors, and in a few minutes people began coming in the more. At 68th District Mission the power of God so fell that in two hours a number were saved and twelve baptized in the Spirit. All who did not run were saved, not a sinner left in the house by the close of the meeting. They fell under conviction and began to fall over all the house, and the "slain of the Lord were many." Even the baptized saints some fell beneath the power of God. The very house shook under the power of the Lord, as if a wind were blowing against it, to which many will testify.

The singing of a song could hardly have been heard, and this sound as of a wind lasted until 4 o'clock in the morning. Many were healed in these meetings while the Spirit was falling so. One man who had tried all kinds of medicines and many physicians all to no avail, afflicted for 45 years, was healed instantly at the command in Jesus' name to be made whole.

**Panama**: We left 68 District for Panama, Oklahoma, stopping off one night with the saints at Pleasant Grove again. Had meeting the night we arrived at Panama, the power falling, people getting saved in their seats during preaching. Four baptized in the Spirit while there, and we promised to return for a regular meeting. . . . Though we are going night and day, the dear Lord is upholding us in a wonderful way. . . . J. A. Corbell and band. (*WaW*, Oct. 1912)

**Brother Collins of Fort Worth, Texas writes:**
An aged Presbyterian minister received a wonderful baptism in the Spirit here last Saturday night. Wife and I were called to his home about 9:30 that night, and found him in his front yard shouting glory to God! The neighbors had run in to see what was the trouble, thinking he was going crazy. Well, Glory to Jesus! (*WaW*, Dec., 1912, page 3)

**Vision and Testimony:**
On the 8th of Nov. God in His mercy took me into His kingdom. I had once before known the Lord, but had departed from God. Now I am back by His grace and intend by His help to go through with Him.

On Nov. 20 while at the altar, seeking Pentecost the Lord wonderfully blessed and anointed me with His Spirit. I was carried away in a vision about 9 o'clock at night, and remained in it under the power of the Spirit till 5 in the morning. (Bro. C. M. Shipley also testifies the same to the Editor.] In the vision I saw them nailing Jesus to the cross. They got after Peter and were going to nail him to the cross too, but Peter denied the Lord, and they let him go.

I was also at the marriage supper in the skies with Jesus. I was allowed to walk the golden streets in glory. I saw Jesus separating a great company to his right and left. Those on the right entered into eternal rest with God in heaven and those on the left went into torment. I saw the fixed gulf which separated them forever! I went through the crucifixion with Jesus.

I counted to 1914 which I supposed meant the time of His coming, though He did not say so. Jesus wrote on a paper the words "too late" and put it beside the gate. By this he showed there is no time to repent at the judgment day. I saw the angels singing and shouting on the streets of gold and was allowed to sing with them the heavenly songs. -- Effie Hile. (*WaW*, Dec., 1912)

## Missionary Reports

**Nikhela, Egypt:**
All is well in Egypt, bless the Lord. Since landing here near the first of last June, the Lord has saved and baptized in the Spirit more than 100 souls. He has also healed many sick people. We praise and give God glory for it all. . . .Last week the Lord gave us some wonderful meetings. The Hall was packed with people. I have not seen since we came, a meeting like last Friday night. When we went to prayer, God poured out his Spirit the more and 4 were baptized with the

# Messengers of An Outpouring

Spirit according to Acts 2:4. We are expecting greater things for Egypt. . .

**Minieh, Egypt:**

The Lord is working blessedly in Egypt, for which we praise Him. One old man walked from another village to find where we lived, said had come to find God. The Lord met him, saved him and baptized him in the Spirit in just a little while. He is about 85. We are expecting God to do greater things. . . .

**Waang Kong, China:**

Six years ago I was an officer in the Salvation Army, and hungry for God's best. When I heard of the outpouring of the Spirit in Los Angeles, I became a seeker, and soon received in Honolulu. I was the first one in that city to receive the baptism with the Spirit. When he came in he took full possession and spoke through me in other tongues. Hallelujah, He abides still! We now realize, as Jesus said, the flowing of the rivers of living waters. . . .

Some weeks ago we secured a building for a mission and moved to this station. On account of the custom in China of having separate meetings for men and women, we started at first to have a meeting for women and children, intending to have a service afterwards for the men. But we were surprised at having our first service broken up by a crowd of angry men on the outside, crying out all sorts of things, declaring it could not be allowed for women to come in first. The women and children inside became almost frantic at their threats, in a rush for the doors, falling over the benches and over one another. We hardly knew what to do, but as the men seemed determined to come in, we opened the doors and they quickly filled the hall. So we preached the gospel to the men first and are doing so yet, having so far been unable to have meetings for these poor enslaved women. . . . There are 20 Pentecostal missionaries in South China. During the last two weeks two of these have gone to be with Jesus -- Sister Nellie Bettex of Canton and Bro. Bartlett of Hong Kong. . . . Elmer B. Hammond, Hong Kong.

**Sai Nam, China:**

We are very, very busy here in Sai Nam Mission just now, teaching an English school, day and night sessions, looking out for the orphans, preaching in the villages every day, etc. . . .

God is blessing our souls. Several have been saved since Sept. 1, and a good many more are seeking the Lord. We have 3 services on Sunday, and the people crowd in to hear the gospel. Praise His name. Everybody seems delighted with the *Word and Witness*. -- Mattie Ledbetter.

**Shanghai, China:**

When I read of the blessed work going on in Texas, from your paper "Word and Witness," and of the wonderful miracles being performed, it sent such a thrill of joy through my soul. In fact, we all had a great time rejoicing, and praising our God, for His "wonderful works to the children of men." That is the Gospel Jesus wants to show to the world. Praise His dear name! We know, and are believing, He is able to do the same things, even among the heathen of China. In fact, we have already witnessed in a small way, some of the same power here in Shanghai.

Glory be to God! Just lately one of our Chinese help was found lying in bed in a paralyzed condition. He could only talk. His limbs and arms were perfectly helpless, but in answer to prayer, and rebuking of the devil, Jesus made him "every whit whole."

Just a short time before this, he was a raw heathen, and one afternoon the power of God struck him, and he was blessedly saved. He shouted and praised the Lord for about an hour, and five others fell under the power at the same time, and one came through speaking in other tongues. The power of God does come down sometimes upon the people in a wonderful way; Praise the Lord! We have 4 Pentecostal missions in the city. -- H. L. Lawler.

**Bro. Anderson in China:**

In the past 5 weeks here in Bro. Hanson's mission the Lord baptized 18 in the Holy Spirit, and two of us two weeks ago baptized 10 in water -- "buried with Christ through baptism." Meeting house packed every night, and can't hold the people. Many seeking after God. Though Jesus is very precious to us in this distant land, still we much need the prayers of the dear saints at home. We expect a newcomer in our home in about 4 weeks. The Spirit is leading to preach very strongly against idolatry and superstition, plainly showing the people how Buddha, Shinto and Confucius have not brought salvation, but left poor China groping in the darkness; and to set forth Jesus Christ as the only Savior. God is giving blessed victory in our souls. T. F. Anderson, Shanghai, China.

**From a Native Indian:**

A missionary from Indianapolis, Ind., who has been in India three years, opened up a work for God in this needy district, and my wife and I felt led to step out on faith and work with her. So a year ago we opened up this work in a village two miles from the railroad. . . .

While one man has stepped out for Christ and is tarrying for the baptism with the Spirit, many are believing and coming for instruction. Many and wonderful have been the healings. I relate one, as we just prayed for her this morning. She is about 8 years old. When we came here she had been sick 5 months. She was all swollen and could not see. They brought her to us at first thinking we had medicine, and when we told them we prayed for the sick they turned away. A month later they brought her back. The mother said she had paid out her last piece and they told her she must now die.

God gave us such a spirit of prayer and all through the night we would awake and pray for her. It seemed the very air was full of demons, contesting against her healing. But Jesus, who took our infirmities and bore our sicknesses, healed her, and in the morning she was well, all the swelling gone. Within two weeks she had gained so much flesh that no trace of her severe illness was left. . . .

At this time of the year our work is attending Melas, or religious fairs, selling gospels, giving the word and instructing in the Zanana homes (the shut-in women). When it gets too hot to go out, we shall take up school work again. We had nearly 100 children in our school, half a day session, when we ceased. Many are giving up their ancient faith in which [they were] brought up. (*WaW*, Dec., 1912)

# Chapter 8

# 1913

**Miraculous Interpretation of English:** [without tongues]
Some time ago I was invited to speak to a congregation of Xosas, and was assured by the native superintendent that a good interpreter would be there. Arriving there I found there was no interpreter and the native minister knew nothing of English. After the Xosa minister had given a short exhortation he sat down and motioned me with a smile to rise and speak.

It was useless to answer in English, so I motioned as definitely as possible that I could not speak the Xosa tongue. He continued motioning and I stood up and began speaking in English. After three or four short sentences had been spoken, to my utter surprise, this dear man jumped up as if forced by a spring, picked the words out of my mouth as fast as I could talk and handed them out to his people in their own tongue.

Only once did he hesitate for an instant, and I put it down to his getting a trifle out of Spirit. When the Lord was through using me I sat down, and immediately the power to understand me had left the Xosa. It was wonderful to me to see God work when man was at the end of his tether. I felt ashamed that I had so limited the Holy One of Israel in days gone by and there and then resolved to put my full and complete trust in Him who is equal to all things.

The poor Xosa man could not tell me his surprise in intelligible words, but let loose a flood of Xosa and the shine on his Jesus-face told me the story he tried to tell. Let us lean hard [on the Lord], for our God is a Rock. -- E. M. Scurrah, Cape Town, S. A. (*TLRE*, Feb., 1913)

## Providential Protection from Storms

How well I remember dear old Dr. Mockridge's testimonies in the old John Street noon-day prayer meetings in New York. How often was I impressed by his quaint way of putting things . . .

He related upon one occasion how he was on his way from a meeting to his home in Philadelphia, and a midsummer storm just about to break. The sky was getting darker, the clouds lowering; the thunder rolled and the lightnings darted hither and thither. He had still ten minutes' walk before him and his old legs would not move very fast, but he bethought himself of his unfailing refuge in God and started to pray, claiming the promises, and especially the fact that a child of God could not be forsaken. It did not seem possible that the storm could hold off any longer -- still he kept on praying, while gradually getting closer to his home.

Finally, reaching his own doorstep and entering the house, his wife, with a startled exclamation, said, "Did you ever see it rain like that?" The rain just then descended in torrents, but not a drop touched him.

About a week after listening to the above testimony I was led into a similar experience of trusting God. The Holy Spirit used our dear brother's words to strengthen my own weak faith. I left my office, near St. Paul's Chapel, for the train to Brooklyn. As I started out I perceived that after an exceedingly sultry afternoon a thunder storm was imminent. In a thin summer suit, without an umbrella, I would be drenched to the skin in a moment; then Dr. Mockridge's testimony recurred to my mind and the Spirit whispered, "Cannot you likewise trust Me?" It seemed, not possible that the rain would hold off for another minute, but I prayed as I hastened along, "Lord, grant that I may not ask presumptuously, but, oh! increase my faith, for Thy servant has no other refuge but Thee.

Here Thy child is praying in Jesus' Name and thou hast promised that whatsoever we shall ask in His Name Thou wilt do." The wind was blowing a gale, the temperature was rapidly falling; on all sides people were running for shelter. The thunder began to roll and the lowering clouds were furiously driven before the storm which was at the point of breaking. I still had a few minutes' walk before me and began to pray more boldly, becoming more importunate as I recalled that Elijah was a man subject to like passions as we are and he prayed earnestly that it might not rain and it rained not for a space of three years and six months.

I told the Lord that here was another child of His who was asking that it might not rain, not for years or months, but for a few moments until he could reach shelter. Meanwhile the sky had fearfully darkened and was illuminated by terrific lightning flashes, and just as I reached the Bridge entrance and was under cover I heard the deafening roar of the pent-up volume of water descending in torrents. Call it coincidence if you will -- I know that my God answered prayer according to His promise.

Since that time I have upon many occasions proved God to be true to His promise. "According to your faith be it unto you." Often, when almost overtaken by drenching rains when out in the open I have invariably been enabled to reach shelter before the storm broke. Once wife and I with baby had driven from our home in Huntington, L.L., to Dix Hills M.E. Church grove-meeting. The preacher of the afternoon service noticed a thunder storm coming up and cut short his sermon, stating that it was going to rain. I had already established communication with my Father when I perceived the wind blowing furiously, swaying the old chestnut trees surrounding the church, and the thunder rolling more threateningly every moment.

As I had been appointed to take charge of the after-meeting I mounted the rough board platform and announced that it was not going to rain just then, but it was God's will that souls should be saved. A few people remained and one precious soul came forward and found Christ, during which time the storm seemed to pass around us. We drove home through the open country, the weather still threatening, and just as I reached the barn and wife had entered the house with the baby the rain descended in veritable torrents, continuing almost without intermission until the following afternoon. [This was back during the horse and buggy days.]

Some far more striking instances to God's direct answers to believing prayer were graciously given to me a few years afterwards, and I take special pains to relate circumstances correctly, so that He who ruleth the winds and waves may be glorified. Our entire family spent the summer vacation in Connecticut, and as the time for our departure for home drew near I engaged staterooms for a certain date and we were to be at the Steamboat Company's wharf at 6 p.m. After an exceedingly dry season it began to rain shortly after dawn on that day, the downpour increasing in intensity, so that at noon it was raining quite heavily.

I realized that my faith would be severely tried, for unless the rain ceased (which seemed altogether improbable), we would be drenched by the time we got to the landing -- a drive of from twelve to fourteen miles. I besought the Lord with trembling -- never before had I realized how weak my faith really was -- to give us fair weather until we got to the boat. I spread the circumstances before Him, as it were, told Him that umbrellas and borrowed blankets and raincoats would be alike ineffectual in an open wagon with such a downpour.

About an hour before we were to start I again went to my room with the rainstorm roaring outside, and got down before God. I then noticed that there was some hindrance to my prayer and realized God was trying to get my attention to speak to me. He spoke to my heart, "Child, you know in the next room lies your father-in-law, an unsaved man who may be upon his death bed. You have several times mentioned salvation to him, but have never definitely pressed upon him an immediate surrender to Me. I want you to clinch that matter with him now."

I knew that God was speaking and dared not disobey. I went in to the old man and found him awake, and no sooner had I spoken to him of salvation than he broke down and weepingly confessed that he was a sinner and wanted to find Jesus as his Savior right now. It was evident the Lord had gone before me and prepared the way. Giving him the simple and beautiful promise of the gospel, I prayed with him, and had the joy of seeing him accept Jesus as his personal Savior, and left him rejoicing.

From that moment my faith took hold of God for a cessation of the rain. I have noticed that implicit obedience always begets faith. Meanwhile, the horse and wagon were in readiness as it was nearly time to start. My family and I knelt with the household and acquaintances -- nearly all formal church members -- and I prayed definitely that the Lord would hold off the rain until we got home. I noticed how peculiarly the dear people regarded me when I told them that the rain would presently cease, while, as if mocking my prayers, the rain roared [outside].

With the little ones all bundled up, and in borrowed raincoats and blankets, we climbed into the wagon. Just then there came a perceptible lull in the storm and in all the hills around the sound of the rain died away. Within one minute from the time of starting the rain had absolutely ceased; a half hour afterwards the sun shone brightly, and we reached the Glastonbury Landing in time, despite the heavy driving through the mud.

At about five o'clock the next morning I was awakened in our stateroom by the rain beating upon the deck above. Looking out upon the Sound I noted that we were opposite Oyster Bay. I then thanked the Lord upon my knees for His mercy to us the preceding afternoon and implored Him for a further continuance of His goodness that we might have fair weather to get home. When I arose from my knees the rain had ceased.

We drove over to Jersey City and through the meadows into A---[sic] in bright sunshine. I had just time to put up the horse and my wife had just entered the house with the little ones when, at that moment, from the seemingly clear sky, the rain descended. Throughout that day and the one following we had an exceptionally heavy downpour, accompanied by thunder and lightning. The Lord had held back the rain to the very minute and then released it again. "If I ever doubted," exclaimed my wife, "I must believe now after seeing such signal answers to prayer. I can doubt no more." (*TLRE*, Feb., 1913)

### He That Gathereth Not, Scattereth: (excerpt)

I was holding a meeting in Boston a few years ago, and as the singer and I were passing along the street we saw a young man standing in a drug store doorway who looked very sad and forlorn. I felt moved to step up to him and put my arm in his and say, "We are holding meetings down this way. Won't you come with us?" He said, "No, I don't think I will." But there was such a sad look on his face I could not leave him, so I took his arm and led him along to the meeting. When I gave the altar call he came headlong and when he got up from his knees the tears were streaming down his face.

He said, "I was standing in the drug store door, ready to enter and purchase some poison to end my wretched life when these brethren came along and literally took hold of me and pulled 'me to the meeting, and now I have found the Lord." -- E. L. Erickson, Chicago. (*TLRE*, May, 1913, page 11)

### Los Angeles Campmeeting:

We have good reports from the Campmeeting at Los Angeles. Word comes to us through letters and telegrams of a large attendance-- fully two thousand [on] Sundays, and that miracles of healing are constantly taking place. Wonderful deliverances have been experienced from incurable and long-standing diseases, including cancers and tumors, and some sufferers have been healed who have sought healing in vain for many years.

At first the meetings suffered because of lack of unity, but weeping and intercessory prayer caused a breaking up that brought the power of God upon the services nightly. We have heard through letters that Saturday, May 3, the sick were miraculously healed as they sat in their seats. A woman who had been in a wheelchair for many years sprang out of it, "leaping and praising God." Following instantly upon this healing, a man waiting to be prayed for, sprang up and was healed.

On May 2, a woman who had been in a wheelchair for seventeen years walked and shouted. From a private letter we quote the following: "A woman came for healing who almost died on the way. Her friends went so far as to bring her grave clothes with them. She had cancer, heart-trouble, and dropsy. Her body was so enlarged by the dropsy that she could not get a gown big enough to wear, but after Sister Etter prayed for her she danced for joy and threw up her arms. The next day she wore a blouse and skirt and is rapidly decreasing in size. Is anything too hard for Him? The lame are made to walk, the deaf receive their hearing, tumors and cancers and other diseases are carried away by the mighty healing power of Jesus." (*TLRE*, May, 1913)

\*\*\*

Brother Bosworth has great faith in the use of the anointed handkerchief in praying for people at a distance. When in Dallas the Lord wonderfully blessed his ministry along this line as the following instances show:

One woman, the wife of a Presbyterian minister, writes that when she opened the letter containing the handkerchief the power of God came on her and she was instantly healed of a serious affliction. Another case is that of a man who was controlled by demon power. Unknown to him the wife placed a leaflet on which hands had been laid in prayer, under his pillow. It was done in faith and the result was deliverance from the evil spirit that had obsessed him.

One woman was healed of cancer on the face and another instantly delivered from a cough. A man at Milford, Texas, writes that he was very ill with pneumonia and when he laid a tract that had been prayed over, on the affected lung all pain and soreness vanished and he drove four miles on a damp day and preached. (*TLRE*, May, 1913)

## A Blessed Revival in Chicago

Glad to report that the God of Pentecost is still with us in the meetings in the Stone Church. I suppose one hundred would be a conservative estimate of the number baptized by speaking in other tongues since the beginning of the meetings. Quite a number have been healed of numerous complaints, and two at least that I suppose would be termed as miracles in healing.

The young girl that I spoke of in last report as her mother testifying of her being healed of deaf and dumbness, but was unable to verify same from my own knowledge; I am now glad to report that the child was actually both made to hear and speak in answer to prayer, she having been deaf and dumb for about eight years. The other case was that of healing of a deaf ear. The sister on whom this miracle was performed, when a girl at the age of about sixteen, was picking her ear with a knitting needle and some one spoke to her when she turned her head striking the other end of the needle against a chair puncturing the ear drum, rendering her totally deaf in that ear for forty-nine years. The accident was so severe she fainted for some time and became very sick.

The other evening she came to the front to be prayed for, for some other ailment, and when Bro. Bosworth spoke to her she turned her head around so he could speak in her good ear. Bro. Bosworth noticed her and asked her if she was deaf in one ear. She said she was and that she didn't have any hopes of ever hearing in that ear again, as the drum had been bursted. However, he assured her that God was able, and suggested that they pray for the deaf ear before praying for the other ailment. He did so, and she was healed and made to hear. That was several days ago, and last night she could stop what was formerly her good ear and listen to the sermon through the ear that had been healed. . . . -- Geo. C. Brinkman. (*WaW*, May, 1913)

## Wonderful Miracles Worked in Jesus' Name:

I want to give you a slight glimpse of what God is doing in the World Wide Camp at Long Hill, Conn. I was never privileged to be where the power of God was so manifestly poured out; many baptized in the Holy Ghost; many speaking in tongues; some powerful cases of salvation to sinners and reclamation of backsliders. God is working on all lines, but particularly in the healing of the sick. The first two weeks there were three hundred and fifty prayed for. A missionary from China carefully tabulated the healings after investigation, and the following list is a part of that table:

| | | |
|---|---|---|
| neuralgia | deafness | kidney trouble |
| neurasthenia | dropsy | heart disease |
| scrofula | goitre | bronchial affections |
| lameness | hernia | bowel ailments |
| mysophobia | grippe | displaced vertebra |
| blindness | catarrh | curvature of spine |

It is difficult to keep track of the healings, they multiply so rapidly. We are now in the third week of the meetings and the power of God is increasing all the time. There is a very large attendance of Pentecostal workers and great unity of the Spirit. A marked feature of the meetings is the strong, direct teaching of the Word, the absence of fanaticism and the repudiation of errors which here and there have crept into Pentecostal work. God Himself is steadying the ark. Bless His precious name!

The unity of spirit in which He holds us all, is most hallowed and deepens from hour to hour. The praises He pours into our hearts and out through our lips are mighty, and on this volume . . .

Oh, praise God for the Latter Rain, the abundant outpouring of the Holy Ghost! It is truly remarkable how God sustains His honored servant, our beloved Sister Etter, who has charge of this camp. At sixty-nine years of age God daily reinforces her strength in the use of the gift of healing, upholding her in arduous labors that, unsustained by God, the vigor of young manhood could not endure. God's miracle in her is greater than all His miracles by her. . . .

There came into this morning's meeting an unconverted mother, bringing her unconverted daughter of seventeen years. The girl had come three hundred and fifty miles for healing of blindness, she having been stone blind since the age of two years. While Sister Etter's hands were on her in prayer, sight was given, and it was most touching to see the mother and daughter weepingly embrace and gaze with joy upon one another. Now, for the first time that she could remember, the girl saw her mother's face.

We are praising here that in so many instances the unconverted come to trust Jesus for healing. . . .

Yesterday morning the presence and power of God came suddenly upon us; while in worship and adoration of Him one fell to the floor under the "weight of glory." Then a clergyman came forth and gave a powerful message in tongues; he seemed not quite to have finished when he, too, was prostrated. Then, with a kind of swishing sound came the "power" and all over the house people fell under it.. I counted fourteen on the platform and just around it-- impossible to say how many fell all over the place, the slain of the Lord were many.

There followed a scene that beggars all description, as under the increasing light and power of God His people worshipped Him, sometimes in hymns, sometimes in the heavenly choir, sometimes in the cooing of the Dove – the Dove of God – the Holy Ghost bringing forth from the innermost depths of their being sweet love notes to Jesus. The voices were many, for all in the tent seemed worshipping; the sound was one, the commingled "sound of many waters." No [trained] choir could have kept in such harmony and unity, with sweetest melody. The bandmaster was evidently the Holy Ghost. He can render music without rehearsals on a company of yielded instruments.

Glory! The "Hallelujah Chorus" was varied by most solemn, searching, loving messages in tongues (with interpretation) and in English.

Meantime many were having visions, some seeing Jesus riding on the white horse of power, some seeing troops of angels hovering over us, one saw blood everywhere and the red horse of war striding on. Crowds of sinners stood on the outskirts of the tent looking on; most respectful and solemn attention was given, and some of the messages were for them, but most were for the saints. . . .

Truly, Apostolic days are upon us! Many hymns and songs of worship were given in tongues. People lying on their backs with eyes closed at a distance from one another would sing these hymns in the same tongue in perfect unison. These duets in tongues were often followed by the song in interpretation. Many of those who had been healed were leaping and dancing under the power, reminding one of the scene in Jerusalem when the onlookers said, "They are filled with new wine." . . .

We soon reassembled and the Spirit held us in His power until 11 p.m., the awe deepening upon us. The majesty and glory of God became so great we could hardly breathe. No one looked to his neighbor, but all felt as though [they were] in the immediate presence of God. . . . No altar service was called and the meeting closed in a death-like stillness. We wended our way home caring to see or speak to no one; the sinners likewise; not a sound was heard as they trooped down the hill to the cars. As we came out of the tent we found "the slain of the Lord" lying all around. . . . Elizabeth Sisson. (*TLRE*, July, 1913)

## Diversities of Operations but the Same Spirit
Report of the Sunderland, England, Convention
Alma E. Doering, Berlin, Germany

The Sixth International Pentecostal Convention at Sunderland [England] has passed into history. Speakers and visitors from Germany, Switzerland, Sweden, Noway, Russia, Holland, Wales, New Zealand, China, India, Japan, Africa, Ireland, Palestine and America were present. As many creeds as countries might also be enumerated. . . .

If we had a doubt as to the reality of the tongues, it has fled. During one of the morning meetings a message in tongues was given by a brother who was greatly agitated and trembled and shook. There might well have been a feeling that his message was not in the Spirit, but we learned through the experience that followed that it is possible for God to give a real message, even when so-called fleshly manifestations accompany it. When the power of God is poured forth through a frail earthen vessel, undue manifestations are only a sign of the weakness of the instrument, not of the absence of power.

In this instance the writer heard words uttered which she understood clearly as the Kifioti language, the first of several Bantu languages she had learned in East and West Central Africa. "Dingalala, dingalala" introduced the message in Kifioti. Immediately she whispered to her German brethren on the platform, "He is speaking a real language," and forthwith began to whisper the interpretation. When the brother who gave the message in tongues had finished, an English speaking person in the audience who sat at quite a distance from the platform began to interpret.

When the part of the message was reached that the writer had understood, the interpreter gave exactly the same interpretation which had been whispered to the German brethren. It was a genuine tongue with a correct interpretation.

The man who had the tongue had no knowledge whatever of the Kifioti language, nor had the lady who gave the interpretation. The tongue *might* have been mere chance but *never* the interpretation. We know that certain combinations of syllables form words which occur in almost every language, but in each language that particular combination of syllables may have a different meaning. . . . (*TLRE*, July, 1913)

> *Book Editor*: Alma Doering (1878-1959) attended Moody Bible Institute, and became a missionary to the Belgian Congo through several different missions societies and was a leader in the Congo Inland Mission.

**From a Letter:**
Extracts from Brother Barker's letter to us, [dated] June 4th, though not intended for publication, will interest our readers:

"I can never overestimate my visit to England last winter, and the new power that came into my life while waiting on God at the home of Mrs. Cantel. Oh, it was then truly wonderful, but now much more so. Away in the heart of Asia Minor, 'the anointing abideth,' yea, increaseth, for while in England I only uttered a few words in an unknown tongue, yet day by day since returning to Turkey the Holy Ghost speaks through me while alone, and it seems a secret valve of power that I never knew before in my life. But, oh such hungering after greater gifts and such gracious assurance that He is leading me on and down, deeper into His perfect will for me.

"I believe I have the confidence of every co-worker (eight in number) on our two stations, and although all is hard to speak of on paper, I must say that love and unity among us has always been real and unbroken. I especially look to God that I may be clothed with my testimony, and that they may see I am a Spirit-filled man, and those who are as I was, dissatisfied with themselves, may receive of the same enduring [baptism in the Holy Spirit]. It has been necessary, however, to report the matter to the Home board, and I leave the result with Him. [Some missionaries were sent home after reporting that they received the baptism in the Holy Spirit.] I am willing for His way and fear nothing but a hard, unbroken spirit. Oh, I am so glad I am in such large field. I am not afraid to trust God, and expect to be true to Him at all cost.

"Thank you in Jesus' Name for your kind interest in us and this work, the expenses of which are so great.... What Turkey needs is not more teaching, but more Spirit-filled lives. I shall ever thank you for your kind interest in this critical period in my life." (*TLRE*, July, 1913)

## The Day of Chicago's Visitation
### The Lame Walk, the Blind See, the Deaf Hear
### Supernatural Power of God Witnessed Daily (July 2--28)

*Book Editor*: The August 1913 issue of *The Latter Rain Evangel* was a very special issue, and was sold separately for several months. I here reprint about 1/2 of that issue that deals with the healing services held at the Stone Church with both Maria Woodworth-Etter and F. F. Bosworth. There is also a teaching article by Sister Etter.

Chicago has just had the mightiest visitation of the supernatural she has ever known. God came down and walked in our midst, fulfilling the word of Israel, "I will bring it health and cure . . . and reveal unto it abundance of peace and truth." Healing streams flowed like rivers and many are rejoicing in miraculous deliverance of body and in the glory of God filling their souls. The month of July has passed into history with its record of hundreds saved and healed, while the faith of thousands has been quickened many-fold.

As arranged, Mrs. M. B. Woodworth-Etter spent the month of July (2nd to 28th) at the Stone Church. Pentecostal scenes as in Apostolic days were daily enacted; the blind received their sight, the deaf heard, paralytics walked, rheumatics were delivered, broken-down nerves restored and demons driven out, in all of which the name of the Lord was magnified.

From the beginning of these special meetings faith was strong and the hearts of the people were open for blessing. The unbroken unity and blessed fellowship that had characterized the revival since March 20th, with continuous showers of blessing, had prepared for the harvest so there was nothing to do but to take the sickle and reap.

All Chicago learned of the mighty workings of God in our midst. The daily papers reported some of the meetings, and though they tried to caricature the proceedings and bring to ridicule the sacred things of God, yet even in this garbled form some truth was presented. "He maketh the wrath of man to praise Him," and since it was admitted that there were healings, the Lord doubtless used these reports to awaken hope in some despairing hearts. Even those who came out of mere curiosity were moved at witnessing the power of God manifested in deliverance to the afflicted.

Well might the on-looker ask, "What means this eager anxious throng?" and as of old it could be said, "Jesus of Nazareth passeth by." Jesus passed by many times; His healing virtue often flowed, and here and there in the audience and at the altar, souls would touch His garment's hem and be made whole.

At first the meetings were advertised by posters in the elevated [train] stations, but after some marked healings occurred this was no longer necessary. People came by car loads on the electric [trolley], they came in automobiles, carriages, ambulances, wheelchairs and afoot from all directions. It was a touching spectacle, reminding one of the Gospel narrative, "And all the city was gathered together at the door."

Earnest interest on the part of the workers was not by any means confined to the Stone Church people or those most intimately connected with the work. It was not a Stone Church affair but catholic [universal] in it broadness.

From all over the city Pentecostal leaders and workers came and participated with as much interest as though the work was in their own missions. All who came -- even those from a distance -- threw themselves into the work of praying with the sick with much earnestness, showing in a marked way the growing spirit of unity. There was no building up on "my work" which naturally characterizes individual effort, but on every hand it was evidenced that all were unselfishly working in the interest of Christ's body, and missions and churches were forgotten in the united effort to get souls through to God.

Not only Chicago Pentecostal saints but God's children in a radius of hundreds of miles have received a mighty impetus to faith in this series of meetings; indeed we believe it is no exaggeration to say that the faith of God's people here has made the most rapid strides of any in modern times -- it has gone forward by leaps and bounds. Ministers who came disheartened and discouraged because of failure, found themselves taking a fresh hold and praying for the sick with marked results.

At the beginning of these special divine-healing meetings Mrs. Etter and several of the brethren strong in faith, unitedly prayed with each individual with laying on of hands, but as the number to be prayed for increased it became necessary to divide the force so that a number of the, sick could be ministered to at the same time. Finally there came to be five chairs occupied at once by those who were being prayed for with laying on of hands and it was not Mrs. Etter's ministry alone that was blessed. God honored the faith of all and people who had their eyes on Him received healing regardless of who prayed for them.

One sick woman who came in mistook one of the sisters for Mrs. Etter and asked her [for] prayers. The sick woman was immediately healed. We hope this will be an encouragement to some sufferers to whom Mrs. Etter cannot minister.

Healing flowed all through the church at different hours; not only in evening meetings but during the day; here and there you would see groups of people praying for the sick and shouts of glory from the suffering ones told that the lightning from heaven had touched their bodies.

When the ministering brethren saw the marvelous way in which healing opened the door to people's hearts and led them to seek salvation, they felt they had neglected one of the mightiest weapons Jesus had given to His disciples. As one remarked, ministers have spent their time in explaining what certain passages in the Bible mean instead of demonstrating to the world that all power has been given to the church.

A man who had received a wonderful experience of salvation, "I never saw or felt such power in a meeting in all my life. Although I was a sinner I felt the power of God." It wasn't so much the preaching that led him to repentance as the manifestation of the power of God.

Brother Argue, who has been traveling over the country visiting assemblies and camp meetings and who had been in the first outpouring of the Spirit six years ago, said this was without doubt the mightiest visitation from God of these latter days.

The revival which has lasted for six months [at the Stone Church] and was at its flood through July, was not due to any distinctions in theology or to the setting forth of any particular doctrine or creed, but because we have been getting back to the simplicity of the Gospel, with much prayer. Results have proved that minute setting forth of doctrine and theological distinctions are not only nonessential but their absence is strongly conducive to the spirituality of the church of God and the success of its work. The absence of all controversy and the beautiful spirit of harmony that characterized these meetings were remarked by all, and at the close Sister Etter said, "Such perfect unity and harmony in meetings I have never known."

Hungry souls that came from a distance were overjoyed because of the spiritual blessing they received; many received the baptism of the Holy Ghost and were more rejoiced over this than in their healing. The power of the Lord was so strongly present that those who had sought the baptism in vain for years were swept into the experience. We heard of one who had been to Los Angeles and traveled all over the country visiting conventions and campmeetings for years, who received the long coveted blessing in these meetings.

After the first two weeks the auditorium would not hold the people who came, and we held an overflow meeting nightly in the vestry, which seats five hundred people, with Brother Kent White in charge. Those who assisted in the overflow meetings said there was equal blessing downstairs; there were some marked cases of salvation and healing and a large number received the Spirit's baptism.

When the Sunday afternoon meetings dismissed at five o'clock people were already coming to the evening meetings, and by 5:30 on the evening of July 27th every seat in the main auditorium was filled. "You are a little late," said an usher to a new comer at 4:30, "the meeting is just about to close." "Oh, I am here for the evening meeting," was the reply.

One of the first healings was that of a Mrs. Pickerell, Kenosha, Wis., who, while she had believed in healing for the body for many years had found her faith waning, and seeing no real miracles being worked today had become discouraged. Last winter she read Mrs. Etter's book, "The Acts of the Holy Ghost," and new faith sprung up within her, so she was ready for healing when she came. We give her testimony in her own words:

"When I came here I had a goitre. It was very large on the inside and it was choking me so I could scarcely swallow food. It also affected my heart so that at times I could not hold anything in my hands and I would have to be helped to a chair. The goitre is all gone on the inside and almost gone on the outside. I had suffered with this goitre for twenty-nine years.

"While I was lying prostrated under the power of God, He also put a new lining in my bowels. I was made new, set free from everything. Seventeen years ago this trouble began. I had an operation, and the doctors cut out two inches of the inner lining of the intestines and also two inches of the muscles. I had not been able to stand on my feet without a support, and suffered constantly. My intestines had the web cut out which fastened them together and when I would lie down I would have to use a pillow to lay them on, all the time suffering from a constant burning. Last night when I took off the support I had been wearing I could walk around the room without any suffering.

"There was also a loose bone in my side that slipped out of place through the operations I had, and God put that back. Three months ago I saw Sister Etter in a vision, and heard a voice saying, 'When she lays hands on you, you will be healed.' Whenever I got discouraged and felt my faith wane, I would get out her book and read it, and my faith would rise."

Another remarkable healing during the first week was that of a Mrs. Dolan from Zion City, Illinois. She was in bed and was given up to die. Had hurt her spine a year ago, and was unable to walk or even stand on her feet. She said:

## Messengers of An Outpouring

"They took me out of bed to bring me to these meetings. I cried all the time they were getting me ready. They brought me in a wheel chair in the baggage car along side of a corpse, but I didn't mind that; I was coming to be healed. I knew when Sister Etter prayed for me I would be healed. I obeyed in everything she told me, and when she laid hands on me and commanded me rise and walk, I did it in Jesus' Name. I had spinal trouble and also suffered from my stomach; both were healed."

She was in such suffering that she could not be lifted out of her chair. The helpers had to carry her chair on to the platform, but after God touched her body in a miraculous way, she walked up and down the aisles, praising the Lord, the people joining with her in glorifying God.

She later testified to the restoration of her voice; said that she had not been able to sing since April 13th, but now was able to sing as well as she had ever done. She stayed during the entire series of meetings, was in attendance regularly without suffering; often testified to the miracle worked in her body, and demonstrated the fact that she was no longer helpless, by running up and down the aisles, glorifying God.

One of the most wonderful healings was that of a paralytic. A man was carried in all bent together -- could not stand upright; his head inclined upon his breast, his knees were bent. He had been paralyzed for eight years. No case seemed more obstinate to the onlooker, and while there are no cases too hard for God, yet humanly speaking, one's heart failed at the sight of his condition. His bones seemed to be ossified, and at first there was no response, no faith looked out from his eyes; but as those around him sounded the praises of God and got him to open his mouth -- his jaw had been locked like his joints -- even though the shout was an inarticulate groan, there was engendered in his heart a tiny spark of faith.

Sister Etter commanded the paralytic spirit to depart, and as she prayed the resurrection life of Jesus began to come into his body and he began to move his limbs. When he became able to stand on his feet the people shouted; then he began to walk to and fro on the platform, first with the aid of the brethren, then alone, and when the meeting closed he started down the aisle and down the steps almost on a run, and when he got out to the street he ran for half a block, praising the Lord. The shouts of the people could not be restrained. They crowded the sidewalk and waved their hats shouting "Hurrah for Jesus!"

On Monday morning, July 14th, four people received the touch of God in their bodies while the song service was going on. All four of them walked either on canes or crutches. One woman had gotten hurt in getting off a street car three years ago; the ligaments in her limb had been broken, and when Mrs. Etter said to her, "Arise and walk," she shook her head, she couldn't. Then Mrs. Etter said, "In the Name of Jesus you can do it," and she started off, walking without any assistance. A man, sixty years old, crippled with rheumatism since he was ten years old, walked without his cane.

Another, lame for a year, couldn't walk without her crutches, was able to walk up and down the aisle unassisted; the doctors had not been able to tell what was the matter with her, but she could not step on the ground with her foot. Another was a girl with hip disease; walked without crutches and without a limp.

All four of these walked up and down the aisles to the strains of "There's wonderful power in the blood." The singing was interspersed with shouts of praises and much rejoicing from the audience. It was a most inspiring sight. We felt like the woman who testified a few nights before, when she said, "I came for the purpose of having an uplift in my faith, but when I saw that paralyzed man healed I said, 'Lord, I do not need to pray for faith now. I have it.'"

A remarkable healing connected with a vision was given by a woman who was healed on July 7th. She said:

"I want to praise God this morning for my healing. I know it was God that healed me. I had never been in a church like this. I was a Christian Scientist for five years and thought I had all there was to be had, but about a year and a half ago, in vision I saw myself in another church than the one I attended. I didn't know anything about this faith, but I saw Mrs. Etter lay her hands on my stomach in which I had been suffering great distress. I didn't understand it at the time; I came in here one Sunday evening and heard the pastor say that every promise in the Bible we could have. I wasn't satisfied and determined I would have every promise in the Bible for my own; so I came again and was saved and received the baptism. Wednesday morning, when I saw Mrs. Etter walk on the platform I recognized her as the one I had seen in the vision a year and a half ago. I saw the rain falling, the latter rain, and I know the vision was of God. Today I am perfectly healed."

Friday, July 25th, was a red letter day for healing. The power was present in greater measure than on any other day and the five chairs on the platform were continually filled with sick, suffering and sinful souls seeking healing and salvation. From one end of the platform to the other the healing power flowed and shouts of glory filled the house. The crowd was so large it was almost impossible to control it, so eager were the people to see and hear.

That evening at 6:30 -- an hour before the meeting began -- the auditorium upstairs was filled, even to the gallery and platform, and at 7:30 the vestry below was crowded. Two services were held that evening, as on many other occasions. The ushers said as many had been turned away from the building as there were people inside. The hearts of the ushers almost failed them as they were compelled to refuse admittance to many who were sick and had traveled long distances, but for whom there was no room. They were not simply curiosity seekers but hungry in heart and afflicted in body. Many had spent all their living on doctors and were "nothing better but rather grew worse."

The reports of the healings had flown on the wings of the wind, and hope sprang up in hearts that had long since given up in despair. A street meeting was held from the overflow of the two meetings, but the crowd was too disappointed to be satisfied. . . .

We had announced from the beginning there would be no meetings on Saturday; on account of the three heavy services on Sunday we felt the ministers needed the rest, but on Saturday night, July 26th, there was a little impromptu meeting, simply because the people came. On this particular evening, a woman came, not knowing there would be no public meeting. She walked with a cane, and as she got off the car at 37th and Indiana Avenue, a German woman seeing she was crippled, said to her, "Where are you going?" She said, "I am going to the Stone Church to be healed." The German said, "There will not be any meeting tonight, but if you come in we will pray for you."

Scarcely had she entered the door when the Lord met her, and as a few earnest ones gathered around and prayed she was healed. She had been afflicted for five years with rheumatism and a growth on her hip, and was not able to bend her knees. She received complete deliverance, knelt down and thanked the Lord, and ran back and forth without [the] cane or any support. She had been to the Christian Scientists for a year but they hadn't been able to help her. After her healing she said she was going home and throw away all her Christian Science literature.

This same evening a woman came on a crutch she had been using for three years. When she saw what God had done for another, her faith reached out for healing and she received perfect deliverance from sciatic nerve trouble. She ran up and down the aisles praising God, perfectly delivered; she then went with a crowd to a street meeting leaving her crutch behind her. Eye witnesses said it was one of the most perfect healings they had ever seen.

That which brought most joy to the little crowd of humble folk present, was the fact that these two notable healings took place, not in the big meeting in which Mrs. Etter and a dozen ministers officiated, but with just a few of God's earnest children. It only goes to prove how easy it is to receive spiritual and physical blessing when the tide is at the flood.

There were a number of healings in the audience and around the altar, without the laying on of hands. A woman suffering from neuralgia said she felt the neuralgia which she had had for several years, going out while sitting in the seat, meditating on the Lord.

Often the workers at the altar, seeing the sick had faith to be healed, prayed for them without taking them to the platform, and they were healed. A woman suffering from rheumatism and open veins said she had not been able to bend her knees for seventeen years. God healed her and she knelt before the audience amid much rejoicing.

Another who had been an invalid for fourteen years testified that the Lord had perfectly healed her body. She said, "I was so sick that life was a burden and many times I wished I would die during the night so I would not wake up in my misery. Now I am glad God saved my life. I had heart trouble, liver trouble, and a floating kidney. My nerves were so exhausted I went into hysterics. I was dead to the world many a time, but I praise god I can stand before this people today and say that He healed me."

Her husband, who had been an infidel, was saved through witnessing the mighty works of God. He said, "I used to curse Jesus for years, but I don't do it any more." Speaking of his wife's healing, he said, "My wife said, 'My kidney is loose. I am going down there to have it put in place.' It was on the side like a big lump. The sister asked Jesus Christ to put that kidney back into place, and she said she could feel it move back just as though somebody pushed it." This man first heard of the work through a little tract handed [to] him by a brother workman. When he read it he said to his wife, "You go down there and get healed." She did, and they both got saved.

A father came from Oklahoma bringing with him two afflicted children; one never had the use of his limbs and never could talk, and the other, a girl twenty-two years of age, was born deaf and dumb. The deaf spirit was cast out, the power of God came down upon her, and she shouted and wept alternately. She was so overjoyed at being able to hear that she walked up and down the platform for half an hour, weeping and praising God.

When her father saw that she could hear, he wept for joy. When she was filled with the power of God she told in her simple way, partly with signs with which she had been accustomed to speak, how Jesus died for us, went down into the grave, arose, and went to heaven, and opened her deaf ears. As we met her after that, at subsequent meetings and in the corridors, her face beamed. God not only opened her ears but brought a wondrous salvation to her soul. She laughed and cried when she heard music and singing for the first time.

A few days later she called her father's attention to the fact that with both ears she heard the piano that was being played in the [apartment] above. She could repeat words after you quite plainly, but her ears will have to become accustomed to sound, and she will have to be taught to speak just as a baby learns to talk.

The little boy also received some blessing, and for the first time in his life was able to raise his arms.

A boy nine years of age, so born, received perfect healing one Sunday morning. A lady meeting him the next night stood behind him and said in a low voice, "God is love;" at once he repeated the words after her. When he received his hearing he danced up and down for joy, and the tears streamed down his face.

A man brought his wife four hundred miles to the meetings; she had been deaf for thirteen years. He said they could now sit in a room and hold an ordinary conversation, and she had no difficulty in hearing him, something she had not been able to do for years.

Brother Bosworth has been used quite a little in opening deaf ears. One day some one called his attention to a deaf and dumb boy waiting for prayer. He immediately went over to him, commanded the deaf spirit to depart, and immediately he could hear well. About fifteen minutes later his mother came along, and not knowing what had happened handed the boy a piece of paper on which was written, "I am deaf," to give to Mrs. Etter. Mr. Bosworth told her, her boy wasn't deaf, and when he himself told her he could hear, she shouted for joy. He repeated words uttered behind him.

A woman received her hearing [during] the sermon. She felt she did want to hear the sermon, and while sitting in the audience, with her heart uplifted to God, suddenly her ears were opened and she heard the entire service. She came out of the meeting with a shining face, saying, "I heard the sermon perfectly."

A boy when three years of age went totally deaf from strong medicine. He was overlooked when they were praying for the afflicted, and when Mr. Bosworth met him, he commanded him to hear in Jesus' name, and he immediately heard in both ears, though not perfectly. For the first time he heard the music.

An old lady over eighty years of age was greatly disappointed at not being prayed with for her deafness. Brother Bosworth said he had faith for her hearing, but she shook her head. She wanted Mrs. Etter to pray for her. He took her in a little side room, rebuked the deafness, and she could hear an ordinary conversation in both ears. She jumped up and down for joy. He met her afterwards telling her friends all about it.

He met an old man, eighty-one years of age, with an ear-trumpet; could hear a little in his right ear, but the other had been stone deaf for nineteen years. Mr. Bosworth commanded his ears to be opened, he was instantly healed so he could hear a low voice with either ear.

A mother brought her daughter from Danville, Illinois, who was stone deaf in one ear for three years. Some years ago she had typhoid fever, and it settled in her ear. When she went to a physician he told her the trouble was in the mastoid bone, that there were three complications, any one of which was dangerous. She had been to the hospital and had a growth taken out of her ear, but got no relief.

The doctor said she could not live unless she was operated on and the pus taken away, for if it went to the brain it would be instant death; even with the operation there was only one chance in a hundred of her recovering. He said her ear drum was destroyed. He closed up her good ear to keep her from hearing, then used an ear trumpet in the deaf ear and shouted so he could be heard a half block away, but she couldn't hear. She told the physician she was coming to Chicago to be healed, and he told her she could travel the world over and not get her hearing restored. God opened her ear instantly, and she heard in the ear where the drum had been destroyed.

The mother was healed of heart trouble. She said the doctor called it *angina pectoralis*; that if anyone had an attack of that they had better be ready to go at any moment. The morning she was healed she had such a bad attack, they thought she was dead; a lump came into her throat so that she could hardly get her breath, and nearly choked.

The mother also said that three years ago she was healed of blindness when three doctors had given her up. She could not see to read at all, and went to a little mission in Danville where they prayed for her, so that she can now read the smallest print without glasses.

A colored woman who had been blind for six years came up for prayer. Soon we heard her scream out, "Oh, I see! I see! I see all your faces! Oh praise the Lord!" Immediately the audience were on their feet, rising in honor to Him who had touched those sightless eyes. She often came back after that and testified to daily improvement in her eyes. She said, a few days later,

"When I went to the chair for prayer I could not see anybody. I tried to see Mrs. Etter but I couldn't. My right eye was entirely blind and I hadn't been able to see much out of my left eye. I can see all over the church this morning. I made up my mind not to go out of this church until I was healed, and I told God so." Later she said, she could see to read and write her own letters.

A woman who was partially blind in one eye testified to healing. For ten or twelve years her eyesight had been partially destroyed, caused by a baby scratching the eye-ball. She had it examined by doctors and they said she would go completely blind in time. She was also healed of spinal trouble from which she had suffered for twenty years.

Mrs. Floyd Reeves of Zion City, Ills., was healed of a double hernia she had suffered from for eight years. A man said, "The Lord healed me last night of a rupture of twenty-three years' standing."

A minister who said he was in a backslidden condition, came for healing of a rupture. He asked Mrs. Etter if he should take off his truss, and she said, "Not until the Lord tells you do." The next day, while sitting in church he felt a peculiar sensation in the region of the rupture and realized it was healing. He immediately took off his truss, and afterwards testified to being perfectly healed.

On July 24th a Roman Catholic came and sat down in the chair where the brethren were praying for the sick, and said he wanted to be saved. In the evening he came back and was healed of a rupture. . . .

A man from this same church had a running sore on his foot from which he had been suffering two years. The doctors had said his foot would have to be amputated; it had been hurt twice in the iron mills and it was killing him. When he first came for prayer he said, "I feel I ought to get right with God first." So he went down stairs where they were holding a prayer service and got a wonderful salvation. He said, "If I never get my foot healed, one thing I know, I have salvation." He came the next day and the foot was healed. The swelling went down at once, and a few days later he said it was almost entirely well. He had his vacation and came early in the morning and stayed until ten o'clock at night, and has been seeking the baptism in the Holy Spirit. They had a little revival in their neighborhood in the Spring, and told him he was saved, but he said he knew he wasn't. Now he knows he is a saved man.

One of the ladies from the neighborhood was healed of poisoning from ivy, and another of stomach and kidney trouble through the prayer of the Bible-class teacher.

A woman testified several times to a healing of cancer on the breast. She said her breast was so sore it could not be touched without pain, and she was frightened when Mrs. Etter slapped the place where the cancer had been, but found it didn't hurt her a particle. The Lord had taken away all the pain and she believes she is healed.

Another woman gave this remarkable testimony a week after she was healed: "I want to praise the Lord for healing me a week ago Friday. I had a tumor in my head, kidney trouble, dropsy, indigestion, and a stroke of paralysis that drew my face to one side. I had everything imaginable and couldn't walk a block without somebody helping me. I had been in this condition since the twentieth of September. I was healed at once, and now can walk anywhere and as fast as anybody."

A number of goitres were healed, some partially, and others entirely. One woman from Indiana said her goitre went down two inches after prayer. She was also healed of Bright's disease and heart trouble caused by the goitre, but what she most rejoiced in was the deep spiritual touch she received from God. She received the baptism in the Holy Ghost and went home, her soul filled with glory.

A woman came on crutches she had used for five or six years. She had been a sufferer for ten years, had tried many doctors, and gone to Hot Springs for healing, but got no help. She came once and could not get in; the second time she came at 4:30 (meetings began at 7:30) and went home healed.

A lady brought a little Jewish girl whose leg was four inches short from hip-disease. Some of the brethren prayed for her and her limb was lengthened so her feet measured even.

Brother Bosworth prayed for a Mrs. Drake, of Zion City, and she was healed of deafness of twelve years' standing.

Mr. Keyes of Zion City said, "I praise God a week ago last Monday morning I was healed of rheumatism I had for eight years and of catarrh which I had for three years. When Sister Etter and one of the brethren prayed for me, the power of God fell, and it was done. It only took about three minutes of their time."

Mr. H. W. Judd, also of Zion City, said, "For sixteen years I have been trusting the Lord as my Healer. Two years ago my little girl had the earache and while we prayed for her we didn't seem to get an answer; so I took a little piece of cotton, dipped it in some hot olive oil and put it in her ear to quiet her and she lost her hearing in the ear. It displeased the Lord. I brought her here today and Sister Etter laid hands on her in the name of Jesus, and I say to the glory of God that little child has her hearing. I tested it this afternoon on the street car. I talked quietly to her and she said she could hear me."

On Thursday afternoon a woman was brought in a wheel chair, paralyzed in lower limbs two and a half years. There was no meeting in the afternoon and she was filled with disappointment that she could not see Mrs. Etter, but the brethren prayed for her, and she got out of her chair and walked around. She walked upstairs to the evening meeting, sat during the entire service, and walked home. [Another two pages of testimonies followed.] . . .

Some amusing incidents occurred, but we were made to feel over and over that the Gospel of healing touches hearts as nothing else does; no amount of reasoning or preaching theories, or denouncing people's sins, convinces the world that God lives and moves on earth today as does the fact that the blind see, the deaf hear and the paralyzed walk. A woman came to one of the ushers and asked, "Will this healing continue all the time?" He said, "Yes," he thought it would. Then she said, "I have just been healed of three ruptures that I have had for eight years and I am going to be one of your regular customers." Some men passed two girls walking on the street and one man remarked to the other, "Those girls go to the 'Glory of God' church." . . .

For the most part there was deep reverence on the part of the spectators; even the curious were respectful, but occasionally there was a skeptical one in the crowd. A young man came into the meeting one night and during the prayer service, mocked and made light of the scene before him. Going home that night he was struck by an automobile about two blocks from the church and was seriously hurt -- leg broken. He sent word to us to pray for him.

Mrs. Etter closed her ministry Sunday night, July 27th, but the meetings have continued with much blessing. All day Monday the people came together in little groups for prayer, and streams of healing flowed. On Monday night, as the brethren prayed, the power of God was present to heal. One older colored woman when the shock from heaven's battery struck her, jumped up and exclaimed, "Oh, praise the Lord! I didn't expect it! I didn't expect it!" and ran down the aisle praising the Lord.

When the sick came seeking deliverance, if they obeyed instructions and praised the Lord even though they did not feel like it, they generally received blessing. Mrs. Etter always called on the sick ones prayed for to raise their hands and praise the Lord, and when they did, with heart and soul open to God, He met them. Brother Kinne gave some valuable instructions to people seeking healing, which we believe will be helpful to others who are suffering:

"It is not only that you should get your mouth open to praise the Lord; He wants your whole being set free to praise Him. These mouths belong to Him and so do these bodies. He wants to heal them and glorify Himself in you. The first thing is to get your soul and body full of the glory of God. The more you praise the Lord the more the resurrection life of Jesus comes in. It is not your old strength that comes back, it is the resurrection life of Jesus flowing into your body. The old strength has not time to come back. It is the same resurrection life that came into Lazarus when he rose from the tomb. When in your homes, in place of giving way to temptations of doubt and discouragement walk through your rooms and praise the Lord, and every step you take will cause your faith to grow and the glory of God increase within you."

Sister Etter emphasized the fact that the sick should first of all get a touch from God in their souls. She inspired them to look up and believe for a real shock from the skies to go through them, and often said unless the Lord met them in spirit, nothing would be accomplished. She endeavored to get the sick to get hold of God for themselves by an actual faith and contact with Him, that they might indeed touch Him and be made whole.

While there are many people who are prayed with who are not healed, we know that it is God's will to heal because Jesus on the cross "took our infirmities and bare our diseases." People must be willing to meet God's conditions. We know unbelief stops God's conditions. We know unbelief stops God. Covenant breakers and those who have drawn back and refused to walk in the light, may find God withholding healing until these evils are corrected. Then there are those who, like Job, find their healing delayed. They are conscious [that] God's hand is on them and a great transforming work is going on in them, perfecting patience, endurance and victory that glorifies God in the fire. In delay their faith may "wax strong," their obedience be made full and a triumphant testimony to healing soon to be given them. God has many such witnesses.

There were many striking and wonderful miracles of healing, but there were other cases in which the healing was but partially realized, and we are constrained to believe that in both classes there are some who did not retain their healing; but this does not disprove that a supernatural work was brought in many at the time they were prayed for. Some failed to return for teaching and, as Christ tells in His parable of the sower, such "withered away because they had no root in themselves." When a soul comes to God for salvation and then goes back among his worldly associates, he is in greater danger of losing his precious inheritance in Christ. "The cares of the world choke the word and he becometh unfruitful." It is the same with healing.

Even though there has been a mighty inflow of the resurrection life of Jesus, if the person is resting in his feelings for the validity of his healing, he goes under at the first breath of testing. Those who are not deeply grounded in the Word and are surrounded by worldly and unbelieving associates are in grave danger of backsliding from any experience they may have in God, whether salvation, healing or the baptism. It is especially incumbent on those who have just been healed to surround themselves with spiritual influences and mingle with those who are strong in faith.

We could fill the paper with testimonies of healings that have stood the test of years, but our present purpose is to show what God is doing in our midst today, for the encouragement of those who have need of healing and help. We cannot refrain, however, from giving a short testimony from our beloved Brother Graves, whose miraculous healing has stood the test of twenty years:

"When I think of those long twenty years of epilepsy that I passed through, listening to the teaching that the day of miracles was past, it doesn't seem possible that I stand before you today, for I never expected to be well again. I had over three hundred attacks; I have fallen under horses' feet and through scaffolding, and yet I live to be fifty-seven years old yesterday.

"With all the quarts and gallons of medicine I took, there came a time when I put them all away; when Jesus said to the spirit of epilepsy, "Come out of him and enter no more into him." This blessed teaching we are having today is the teaching that brought me deliverance. 'Jesus Christ, the same yesterday, today and forever!' I thank God for the dear brother that held that up before me day after day, and day after day until it was made real in my life. My healing has stood these twenty years. What are we going to do with the teaching that the day of miracles is past in the face of such testimonies?" ... Anna C. Reiff. (*TLRE*, Aug., 1913)

## Neglect Not the Gift that is in Thee
### Instructions to Ministers and Christian Workers
### Mrs. M. B. Woodworth-Etter in the Stone Church

*TLRE Note*: One of the most deeply solemn meetings was that in which seventy elders, evangelists and helpers had hands laid on them that they might receive a fresh anointing of the Spirit and have more power in their ministry. A holy hush fell on all and the slaying power of the Lord was strongly manifested. One after another they were prostrated under the power until the large platform looked like a battlefield.

Then came a cry from those who worked in hospitals and visited the sick, that they might have more power to bring blessings to the suffering, and Sister Etter and several of the brethren prayed for nearly fifty. Again, as other ministers and workers came in at the close of the month's meetings, there was another service of this nature on Sunday, July 27th, in which fifty more were prayed for. All present were deeply affected by seeing the mighty power of God resting upon His workers. The faces of many were wet with tears as they looked upon the scene.

On July 17th, before giving a talk to the ministers and Christian workers, Sister Etter made a few introductory remarks, in which she said she was not sending them out with license to preach, but that she did believe in many there were gifts lying dormant and that she felt part of her mission was to stir up the gifts in her brethren. She said: "I have no authority to send you out. My prayer is that God will give you authority. We can be of the same mind and same spirit though separated a thousand miles. God has wonderfully blessed me by imparting gifts, and many have received the baptism when I laid hands on them. You are going out with a courage you never had before. We don't want to be a hissing and a by-word. We don't want to run ahead of the Lord nor lag behind. Let us get deep in the Spirit, so the power will come on us this morning."

Brother Argue spoke of the fresh anointing that had come to many at the Los Angeles Campmeeting through a similar service, and also emphasized the fact that these ministers who were about to be prayed for with the laying on of hands were not being sent out by Sister Etter or to claim any authority from her or the Stone Church, but that they might go away from this service with more power, a new courage and a stronger faith. He spoke of the great need of wisdom; that some had not exercised wisdom and had gone out claiming authority from certain missions because hands were laid on them in that place. Everyone was committed to God and made to feel his responsibility to God. Many other valuable instructions were given fitting the hour, but lack of space forbids us recording them further. We give below the address given by Mrs. Etter. All felt the hush of the presence of the Lord, and it was a time of real solemnity to many hearts.

*"And this Gospel shall be preached unto all the world for a witness, and then shall the end come."*

The Holy Ghost said, *"Separate me, Barnabas and Saul, for the work whereunto I have called them."* They had been called and were working, but now they were to be set apart in a special way. The Holy Ghost has to call you, quality you. Jesus Christ has to send you forth.

*"And when they had fasted and prayed, and laid their hands on them, they sent them away. So they being sent forth by the Holy Ghost, departed."* Has God sent you? The Holy Ghost has to qualify you. Our laying on of hands would do no good unless the Holy Ghost comes in to work mightily. The Holy, Ghost said, "separate."

These men had been called and chosen; chosen for the special work to which they had already been called.

Now in the tenth chapter of Luke we read that the Lord appointed the seventy and sent them forth two and two before His face. He said, "Behold, I send you forth as lambs"-- let us remain lambs, and not become wolves to bite and snatch and tear and antagonize everybody. "Behold, I send you forth as lambs among wolves" -- but remember the wolves won't devour you. "Carry neither purse nor scrip." Don't be overanxious about anything.

Verse 19: *"Behold, I give you power to tread on serpents and scorpions, and over all the power of the enemy: and nothing shall by any means hurt you."*

Then He told them not to rejoice because they had power over the spirits but rather rejoice that they are children of God. Don't be puffed up by the miracles, don't get your eyes on them, but keep your eyes on Jesus. You are not saved by miracles. You are saved and kept by the power of God. The miracles are the work of the Holy Ghost. You will get a reward for the works of the Holy Ghost that are worked through you; they are going to make your crown, but they will never save you.

If a hundred thousand were healed through my prayers a day I could not pin my salvation to that. We are not saved by works, but through faith in Jesus, through living, constant faith and prayer. We are kept by the power of God. The works are thrown in and there will be a great reward for them; our crown will be the brighter.

Now in Moses' day the work was great as it is now and the time came when the force of workers had to be enlarged. The Lord told Moses to select seventy men of good report, elders of the people, and bring them together to the tent of meeting that he might take of the Spirit that was upon Moses and put it upon them.

He said that they should be used in the same way as Moses; and so it was, the Spirit that rested on Moses came upon the seventy and they all began to prophesy. Then they were sent out to work. When the Spirit of God comes on you, you are not going to sit around idle and do nothing. And the Spirit fell upon two men who had stayed in the camp. They had not been brought into the tent by Moses, yet the Spirit fell upon them.

That made some feel jealous and you will find the same spirit today -- jealousy of those who are being blessed. Are you jealous for the cause or jealous for yourself? It wasn't for God's glory that Joshua asked Moses to forbid the prophesying of these men. Thank God for Moses' answer, "Would that all the Lord's people were prophets." You must have the Spirit resting upon you if you are to do anything for God, either at home or abroad. You are not fit for work unless you have Him, and those who serve at home must have Him the same as those who go to China or Africa.

God is not calling everyone to the foreign field, but God is calling everyone in some way. Many make the mistake of going out whom God has not called, and many spend all their time running around to camp-meetings. Let us make every place a tent of meeting with the Lord and the Spirit may fall on us as on Eldad and Medad, who were not called to the tent of meeting. And if you are not called to the foreign field, get to work in the place in which God does call you to labor.

If you cannot get victory for God you are not called. The hardest place God sends you to is just the place where he is going to give the greatest victory. But if you have not the Spirit and power of the Holy Ghost to energize you, you will be stranded. God expects us to be qualified by the Spirit resting upon us even more in these last days than in the time of Moses. The seventy that Christ sent out had power, and how much more should we have power now that Christ is glorified? So we are expected to do all these great things set forth in the last chapter of Mark.

Now in the 24th chapter of Matthew it says this Gospel of the kingdom shall be preached to all nations as a witness and then shall the end come. Friends, you and I cannot go out and preach as we used to do. Many sermons that God wonderfully blessed in the past I cannot preach now. I used to preach hell fire, so you could nearly see the fire, and it took effect then, but the call today is for a different ministry. It is not so much in the might of preaching but in the demonstration of the Spirit. Sinners are more hard-hearted than they used to be. You can preach hell until they see the blaze and yet they will stand and look you calmly in the face; but let them see the mighty power of God manifested and they are convicted.

The disciples came to Jesus privately and asked Him what should be the sign of His coming and of the end of the world and He answered these questions. The same questions are being asked today: *"How will people know when He is coming back again? And then what will be the sign of the end when the tribulation is over?"* Now, we are given signs that we may know Jesus is coming soon. He goes on to tell many things that will happen by which we may know. He says this Gospel must be preached all over the world as a witness and then shall the end come. This is our business, to sound the midnight cry, to herald the King.

It is our mission to blow the trumpet in Zion among the saints for the day of the Lord is at hand. It is near, even at the door. Jesus says in the same chapter, "Now from the fig tree learn her parable; when the branch putteth forth its leaves ye know that the summer is nigh; even so ye also, when ye see all these things know that He is nigh, even at the doors."

He had just been saying that the Lord would send forth His angels with a great sound of the trumpet to gather together the elect from the four winds. These are not actual angels but God's servants. The Greek word translated angel means messenger. You see the herald is going forth giving this last message of the kingdom, having power in the Holy Ghost, "Signs and Wonders" following; then know that the coming of the Lord is near at hand.

The Lord has given me a special mission to bring about a spirit of unity and love and God is raising up people in every land who are reaching out after more of God and saying, "Come and help us. We want the spirit of love. We want the signs and wonders."

The Lord showed me last night as I lay awake the most of the night, to gather together the ministers as far as I could, that we might see eye to eye, preach the same Gospel and have the same signs following. The word is going forth and the multitude is going to take it up and publish it everywhere -- this Gospel of the kingdom, our last commission. So you see the saints going out to give this last message, telling the people that Jesus is coming soon.

Our Lord told us, as it was in the days of Noah so shall it be in our day. While the great mass of people are busy with the affairs of this life a little band like Noah and his family are preparing to be hidden away in Christ from the disaster that will come upon the world. And we are told in the "time of the end" the book of Daniel will be read and understood. Daniel had called upon God to show him the future and he was given a vision of great things taking place; but the Lord said, "It is not for this people, Daniel. It is for the people you ask about in the 'time of the end.' Seal up the book; they won't know anything about it now."

The book of Daniel is for our time and God is now opening His word. The light of heaven is shining upon us; God is unveiling it to us. He is giving us light on these things as never before. He says positively, "They that be wise shall understand." We are going to know before Jesus comes. Nearly everyone that is carried away in a vision gets the message, "Jesus is coming soon. Tell the people to be ready."

God expects us as ambassadors, as teachers, as messengers of His kingdom to blow the trumpet that sounds the alarm to those who are not ready for His coming. He expects us to prove by His word, and by the signs and wonders following our ministry, make it plain that Jesus is coming soon. His ambassadors must stop all-contention, all hair-splitting theories must be dropped; this hobby and that hobby with continual harping on "finished work" or "sanctification" that antagonizes the saints must be put away.

We are going out to lift up Jesus. Not many sinners come in by our preaching red-hot judgment these days. Paul says preaching has to be with demonstration of the Spirit and of power. The Holy Ghost bears witness with signs and miracles; unless these attend our ministry we cannot succeed.

There are scores and hundreds getting saved. They come from all parts of the country to get healed. The ministry of healing brings people more than anything else and if you can lay hands on the sick and they recover, you will not have to preach to empty seats. You "produce the goods" of heaven, and people want the goods. Let the word go forth in demonstration and power so people can see what God has for them. There will be no failure in your ministry when they see the power of the Lord present to heal.

The main thing to keep before the people is the near coming of Jesus. We are not to set the day -- God forbid; but the saints will know as the day draws nigh. We can tell by the signs that it is near. God expects you to preach as one having authority. This is a generation that will go up without dying. Christ looked down the age to our day and saw the whole world in unbelief, men fainting and their hearts failing them for fear of the things that were coming upon the earth and Daniel prophesied and said the wicked should grow worse and worse and none of the wicked should understand, but the wise shall understand.

Then the Lord gave Daniel another picture. He saw on the land and on the sea, here and there, messengers blowing trumpets, hailing each other as they pass along. For years back whenever I met a child of God my greeting has been, "Watchman, what of the night?" and from those who have much of the Spirit of God the answer comes, "the morning cometh." But the night is here, too. We have to preach that.

We know the darkness of hell is spreading over the earth and it will soon be a fearful scene, a regular deluge of blood. We have to sound the alarm and give the message that the King is coming. Some will be accounted worthy to escape all these things and stand before the Son of Man.

There is loving unity here. So far as I can see there is not a dissenting voice. There is not much wild fire. God will not permit it and no one dares to chime in: saying, "I am a dove" when he is a raven. No one dares to join us but to magnify God. Those just starting in the life of the Spirit will run off in the flesh more or less, but if they are honest they will recover themselves and fall into their places. There is room for everything in the meeting but the devil. We don't want to give him a place. I haven't heard any hobby [= hobby-horse?] aired here.

Christ finished the work on Calvary, the wonderful plan of salvation, but I do not consider the great work of the baptism was finished until after He went to glory, because the Holy Ghost could not be poured forth until after His ascension. That brings us into the heavenly places and leads us on in the way. There are powers and gifts and greater gifts; we are to go on from glory to glory. God didn't send us out to ride hobbies, to hold up this term or that term, but hold up Jesus. He didn't send us out to tear down, churches.

When Christ sent out His workers He said, "If you go to a city don"t go gadding about. Abide in one place and be much in prayer and don't be worried about the money not coming in, for the laborer is worthy of his hire." Give yourself wholly to your ministry. If you are in the will of God He will provide for you. And eat such things as are set before you; don't have some fad about diet. Don't say, "I don't eat this," or "I don't eat that." If you don't eat it, let it alone, but don't air your opinion about it. The Lord says, "He that receiveth you in my name receiveth me," and we want to represent Him worthily.

As for forbidding to marry or having spiritual "affinities" -- shun such things as you would a deadly viper. But you don't need to talk about these things. Just hold up Jesus. God doesn't want you to be personal about these sins. Let Jesus have the preeminence. The more He is held up, the deeper people get in love with Him the quicker they will drop everything else. So let us hold up Jesus and herald the coming of the King. Show them the great danger of the tribulation. Preach Jesus and hold unto God until the signs follow. There is something wrong unless they do follow. Don't wait until you have any special gift. Believe you can do it and it will be done. Not only send forth the prayer, but look to God for courage, command the devil to go and you will see victory perched on your banner.

People are affected every day by seeing the wonderful miracles. There are different degrees in heavenly places; there are the moon and the sun and the stars.

The time has come when we have to be something more than the moon. We have to be as the sun. They that be wise shall shine as the brightness of the firmament.

Don't denounce churches. Don't denounce the Catholics. Catholics won't come in for fear you will denounce them. I never mention Catholics. I never denounce any particular church. We can show the signs of the formalist in a general way, and they [will] see they have been fed on chaff, and they [will] know they are frozen to death and will want to get alive.

Let us hold up Jesus and if we do that, these antagonistic spirits will get ashamed. They will find themselves lacking. If you blow the trumpet, show the people a supernatural God, and give them the light on what is coming in the Millennial age-- that they will be Kings and priests --they will realize that the King is in our midst in power and might and glory. Any one that will call upon God in the right way shall be saved. He is pouring out His Spirit upon the sons and daughters. There is a special ministry for the women in these days. The sign that brought the people together when the 5000 were converted, was healing, and there would have probably been ten thousand if they hadn't broken up the meeting. Five thousand as the result of this one man being healed, and for that healing the disciples preached the mighty works of God.

So the great revivals all through the New Testament were the result of somebody getting healed. Eneas was eight years afflicted, like the man we prayed for the other day, only this man was probably in a worse condition than Eneas. He could not bend himself, could not open his mouth, could not even move his eye or his head. Soon he was able to stand on his feet; he had been carried in and while we were singing, he ran down the aisle, and down the stairs without taking hold of the banister, and down the street. All that saw him glorified God as the people did when Eneas was healed. There are scores who get saved and healed, so you will always have the miraculous, if the signs follow. God is going to draw in such as can be saved, to see the mighty works.

Paul said to Timothy, "Stir up the gift of God which is in thee." If there is any gift God is showing you you ought to have, you can receive it by the laying on of hands. It is not so much what you say about the baptism and the Holy Spirit, but what they see you have. We can talk until we are hoarse and they won't be convinced, but the power of God convinces them.

Don't wait for manifestations before you go forth and do something. When you are weakest, then you are strong. Let us go out and work miracles. Then the people will glorify God. (*TLRE*, August, 1913)

## Additional Notes of July Meetings

God blessed in the anointing of handkerchiefs. A man in Winnipeg wrote to Brother Argue asking for prayer for the healing of a rupture. Prayer was offered and a handkerchief sent in the name of the Lord, but before he got the handkerchief he realized the healing was taking place. When he received the handkerchief his whole body was filled with the power of God. He went to the mission and told the people what God had done, the power fell, and they had three wonderful cases of healing.

Mrs. Hawkins testified to the healing of a fibroid tumor last winter while in the hospital waiting for an operation. A friend sent a handkerchief to Sister Etter in Dallas, and when it was laid on her body in faith, the tumor disappeared. She had suffered intense pain from the tumor, but God healed her.

There is a blessing in the use of the anointed handkerchief if those who receive them use them in faith.

Tommy Griffin: "I went out to Oak Forest last Saturday and a woman who was making all preparations to die and had asked me to take care of her body so the doctors would not get it, was wonderfully healed by the Lord. I am glad to be so privileged as to live in these days. Eleven years ago I was a poor, drunken gambler, dying of consumption of the lungs. Though I was a Roman Catholic the priest would not come to see me; but the Lord Jesus Christ came into my life and healed me. I was also healed of a disease contracted through sin, and not a mark or scar is left. God has restored the years that the canker-worm and locust had eaten. I was prejudiced against Sister Etter because of reports I had heard, but I came praying and I saw it was God's eternal truth she was preaching; and since these meetings opened, God has really blessed my ministry in the slums as never before." . . .

**The Stone Church, Chicago**

A number of people told of visions that God had given them. On the night of July 7th, while sitting in the auditorium a sister had a vision of a great wall around the platform. This wall stood between the people and God. All at once she saw the wall tottering, and the Scripture came to her, "By faith the walls of Jericho came down," the Lord showed her that it was the prayer of faith that was causing this wall to fall. As the prayer of faith ascended, the wall came down.

She also told us that while living in her home in Danville, she would be led to get up at night and pray. One night last Fall she was praying, and going out on the porch she saw the letter "Z" in the sky, beautifully and perfectly formed of stars. While praying what it meant, the Lord said to her, "I am the Alpha and Omega, the beginning and the end," and revealed to her that the time of the end had come.

During the service a sister saw a hand stretched out on the south side of the building, and as she looked, that hand enlarged and stretched out over the congregation -- the hand of the Lord stretched out in power to heal.

# Messengers of An Outpouring

Another had a vision of angels surrounding the platform, with Jesus in the midst. Then a cloud of glory came down and rested upon the congregation.

A little Jewish girl, about twelve years of age, told of a vision God had given her. She was baptized in the Spirit about three months ago, and recently while in prayer she was carried away in spirit. She said, "I saw Jesus and the white angels standing by His side. His face was shining as the sun. I saw a great multitude of people and the angel blew the trumpet. Then I heard a loud voice saying, 'Woe, woe to this generation;' and another voice saying, 'Woe, woe to the inhabitants of the earth.'" [WW1 started one year after this paper came out. But horrible things were already happening, such as the Armenian genocide, earthquakes, famines, etc.]

Messages in tongues were given and interpreted at a great many of the services. They were messages of exhortation, of warning, encouragement and prophetic utterances of the coming of the Lord, warning people of the nearness of the time of the end. The following is one of many that stirred the hearts of the people:

"The Lord is about to burst forth upon this old earth and among the children of men with majesty and glory and power. Are you ready for Him to take hold of you? Are you awake? Are you aroused by the Spirit of God or are you full of half-heartedness and lukewarmness? Are you insulated from the things of this world or are you in contact with them so that God's power cannot come upon you? Are you asleep in the most perilous hours the world has ever seen? Are you asleep in the most gracious hours that have ever come to this world? Are you half-hearted, lethargic and thoughtless? Behold the Bridegroom will descend in majesty and glory and power and might and snatch away those that are ready, and you who are not ready will be left behind. What can be said to the people of God more than has been said to awaken them? What can be done for the people that has not been done to arouse them? What binds you? What hinders you? Will you seek the Lord? Will you find out what holds you back from the power of God? Seek the Lord until you find Him in the power and majesty and glory of His mighty revelation." (*TLRE*, Aug., 1913)

**Also from Michael D. Fortner**
*Satan's False Prophets Exposed*
*Editing God: Textual Criticism and Modern Bibles Analyzed*
*Bible Prophecy Revealed*
*The Fall of Babylon and The Final Antichrist*

**Also from Trumpet Press:**
*With Signs Following by Stanley H. Frodsham*

www.ingramcontent.com/pod-product-compliance
Lightning Source LLC
Chambersburg PA
CBHW080224100526
44583CB00020BA/2546